m

GREENFIELD ON EDUCATIONAL ADMINISTRATION

This collection is a representative set of ten of the key papers which Thomas Greenfield, arguably the doyen of contemporary theorists of educational administration, has published over the last twenty years. His writings as they appear are eagerly sought after and studied by scholars, students and practitioners in Britain and across the English-speaking world, and increasingly beyond it, but are not always readily available individually.

The collection charts the development of Greenfield's views of social reality as human invention, and explores strands of argument on the nature of knowledge, on administrative theory and research, on values, on the limits of science and the importance of human subjectivity, truth and reality. The volume is concluded by a discussion between Thomas Greenfield and Peter Ribbins, which reflects on Greenfield's career and elaborates on the range of his complex and often controversial ideas.

Thomas Greenfield was formerly Professor at the Ontario Institute for Studies in Education. **Peter Ribbins** is Reader in Educational Management at the University of Birmingham.

GREENFIELD ON EDUCATIONAL ADMINISTRATION

Towards a Humane Science

Thomas Greenfield
and
Peter Ribbins

London and New York

First published 1993
by Routledge
11 New Fetter Lane, London EC4P 4EE

Simultaneously published in the USA and Canada
by Routledge
29 West 35th Street, New York, NY 10001

© 1993 Thomas Greenfield and Peter Ribbins

Typeset in Baskerville by LaserScript, Mitcham, Surrey
Printed and bound in Great Britain by
Mackays of Chatham PLC, Chatham, Kent

British Library Cataloguing-in-Publication Data

A catalogue record for this book is available from the British Library.

ISBN 0–415–08045–2 (hbk)
0–415–08080–0 (pbk)

Library of Congress Cataloging in Publication Data
Greenfield, Thomas Barr.
Greenfield on educational administration: towards a humane
science/by Thomas Greenfield and Peter Ribbins; with a
foreword by Christopher Hodgkinson.
p. cm.
Includes bibliographical references.
ISBN 0–415–08045–2. – ISBN 0–415–08080–0 (pbk)
1. School management and organization. 2. School management
and organization – Social aspects. I. Ribbins, Peter. II. Title.
III. Title: On educational administration.
LB2805.G695   1993   92-160303
CIP

What a piece of work is man, how noble in reason, how infinite in faculties, in form and moving how express and admirable, in action how like an angel, in apprehension how like a god; the beauty of the world, a paragon of animals.

Hamlet, William Shakespeare

CONTENTS

CONTENTS

ix

FOREWORD

It is not possible to properly comprehend the contemporary discipline of educational administration without some familiarity and acquaintanceship with the thought of Thomas Barr Greenfield. That is the main *raison d'être* for this book and ought to be the chief motivation of its readers. But is this strong assertion truly justified?

I shall argue that it is on several grounds. To begin, consider the fact that educational administration is neither unitary nor homogeneous nor monolithic. It is fragmented and factional, obscure in its dimensions, vague in its ends, and contentious in its methodologies. But above all it is divided along a major fault line into two camps or schools of thought, two *Weltanschauungen*. These outlooks and their infinite ramifications have not only been clarified by Greenfield, their greatest expositor, but in a sense have been initiated by him, a point to which I shall advert later. Which is why this text and its collation is so sorely needed. It deserves and will certainly reward study by graduate students, practitioners, and theorists alike.

The content of this book reaches beyond the conventional boundaries of educational administration into that general subset of human behaviour known severally by such deceptive names as administration, management, leadership, policy making, and executive skills. Since all of these activities are real and all of fundamental importance to the quality of human life, not to mention the quality of life in that other set of mysteries called education and schooling, it follows that enlightenment about them is eminently desirable. Greenfield throws such light.

But there are, as it happens, two unevenly matched contenders for the role of light-bearer. Science and art. Both lay their claims to the territory of educational administration. To be sure it is not a simple matter of either–or and of course it is a complex bedevilment of both–and. Nevertheless, there is little doubt which is to bear the burden of Lucifer when the author quotes Hoy and Miskel's text as aspiring to make educational administration 'more of a science and less of an art'. Hoy and Miskel as standard-bearers of the science-oriented camp do seek, in the best (but somewhat jaded) spirit of American pragmatic empiricism, for an explanatory order of things, for predictabilities, for law-like interpretations of complex social phenomena, perhaps even for a mechanism or quasi-mechanistic system of interactions which can be managed, directed, planned and, above all, comprehended. It follows inescapably that this project, often unkindly described as *scientistic*, inclines towards the quantitative in methodology and the realistic in epistemology. It tends to eschew the qualitative, the imponderable, the intractable, and to avow the early Wittgenstein's, 'Whereof one cannot speak, thereof one must remain silent.'[1] Indeed, the philosophical battlefield upon which Greenfield has chosen to fight is very much demarcated by the differences between the earlier and the later Wittgenstein.

It is to be noted that the former is associated with the school of logical positivism or logical empiricism and it is also to be noted that these schools of thought are alive and flourishing today and even dominant despite considerable technical discrediting. Notwithstanding protestations to the contrary, their central ideas are to be discovered behind the façades of American pragmatism and realism, in post-structuralism and deconstructionism in the humanities, and in systems thinking and neo-Taylorism in organization and administrative theory. I make the point to show that Greenfield is not tilting at windmills. His chosen enemy on the battlefield of ideas is a real one. A Goliath even.

The division which Greenfield explicates goes far beyond the frontiers of educational administration. It represents the central dilemma of our times. George Steiner traces the roots of this problem to the Enlightenment era of European rationalism and goes so far as to assert that we are now living in the period of the Epilogue or Afterword.[2] That is, ever since the death of God announced by Nietzsche and confirmed by Freud and ever since the logical positivists rendered triumphant the ascendency of modern science and its handmaiden technology it no longer makes 'sense' to claim that 'in the beginning was the word (*logos*), and the word was with God, and the word was God'. Rather we live now in the epilogue, the afterword, for what science has done for the natural world deconstructionism in literature and the arts, behaviourism in psychology, and pragmatic positivism (veiled or blatant) has done for cultural interactions, administration, and the affairs of men. Orwell rightly forecast the newspeak that takes the current form of political correctitude. Values tend to be preferential, hedonistic, pluralistic, relativistic, and nihilistic. Our times, Greenfield's times, are those in which, as Yeats would insist, 'The best lack all conviction while the worst are full of passionate intensity.' The word has yielded to the number, the humane to the microchip, the individual to the statistic. God the mathematician has distanced Himself. *Deus absconditus*. It is as Nietzsche would have it, 'getting colder'.

Such is the cultural background against which Greenfield prophesies and excoriates. And without his voice it would be all the easier to succumb, to submit to the logic of pseudo-scientific authoritarianism.

But let us consider just a moment longer this great cultural rift, this tear in the fabric of our ethos. There is another way in which it can be expressed. It is, as I have tried to show elsewhere, the radical and abysmal distinction between value and fact:

The world of fact is given, the world of value made.

We discover facts and impose value.

There is nothing at all valuable or beautiful or good *out there*, only in *here*.

Valuation precedes rationality. One can only be rational within the limits set by value.[3]

These are all propositions with which Greenfield concurs and all are themes that he elaborates and enlightens us about. For he is always the teacher and administrator.

This great distinction is disguised and muddied in educational administration but remains there too as ineluctable and inescapable as it is in the culture at large. In the theory of educational administration – and re-member that one can hardly have a science without a theory – the division is subsumed in the now classical Getzels–Guba model which discriminates between the dimensions of collectivity (nomothetic) and individuality (idiographic). The sceptical might be inclined to view this conceptual silence as an elaborate restatement of the obvious, but how many students, to this day, embark on advanced studies in educational administration by way of this model? And how many of them fail to comprehend, unless they are fortunate enough to encounter Greenfield, that this *Ur*-distinction overlays the value–fact dichotomy and cannot be trivialized away by loose or muddle-headed talk of transactional leadership?

In the tension between individual and organization or between child and school, or between entropy and negentropy, there is more than mere dialectical conflict. There can also be a chasm, a Great Divide, an abyss. A fact can *never* entail a value, an individual can *never* become collective. Living tissue is radically distinct from dead tissue. One cannot compromise with pregnancy. Or the arrow of time. The quantitative cannot become qualitative, what is unconscious is by definition *not* conscious, and brain is not the same as mind. All of this is the human condition. To look hard at it is often neither easy nor compelling. Easier by far to elide these difficulties altogether and to study organizational life as if it were somehow inorganic.

Yet who, if not administrative theorists, ought to be more concerned with the human condition, with the profound difficulties that attend the analysis of human nature, with the problem of good and evil, virtue and wickedness? Of course this makes things conceptually messy and even allows the camel's head of polemic to enter the tent of academic objectivity. But it is to Greenfield's everlasting credit that he neither fails to follow where his arguments lead nor hesitates to challenge the sanctity of conventional wisdom. That challenge began with his famous IIP paper and led to what is not inaccurately called the Greenfield Revolution.[4] It continues with waxing and waning, heat and light, but with generally sustained impetus into this publication.

The style of writing in this compendium may disconcert some readers. Its lucidity and literary persuasiveness are unusual in the field and may deflect a certain consciousness of the underlying technical difficulties. Yet how different this is from the cookbook verities and banalities of the conventional textbook in the field. We are seduced even by the titles:

The Man Who Comes Back Through the Door in the Wall: Discovering Truth, Discovering Self, Discovering Organizations,

Against Group Mind: An Anarchistic Theory of Organization,

. . . The Truths of Irreconcilable Realities,

. . . Whence and When Cometh the Phoenix?

Suddenly the real world is not so solid anymore. The cement beneath our feet becomes sand. And shifts.

Philosophically Greenfield is existentialist. Not that that inflated category conveys much meaning except to stress that he is a believer in the freedom of the will, the possibility of intention, and hence morality. For he is a moralist and, in the last analysis, an idealist. He is not in the camp of Dewey, Russell, or Quine. Nor within the discipline does he share the epistemology of the philosopher Evers. It is rather Max Weber with whom he shares the greatest affinity; Weber that polymath and monumental Teutonic scholar whose influence on administrative thought is so pervasive and whose status as politico–social prophet is so superior to that of Marx.

In educational administration we are inclined to trivialize Weber. Our graduate students tend to make a superficial acquaintance with his theories of bureaucracy, power, authority, and leadership but rarely, I imagine, do they come to grips with the subtlety of his thought about ideology and values. Yet he is an important source for Greenfield, and Weber's concept of *Verstehen* and its cognate methodology of hermeneutics is referred to and elucidated in the work presented here. Consider also Greenfield's affinity for drama. In the end the only way to explicate or critique or probe the meaning of a dramatic work of art is by hermeneutically staging and performing it. By analogy the only way to truly understand a school is by enacting its scripts, participating in its scenarios, yet somehow discriminating always between the actor and the role. Greenfield, Weber, and

Goffman triangulate this methodology. Observing the world, their impulse is less to explain than to *interpret*, to communicate meaning from one life-space and language game to another. In this way we may come, not to a manipulative technology of power but to a *Verstehen*, a comprehension of the value-dynamic complex of a real situation that is always the time-bound, and culture specific. Greenfield thus shows traditional theory an alternative face and he fondly quotes Protagoras, 'Man is the measure of all things, of things that are, that they are, and of things that are not, that they are not.'[5] But still Quine and Evers seek for bedrock and the search probes and penetrates the most esoteric reaches of brain chemistry and ever more attenuated neural mechanisms in the hope that man may one day find his ultimate measure in the natural world. Such is *their* privilege and *their* measure of things. The philosophical stage is large and can field many actors, portray an infinity of messages.

But let us put philosophical differences aside and turn to the profession itself. Greenfield's relationship with the profession has been adequately documented in the work of Peter Gronn[6] and, more lately, in a chapter in Evers and Lakomski.[7] It embraces the now historical debates with Griffiths and Hills and extends to the contemporary reactions of Professor Willower among American authorities. All in all the cut and thrust of controversy covers the best part of a quarter-century, despite the many and various attempts that have been made throughout that period to dispose of or bury Greenfield once and for all. About this several points need to be made.

First, and most important, is that the tension between the opposing positions – qualitative–quantitative, art–science, subjective–objective, individual–collective, phenomenological–logical – has never been resolved. In terms of Hegelian dialectics no synthesis has been achieved. As the author puts it in his penultimate chapter, no phoenix has arisen from the ashes because there are no ashes.[8] Nor, despite protestations by the late William Walker, is there any intellectually defensible melding of the opposing positions about the truth and nature of organizational life. Willower's neo-Deweyan pragmatism is certainly no synthetic resolution; nor is the coherentist physicalism of Evers and Lakomski. And the complementary notion of unity in diversity expounded by Boyan, McCarthy, and Pitner[9] represents an understandable but in the end tender-minded abdication of the attempt to define a new paradigm.

What all this amounts to is simply that the game begun by Greenfield is still in play. Sides can be and are taken and, though the mêlée rages and subsides with the varied distractions of a changing ethos, and with the energies of the contestants, still time cannot be called. Greenfield remains a stimulating irritant to the ranks of the professoriate. For some a burr under their saddles, for others a continuing inspiration.

Second, the geography of Greenfield's academic reception is curious. This book is published in England yet Greenfield speaks first from and to

North America. It is not that he is a prophet without honour in his own country. In his native Canada he is generally revered and has influenced generations of students, not to mention that sizeable contingent of colleagues persuaded to his viewpoint. Abroad his works have been translated into Hebrew and the major European languages while Chinese students have remarked to me on the popularity of his works in the People's Republic. Yet, curiously, it is only in the United States that Greenfield seems to encounter extended contention and opposition. Many of his writings have indeed been published there but sometimes only with difficulty and sometimes not at all. What is it about the ideas that provokes this American resistance? What is the threat? These are interesting questions because they seem to touch upon deep-seated philosophical differences between the USA and the rest of the English-speaking and European world. From the Canadian perspective it is even more interesting in that superficially the educational structures and the ethos of the two neighbouring nations are so similar. Is it perhaps an artefact of the differing command systems of the sociology of knowledge in the USA and Canada, that is, different cohorts of professional vested interest? Or does it go beyond this to some threatening aspect of the value-based approach to educational organizations? Or to the tacit philosophy of pragmatism and its underlying ideology of positivism? Could it be that Greenfield strikes at the American roots? Does he, as the Romans used to say, touch the point with a needle?

Third, if the arguments of this book are to be taken seriously in the academy and in the field then there are implications, even entailments, for the training and preparation of administrators. Practitioners can no longer be considered as managers, factotums, or functionaries dedicated to some gospel of efficiency and effectiveness in the tradition of Herbert A. Simon, his heirs and successors. On the contrary they must become, in addition to all that, active philosophers, reflexive about practice and reflective about praxis. As the doctorate becomes more and more the *sine qua non* of career accreditation then the burden will increasingly fall on the academy to consider Greenfield's proposals for curriculum and his general directions for research methodology. Hermeneutics, ethnography, value analysis, and qualitative approaches generally must come to supersede, without displacing, the established habits of quantifying and correlating variables. Multiple regression has its place but not pride of place.

Finally, all the implications of this book, which could well have been entitled 'Towards a New Educational Leadership' point to a renaissance of interest in the problem of value. We can no longer act as if all teachers, all administrators, all professors, all participants in the Great Game of education could be assumed to be honourable men and women. Such presumption is as patently false as the American Constitution's absurd declaration that all men are created equal. The concepts of honour and equality themselves deserve scrutiny. And certainly the reality of wickedness must be faced.[10] Nor can we any longer accept Simon's dictum that an organization is a bus and its executive the driver.[11] The education of administrators and aspirants to leadership must be vigorously concerned with the raising of consciousness about value problems and with increasing sophistication about the nature of value. Such knowledge today is deficient in the discipline and in the field. Yet it need not be and Greenfield would have it otherwise. His opus is sustained argument for research and creative scholarship in this domain. The phenomena of value are still phenomena and they can be studied. The new administrative syllabus would carry that study beyond the usual nods of recognition to Machiavelli.

It is instructive too that this book comes to press at a time when the great administrative ideology of totalitarian Marxism has collapsed. The reasons for that failure now seem with all the clarity of hindsight to be self evident: basic fallacies of value and of fact. Of fact in that market mechanisms are more efficient and effective than central planning, which is to say that the 'irrational' supervenes the 'rational'. Of value because the Utopian value orientation and its assumptions about the nature of man have proved to be a terrifying misinterpretation of the truth.

Now educational administration is rife with planners and the education profession has always been in dalliance with Utopian attempts at social engineering. The leap to totalitarianism is not unthinkable. Authoritarian inhibitions to freedom of speech already exist on many campuses.[12] And the Orwellian Newspeak of Political Correctness is well established on this continent. It is as an antidote to or a defence against these dangerous errors that the wisdom of these pages is especially valuable, for Greenfield is a great humanist, a great educator. His light has been hidden too long beneath a bushel of journals. Like Wittgenstein his influence and ideas have made the largest mark upon his students and it is they who leaven our profession today. But there is word of mouth and word of text and it is good that at last his major writing and the corpus of his ideas can be accessible within a single cover.

The problems Professor Greenfield raises are dialectical. They are not susceptible of simple answers or binary logic but the creative tension which they engender, his exposition of that tension, and the reader's own commitment can lead to a dynamic which can humanize and sophisticate our art of educational administration. One can be confident that the ideas expressed below will, again *pace* Wittgenstein, extend the limits of our language and therefore of our world. To understand Greenfield, whether one agrees with him or not, is to understand the nature of organizational reality better and to be better able to advance the state of the art.

Christopher Hodgkinson
Professor of Educational and Public Administration
University of Victoria
British Columbia

NOTES

1 Ludwig Wittgenstein, *Tractatus Logico–Philosophicus* (Henley: Routledge & Kegan Paul, 1922).

2 George Steiner, *Real Presences* (Chicago: University of Chicago, 1989).

3 Christopher Hodgkinson, *Towards a Philosophy of Administration* (Oxford: Basil Blackwell, 1978), 220.

4 Colin Evers and Gabriele Lakomski, *Knowing Educational Administration* (Oxford: Pergamon, 1991), 76–97.

5 Thomas B. Greenfield, 'Still Waiting for an Answer', *Curriculum Inquiry* 19, 1 (1989), 1–9.

6 Peter C. Gronn, ed., *Rethinking Educational Administration: T. B. Greenfield and his Critics* (Geelong: Deakin University, 1983).

7 Evers and Lakomski, *Knowing Educational Administration*, 76–97.

8 See p. 160.

9 Cf. N. J. Boyan, 'Follow the Leader: Commentary on Research in Educational Administration', *Educational Researcher* 19, 2 (1989): 6–13; M. McCarthy, 'Research in Educational Administration: Promising signs for the Future', *Educational Administration Quarterly* 22, 1 (1986): 3; Nancy Pitner, 'The Study of Administrator Effects and Effectiveness', in *Handbook of Research in Educational Administration*, ed. N. J. Boyan (New York: Longman, 1988), 99–122.

10 Mary Midgley, *Wickedness* (London: Routledge & Kegan Paul, 1984).

11 Herbert A. Simon, *Administrative Behavior*, 2nd edn (New York: Free Press, 1957 [1945]).

12 C. Vann Woodward, 'Freedom and the Universities', *New York Review of Books* 38, 13 (18 July, 1991): 32–37.

1

THEORY ABOUT ORGANIZATION

A new perspective and its implications for schools

In common parlance we speak of organizations as if they were real. Neither scholar nor layman finds difficulty with talk in which organizations 'serve functions', 'adapt to their environment', 'clarify their goals' or 'act to implement policy'. What it is that serves, adapts, clarifies or acts seldom comes into question. Underlying widely accepted notions about organizations, therefore, stands the apparent assumption that organizations are not only real but also distinct from the actions, feelings and purposes of people. This mode of thought provides the platform for a long-standing debate about organizations and people. Is it organizations which oppress and harass people or is it fallible people who fail to carry out the well-intentioned aims of organizations? The debate continues on issues such as whether it is better to abolish organizations, to reshape them along more humane lines, or to train people to recognize the goals of organizations more clearly and to serve them more faithfully.

In contrast, this chapter rejects the dualism which conveniently separates people and organizations; instead it argues that a mistaken belief in the reality of organizations has diverted our attention from human action and intention as the stuff from which organizations are made. As a result, theory and research have frequently set out on a false path in trying to understand organizations and have given us a misplaced confidence in our ability to deal with their problems. If we see organizations and individuals as inextricably intertwined, it may not be so easy to alter organizations, or to lead them, or to administer them without touching something un-expectedly human. More importantly, the view that people and organizations are inseparable requires us to reassess the commonly accepted claim that there exists a body of theory and principle which provides the touchstone for effective administrative action in organizations. The belief in the reality and independence of organizations permits us to separate the study of organizations from the study of people and their particular values, habits and beliefs. The common view in organization studies holds that

1

people occupy organizations in somewhat the same way as they inhabit houses. The tenants may change but, apart from wear and tear, the basic structure remains and in some way shapes the behaviour of people within. Studies have therefore focused largely on the variety of organizational structures and their effects upon people. These structures are usually seen as invariate over time and place, as universal forms into which individuals may move from time to time, bringing with them idiosyncrasies which colour their performance of the roles prescribed by the organization (Getzels, 1958, 156).

ORGANIZATIONAL SCIENCE AND THE PROFESSION OF ADMINISTRATION

The science of organization has found its way into studies of schools and influenced the training of those who are to administer schools. In this science, schools are a variety of the species organization which can be distinguished chiefly by the nature of their goals and their bureaucratic structure (Bidwell, 1965, 973–974). The science of organization is, therefore, assumed to provide useful knowledge about schools even as it does about other kinds of organizations. Accepting this position, Griffiths (1964, 3) rejects 'the opinion that educational administration is a unique activity, differing greatly from business, military, hospital and other varieties of administration' and endorses (p. 118) a 'general theory which enables the researcher to describe, explain, and predict a wide range of human behavior within organizations'.

In a profession of administration based upon organizational science, the task of the administrator is to bring people and organizations together in a fruitful and satisfying union. In so doing, the work of the administrator carries the justification of the larger social order (Getzels, 1958, 156), since he works to link day-to-day activity in organizations to that social order. In schools, the administrator may be director or superintendent, principal or headmaster, department head or supervisor. Whatever their titles, their tasks are always the same. They bring people and resources together so that the goals of the organization and presumably of an encompassing social order may be met (Gregg, 1957, 269–270). No matter what circumstances he finds himself in, the administrator mediates between the organization and the people within it. The task is difficult; he needs help with it. As the argument runs, such help is fortunately to be found in the emerging science of organizations. Since organizations do have a human component, knowledge about organizations is usually described as a social science. But social or not, this science like all others is seen as universal, timeless, and imperfect only in its incompleteness.

The claims for a science of organization and for a profession of administration based upon that science have in recent times made a marked impact upon education. For over two decades now, scholars have attempted to improve education by applying organization theory to the conduct of affairs in schools and by training educational administrators in that science (Culbertson and Shibles, 1973). Celebrating its emancipation from the press of immediate practical affairs, the field now sought to uncover the basic relationships and principles which underlie day-to-day concerns (Griffiths, 1964). The professor supplanted the practitioner as the source of valid knowledge about administration. If practitioners did not know or accept that they were no longer masters of the basic knowledge which underlay their craft, it did not matter. Even the scholar-practitioner, Chester Barnard, in introducing Simon's classic writings claimed that it was the scholar's knowledge of the 'abstract principles of structure' rather than the practitioner's knowledge of 'concrete behavior' which leads to an understanding of 'organizations of great variety' (Simon, 1957, xlii–xliv). Things are not what they seem, in educational administration as in other realms of reality. We need the scientist and his theory to interpret them to us. His knowledge, though it may be incomplete and is certainly subject to improvement, has the virtue of universal applicability. Acting on this conviction, scholars in educational administration have sought to understand how organizations really work and to use this knowledge towards the improvement of educational practice.

A survey of representative writing in educational administration (see Campbell and Gregg, 1957; Halpin, 1958; Griffiths, 1964; Getzels, Lipham and Campbell, 1968; Milstein and Belasco, 1973) reveals that enquiry in this field has leaned heavily on the belief that a general science of organizations has provided the needed theoretical underpinnings for understanding schools and for the training of the administrators who are to run them. While a general theory of organizations provided the rationale for understanding schools, the sister social sciences provided the research tools and the 'sensitizing concepts' needed to identify and resolve their administrative problems (Downey and Enns, 1963; Tope *et al.*, 1965). Since this happy combination of theory and method yields an understanding of organizations as they really are, it then becomes possible to say how educational administrators may be trained to improve organizations and administrative practice within them (Culbertson *et al.*, 1973). Although the claim is seldom if ever made explicitly, this line of reasoning, linking a general theory of organizations to the training of administrators, implies that we have at hand both the theory and method which permit us to improve schools and the quality of whatever it is that goes on within them. That change in schools proceeds without assistance from an applied organization theory or, indeed, in contravention to it (Fullan, 1972), usually fails to shake our faith in such theory.

It will surely come as no surprise to anyone who examines the references cited to this point that most of them are American in origin, since it was in

3

the United States that the movement to conceive educational administration as a social science arose in the early years of the 1950s. By the end
of that decade the movement had taken hold in Canada and some time
later in Australia and Britain. As the concept of educational administration
as a profession and social science gains ever wider recognition and acceptance, it becomes appropriate to examine the theory and assumptions
which underlie the field. In particular we need to ask whether the theory
and assumptions still appear to hold in the settings where they were
developed before they are recommended and applied to totally new
settings. Such an examination is not only appropriate but essential in the
face of an alternative view which sees organizations not as structures subject
to universal laws but as cultural artefacts dependent upon the specific
meaning and intention of people within them. This alternative view, which
stems from nineteenth-century German idealism (Deutscher, 1973, 326),
bears the awkward name phenomenology (Phillipson, 1972), though it
might with equal justification be called the method of understanding, as it
is in the work of Max Weber (Eldridge, 1971, 28). What we call the view is
not important. What matters is that there exists a body of theory and
assumption which runs squarely at odds with that which has provided the
ideological underpinnings of educational administration as it has
developed over the past two decades. The ideological conflicts between
these views rest on two fundamentally different ways of looking at the
world. One is the established view both in the study of organizations
generally and in the study of educational administration. In this chapter, I
will outline the alternative view and recommend its application both in
organization and administrative theory.

It is no accident that the alternative view has its roots in European
philosophy and social science. And it is at least noteworthy that this view has
a current flowering in Britain, where it is exerting a strong influence in both
sociology (Filmer, *et al.*, 1972; Dawe, 1970; Brittan, 1973) and in education
(Young, 1971, Cosin *et al.*, 1971). I do not wish to drive the differences in the
views to the point of a spurious contrast between American and European
social science. The alternative view which I will outline has its supporters in
the United States too (Garfinkel, 1967; Cicourel, 1964; Louch, 1966; Wilson,
1970). Two points should be made here. First, and of lesser importance,
phenomenology has yet to influence the study of organizations in the
United States despite the existence of a long-standing phenomenological
tradition in some sociological schools of thought in that country.[1] In Britain,
both theory and research on organizations reflect the phenomenological
perspective (Tipton, 1973; Silverman, 1970). Second, and more important
since it relates to the heart of the issue, the existence of the two competing
ideologies illustrates the fundamental contention of phenomenology that
there are no fixed ways for construing the social world around us. These
ways are products of particular settings and circumstances rather than

4

expressions of universal ideas and values. Our concepts of organizations must therefore rest upon the views of people in particular times and places, and any effort to understand them in terms of a single set of ideas, values and laws must be doomed to failure.

The alternative view rejects the assumption, underlying much of organization theory, that organizations belong to a single species which behaves in predictable ways according to common laws. This view finds forceful expression in the work of Mayntz (1964, 113–114), a European scholar of organizations:

> Propositions which hold for such diverse phenomena as an army, a trade union, and a university . . . must necessarily be either trivial or so abstract as to tell hardly anything of interest about concrete reality. . . . After all, the distinct character of an organization is certainly determined, among other things, by the nature, interests, and values of those who are instrumental in maintaining it.

If people are inherently part of organizations, if organizations themselves are expressions of how people believe they should relate to each other, we then have good grounds to question an organization theory which assumes the universality of organizational forms and effects. This argument suggests that organization theorists have been so busy defining the forest that they have failed to notice differences among the trees – and worse, have ignored objects in the forest that are not trees at all. It suggests, too, that an academic industry which trains administrators by disclosing to them the social–scientific secrets of how organizations work or how policy should be made indulges at best in a premature hope and at worst in a delusion.

TWO VIEWS OF SOCIAL REALITY

The conflicting views on organizations of which I have been speaking represent vastly different ways of looking at social reality and rest on sharply contrasting processes for interpreting it. These contrasts are summarized in Table 1.1 in which I have compared the two views and suggested how they differ with respect to a number of critical issues. Each of these issues has implications for the theory of organizations and for research undertaken in line with such theory. Necessarily then, these contrasts also have implications for a number of practical questions in the conduct of affairs in organizations. Some of these will be explored in the concluding section of this chapter. Although there are no generally accepted names for identifying the two views contrasted in Table 1.1, it may suffice to note that the crux of the issue is whether social reality is based upon naturally existing systems or upon human invention of social forms. Social reality is usually construed as a natural and necessary order which, as it unfolds, permits human society to exist and people within it to meet their basic needs. Alternatively, social reality may be construed as images in the mind of man having no necessary or inevitable forms except as man creates them and endows them with reality and authority. In the one perspective, organizations are natural objects – systems of being which man discovers; in the other, organizations are cultural artefacts which man shapes within limits given only by his perception and the boundaries of his life as a human animal.

The systems notion posits an organizational force or framework which encompasses and gives order to people and events within it. The system – unseen behind everyday affairs – is real; it *is* the organization. The force of 'natural' in the descriptor is to evoke the view common in systems theory that organizational forms are shaped by powerful forces which in large measure act independently of man. The organizations so formed will be right and good, if the natural forces are allowed free play. Mayntz (1964, 105, 115) has noted that such views in which an unseen organizational hand works for the greater social good are likely to be most congenial to scholars who share a faith in the ideals of the Western liberal democracies. In identifying organizations as social invention, the alternative view identifies organization with man's image of himself and with the particular and distinctive ways in which people see the world around them and their place in it. This view is the perspective of phenomenology. In it organizations are the perceived social reality within which people make decisions and take actions which seem right and proper to them (Greenfield, 1973, 557). The heart of the view is not a single abstraction called organization, but rather varied perceptions by individuals of what they can, should, or must do in dealing with others within the circumstances in which they find themselves. It is noteworthy that this tradition – the decision-making tradition (Cyert and March, 1963; Simon, 1964) in organization theory – is frequently cited in scholarly writing, but seldom followed in analyses of organizations. This tradition, culminating currently in the creative insights of James March (1972) into organizational realities, reaches back to the work of Max Weber (1946) and to the German philosophers and sociologists of the phenomenological tradition (Deutscher, 1973, 327; Silverman, 1972, 184–185).

What are some of the particular issues involved in the contrast between the systems and phenomenological views? These are suggested in Table 1.1 where the two views are compared on a number of points. In the discussion which follows, the phenomenological view is emphasized, since it is assumed that the foundations of the system view are the more familiar of the two views.

Philosophical basis

The system view assumes that the world is knowable as it is. Although the acquisition of such knowledge requires the intervention and help of scientists, theorists and scholars, there exists an ultimate reality which may be discovered by application of the scientific method and similar forms of

6

Table 1.1 Alternative bases for interpreting social reality

Dimensions of comparison	What is social reality?	
	A natural system	*Human invention*
Philosophical basis	Realism: the world exists and is knowable as it really is. Organizations are real entities with a life of their own.	Subjectivism: the world exists but different people construe it in very different ways. Organizations are invented social reality.
The role of social science	Discovering the universal laws of society and human conduct within it.	Discovering how different people interpret the world in which they live.
Basic units of social reality	The collectivity: society or organizations.	Individuals acting singly or together.
Method of understanding	Identifying conditions or relationships which permit the collectivity to exist. Conceiving what these conditions and relationships are.	Interpretation of the subjective meanings which individuals place upon their action. Discovering the subjective rules for such action.
Theory	A rational edifice built by scientists to explain human behaviour.	Sets of meanings which people use to make sense of their world and action within it.
Research	Experimental or quasi-experimental validation of theory.	The search for meaningful relationships and the discovery of their consequences for action.
Methodology	Abstraction of reality, especially through mathematical models and quantitative analysis.	The representation of reality for purposes of comparison. Analysis of language and meaning.
Society	Ordered. Governed by a uniform set of values and made possible only by those values.	Conflicted. Governed by the values of people with access to power.
Organizations	Goal oriented. Independent of people. Instruments of order in society serving both society and the individual.	Dependent upon people and their goals. Instruments of power which some people control and can use to attain ends which seem good to them.
Organizational pathologies	Organizations get out of kilter with social values and individual needs.	Given diverse human ends, there is always conflict among people acting to pursue them.
Prescription for curing organizational ills	Change the structure of the organization to meet social values and individual needs.	Find out what values are embodied in organizational action and whose they are. Change the people or change their values if you can.

rational analysis. In systems theory, the prevailing image of the organization is that of an organism. Organizations exists; they are observable entities with many human properties. They have goals towards which they direct their activities; they respond and adapt to their environments. Nor can organizations escape the fate of organisms ill-adapted to their environments. Indeed, the fate of organizations depends upon their ability to adapt to an increasingly complex and turbulent environment. Following the Darwinian logic inherent in their image of the organization, system theorists see small, quick-witted, democratic organizations replacing the ponderous bureaucratic forms now expiring around us (Bennis, 1968). The fact that bureaucratic organizations appear as large, robust and formidable as ever does not appear to shake belief in organizations as living entities subject to stringent laws permitting only the fittest to survive. Indeed, our belief in the living organization is likely to be so strong that we fail to notice that system theorists have shifted from telling us about the way organizations are to telling us how they ought to be. 'If only organization were adapted to their environments', the argument runs, 'imagine how quickly these bureaucratic forms would disappear.' In thinking about the dazzling prospect of a world in which organizations were creatures closely adapted to a benign, well-intentioned environment, we forget that the role of the theory is to tell us the way things are rather than how they ought to be or how we should like them to be. Our image of the organization as an entity, as a living entity, rests upon an analogy. But we fail to draw the conclusion (Willer, 1967, 33) that the analogy is useless when discrepancies appear between the image and the phenomena observed.

Reality in systems theory contrasts sharply with the phenomenological view of it. This view has its origin in the distinction Kant drew between the noumenal world (the world as it is) and the phenomenal world (the world as we see it). For Kant, a world of reality does indeed exist, but man can never perceive it directly; reality is always glossed over with human interpretations which themselves become the realities to which man responds. And man is always learning, always interpreting, always inventing the 'reality' which he sees about him. In popular form, the Kantian philosophy has been expressed as follows: 'Man does not make his world, but he does create it.' It therefore comes as no surprise to the phenomenologist that people are killed by 'empty' guns. But for the phenomenologist beliefs are always of greater consequence than facts in shaping behaviour. The bullet may indeed be in the gun, but it is the individual's belief about an empty chamber which causes him idly to pull the trigger. Deutscher (1973) summarizes the phenomenological view as follows:

> The phenomenological orientation always sees reality as constructed
> by men in the process of thinking about it. It is social version of

8

Descartes' *Cogito, ergo sum.* For the phenomenologist it becomes *Cogitamus, ergo est* – we think, therefore it is! (p. 328)

The role of social science

The implications of the phenomenological view are of critical importance in shaping our views both of the social sciences and of a study of organizations founded on them, as may be seen in the contrasting positions taken by Weber and Durkheim (Bendix and Roth, 1971, 286). Working within his 'method of understanding', Weber concluded 'there is no such thing as a collective personality which "acts", only individuals acting on their interpretations of reality'. In contrast, Durkheim, convinced of an ultimate, knowable social reality, sought to eliminate the perceptions of individuals and to find 'the explanation of social life in the nature of society itself' (Bendix and Roth, 1971, 291). Thus Durkheim spent his life building a sociology around notions of 'elemental' forms which provide the invariable units out of which social life is built. Weber, on the other hand, explored the ideas, doctrines and beliefs with which men endowed their organizations and which provided the motivation for action within them. Durkheim's path leads to generality, abstraction and universality in the study of organizations; Weber's leads to the particularistic, the concrete, and the experience-based study of organizations. Durkheim's path leads to an asceptic study of organizations, Weber's to one that smells of reality.

The phenomenological view leads to the concept of organizations as 'invented social reality' (Greenfield, 1973, 556) and to the paradox that, having invented such reality, man is perfectly capable of responding to it as though it were not of his own invention (Silverman, 1970, 133). More basically, however, the phenomenological perspective questions the possibility of objectivity in what Weber calls 'the cultural sciences'. While it is possible for such sciences to pursue inquiry within a logically rigorous methodology and for them to take into account certain basic social facts such as where people live and what they do, it is not possible for cultural scientists to give us 'a direct awareness of the structure of human actions in all their reality' (Eldridge, 1971, 16). Thus the notion of discovering the ultimate laws which govern social reality becomes an ever receding fantasy which retreats as we attempt to approach it. Such bogus 'laws' as the law of supply and demand were, both for Weber and Durkheim, 'maxims for action', advice to people on how to protect their interests if they wished to be 'fair and logical' (Eldridge, 1971, 18). In Weber's view, then, it is impossible for the cultural sciences to penetrate behind social perception to reach objective social reality. Paradoxically, this limitation on the cultural sciences is also their strength, since it permits them to do what is never possible in the physical sciences: the cultural scientist may enter into and take the viewpoint of the actor whose behaviour is to be explained.

9

> We can accomplish something which is never attainable in the natural sciences, namely the subjective understanding of the action of component individuals. . . . We do not 'understand' the behaviour of cells, but can only observe the relevant functional relationships and generalize on the basis of these observations. (Weber, 1947, 103–104)

While the cultural scientist may not discover ultimate social reality, he can interpret what people see as social reality and, indeed, he must do so according to a consistent, logical, and rigorous methodology (Eldridge, 1971, 9–10). It is such a discipline for interpreting human experience which provides the science in the cultural scientist's work, not his ability to discover ultimate truths about social structure. Thus the purpose of social science is to understand social reality as different people see it and to demonstrate how their views shape the action which they take within that reality. Since the social sciences cannot penetrate to what lies behind social reality, they must work directly with man's definitions of reality and with the rules he devises for coping with it. While the social sciences do not reveal ultimate truth, they do help us to make sense of our world. What the social sciences offer is explanation, clarification and demystification of the social forms which man has created around himself. In the view of some (Dawe, 1970, 211), the social sciences may lead us to enlightenment and to liberation from the forces which oppress man. In the phenomenological view, these forces stem from man himself, not from abstractions which lie behind social reality and control man's behaviour within that reality.

Theory about what?

The two views give rise to opposing theories about the world and the way it works, since each sees reality in different kinds of things. Each approaches theory building from a point of view which is normative rather than descriptive. In the natural systems view, the basic reality is the collectivity; reality is in society and its organizations. Assuming the existence of an ultimate social reality, the role of theory is to say how it hangs together or how it might be changed so that it would hang together even more effectively (Merton, 1957; Etzioni, 1960). Thus functional analysis – the theory associated with the systems view – becomes a justification of the way social reality is organized rather than an explanation of it. In this view, the theory becomes more important than the research because it tells us what we can never perceive directly with our senses: it tells us the ultimate reality behind the appearance of things and it establishes a view which is essentially beyond confirmation or disproof by mere research.

The phenomenological view begins with the individual and seeks to understand the interpretations of the world around him. The theory which emerges must be grounded in data from particular organizations (Glaser

10

and Strauss, 1967). That these data will be glossed with the meanings and purposes of those people and places is the whole point of this philosophical view. Thus the aim of scientific investigation is to understand how that glossing of reality goes on in different times and places. Similarly organizations are to be understood in term of people's beliefs about their behaviour within them. If we are to understand organizations, we must understand what people within them think of as right and proper to do. Within this framework we would certainly not expect people everywhere to have the same views. In fact, it is the existence of differences in belief structures which provides us with the key to interpreting them. People are not likely to think of their own views as strange. Indeed it is only in contrast to other views that we come to understand our own. Theory thus becomes the sets of meanings which yield insight and understanding of people's behaviour. These theories are likely to be as diverse as the sets of human meanings and understandings which they are to explain. In the phenomenological perspective, the hope for universal theory of organizations collapses into multifaceted images of organizations as varied as the cultures which support them.

The view of theory as arising from our understanding is expressed by Walsh (1972):

> The point about the social world is that it has been preselected and preinterpreted by its members in terms of a series of commonsense assumptions which constitute a taken-for-granted scheme of reference. . . . In this manner factual reality is conferred upon the social world by the routine interpretive practices of its members. The implication of this is that every man is a practical theorist when it comes to investigating the social world, and not just the sociologist. (p. 26)

Thus, the naturalist tries to devise general theories of social behaviour and to validate them through ever more complex research methodologies which push him further from the experience and understanding of the everyday world. The phenomenologist works directly with such experience and understanding to build his theory upon them. As Kuhn (1970) points out, our theories are not just possible explanations of reality; they are sets of instructions for looking at reality. Thus choice among theories and among approaches to theory building involves normative and – especially in the social sciences – moral questions. Choice among them is in part a matter of preference, but choice may also be made on the basis of which theories direct us to the most useful problems and which provide the most helpful insights into them.

11

Research and methodology

In the systems view, research is directed at confirming theory. Theory, in this view, is something which scientists build, largely from the armchair, by thinking up what must be the ultimate explanation for the phenomena observed. Contrary to accepted opinion, Kuhn (1970, 16) has argued that such theory is never open to disproof and serves instead as a 'consensual agreement among scientists about what procedures shall constitute scientific activity and hence which explanations will count as scientific explanations' (Walsh, 1972, 250).

From the phenomenological perspective research, theory and methodology must be closely associated. Theory must arise out of the process of inquiry itself and be intimately connected with the data under investigation. In this view, the aim of theory should be explanation and clarification. Thus research and theory which fulfils this aim must depend not only upon what is being explained but also upon to whom it is explained, and with what. Louch (1966, 233) argues this view as follows:

> Explanation, in Wittgenstein's phrase, is a family of cases joined together only by a common aim, to make something plain or clear. This suggests that a coherent account of explanation could not be given without attending to the audience to whom an explanation is offered or the source of puzzlement that requires an explanation to be given. There are many audiences, many puzzles.

Research in the naturalist mode is prone to use experimental methods to establish relationships among variables. The research often substitutes mathematical models for the substantive theoretical model and is satisfied if statistically significant relationships are found among the variables of the mathematical model. The aim is to relate variables x and y usually with a host of other variables 'held constant'. Little effort is spent on determining whether x and y exist in any form which is meaningful to or has consequences for actors within a social situation. Nor is there much effort to ask whether holding one or more variables constant yields an interpretable result among those remaining. In physical systems, we can understand what it means to hold volume constant, for example, while we raise the temperature of a gas and observe the effect on pressure. But what does it mean when we come to a social system and speak, as some researches do, of holding social class constant while we observe the effect of school resources upon achievement? Whereas the physicist manipulates materials and apparatus in specific, understandable ways, the social researcher frequently makes no intervention at all in the social system that he is attempting to explain. Instead, he does the manipulation of variables in his mind, or in the workings of his computer. Can we rely on the suggestion that if we manipulate variables in a social system, we will get the same results the researcher gets from his intellectual manipulation of them? The doubt is growing that we will not, as is apparent, for example, (Spady, 1973, 139) from critiques of school effects research demonstrating that schools may account for a great deal or virtually nothing at all of pupil achievement, depending on which of several alternative but statistically acceptable procedures the researcher chooses for his analysis.

Phenomenologically based research, on the other hand, aims at dealing with the experience of people in specific situations. Therefore the case study and comparative and historical methods become the preferred means of analysis. These methods are perhaps found in their most developed form in the work Weber did in building ideal types for organizational analysis. These types should be seen as 'characterizations or impressions of ways of thought and styles of living' which permit comparison and understanding of them (Louch, 1966, 172). What Weber did in building these ideal types was to worm his way into heads of bureaucrats, clerics and commercial men in order 'to discern logical connections among propositions expressing [their] beliefs about the world' (Louch, 1966, 173). The moral consequences of these beliefs may also be made plain and checked against 'reality'. The close connections among theory, research and ethics thus become obvious.

Thus an organizational theory based upon understanding rejects the emphasis which much of contemporary social science places upon quantification, more complex mathematical models, and bigger number crunchers in the shape of better and faster computers. As Burns (1967, 127) has pointed out, better manipulation of numbers cannot substitute for the emptiness of the concepts to which they apply. This fixation on numbers without concern for the concepts they are thought to represent leads to a sickness of social science which Sorokin has called 'quantophrenia' and which Rothkopf (1973, 6) likens to the *Leerlauf* reactions described by Lorenz. In such 'empty running', animals go through elaborate stereotyped performances for hunting or mating when no other living creature is there to see or respond to their behaviour.

If we move towards improved understanding in our research, we might change our image of what constitutes *the* essential research tool and supplant the computer with Weber's notion of the ideal type. An ideal type provides us with an image of a social situation at a particular time and place. We may then surround this image with others made of different organizations or of the same organization at other times. By looking at these images comparatively, by seeing them almost as the frames of a motion picture, we begin to understand our world better and to comprehend its differences and the processes of change occurring within it. This direction in theory and research leads to an investigation of language and the categories it contains for understanding the world (Bernstein, 1971a; 1971b). It leads also to an investigation of the processes by which we negotiate with each other and so come to define what we will pay attention to in our environment and our organizations (Scheff, 1973; Garfinkel, 1964).

Society and its organizations

In the systems view, the problem of society is the problem of order. Without society and its organizations, chaos and anarchy would result. The social order is seen as a basically well-working system governed by universal values. In the phenomenological view, the organization as an entity striving to achieve a single goal or set of goals is resolved into the meaningful actions of individuals. Organizations do not think, act, have goals or make decisions. People do (Georgiou, 1973; Greenfield, 1973), but they do not all think, act and decide according to preordained goals. Thus the notion of the organization as a necessary order-maintaining instrument falls and the notion of organization as the expression of particular human ideologies takes its place. In this way, the problem of order becomes the problem of control (Dawe, 1970, 212). Or, to put the question otherwise, the problem is not whether order shall be maintained but rather who maintains it, how, and with what consequences. The image which this view calls to mind is the organization as a battlefield rather than the organization as an instrument of order. People strive to impose their interpretations of social reality upon others and to gain command of the organizational resources which will permit them to do so. The warfare in this battlefield usually takes the form of linguistic attack and defence, although the physical forms of warfare fit just as comfortably within the perspective.

Take as an example this exchange between a principal and a new social worker after the social worker has spent considerable time counselling a student who had been persistently truant and tardy.[2]

Pr: It was really simpler and more effective in the old days when the truant officer just went straight to the student's home and brought him back to school.

SW: Actually, I do the work truant officers did, but I do it a different way.

Pr: That may be so, but we used to get results more quickly. If the students wouldn't come to school, we expelled them. They had to recognize our authority or quit school. That's what I mean by simple. Now everything is complicated. Why can't we deal with these cases without a lot of red tape?

SW: I prefer to see my work as treatment. The aim is not to wind up a case quickly but to keep the student in school and learning. And in any case, Mr Principal, legally I am the truant officer and you need my backing to expel a student for truancy.

14

It is surely not hard to see in this exchange a battle going on over what the job of the social worker should be and behind that a struggle over how the school should define its responsibilities to students. The issue is how the job of the social worker shall be defined and who shall control the school's power of expulsion. Each of the protagonists is inviting (and threatening) the other to accept a particular definition of the situation and the way it is proper to act within it.

The conflict view of organizations thus links up neatly with the decision-making tradition in organizational analysis. In a recent significant contribution Perrow (1972, 145–176) demonstrates how this tradition, seen also in the work of March and Simon (1958), complements the insights of Weber. A major concern of Weber was for the way in which the power of bureaucracies would be used outside the organization. March and Simon demonstrate how power may be marshalled within the organization. As Perrow points out (p. 196), the supposed plight of professionals within bureaucracies is a minor complaint compared to what others have suffered from professionals who have been able to act out their ideological beliefs through their control of organizations.

We should also be grateful to Perrow (p. 90) for pointing out the contrasts between Barnard's theory and his practice. For Barnard (1938, 46–61) organizations were by their very nature cooperative enterprises. In this respect, Barnard was a good systems theorist whose theory dealt with abstractions about organizations and not with the ideologies of those who ran them. In an astonishing case study, Barnard (1948, 64) spoke in the following terms to a group of the unemployed who had recently seen 'police clubs flying, women trampled, men knocked down':

> I'll be God damned if I will do anything for you on the basis that you ought to have it just because you want it, or because you organize mass meetings, or what you will. I'll do my best to do what ought to be done, but I won't give you a nickel on any other basis. (pp. 73–74)

In his commentary on this situation, Barnard makes it clear he realized he was in a position of conflict over ideology. But his theoretical concern lies not with the ideologies, but with his position that men under 'states of tension' will do what is 'utterly contrary to that which is normally observed in them' (p. 62). While he explains in detail how he won the ideological battle that gave him power to decide what the men 'ought to have', he makes no mention of his final decision. The content of decisions is not important in systems theory. However, Barnard does take pains to denigrate the ideology of the unemployed workers and their claims for better treatment. He also considers in a footnote (pp. 73–74) whether a person of 'superior position' should swear in front of those of 'inferior status', and confides that the 'oath was deliberate and accompanied by hard pounding on the table'.

15

In this example, Barnard as theorist merely adds the notion of 'states of tension' to his earlier developed principles of cooperative action in organizations. Do these ideas tell us the significant aspects about organizational life with Chester Barnard? The phenomenologist holds that Barnard's ideology is the significant variable shaping the experience of many people in the organizations which he controlled. Without understanding the ideological issues involved in an organization, and in particular without knowing what ideology is in control, the general principles of organization mean relatively little in terms of what people experience in an organization.

Organizational pathologies and cures

The systems theorist looks for pathologies in the body of the organization itself. These stem from ill adaptations of the organization to its environment, to the ultimate goals it should serve, or to the needs of individuals. The solution to these pathologies is obvious: change the structure of the organization to improve the adaptation and thus the performance of the organization. The phenomenologist, on the other hand, sees structure as simply the reflection of human beliefs. If there are problems in organizations – and problems are certainly to be expected – they must therefore rest in conflicting beliefs held by individuals. Solutions to such problems cannot be found simply by changing structures. As Schein (1973, 780) says, the root of the problem lies in people's beliefs and in their ability to act upon them.

> Thus the argument that we must make organizations more liveable, more congruent with human values and motives, ignores the fact that it is one set of human motives and values which is in conflict with another set of motives and values. There is no abstract entity called organization which can be held accountable – only other people.

Our penchant for thinking about organizations as entities, as things with a life of their own, blinds us to their complexity and to the human actions which constitute the façade which we call organization. It leads us to believe that we must change some abstract thing called 'organization' rather than the beliefs of people about what they should do and how they should behave towards each other. The more closely we look at organizations, the more likely we are to find expressions of diverse human meanings. The focus of our efforts to improve organizations should not be, 'What can be done to change the structure of this organization?' but, 'Whose intentions define what is right to do among people here involved with one another?' and 'How might these intentions be changed?' The task of changing organizations depends, first, upon the varieties of reality that individuals see in existing organizations, and secondly, upon their acceptance of new ideas of what can or should be achieved through social action. We know

16

little about either, but it is clear we should understand the first before we attempt to direct the second.

IMPLICATIONS

Where do the ideas based in phenomenology leave the notion of 'organization'? And what of the science that studies organizations? And where does a profession of educational administration which bases its practice on this science now find itself? In conclusion, let me briefly develop some answers to these questions and suggest some directions for future study.

1. Organizations are definitions of social reality. Some people may make these definitions by virtue of their access to power while others must pay attention to them. Organizations are mechanisms for transforming our desires into social realities. But the transforming mechanism lies within individuals. It is found in individuals striving to change their demands or beliefs into definitions of reality that others must regard as valid and accept as limitations on their actions. This notion of organizations as dependent upon the meanings and purposes which individuals bring to them does not require that all individuals share the same meaning and purposes. On the contrary, the views I am outlining here should make us seek to discover the varying meanings and objectives that individuals bring to the organizations of which they are a part. We should look more carefully too for differences in objectives among different kinds of people in organizations and begin to relate these to differences in power or access to resources. Although this concept of organization permits us to speak of the dominating demands and beliefs of some individuals, and allows us to explore how those with dominating views use the advantage of their position, we need not think of these dominating views as 'necessary', 'efficient', 'satisfying' or even 'functional', but merely as an invented social reality, which holds for a time and is then vulnerable to redefinition through changing demands and beliefs among people. Where then may we go from here? Let me suggest some lines of development.

2. We should begin to regard with healthy scepticism the claim that a general science of organization and administration is at hand. Such theories carry with them not only culturally dependent notions of what is important in an organization but also prescriptive ideas of how study and enquiry into organizational problems should go forward. The movement toward international associations for the study of educational administration should be welcomed, but these associations should open windows on our understanding of organizations rather than propagate received notions of organization theory. If the movement can provide a comparative and critical perspective on schools and on our notions of how they should be run, the association will serve a valuable role. Since the dominant

theories of organization and administration have their source in the United States, it is these ideas which should receive searching analysis before they are blindly applied in other cultural settings. In Britain, this critical examination of theory and its policy implications has already begun (Baron and Taylor, 1969; Halsey, 1972), though one is hard pressed to find similar critical examinations in other national or cultural settings.

3. Willy nilly, the world does seem to be shrinking towards the global village. Yet there are still strong forces that maintain vivid cultural distinctions within it. Despite these forces, the interests of the mass media, which the academic community seems all too ready to ape (Perrow, 1972, 198), direct attention more frequently to the symptoms of social problems rather than to their sources. While the mass media are usually ready with prefabricated solutions to these problems, students of organizations should doubt the utility of solutions that ignore their sources in the truly critical and powerful organizations of our societies. If we are unwilling to understand our own organizations, or if we regard acquiring such understanding as a trivial task, we should be aware that there are often others willing and waiting to apply their own preconceptions and answers to the tasks of defining the organization, identifying its problems, and prescribing solutions to them. Our own experience of our own organizations is a valuable resource. It is with this experience that the organization theorist must begin to understand the nature of organizations. Since an understanding of organizations is closely linked to control of them and to the possibility of change within them, the phenomenological perspective points to issues of crucial importance both to the theorist and to the man of practical affairs.

4. The possibility of training administrators through the study of organization theory has been seriously overestimated. Such theory does not appear to offer ready-made keys to the problems of how to run an organization. Through credentials, such training does appear to offer sound prospects for advancement within administrative systems. While such training may increase social mobility, each society must decide whether it wishes to pursue this goal and, if it does, whether this method is the most appropriate for doing so. If training of administrators is to serve its avowed purposes, then it seems clear that the nature of the training must move in virtually the opposite direction from that advocated in recent years. This is to say, training should move away from attempts to teach a broad social science of organizations-in-general towards a familiarity with specific organizations and their problems. That the training should continue to have critical and reflective dimensions should not conflict with this redirection of training programmes. It appears essential also for training programmes to develop a much stronger clinical base than is now common in most of them. In such training, both the theoretician and the practitioner must be intimately involved.

18

5. Research into organizational problems should consider and begin to use the phenomenological perspective. This redirection of research should awaken interest in the decision-making tradition of organization theory and in the institutional school of organizational analysis with its emphasis on the *exposé* and ideological analysis of specific organizations (Perrow, 1972, 177–204; Bendix, 1956). In methodology, research should turn to those methods which attempt to represent perceived reality more faithfully and fully than do the present highly quantified and abstruse techniques. And researchers should avoid prescribing solutions to pressing social problems on the basis of prescriptive theory and research. For example, those who concluded on the basis of the Coleman study that the achievement of black students in American schools might be raised by integrating black and white students were dazzled by the naturalist assumption that a statistical relationship represents social reality. They therefore were led to the error of believing that social relationships may be manipulated in the same way in which variables from the research design can be manipulated. In doing so, they failed to reckon with the reaction of black students to greater integration as a 'solution' to their problems (Carlson, 1972). Indeed researchers and social scientists might consider the cultural imperialism which is frequently inherent in their recommendations for solving problems and strive first to understand the social and organizational world for which they hope to prescribe solutions (Bernstein, 1971b; Holbrook, 1964; Sarason, 1971).

What is needed for better research on schools is better images of what schools are and what goes on in them. 'Better' in this case means creating images of schools that reflect their character and quality and that tell us something of what the experience of schooling is like. Since schools are made up of different people in different times and places, it is to be expected that images which reflect the experience of schooling must be many and varied. These images would be sets of 'one-sided viewpoints', as Weber called them (Eldridge, 1971, 12), each throwing 'shafts of light' upon social reality in schools.

As natural systems have been the dominating model in studies of organizations (Mayntz, 1964, 116), so also the image of the unit of production prevails in researches about schools (Levine, 1973; Spady, 1973). The production model of the school is a systems variant which sees the school as a set of roles and resources arranged to yield a product which conforms to predetermined goals. We are often so accustomed to this model that we fail to notice the enormous discrepancies between it and what typically goes on in schools. To begin with, most sets of official educational goals would justify schools doing virtually any good thing for the individual or the society in which he lives. Second, the products of school are nearly impossible to identify, if by product we mean something which is unmistakably due to the efforts of the school itself. The clearest measure of school product – the results students obtain on standardized and other kinds of tests – correspond poorly to the goals of education and are usually accounted for most readily by influences outside the school. Thus whether schools do anything to achieve a set of vague goals can never be determined within the model of the school as a unit of production.

If we shear from our image of schools the notion of overriding goals and visible products, what are we left with? The image is now that of pure process in which people strive to shape a social environment which is congenial to them and which they believe serves *their* purposes or the purposes which other people ought to have. The image of the school is now not the factory or the system but the public utility which produces a service which people use for their own ends (Pincus, 1974). It is not surprising in this conception of the school that people involved with it – teachers administrators, pupils, parents, etc. – have strong feelings about what services should be provided and how they should be provided. Moreover, it should be apparent that experience with the school's services leads to strong, though not necessarily universally accepted, beliefs about what kinds of service are good and bad and to convictions about which of them are effective and ineffective. Lacking objective criteria to judge the relevance and validity of their claims, and lacking even a common basis of experience with the school's services, people holding these beliefs and convictions are likely to clash with others having different but equally firmly held convictions. We learn to believe in our own experience of school process and to doubt the validity of others' beliefs. In this way, the proposed model accounts both for apparent stability of schools – their resistance to change – and for the continuing conflict about what schools are for and how they should be organized and run. It suggests as well that the path to understanding more about schools must lie through interpretations and analysis of the experience of people in schools, not through attempts to decide which structural elements of schools yield outcomes that best approximate their ultimate purposes.

6. The research advocated above and the rationale for it developed earlier in this article does not imply only the description and analysis of subjective states. Weber is said to have advised researchers to get first the facts about the basic elements of social situations and then to move to a subjective interpretation of them (Eldridge, 1971, 19; Bendix and Roth, 1971, 286–291). The 'facts' Weber had in mind were such matters as wages, costs of materials, the people involved, and descriptions of them in demographic terms. These are the typical resources variables which are of frequent concern in analyses of the school from the perspective of the production model. The questions usually investigated are whether the school is making effective and efficient use of its resources in pursuit of predetermined educational goals. Answers to such questions are complex, contradictory

and unconvincing, as Spady (1973) has demonstrated. The reasons for such unsatisfactory outcomes are obvious when pointed out, as Gagné (1970) has done. Children do not learn from 'environments', from 'resources' or from the 'characteristics of teachers'. They learn from their specific involvement with people, things and events around them. Thus knowledge of the basic facts about social situation is only the beginning of an understanding of it. What is needed beyond these basic facts is a knowledge of how people in a social situation construe it, what they see as its significant features, and how they act within it. Such knowledge can only come from the interpretation of particular experiences in specific situations.

In this respect, it might be useful to think of two kinds of variables in a social situation – outside and inside variables. The outside variables are those which lend themselves readily to quantification and which involve a minimum of interpretation. As has been suggested, these variables provide information about the characteristics of the people and resources found in a social situation. The inside variables are those which may only be expressed through interpretation of experience. Both kinds of variables are important, though in most organizational studies of schools, emphasis has usually fallen exclusively on the former category.

It would be helpful to replace our usual notion of the school as a system with the idea of the school as a set. Where the system implies preordained order and functions in the school, the notion of set leaves completely open both the definition of the elements of the school and the description of relationships among them. Defining the school as a set leaves as a problem for investigation what the elements of the situations are and what the meanings of relationships among the elements are. With such a view of the school, we might recognize both external and internal variables, as follows.

External variables. Pupil characteristics: their age, sex, home background, individual abilities and previous learning. School characteristics: building design, facilities and equipment. Classrooms: number of pupils, subjects of study, methodology. Teacher characteristics: training and length of service, personality, intelligence, abilities and interests.

Internal variables. What is the quality of relationships among teachers, pupils and others in the school? What experiences do they have in terms of (a) their expectations for the environment, (b) the opportunities and problems they perceive, (c) the efforts they make to learn, help or teach, (d) their feelings of accomplishment or failure? What decisions do different people in the school make and why do they make them? How are people and situations defined and evaluated?

21

The variables listed above are intended to be suggestive rather than exhaustive. The final point to be made about them is that both of these major dimensions are essential for describing and understanding schools fully. In fact, some of the most revealing analyses will arise from contrasts between the school seen in terms of external variables and the schools seen in terms of internal variables. That organizational theory has too frequently directed attention to the external variables and that it has presumed rather than explored their relationships to internal variables are points which have already been made at length.

7. A continued study of organizations from the perspectives of the social sciences is certainly warranted. Schools as one of the most significant of our social institutions deserve particular attention. It seems appropriate, however, for students of schools as organizations to consider the meaning of their studies and to redirect them towards investigations which increase our understanding of organizations as they are before attempts are made to change them. Paradoxically, the efforts which promise to yield the most penetrating insights into organization and the most practical strategies for improving them are those efforts which deal with the way people construe organizational reality and with the moral and ethical issues involved in these construings (March, 1972).

If, as the phenomenologist holds, our ideas for understanding the world determine our action within it, then our ideas about the world – what really exists in it, how we should behave in it – are of the utmost importance. And if our ideas about the world are shaped by our experience, then the interpretation of experience is also of paramount importance. It is this process, the placing of meaning upon experience, which shapes what we call our organizations and it is this process which should be the focus of the organization theorist's work. Unless we wish to yield to universal forces for determining our experience, we must look to theories of organization based upon diverse meanings and interpretations of our experience.

NOTES

1 Deutscher (1973, 324ff) describes these schools of thought and their connections with idealistic philosophy. He also points out (p. 325n) that those he calls the 'Harvard functionalists' make no mention of phenomenology or its proponents in their encyclopedic history of theories of society. See Parsons *et al.* (1961).
2 Personal communication to the author.

REFERENCES

Barnard, C. I. 1938. *The Functions of the Executive.* Cambridge, MA: Harvard.
—— 1948. *Organization and Management.* Cambridge, MA: Harvard.
Baron, G. and Taylor, W. eds 1969. *Educational Administration and the Social Sciences.* London: Athlone.

Bendix, R. 1956. *Work and Authority in Industry: Ideologies in the Course of Industrialization*. New York: Wiley.
Bendix, R., and Roth, G. 1971. *Scholarship and Partisanship: Essays on Max Weber*. Berkeley: University of California.
Bennis, W. G. 1968. 'Beyond Bureaucracy', in *The Temporary Society*, ed. W. G. Bennis and P. Slater, 53–76. New York: Harper and Row.
Bernstein, B. 1971a. *Class, Codes and Control: Theoretical Studies towards a Sociology of Language*. London: Routledge & Kegan Paul.
—— 1971b. 'Education Cannot Compensate for Society'. In *School and Society: A Sociological Reader*, eds B. R. Cosin *et al.*, 61–66. London: Routledge & Kegan Paul.
Bidwell, C. E. 1965. 'The School as a Formal Organization'. In *Handbook of Organizations*, ed. J. G. March, 972–1022. Chicago: Rand McNally.
Brittan, A. 1973. *Meanings and Situations*. London: Routledge & Kegan Paul.
Burns, T. 1967. 'The Comparative Study of Organizations'. In *Methods of Organizational Research*, ed. V. Vroom, 118–170. Pittsburgh: University of Pittsburg.
Campbell, R. F. and Gregg, R. T. eds 1957. *Administrative Behavior in Education*. New York: Harper and Row.
Carlson, K. 1972. 'Equalizing Educational Opportunity'. *Review of Educational Research* 42, 4: 453–475.
Cicourel, A. 1964. *Method and Measurement in Sociology*. New York: Free Press.
Cosin, B. R., Dale, J., Esland, G. and Swift, D. eds 1971. *School and Society: A Sociological Reader*. London: Routledge & Kegan Paul.
Culbertson, J. and Shibles, M. 1973. 'The Social Sciences and the Issue of Relevance'. In *Social Science Content for Preparing Educational Leaders*, eds J. Culbertson *et al.*, 3–32. Columbus: Merrill.
Culbertson, J., Farquhar, R., Fogarty, G. and Shibles, M. eds 1973. *Social Science Content for Preparing Educational Leaders*. Columbus: Merrill.
Cyert, R. M. and March, J. G. 1963. *A Behavioral Theory of the Firm*. Englewood Cliffs, NJ: Prentice Hall.
Dawe, A. 1970. 'The Two Sociologies'. *British Journal of Sociology* 21, 2: 207–218.
Deutscher, I. 1973. *What We Say/What We Do: Sentiments and Acts*. Glenview, IL: Scott, Foresman.
Downey, L. W. and Enns, F. eds. 1963. *The Social Sciences and Educational Administration*. Edmonton: University of Alberta.
Eldridge, J. E. T. ed. 1971. *Max Weber: The Interpretation of Social Reality*. London: Michael Joseph.
Etzioni, A. (1960), 'Two Approaches to Organizational Analysis: A Critique and a Suggestion'. *Administrative Science Quarterly* 5, 2: 257–278.
Filmer, P., Phillipson, M., Silverman, D. and Walsh, D. 1972. *New Directions in Sociological Theory*. London: Collier-Macmillan.
Fullan, M. 1972. 'Overview of the Innovative Process and the User'. *Interchange* 3, 2–3: 1–46.
Gagné, R. M. 1970. 'Policy Implications and Future Research: A Response'. In *Do Teachers Make A Difference?*, ed. A. Mood. Washington: US Office of Education.
Garfinkel, H. 1964. 'The Relevance of Common Understandings to the Fact That Models of Man in Society Portray Him as a Judgmental Dope'. In *What We Say/What We Do: Sentiments and Acts*, ed. I. Deutscher, 330–338. Glenview, IL: Scott, Foresman.
—— 1967. *Studies in Ethnomethodology*. Englewood Cliffs, NJ: Prentice Hall.
Georgiou, P. 1973. 'The Goal Paradigm and Notes towards a Counter Paradigm'. *Administrative Science Quarterly* 18, 3: 291–310.

Getzels, J. W. 1958. 'Administration as a Social Process'. In *Administrative Theory in Education*, ed. A. W. Halpin, 150–63. New York: Macmillan.

Getzels, J. W., Lipham, J. M. and Campbell, R. F. 1968. *Educational Administration as a Social Process: Theory, Research, Practice.* New York: Harper and Row.

Glaser, B. G. and Strauss, A. L. 1967. *The Discovery of Grounded Theory.* Chicago: Aldine.

Greenfield, T. B. 1973. 'Organizations as Social Inventions: Rethinking Assumptions About Change'. *Journal of Applied Behavioral Science* 9, 5: 551–574.

Gregg, R. T. 1957. 'The Administrative Process'. In *Administrative Behavior in Education*, eds R. F. Campbell and R. T. Gregg, 269–317. New York: Harper and Row.

Griffiths, D. E., ed. 1964. *Behavioral Science and Educational Administration.* The Sixty-third Yearbook of the National Society for the Study of Education. Chicago: University of Chicago.

Halpin, A. W., ed. 1958. *Administrative Theory in Education.* New York: Macmillan.

Halsey, A. H., ed. 1972. *Educational Priority: E. P. A. Problems and Policies.* Vol. I. London: HMSO.

Holbrook, D. 1964. *English for the Rejected.* Cambridge: Cambridge University.

Kuhn, T. 1970. *The Structure of Scientific Revolution.* Chicago: University of Chicago.

Levine, D. M. 1973. 'Educational Policy After Inequality'. *Teachers College Record* 75, 2: 149–179.

Louch, A. R. 1966. *Explanation and Human Action.* Berkeley: University of California.

March, J. G. 1972. 'Model Bias in Social Action'. *Review of Educational Research* 42, 4: 413–429.

March, J. G. and Simon, H. A. 1958. *Organizations.* New York: Wiley.

Mayntz, R. 1964. 'The Study of Organizations'. *Current Sociology* 13, 3: 95–155.

Merton, R. K. 1957. *Social Theory and Social Structure.* New York: Free Press.

Milstein, M. M. and Belasco, J. A. eds 1973. *Educational Administration and the Social Sciences: A Systems Perspective.* Boston: Allyn and Bacon.

Parsons, T., Skils, E., Naegele, K. and Pitts, J. 1961. *Theories of Society: Foundations of Modern Sociological Theory.* New York: Free Press.

Perrow, C. 1972. *Complex Organizations: A Critical Essay.* Glenview, IL: Scott, Foresman.

Phillipson, M. 1972. 'Phenomenological Philosophy and Sociology'. In *New Directions in Sociological Theory*, eds P. Filmer *et al.*, 119–163. London: Collier-Macmillan.

Pincus, J. 1974. 'Incentives for Innovation in the Public Schools'. *Review of Educational Research* 44, 1: 113–143.

Rothkopf, E. Z. 1973. 'What Are We Trying to Understand and Improve? Educational research as *Leerlaufreaktion*'. Invited address to the meeting of the American Educational Research Association, New Orleans.

Sarason, S. B. 1971. *The Culture of the School and the Problem of Change.* Boston: Allyn and Bacon.

Scheff, T. J. 1973. 'Negotiating Reality: Notes on Power in the Assessment of Responsibility'. In *What We Say/What We Do: Sentiments and Acts*, ed. I. Deutscher, 338–358. Glenview, IL: Scott, Foresman.

Schein, E. H. 1973. 'Can One Change Organizations, or Only People in Organizations?'. *Journal of Applied Behavioral Science* 9, 6: 780–785.

Silverman D. 1970. *The Theory of Organizations.* London: Heinemann.

—— 1972. 'Methodology and Meaning'. In *New Directions in Sociological Theory*, eds P. Filmer *et al.*, 183–200. London: Collier-Macmillan.

Simon, H. A. 1957 [1945]. *Administrative Behavior: A Study of Decision-Making Process in Administrative Organization*, 2nd edn. New York: Free Press.

—— 1964. 'On the Concept of Organizational Goal'. *Administrative Science Quarterly* 9, 1: 1–22.

Spady, W. G. 1973. 'The Impact of School Resources on Students'. In *Review of Research in Education*, No. I, ed. F. N. Kerlinger, 135–177. Itasca, IL: Peacock.

Tipton, B. F. A. 1973. *Conflict and Change in a Technical College*. London: Hutchinson.

Tope, D. E. *et al.* 1965. *The Social Sciences View School Administration*. Englewood Cliffs, NJ: Prentice Hall.

Walsh, D. (1972), 'Sociology and the Social World'. In *New Directions in Sociological Theory*, eds P. Filmer *et al.*, 15–35. London: Collier-Macmillan.

Weber, M. 1946. *From Max Weber: Essays in Sociology*. Trans. H. H. Gerth and C. W. Mills. Oxford: Oxford University.

—— 1947. *The Theory of Social and Economic Organizations*. Trans. T. Parsons. London: William Hodge.

Willer, D. 1967. *Scientific Sociology: Theory and Method*. Englewood Cliffs, NJ: Prentice Hall.

Wilson, T. P. 1970. 'Conceptions of Interaction and Forms of Sociological Explanation'. *American Sociological Review* 35, 4: 697–710.

Young, M. F. D., ed. 1971. *Knowledge and Control: New Directions for the Sociology of Education*. London: Collier-Macmillan.

2

RESEARCH IN EDUCATIONAL ADMINISTRATION IN THE UNITED STATES AND CANADA

An overview and critique[1]

The task set for this paper is easily accomplished in one sense and virtually impossible in another. The organizers of this conference have asked me to 'help them to take cognizance of the not inconsiderable effort put into educational administration research in North America over a generation or more'. Those who know I hold the view that positivistic social science has simply and plainly failed to unlock the puzzles of administrative and organizational process may wonder why I have been asked to undertake this task. Knowing my concern for the cultural and linguistic bases of social action (Greenfield, 1976), others will recognize why I have used the phrase 'United States and Canada' in the title of this paper rather than the term 'North America' that was contained in the invitation. In their patterns of language and culture, in their approach to educational research and in many other respects, Canada and the United States are not North America; nor is North America the world. That theme has marked another of my criticisms of 'North American' research in educational administration: it has too often ignored the cultural forces that condition the 'findings' of research and has been too quick to promulgate a universal set of truths about the nature of organizations and how they work (Greenfield, 1975).

Accomplishing the purpose set for this paper thus requires me to review research from those countries that have been the very cradle for the idea that social science can solve social problems in the same way that physical science has enabled us to understand and master much of the natural world. Applied to education, this credo has led to the belief that a science of administration would bring us happier and more effective teachers and lead ultimately to better schools where students learned and parents were satisfied. My criticisms contend that this promise has obviously not been fulfilled, that the research in the field has made no marked advance towards substantive knowledge and has often exalted trivial and banal findings by proclaiming them general laws and fundamental insights.

These failures stem, in my view, from an inappropriate paradigm or ideological theory that has pervaded, if not dominated, the field. Some of you may doubt, therefore, the wisdom of asking me to review research in educational administration from the United States and Canada on the grounds that such action is tantamount to setting a fiery-eyed, radical cat among some honoured scientific pigeons.

Let me try, if I can, to set your minds at rest on that score. In the first place, it is impossible for me to review all the research that falls within the topic I have been assigned. Second, I cannot fault the integrity and good intentions of those in the United States and Canada who have attempted to pursue administrative research within a strong scientific framework over the last two decades or more. I have been involved in such an effort for the large part of that time, first as a student who began master's level studies in 1959 and later as a researcher and professor with formal responsibilities for one of the major centres for the study of educational administration in Canada. My comments in this paper must therefore be limited to looking at the theoretical foundations of what Andrew Halpin (1970, 159) has called the 'New Movement' in educational administration and to asking where all of the research conducted in the name of this theory has brought us. I cannot offer you detailed summaries of the administrative research such as used to appear in the *Review of Educational Research*. These triennial reviews were discontinued in 1967 by the *Review*'s publishers, the American Educational Research Association, who at about that time abandoned their policy of focusing the reviews within the disciplinary frameworks provided by the sub-fields of education such as administration, psychology, curriculum and so on. Since that time it is perhaps worth noting that the *Review* has published articles along topical lines and that few, if any, of the resulting issues of the journal have reflected themes readily recognised as the usual concerns of those involved in organizational and administrative studies. Instead, scholars in the field of educational administration have produced a number of their own critical and retrospective reviews. While these are few in number, they are comprehensive and searching, thereby providing me with a reason for directing this paper to tasks that will not duplicate their extensive critical efforts.

THEORETICAL FOUNDATIONS OF ADMINISTRATIVE RESEARCH

Two observations struck me as I reviewed the research conducted in the United States and Canada over almost a quarter of a century. The review has served to demonstrate that the critical stance I have taken with respect to theory and research in educational administration is by no means unique, though other critics have perhaps cast their conclusions in more cautious terms and have seen very different implications in them. The scope of my review extended from the present back to that point of time in the intellectual history of America when a small group of social scientists shocked and disturbed practising school administrators during the 1950s by telling them that rigorous, theory-based research would shortly make obsolete the knowledge on which they based their profession. The first observation concerns the attitudes of the social scientists to their knowledge and to those whom they thought could benefit from it. They soon realised the hubris, the intellectual arrogance, that had swept them to make a promise that, on the basis of closer contact with the field and its problems, they realised they could not keep. The scientists' attitude of disdain towards the practitioner's knowledge appeared to change little, however. Their attitude was perhaps somewhat like that of the Oxford professor who characterized his knowledge and his relationship to his students as follows: The pearls I cast may be false, but the swine are real.

The second observation concerns the substance of the research itself. Repeatedly, the scholarly reviews of research in educational administration have demonstrated the inadequacy of the basic theory and the weakness of narrowly empirical research as tools for understanding and controlling the problems of organization and administration. Nevertheless, for all these demonstrations of the failures of administrative research, its manifest shortcomings have totally failed to shake the commitment to the *idea* of theory as a guide to practical action in administration. The faith of the scholarly community in theory-based research remains virtually unshaken. So we have the anomaly that the more the research fails, the more do the scholars of our field defend theory and the more do they proclaim – at least in textbooks directed at large audiences of students and practising administrators – that theory and research in educational administration provide the soundest and most reliable guide to practical action and offer, as well, a general understanding of organizations and how they work. When one points out this discrepancy between faith and evidence, as I have done (Greenfield, 1975), the results are curious. In response to the issues I raised at the 1974 International Intervisitation Program and in later publications, the organizers of the 1978 IIP simply chose to overlook the controversy that had developed in the ensuing years (Layton, 1978, 8). But the issues will not go away. Daniel Griffiths, for example, will shortly deliver an invited address to the 1979 Annual Conference of AERA and his remarks will bear the title: 'Intellectual Turmoil in Educational Administration'. Something is not right in research in educational administration. I propose to identify what that something is by reviewing the intellectual history of the Movement and by examining those reviews of research that show what the movement has accomplished.

Intellectual orientations in the field

If I were to add a sub-title to this paper, it would run, 'Whatever happened to Andrew Halpin?' Halpin, of course, was one of the small group of social scientists who first took an interest in the scientific approach to the study of educational administration. As a social scientist he was instrumental also in developing the conviction that *behavioural* science and its methods of inquiry could bring order, understanding and control to the problems that beset educational administrators. Writing in retrospect, Halpin (1970, 159–160) described how the 'New Movement' in educational administration came about in America. From that vantage point, he noted the role of the National Conference of Professors of Educational Administration – the NCPEA – that had been formed in 1947 to improve the training of administrators. The need for the organization was grounded in the circumstance that professors of educational administration in those days were drawn almost exclusively from the ranks of former administrators in school systems. They were those, according to Halpin (1970, 159–160) who had 'chosen the professorship as a form of early retirement' and who 'regaled their protégés with their own personal experiences as school administrators'. In the style that came to characterize his later writings, Halpin went on to say that 'instruction was by anecdote, often given by men in their anecdotage'. The solution that Halpin and a small group of others saw for this problem required that instruction for administrators be provided by behavioural scientists with training in rigorous research methodologies and with a clear grasp of theories that would make sense of the administrators' perplexing world – a sense, of course, that would not be readily apparent to the administrators themselves without the theories and research tools that only the behavioural scientists could understand and manipulate. Halpin (1970, 161) describes what happened when he and two other scientists brought this good news to the administrators at a meeting of NCPEA held in August, 1954:

> At that meeting the first 'real' confrontation between behavioral scientists and professors of educational administration took place. Coladarci (of Stanford) Getzels (of Chicago) and Halpin (then of Ohio State University) pointed out to the group – and not gently – that what the CPEA Centers and the members of NCPEA were doing in the name of research was distinctly a-theoretical in character and sloppy in quality. The reception that these three behavioral scientists received at the meeting can scarcely be described as cordial.

What is the point, you may ask, of these historical and intellectual perspectives in an article that is supposed to be dealing with the findings of research? Their relevance appears most forcefully if one looks at what else Halpin was saying about research and theory in the same article in which he launched the above trenchant criticisms of administrators for their failure to grasp the meaning and importance of the 'New Movement', the theory–research movement in educational administration. Halpin (1970) opened his reflective, retrospective article by examining two of the corner-stone writings in the New Movement dogma. One of these is *Administrative Theory in Education* (Halpin, 1958), a collection of the New Administrative Thinking that Halpin edited in 1958. At the same time, he comments on his book, *Theory and Research in Administration* (Halpin, 1966). While this later work contains some materials representing the revolutionary, opti-mistic view of the 1950s, it also contains later and more sombre and pessimistic writings. When Halpin (1970) was writing under the title: 'Administrative Theory: The Fumbled Torch', his view of the value and validity of administrative theory had shifted from messianic fervour to iconoclastic condemnation.

Thus I reach one of the major conclusions that this analysis has brought me to. Shrinking faith among academics about the validity of adminis-trative theory and their growing doubts about even the existence of such theory have not served to shake their commitment to research conducted in the name of that theory. On the contrary, academic populists ever more strongly advocate research as a guide for practical administrative action. Concurrently with such advocacy, one also finds that the founding geniuses, the Newtonian theoreticians of the New Movement and their latter-day saints are confessing a sin of commission. There is growing among them the recognition that the general administrative science that they so confidently – and even a little arrogantly – offered to practitioners some years ago, contains flaws major enough to render it virtually useless. For example, Halpin (1966; 1970) in his later writings reasserts the intel-lectual scorn that behavioural scientists felt for the practising administrator at the time when the New Movement was blossoming in the United States. Now, however, one can see juxtaposed against these attitudes a flat state-ment, a confession in effect, that the promise of administrative theory was an illusion – a wild chimera, in fact – that served to mislead the credulous and to distract attention from real problems.

In his bleak, almost despairing article: 'Administrative Theory: The Fumbled Torch', Halpin (1970, 157) hammers home the shortcomings of the original theory with particular force. Speaking of some of his own early writings, he also criticizes by implication the basic theoretical foundations of the field:

> The book does not present a single theory of administration in education, simply because there is no theory worthy of the name available to report at the present time. And even last week I finished teaching a course at the University of Georgia that is entitled: 'Basic Theories of Administration'. I assuaged my conscience by conceding

that this course title was already on the books and by telling myself, *sotto voce*, that any student who still expected a necessary relationship between the title and content of a course in education was too innocent to belong in graduate school.

Even in his earlier work, Halpin (1966, 284–285) had expressed what he called 'qualms about the role of theory'. He pointed then to another influential and basic set of writings in the field by Campbell and Lipham (1960) with the ringing title: *Administrative Theory as a Guide to Action.* Does not such a title invite us to put it into question form? Unfortunately, it does exactly that, as Halpin admits, and we may thereby be encouraged to ask the question: 'How can administrative theory be applied by the super-intendent?' The error that Halpin saw in this question occurs because administrative theory (which he then apparently still believed in) does not tell the administrator what to do: it will simply serve to 'sharpen his analysis of the social situations with which he must deal' and 'thus enable him to make wiser decisions' (Halpin, 1966, 285). Wiser decisions? Whatever happened to the fundamental distinction that the earlier writings about theory had taught us to make between 'is' and 'ought'? And whatever happened to a theory based on conceptual relationships that would eluci-date the 'why' and 'how' of things? Sharpening the 'analytical skills' of administrators is surely a long way from offering the administrator a research-based theory of why things are as they are; and it surely falls short of any insight into how variables can be manipulated to make the adminis-trative world otherwise than it is.

Griffiths (1957, 364), writing in *Administrative Behavior in Education,* another of the basic manifestos of the New Movement, had no doubt about the utility of theory for the administrator. There he proclaimed that '*Theory as guide to action* has first place in administration.' The only limitation he saw on the role of theory was its inapplicability in the world of values. He asks whether theory can tell the administrator what he ought to do and answers, 'Apparently no.' The reason for theory's incapacity in the face of values lies in the positivistic separation of facts and values. Theory, in this view, deals with means while values deal with the ends to which means may be applied. Griffiths (1957, 365–366) elaborates this distinction as follows:

> Since theory is finally validated entirely by empirical means it would be a serious error to think of theory in terms of setting ethical standards for administrators to meet. The use of theory must be restricted to factual content. The 'oughtness' of administrative action is derived from the set of values to which the administrator adheres. Science is in and of itself ethically neutral.

The difficulty with this position began to bother Halpin (1960) even in the early days of the march towards the New Movement science of educational administration. The trouble arises from its neat separation of fact and value. While theory, logic and positivistic science may conveniently separate fact and value, the administrator cannot. They are inextricably intertwined in the world administrators deal with. Halpin (1960; 1966, 284) grants that administrators have good cause to be uneasy about theory because it leaves out of consideration the critical realities they must cope with:

> There is indeed something missing. The fault is that the scientist's theoretical models of administration are too rational, too tidy, to aseptic. They remind us of the photographs in magazines devoted too home decorating – glossy pictures of dramatic and pristine living room interiors . . . The Superintendent distrusts such tidiness in administrative theory and senses intuitively that the theoretical–analytical approach has ignored much that is reality. That is why I think we had better examine afresh our present perspectives in educational administration. We had better be sure that the current slant on administrative theory is taking us where we want to go.

This warning has been ignored for more than a decade. Only in recent years have Halpin's latter-day doubts been noted, let alone seriously considered. Halpin concluded his 1966 text on theory and research in administration – which he later admitted contained no theory at all – with a plea for greater tolerance for those who seek different roads to administrative truth and for those who recognize that there are many ways by which we can come to know things. He was then (1966, 296) less sure that either the practitioner's grasp of detail or the theoretician's retreat to abstraction constituted the only roads to knowledge and that one of them must be the true path and the other the false:

> I suggest that the crux of all science, of all practice and of all wisdom lies in a careful, sensitive observation of what is indeed 'out there'. But it is easy to be blinded, whether by the slogans of the practitioners' work-a-day world or by the jargon of the scientists' never-never land.

His solution, which he was sure would alienate him from both superintendents and scientists, was to turn to that tradition which both sides 'have studiously ignored: the heritage of the humanities' (1966, 296). This occasion is not the appropriate one to consider the implications of this statement further, but it should at least be noted now that critics of research in educational administration such as Hodgkinson (1978b) and Greenfield (1979b) see philosophical and value questions as constituting the heart of administrative action. From this perspective, no theory of administration or methodology of research can be adequate unless it comes to terms with that condition of human life which inextricably interweaves fact and value. It is this circumstance, this recognition of the

32

complexity and drama in human life, that burdens administrative studies with enormously difficult problems while surrounding them also with the sense of urgency and inevitability that attends upon matters of great importance.

It is perhaps now becoming clear why I said at the outset of this paper that its purpose might easily be fulfilled. If major cracks have appeared in the theoretical foundation of an administrative science constructed to guide practical action – as I believe they have – what is the point in reviewing the content of research that has been conducted within the framework of such theory? I have suggested here why I think such short-comings do exist in the basic theory and given arguments elsewhere to support this view (Greenfield, 1975; 1979a). It is clear, however, that contention still surrounds this point of view (Griffiths, 1977; Greenfield, 1978) and that further argument is needed to support it. Justification for this position can perhaps best be provided by examining the conclusions reached by authors who have conducted comprehensive reviews of research in educational administration. To my mind, examination of these reviews reveals major flaws in administrative theory and obvious in-adequacies in the research; they reveal as well a sharp contrast between the substance of the theory and research on the one hand and a continuing, optimistic faith on the other hand, that still prevails among many pro-fessors of educational administration and so enables them to go on propagating belief in the possibility, power and usefulness of a science of administration. The implications of this gulf between evidence and faith will be taken up again.

REVIEWING THE REVIEWS

Before turning to the major reviews of research in educational adminis-tration, let us be quite clear about the ideological base on which the New Movement stood. And let us be clear too, what the Movement meant by 'theory' and 'research'. Once again, Halpin provides invaluable assistance in exploring these points. He outlines the basic assumptions of New Move-ment ideology and their implications for the study of administration in three short statements. I am sure that anyone familiar with either classic or contemporary literature of the Movement will recognize them as accurate descriptions of how the Movement conceived its task as it set out to solve the problems of administration action.

1 That the role of theory be recognized and that 'nakedly empirical research' be rejected in favour of hypothetico–deductive research rooted in theory.
2 That educational administration not be viewed provincially, and especi-ally as distinct from other kinds of administration. That administration,

as administration, without adjectival qualifiers, is a proper subject for study and research.

3 That, because education can be construed best as a social system, educational administration must, in turn, draw heavily from insights furnished by the behavioral sciences (Halpin, 1970, 162–163).

The theories sought by the founders of the New Movement were to be something like Newton's laws of dynamics: mathematical formulae relating operationally defined concepts would direct researchers to reason how the administrative world was constructed; it would enable them to devise strong hypotheses for checking their reasoning and direct them to the data relevant to such experimentation. Certainly it is such an approach that Griffiths (1957) defined and advocated in the early phase of the Movement. In this approach to theory and research, facts are important, but only facts of a certain kind. At that time Griffiths (1957, 361–362) made the researcher the judge of what it is to be considered a fact and of what facts are relevant in research. He then cited the psychologist, Guthrie, and asserts that 'objective evidence' is that based upon 'facts open to the observation of all' and '*accepted by other scientists*'. I have added the emphasis in the previous quotation because it makes it clear that the researchers of New Movement administrative science were themselves the ultimate criterion for determining what was 'fact' in the social world they were studying. As Schumacher (1977, 3–4) points out, this approach makes the scientist the map-maker of reality:

> The philosophical maps with which I supplied at school and university . . . failed to show large 'unorthodox' sections of both theory and practice in medicine, agriculture, psychology, and the social and political sciences, not to mention art and so-called occult or paranormal phenomena, the mention of which was considered to be a sign of mental deficiency. In particular, all the most prominent doctrines shown on the 'map' accepted art only as self-expression or as escape from reality. Even in nature there was nothing artistic except by chance, that is to say, even the most beautiful appearances could be fully accounted for – so we were told – by their utility in reproduction, as affecting natural selection. In fact, apart from 'museums' the entire map from right to left and from top to bottom was drawn in utilitarian colours: hardly anything was shown as existing unless it could be interpreted as profitable for man's comfort or useful in the universal battle for survival.

So theorists in administrative science faced a problem: Of the facts in their subjective world, what should they pay attention to? Griffiths answers this puzzling question by returning to the theory itself. It is theory that tells us what facts to look for. So within a few pages Griffiths (1957, 364–366) tells his readers, on the one hand, that '*theory as a guide to action* has first place in administration' and, on the other hand, that '*theory is a guide to the collection of facts*'. The emphasis in these quotations is in the text and should serve now to reveal the circularity of the logic that it contains. Theory in this argument is both a guide for action and the standard for identifying data to test the validity of the theory.

From this review of the foundations of administrative research, it should be clear theory itself played a paramount role in determining what scientists saw as true and in directing their attention to certain facts. But where was the theory? It is extraordinary now to look back at the writings of the New Movement and to realize, as Halpin (1960, 1966) did, how little theory the behavioural scientists offered as explanation for administrative action. It is for this reason that theorists reached, as I have argued elsewhere (Greenfield, 1975) for the systems ideas to explain the social fabric. The Parsonian systems view explained everything at such a level of generality that the myriad of micro-empirical studies that blossomed under its aegis found either nothing of significance or reported findings of such tiny scope that the massive edifice of the overriding 'theory' was never supported or threatened by them. It was Halpin who first began to point to the absence of theory of the rigorous hypothetico–deductive kind that the Movement itself called for. 'Where is it?' he asked, and got little answer. 'Bring on the theory', is the repeated theme in Halpin's later writings, 'it must exist somewhere.' Or, as Stephen Sondheim in his almost popular song might sing, 'Bring on the clowns, there's got to be clowns.'

Halpin's review

In his review conducted in 1969, Halpin (1970) reports finding no theory defining *the content* of administration and only five 'major research contributions' that can be attributed to the New Movement. Given the need for hypothetico–deductive theory to guide research, it is not clear how the research constitutes 'substantive achievements', as Halpin (1970, 163) claims it does. This anomaly is not a matter Halpin deals with in his review. The five studies he cites are well-known but a rather curious collection if one takes seriously the claim that research should rest on a foundation of hypothetico–deductive theory. In chronological order he lists them as (1) his own work with the Leader Behavior Description Questionnaire (LBDQ), completed in 1956 (Halpin, 1966); (2) the model of administration as a social process developed by Getzels and Guba (Getzels and Guba, 1957; Halpin, 1958); (3) the study, *Administrative Performance and Personality* by Hemphill, Griffiths and Frederickson (1962); (4) Carlson's *Executive Succession and Organizational Change* (1962); and (5) Halpin and Croft's examination of the organizational climate of schools with a new instrument, the OCDQ. This instrument turned out, of course, to be as

35

adaptable to computer technology and to sophisticated statistical pressure-cooking as had the earlier LBDQ.

If these are the major achievements of administrative science in education to the year 1969, they surely justify a scepticism on the part of practitioners that leads them to conclude that such science provides no guide to action and offers little insight into the process of administration. All of the studies rest on *ex post facto* designs. This weakness in research design all too frequently makes the researchers yield to temptation and to read the resulting correlations – obtained often by torturing the data in the computer – as causalities. Many of these studies might well be described by Halpin's own *Schimpfwort*, 'naked empiricism'. Reviews that have examined the flood of leadership and climate studies (Greenfield, 1968; Andrews, 1965) have found serious limitations in their validity and have suggested basic theoretical problems not dealt with in the research. The study of administrative performance and personality and the study of executive succession also suffer from the shortcomings of *ex post facto* research design. Even if one accepts their findings as explanations, how can one use them as a guide for action? The personalities of administrators and the cosmopolitan orientations of chief executive officers do not lend themselves to ready manipulation, even if one is convinced that these are indeed the critical variables that determine administrative action and organizational change.

And what of the famed Getzels–Guba model? is it not odd that Halpin accepts this model as research? What the model does, in fact, is draw a picture of the social world in the manner so favoured by theorists of administration. The reader is presented with a set of boxes connected by directional arrows to make the point that a person's behaviour stems in part from unique elements within the individual and in part from broader social realities. This insight is summed up in the speciously precise formula $B = f(R \times P)$, to tell us that behaviour is a function of role and personality. While its over-simplifications may have launched a thousand doctoral theses, the Getzels–Guba model is more like a Mercator projection of the social world than it is like the hypothetico–deductive theory that Halpin (1957, 156) and Griffiths (1957, 359–360) advocated in their early attempts to establish the New Movement science of educational administration. Instead of precise operationally-defined concepts linked by strong logic, the Getzels–Guba model merely views the social world from a lofty distance. From this vantage-point it then manages to reduce the puzzles, conflicts and pain of life in organizations to a few neatly working regularities by applying some very special assumptions to the mysteries of existence.

The review of educational research

Over the decade beginning in 1958 the American Educational Research Association devoted three issues of its journal, the *Review of Educational*

Research, to studies of research in educational administration. This decade begins at the moment when the New Movement was, as it were, springing full-grown and confident out of the mind of Zeus, and it spans the years of the Movement's growth to some maturity. The research reviewed in these volumes therefore provides a fair and reasonable basis for assessing the fruits of the New Movement as seen in its research and theory. A look at what is said in the reviews reveals a strange paradox: critics writing at the time reported their growing disillusionment with theory and their recognition of the enormous difficulties involved in achieving high-quality research. Divided opinion about the possibility of a science of administration is also apparent in the reviews.

In the 1958 *Review*, Griffiths and Iannaccone (1958) provided the major contribution. Writing from the perspective of the New Movement, they demanded cogent theory and stringent research from the studies they reviewed and found these qualities generally lacking in the work before them. In their conclusions, Griffiths and Iannaccone (1958, 350) complain first that they were

> faced at the outset with the almost impossible task of evaluating the rigor of the research reported. Of the hundred or so articles which by the most generous stretch of the imagination can be considered reports of research, only an extremely small proportion give exact information concerning either conceptual or technical tools used.

They go on (p. 351) to condemn the reliance upon questionnaires built on the assumption that self-reports by respondents give reliable insights into 'behavior, human relationships, and administrative process'. Despite these damning judgements, they end their review (p. 352) by noting a commendable trend towards group-based interdisciplinary research and by pointing to its desirable focus upon administration as a dynamic phenomenon. In their final words they note progress toward 'solution of the criteria problem' and 'a movement toward theory and away from naked empiricism'.

By the time the next volume appeared in 1964, the New Movement had been in progress some time and one might expect to see some major improvement in the quality of research and indications of substantive findings. In his central chapter in the 1964 *Review*, Lipham's (1964, 450) critique finds that the studies reviewed have 'focused upon behavioral antecedents, rather than upon behavior *per se*'. He sees important gaps still to be filled. His final comments (p. 450) focus upon the inadequacies of the leadership studies then in vogue:

> Yet the veridicality of existing measures of leader behavior as well as their relevance for describing leadership in the educational organization must be continuously tested, lest educational researchers

erroneously assume that their present knowledge of leader behavior is more secure than in fact it is.

Despite this sombre warning from Lipham, two other critics, Briner and Campbell (1964, 485), announced in the same volume of the *Review* that 'a science of administration is emerging'. They did not dwell, however, on what the essence of that science was. Instead, they engaged in the long-standing game of theorizing about theory and reported various disparate empirical findings from research. One thing is clear from their article, however. They are in favour of change in education and take administrators and teachers to task for their slowness in adopting innovations. Adopting an analogy between agriculture and administration, they note how social science has assisted government to persuade farmers to use hybrid corn seed that possessed demonstrably superior growing qualities. From this discussion (p. 486) they turn to note that 'administrators and researchers in education also have been slow to accept and to use scientific inquiry'. This failing they attributed, on the basis of social scientific research, to 'habits and beliefs' that preclude 'intelligent consideration of theory in administration'. Among these unfortunate habits and beliefs they included 'fear of theorizing and lack of appropriate language'. In these days, when a considerably part of many educational changes wrought in recent years begin to appear faddish and possibly ill-advised, these claims that science is on the side of educational change appear remarkable indeed.

The 1967 volume of the *Review* is noteworthy in two respects. Brown and House (1967, 412) report a surprising shortage of quality research. They point to the 'immensity of the practical problems confronting school administrators today' (p. 413) but conclude (p. 412) that 'it would be misleading to suggest that educational administration researchers are developing a massive attack upon the nature and functioning of organizations in education'. Despite the rhetoric about the power of administrative science and theory, they find that the sheer quantity of research supporting this flow of words is surprisingly small.

Donald Erickson who acted as chairman of the committee supervising the preparation of the 1967 review, underscores this judgement in his own critical article reviewing research on the school administrator. He delivers his judgement on this branch of research in administrative science as follows:

It would appear that research on the school administrator represents an immature field, lacking well established canons of inquiry of any notable rigor and suffering still from efforts that reflect little awareness of previous developments. A strong cross-fire of collegial criticism might be salutary at this point. (Erickson, 1967, 430)

Erickson goes on, nevertheless, to express some optimism for research in the field on the strength of the 'sustained attention' and 'seminal concepts' that 'a growing coterie of capable scholars' have given to 'relevant issues' (p. 430). Included in his hagiography of capable scholars are the familiar names of Griffiths, Gross, Hemphill, Campbell, Getzels and 'especially Halpin'. Erickson's overall view of the field at that time was much less sanguine than the hopes he placed in a coterie of capable scholars. In his foreword to the 1967 *Review* (p. 376), his view is at best equivocal on the prospect for establishing an administrative science in education:

> The field is very much in flux. The erstwhile search for 'administrative theory', for example, seems virtually abandoned today, thought a few scholars still attempt to explain important events in terms of what The Leader is or does. . . . There is still enough second-rate research in the area to justify humility. . . . Among the questionnaire lionizers are appearing a few validators.

Erickson's hopefulness expressed in 1967 does not persist, however, as we shall see when we examine his later opinions.

The study of educational administration

Perhaps the most succinct and comprehensive review of research in educational administration is that provided by Immegart (1977). His review is but one article in the publication which arose from the 1975 conference held at the Ohio State University under the title: 'Educational Administration Twenty Years Later: 1954–1974'. There are several important contributions in the publication (Cunningham, Hack and Nystrand, 1977) but they are best seen against Immegart's review of the research. To being with, his review was extraordinarily painstaking. The substance of his findings, however, is not much different from that already reported from the special issues of the *Review of Educational Research*. Immegart's conclusions are, however, set out with almost brutal clarity. Although his tone is generally charitable and optimistic, the substance of what he says identifies major problems in the study of educational administration. In his conclusions, Immegart (1977, 315) finds that the research over the twenty years reviewed has increased in both quality and quantity but 'not so dramatically as many think' and 'not to the degree hoped for'. He finds (p. 317) 'substantive dialogue and interaction conspicuously absent in the published literature' and notes (p. 316) that 'research tends to follow hot topics, social concerns, popular concepts, theory, or models'. Improvements in the methodology of studies were apparent, but these yielded more by way of sophistication of techniques than in validity of findings. In other words, the studies are characterized by changes in style without corresponding increases in their contributions to knowledge.

39

A great range of methodologies has been tried from case studies to experiments . . ., but advances in sophistication are most notable in terms of instruments for gathering data and procedures or approaches for analyzing data. More broadly conceived in terms of study design, problem development, time perspective, and 'controls', methodological improvement has been less obvious.

Thus methodology is becoming an end in itself in administrative studies and the realization of the great promise of the theory movement seems as far away as ever.

The 1977 seminar on theory and research

A landmark event in the development of the New Movement in educational administration was the seminar on the 'role of theory in educational administration' (Halpin, 1958) sponsored by the University Council on Educational Administration (UCEA) and the Midwest Administration Center of the University of Chicago. In 1959 there followed another seminar sponsored by the Midwest Administration Center, directed at 'further exploration concerning the relevance of different theoretical approaches for the practice of educational administration' (Campbell and Lipham, 1960, vii). Halpin's retrospective view (1970, 157) of such seminars regarded them as largely empty of substantive theory about administration. Instead, these seminars provided platforms for those who wished to argue for theory-based research in administration. Perhaps recognizing that further advocacy of this idea was not required, no institution sponsored a similar seminar for nearly twenty years. In 1977, UCEA and the University of Rochester sponsored such a seminar and directed it to look not only at problems in theory and research methodology, but also to examine the substantive outcomes of research in educational administration. The proceedings of this seminar will appear in print shortly (Immegart and Boyd, 1979). They make interesting reading. A battle is apparent in the proceedings between those who seek on the one hand to improve administrative theory by better and more sophisticated technology and those (Greenfield, 1979a; Griffiths, 1979) who argue on the other hand that such improvements can come only through new methodologies and different ideas for understanding and directing them.

In perhaps one of the most significant comments made to the seminar, Griffiths (1979, 51) repudiated the paradigm of the past that saw organizations as goal-dominated, administrative behaviour as rational and member motivation as ordered, though perhaps imperfectly, around bureaucratic rules and legitimate power. This paradigm, he said,

is neither useful nor appropriate because it is no longer fruitful in generating powerful concepts and hypotheses: it does not allow us to describe either modern organizations or the people in them and, as a result, it is not helpful to administrators.

The issue raised here is the goodness-of-fit problem. How are we to conceive organizations? What ideas will help us to understand them either theoretically or in 'reality'? These are, indeed, major questions, and to hear Griffiths voice them means that one of the pioneers of the New Movement in administration has conceded that, twenty years or more after its inception, the New Movement is still struggling to find a theoretical base from which to launch productive research. As I have argued elsewhere (Greenfield, 1979a), the recognition of this goodness-of-fit problem is the first step in its solution, though we must recognize as well that the solution will probably bring with it the destruction of the notion of a science of administration, a notion to which the New Movement has devoted so much time and effort.

The Ericksonian critique

Donald Erickson (1977a) has produced another of the recent and valuable critiques of research in educational administration. His work is part exemplar of selected research and part argument for 'a paradigm shift' in the study of educational administration, shift that he (1977b; 1979) has argued for elsewhere as well. Significantly, very few of the exemplars are drawn from studies conducted within the field of educational administration. Moreover, despite his contention (1977a, x–xi) that one criterion for the selection of the studies was their practically, it appears that these studies no more provided a guide for action than did the earlier efforts that Halpin (1966, 283–346) so trenchantly criticized when he urged researchers to reach beyond the 'glyphs and graphs' of stereotyped social science research.

Erickson does identify and recommend a new emphasis in the study of educational administration. His preference for 'practical' studies is also reflected in the summary chapter of Immegart and Boyd (1979) where they call for policy-oriented research. Expressing what may be an emerging new emphasis in the field, these critics contend that research in educational administration has taken too narrow and self-serving a view of the problems of administration. Researchers' concerns have too often focused on the administrators themselves or perhaps, in a somewhat wider conception of the field, upon administrators and teachers. In any case, the central questions pursued in many researches have directed attention to the effect of organizations on people, with 'people' being effectively defined as administrators and teachers. Other dynamics within the organization have been of lesser interest to researchers. Similarly, these critics are arguing that the field has ignored large contextual effects on schools. The implications of the Coleman *et al.* (1966) and Jencks *et al.* (1972) studies have scarcely been acknowledged by researchers in educational administration. The reason for this indifference is to be found, they argue further, in the fact that these studies suggest that schools have less impact upon learning than administrators and those who study them would like to believe.

Texts in educational administration

Before leaving this section reviewing the reviews, I would like to look briefly at another body of literature. While it is not a source usually cited in scholarly reviews, it is one that sheds important light on how the field of educational administration has interpreted administrative theory and the research that supposedly supports it. The literature I refer to is that found in texts used in training programmes for educational administrators. I have chosen an unscientific sample of these texts by the simple expedient of standing in front of that section in the stacks of my university library devoted to writings in educational administration. From this collection I drew some well-known texts produced over a period of several years and examined them to determine what knowledge professors of education administration set before their students. The sample is small, but contains authors whose names (Morphet, Johns and Reller, 1959, 1967; Getzels, Lipham and Campbell, 1968; Granger, 1971; Milstein and Belasco, 1973; and Hoy and Miskel, 1978) would be familiar to those who know the prominent members of the American professional associations in the study of educational administration. With a single exception, the overwhelming emphasis in these texts is upon theory and explanation. Critical attention to research is notably absent in all but one text – that by Getzels, Lipham and Campbell (1968). In all of the texts, moreover, research where it appears is invariably used to support and confirm the theories presented. Doubts about the quality of research or the validity of the theory may be readily found in the scholarly literature, as has been argued above, but doubts of this kind do not make their way into these texts. The difficulties of conducting research based on hypothetico–deductive theory – and indeed, as some critics would argue, the simple absence of theory – does not appear to trouble the authors of these texts. Their aim, after all, is to help other professors to train educational administrators and to present them with an ordered and explainable picture of organizations and administration. In this they certainly succeed. The problem in presenting such a picture of administrative science, as I have already suggested, is that it stands at sharp variance with the scholarly reviews of research that repeatedly show a lack of research-validated theories and continuing methodological and conceptual problems.

These difficulties are barely mentioned or totally ignored in these texts, which are bent upon demonstrating that administration is a science or, at least, that it is more science than art and that a substantial body of know-ledge exists that will make those who master it better administrators. Hodg-kinson (1978a) has asked how this state of affairs came to be and points to Litchfield's (1956) classic article, 'Notes Towards a General Theory of Administration', written for the founding issue of the *Administrative Science Quarterly*. The article stated only general propositions and left the details, as it were, to be worked out by later theoreticians and researchers. Hodg-kinson concurs with other scholarly critics in concluding that this elabora-tion has never been fulfilled and that the field is still subject to Simon's (1957, 20) castigation as a set of mutually contradictory 'proverbs'. The explanation of this failure, according to Hodgkinson (1978a, 272), is found in the 'stupefyingly simple reason that the central questions of adminis-tration are not scientific at all. They are philosophical'.

From this point, Hodgkinson goes on to make a distinction between administrative theory and organization theory. He sees administrative theory as dealing with the existential realities of making decisions and wielding power. But it is exactly these kinds of concerns that are missing from the textbooks on the science of educational administration. They deal instead with organizations and the relationships people have to them. These relationships are modeled and described in a myriad of ways, all of which seem to say that organizations and the people in them can be conceived as a set of complex variables in interaction. The assumption is that, if one can only picture the variables, one can also control them. Questions, of what the administrator ought to do or what it means to have power and use it are barely mentioned or totally ignored.

This characterization is probably unfair in some respects to the texts I have reviewed, or to others I have not reviewed, but I believe it is justified as a general assessment of them. The most recent of them, the text by Hoy and Miskel (1978), is the text that perhaps best illustrates my point. It is replete with diagrams and models showing how organizations work. Administration is conceived as a technical problem in achieving goals and science is invoked to provide the administrator with the skills needed to make the organization achieve its goals and to keep people happy, moti-vated and productive. The text discusses no substantive issues in the con-duct of schools; no words speak of segregation or other common problems arising from culture, language, religion and disagreements over curri-culum and evaluation. They remain silent that public faith in schools may be waning while doubts grow and shake our conviction that schools are good and serve useful purposes. Instead Hoy and Miskel (1978, vii) open their text by directing it to

> educational administrators who want to make their administrative
> practice less of an art and more of a science. . . . To this end, the focus
> of the analysis was on social systems, bureaucracy, professionalism,

work motivation, job satisfaction, organizational climate, leadership, decision making, and communication. We believe that our work reflects the current 'state of the science' in educational administration.

If it does reflect the state of administrative science in education, it does so without ever referring to values, philosophy, conflict, the 'hidden injuries' of school, the debate about phenomenology, or to what Daniel Griffiths now describes as the 'turmoil' in the field of educational administration.

THE FUTURE OF RESEARCH IN EDUCATIONAL ADMINISTRATION

This review of research in educational administration has certainly been too brief to do full justice to the efforts that many researchers have made over nearly a quarter of a century. It may serve, however, to identify certain recurring difficulties in the field and to suggest the cause of them. I have limited my aim to describing the larger trends in research and to identifying some of its adequacies. Comment about the future of research in the field may be appropriate now as a conclusion for the article.

Shadow and substance

Words bewitch us. Their meanings and connotations can take on greater reality to us than the substance they are supposed to denote. We become prisoners of our ideas, of our thinking. And so we lose the power to deal effectively with each other and with that puzzling entity we call 'the world'. William James spoke of reality as a buzzing, blooming welter that we are left to make sense of. What appears to have happened in the study of educational administration in the United States and Canada is that the ideas, assumptions and convictions – the theories – that academics use to describe organizations and administration now exist in a world of their own. At least, they stand in marked contrast to what many others in schools understand as their realities. Science-making in educational administration has become an end in itself; it does not seriously or meaningfully impinge upon the world of administrators, teachers, students and all those concerned for what goes on in schools. The academic study of educational administration goes on, in Sylvia Plath's plangent term, like life under a bell jar. It is sealed from the larger world, but the barrier is noticed by virtually no one in the oppressive, airless environment.

Perhaps I exaggerate here to make a point, but the problem is certainly one that others have identified. Halpin and Hayes (1977, 287–288) speak of the 'language' of administrative theory, a language that the New Movement introduced to the world. This language, they assert, has become part of the 'conventional wisdom' in educational administration and continues as a medium of discourse apart from any relevance to basic issues and practical realities. They contend, moreover, that the understanding of pivotal concepts by many professors of educational administration is 'word deep':

> The ability to match the names of investigators with names of the specific concepts with which they are associated is not enough: it would be helpful if one also *understood* the concepts themselves.

Empirical studies confirm this rather depressing judgement. Hills (1965, 63) found that a large proportion of professors of educational administration could not recognize the difference between 'facts' and conceptual relationships. When asked to consider the statement: 'The expectations that teachers hold for administrators are, in part, a function of their personalities', nearly forty per cent of the respondents thought the statement was either factual or a description of a directly observable relation between events. Campbell and Newell (1973) further confirm these difficulties and report, on the basis of a national survey, a low commitment on the part of many professors of educational administration to theory development and research.

Faced with these observations, Halpin (Halpin and Hayes, 1977, 288–289; Halpin, 1969, 6–7) sees only a lack of talent in young professors and the failure of research training programmes. No one, he feels, was there to catch the flame that the first Olympians threw to later researchers. As a consequence, the torch of competent research was 'fumbled' (Halpin, 1970). But the problem is surely deeper than that. In fact, the contrary appears to be true. Younger researchers in the United States and Canada have certainly picked up the torch of positivistic science (Greenfield, 1979a, 168–175). They display with ease the methods derived from the legacy of hypothetico–deductive theory that the pioneer behavioural scientists in the field left them. The greater availability of computing technology and 'packages' for statistical analysis has worsened, not improved, the problem as Halpin and Hayes (1977, 289) argue it could.[2]

For example, a recent issue of the *Educational Administration Quarterly* contains a report of research that purports to study charismatic leadership among school superintendents in Kentucky by means of an instrument called the Charismatic Authority Scale (Scott, 1978). The study reports that tenured superintendents were more charismatic 'than superintendents in the low and medium tenure groups' (Scott, 1978, 43). Despite the fact that the author reports high validity and reliability (0.97 and 0.96) for the scale, it is hard to imagine a finding that runs more strongly at odds with Weber's basic notion of charisma. One suspects that if by some highly improbable circumstance the researcher could measure the Ayatollah Ruhollah Khomaini on his scale, the Ayatollah would score low on it.

Yes, our words do bewitch us and so, too, do the methods of the positivistic science in studies of administration that too often make us see and believe in what is not there or is of little importance if it is there. More importantly, it keeps us as scientists firmly under the bell jar so we fail to note shattering events that are going on in the world around us.

Policy and the practical

In response to the manifest failures of administrative theory and research, some scholars (Immegart and Boyd, 1979; Erickson, 1977b; 1979) are urging the field to turn from its past concerns to new emphases upon policy studies and 'practical issues'. If administrative theory is to be of some consequences in this world, these authors argue, scholars must turn their minds to matters recognized as important in the world at large. Two difficulties may be identified in this connection. First, these new directions seem a little faddish; they reflect a growing mood of conservatism among the electorates of the United States and Canada. This mood drives towards the elimination of government services that only a few years ago were welcomed as essential pillars of the good society. Conventional wisdom in both popular and academic circles are likely – at least in the United States – to see the effectiveness of schools as determined by factors essentially outside the control of schools. Such argument thus helps those who would reduce the public financial support given to schools. Contrary opinions on this matter are held in Canada, where belief in government as an instrument for achieving social ends is stronger than in the United States. Canadian schools are now increasingly used to give students second-language competence in pursuit of social and political purposes that are possibly vital to the survival of the country. Yet this example of a 'school effect' is one that makes little sense in the American context (Holmes, 1978). We seem to be more confident in Canada than in the United States that schools do have real effects and that it is worth putting money into them.

The basic difficulty with policy studies is not whether they would be of value, but rather if they are possible. The basic question is whether social science *can* improve policy-making. I have already suggested that cultural circumstances alter the views that scholars take about a given issue, for example, on the question of 'school effects'. The literature on policy-making is, of course, large and complex (Stufflebeam *et al.*, 1971). Experienced scholars in the field are now likely to argue that social science can make only a small contribution to 'effective policy-making' – whatever this high-sounding but ambiguous term might turn out to mean. Along this line, Levin (1975, 236) argues

> that the social sciences cannot produce conclusive results that would
> support a particular educational strategy for improving the life

attainments of students from low income and minority families. Also, it has been asserted that the evidence that does enter the courts or policy arena is considered and utilized on the basis of factors other than its scientific 'validity'.

The danger in the move towards policy studies in educational administration is, therefore, that 'science' will be no more effective in solving educational policy questions than the New Movement in educational administration was in improving our understanding of organization and administration. But, even as the New Movement succeeded in establishing an academic industry devoted to the study of the 'science' of administration, the new movement towards policy might well end with another academic establishment under the bell jar whose relevance to the practicalities of the outside world is no greater than that of the scientific movement in the study of administration.

Similar difficulties will surely also stand in the path of Erickson's plan for 'practical' studies in administration. He calls for rigorous research that will link administrative behaviour with student outcomes. Alas, our field has travelled this path before, as Erickson should know. Halpin's (1957) 'paradigm for research on administrator behavior' was published twenty-two years ago and provides what is surely the most complete and careful design for research that might link what administrators do to demonstrable outcomes. Research that fully explores the implication of this model has never been carried out in educational administration. This failure testifies not to the incompetence of researchers or even to their lack of diligence. It is evidence, rather, that there is something wrong with the paradigm. To begin with, it identifies and links conceptually a bewildering array of variables. Virtually everything is thrown into the analytical pot and, as with such approaches to reality, the task of sorting out the effect of one variable from the many intertwined in the phenomena under investigation is virtually impossible. And furthermore, the paradigm rests on the assumptions of positivistic science and therefore omits all that lies in the domain of value and will. For these two reasons, the complexity of the variables and the omission of human purposefulness, the paradigm has failed in the past to tell us much about what makes effective administrators and efficient organizations. Similar models are likely to fail again in the future despite Erickson's otherwise cogent arguments in favour of the attempt. However desirable it might be to have the knowledge that such models promise, the bleak fact is that the complexity and mystery of the human condition will likely deny it to us again as it has so often in the past. To repeat from Hodgkinson: The central questions of administration are not scientific but philosophic.

An alternative?

Readers of this paper will almost certainly tell me what I have heard before. 'You destroy existing achievements but offer nothing in their place.' If 'achievements' in administration are so readily destroyed, I can feel little regret at their loss. My answer now to this charge is to repeat what I have said before. The act of destruction is also an act of creation. We cannot abandon old ways of thinking without putting new ones in their place. I can make only two suggestions to guide further research. One is to place greater emphasis upon the specific as opposed to the general as a starting point for enquiry. Social science has been too successful in teaching us to see truth in numbers and to insist that nothing is true unless it is true everywhere. Since I have written about these ideas elsewhere (1978; 1979a) I will not elaborate them at the end of this lengthening paper. My second suggestion is to take seriously again a basic theoretical and methodological question: what is the relation between the unique event and the context in which it exists?

Explorations of these questions will take us into the philosophy of science and the philosophy of action. Are these suggestions too remote from what one might normally consider as educational administration? I don't know. I am coming not to know what educational administration is and to doubt that it ought to continue an existence as an independent field of inquiry. In its place, I am beginning to believe in basic studies in the humanities and a consideration of the existential realities experienced by those who wield power in schools and by those who suffer its application.

I will close with some quotations evocative of the alternative direction towards which I am groping. The first two are from Hodgkinson (1978a, 272–273):

> As a philosopher I feel justified in talking about number magic since I have never yet been able to actually find such a thing as a *number* in the empirical world.

> Arrow's General Impossibility Theorem . . . would certainly blow a lot of administrative battleships out of the water. Arrow's dilemma may be expressed as follows: Either we must accept the Fascistic notion of some kind of group mind, or else the group leader must himself impose his own will by force or guile – both of which are alternatives thoroughly distasteful to adherents of the contemporary rhetoric in administrative theory.

The following insights come from Sir Geoffrey Vickers who refers to the social–political impasse that occurred in Britain during the winter of 1978–79 when trade unionists precipitated a series of irregular strikes and walkouts to protest the policy that the Labour government thought would control inflation and thereby serve everyone's interests including those of unionists:[3]

How specific should we, can we be? Some millions of people here are acting in ways which their fellows regard as both wrong and self-defeating, because they are defining too narrowly the contexts in which they are acting. If they were more aware of the systematic relations between their collective demands, the sources from which these could be met and their effect as communications, they might act differently. But there are powerful historical reasons as well as other reasons why, if you are a trade unionist, you should exclude doubts about the desirability of 'winning' a strike.

So the contrast between the specific and the general is not all that sharp.

Schon and Argyris, in their book *Theory in Practice* define a theory as any proposition which can be put in the form of 'if this, then that'. But what if the 'this' be an unique contextual configuration, unique both in its own constituents and in the minds of all the participants, themselves uniquely constituted by their historic situation, which is itself continuously on the march? And 'that' be dependent among other things on what all the participants regard as 'this'? Everyone in daily life, including school administrators, knows that the world they live in is a subjective and inter-subjective interpretation of such unique contextual configurations. And more, the good ones manage very well in it.

If there is a lesson in all this, it is that the path to scientific administration is a hard road. Progress along it is difficult for those who would follow it. In the United States and Canada it has led to few real achievements. Perhaps it is time now to set out in new directions and in pursuit of new aims.

NOTES

1 First presented as a paper to the British Educational Administration Society (BEAS) Research Seminar, University of Birmingham, March 1979.
2 This argument is given at greater length in Greenfield (1979, 170–173). In this collection it is made again on pp. 13 and 64.
3 Sir Geoffrey Vickers, letter to TBG, 27 February 1979.

REFERENCES

Andrews, J. H. M. 1965. 'School Organizational Climate: Some Validity Studies'. *Canadian Education and Research Digest* 5, 4: 317–334.
Briner, C. and Campbell, R.F. 1964. 'The Science of Administration'. *Review of Educational Research* 37, 4: 485–492.
Brown, A. F. and House, J.H. 1967. 'The Organizational Component in Education'. *Review of Educational Research* 37, 4: 399–416.
Campbell, R.F. and Lipham, J. M. eds. 1960. *Administrative Theory as a Guide to Action*. Chicago: Midwest Administration Center, University of Chicago.

Campbell, R. F. and Lipham, J. M. 1973. *A Study of Professors of Educational Administration*. Colombus: University Council of Educational Administration.

Carlson, R. O. 1962. *Executive Succession and Organizational Change*. Chicago: Midwest Administration Center, University of Chicago.

Coleman, J., Campbell, E., Hobson, C., McPartland, H., Mood, W. F. and York, R. 1966. *Equality of Educational Opportunity*. Washington: U.S. Government Printing Office.

Erickson, D. A. 1967. 'Foreword'. In *Review of Educational Research* 37: 4.

Erickson, D. A., ed. 1977a. *Educational Organization and Administration*. Berkeley: McCutchan.

—— 1977b. 'An Overdue Paradigm Shift in Educational Administration, Or, How Can We Get That Idiot Off The Freeway?' In *Educational Administration: The Developing Decades*, eds L. L. Cunningham, W. G. Hack, and R. O. Nystrand, 119–143. Berkeley: McCutchan.

—— 1979. 'Research on Educational Administration: The State of the Art'. *Educational Review* 8, 3: 9–14.

Getzels, J. W. and Guba, E. G. 1957. 'Social Behavior and the Administrative Process'. *School Review* 65: 423–441.

Getzels, J. W., Lipham, J. M. and Campbell, R. F. 1968. *Educational Administration as a Social Process: Theory, Research Practice*. New York: Harper and Row.

Granger, R. L. 1971. *Educational Leadership: An Interdisciplinary Perspective*. Scranton: Intext.

Greenfield, T. B. 1968. 'Research on the Behavior of Leaders: Critique of a Tradition'. *Alberta Journal of Educational Research* 14, 1: 55–75.

—— 1975. 'Theory about Organization: A New Perspective and its Implications for Schools'. In *Administering Education: International Challenge*, ed. M. Hughes, 71–99. London: Athlone.

—— 1976. 'Bilingualism, Multiculturalism, and the Crisis of Purpose in Canadian Culture', In *Bilingualism in Canadian Education: Issues and Research*, ed. M. Swain, 107–136. Yearbook of the Canadian Society for the Study of Education. Edmonton: The Society.

—— 1978. 'Reflections on Organization Theory and the Truths of Irreconcilable Realities'. *Educational Administration Quarterly* 14, 2: 1–23.

—— 1979a. 'Ideas Versus Data, or, How Can the Data Speak for Themselves?' In *Problem Finding in Educational Administration: Trends in Research and Theory*, eds G. L. Immegart and W. L. Boyd, 167–190. Lexington, MA: D. C. Heath.

—— 1979b. 'Organization Theory as Ideology'. *Curriculum Inquiry* 9, 2: 97–112.

Griffiths, D. E. 1957. 'Towards a Theory of Administrative Behavior'. In *Administrative Behavior in Education*, eds R. F. Campbell and R. T. Gregg, 354–390. New York: Harper.

—— 1977. 'The Individual in Organization: A Theoretical Perspective'. *Educational Administration Quarterly* 13, 2: 1–18.

—— 1979. 'Another Look at Research on the Behavior of Administrators'. In *Problem-Finding in Educational Administration: Trends in Research and Theory*, eds G. L. Immegart and W. L. Boyd, 41–62. Lexington, MA: D. C. Heath.

Griffiths, D. E. and Iannaccone, L. 1958. 'Administrative Theory, Relationships, and Preparation'. *Review of Educational Research* 28, 4: 334–357.

Halpin, A. W. 1957. 'A Paradigm for Research on Administrative Behavior'. In *Administrative Behavior in Education*, eds R. F. Campbell and R. T. Gregg, 155–199. New York: Harper.

—— ed. 1958. *Administrative Theory in Education*. Chicago: Midwest Administration Center, University of Chicago.

—— 1960. 'Ways of Knowing'. In *Administrative Theory as a Guide to Action*, eds R. F. Campbell and J. M. Lipham, 3–20. Chicago: Midwest Administration Center, University of Chicago.

—— 1966. *Theory and Research in Administration*. New York: Macmillan.

—— 1969. 'A Foggy View from Olympus', *Journal of Educational Administration* 7, 1: 3–18.

—— 1970. 'Administrative Theory: The Fumbled Torch'. In *Issues in American Education*, ed. A. M. Kroll, 156–183. New York: Oxford.

Halpin, A. W. and Croft, D. B. 1963. *The Organizational Climate of Schools*. Chicago: Midwest Administration Center, University of Chicago.

Halpin, A. W. and Hayes, A. W. 1977. 'The Broken Ikon, Or, What Ever Happened to Theory?' In *Educational Administration: The Developing Decade*, eds L. L. Cunningham, W. G. Hack and R. O. Nystrand, 261–297. Berkeley: McCutchan.

Hemphill, J. K., Griffiths, D. E. and Frederickson, N. 1962. *Administrative Performance and Personality*. New York: Teachers College, Columbia.

Hills, J. 1965. 'Educational Administration as a Field in Transition'. In *Educational Administration Quarterly* 1, 1: 55–66.

Hodgkinson, C. 1978a. 'The Failure of Organizational and Administrative Theory'. *McGill Journal of Education* 13, 3: 271–278.

—— 1978b. *Towards a Philosophy of Administration*. Oxford: Basil Blackwell.

Holmes, M. 1978. 'Formal Education and Its Effects on Academic Achievement'. *Canadian Journal of Education* 3, 3: 55–70.

Hoy, W. K. and Miskel, C. G. 1978. *Educational Administration: Theory, Research, and Practice*. New York: Random House.

Immegart, G. L. 1977. 'The Study of Educational Administration, 1954–1974'. In *Educational Administration: The Developing Decades*, eds L. L. Cunningham, W. G. Hack and R. O. Nystrand, 298–326. Berkeley: McCutchan.

Immegart, G. L. and Boyd, W.L. 1979. 'Education's Turbulent Environment and Problem-Finding: Lines of Convergence'. In *Problem-Finding in Educational Administration: Trends in Research and Theory*, eds G. L. Immegart and W. L. Boyd, 275–289. Lexington, MA: D. C. Heath.

Jencks, C., Smith, M., Ackland, H., Bane, M., Cohen, D., Grintis, H., Hegus, B. and Micholson, N. 1972. *Inequality: A Reassessment of the Effect of Family and Schooling in America*. New York: Basic Books.

Layton, D. H. 1978. 'The Canadian International Intervisitation Program'. *UCEA Review* 20, 1: 1–10.

Levin, H. M. 1975. 'Education, Life Chances, and the Courts: The Role of Social Science Evidence'. *Law and Contemporary Problems*, 39, 2: 217–240.

Lipham, J. M. 1964. 'Organizational Character of Education: Administrative Behavior'. *Review of Educational Research* 34, 4: 435–454.

Litchfield, E. H. 1956. 'Notes on a General Theory of Administration'. *Administrative Science Quarterly* 1, 1: 3–29.

Milstein, M. M. and Belasco, J. A., eds. 1973. *Educational Administration and the Behavioral Sciences: A Systems Perspective*. Boston: Allyn and Bacon.

Morphet, E. L., Roe, L. and Reller, T. L. 1967 [1959]. *Educational Organization and Administration: Concepts, Practices, and Issues*, 2nd edn. Englewood Cliffs: Prentice Hall.

Schumacher, E. F. 1977. *A Guide for the Perplexed*. New York: Harper Colophon.

Scott, L. K. 1978. 'Charismatic Authority in the Rational Organization'. *Education Administration Quarterly* 14, 2: 43–62.

Simon, H. A. 1957 [1945]. *Administrative Behavior*, 2nd edn. New York: Free Press.

Stufflebeam, D. L., *et al.* 1971. *Educational Evaluation and Decision Making.* The Phi Delta Kappa National Study Committee on Evaluation. Itasca, IL: F. E. Peacock.

3

ORGANIZATIONS AS TALK, CHANCE, ACTION AND EXPERIENCE[1]

The world is all that is the case.
We make pictures of the facts for ourselves.
Nothing in the field of vision itself causes one to conclude that an eye sees it.
Everything could be different than we see it.
The world is independent of my will.

Ludwig Wittgenstein[2]

The error most theorists make in thinking about organizations is to conceive them as somehow separate from life, love, sex, growth, self, conflict, accomplishment, decay, death, and chance. If we seek to understand the world as people experience it, we come to see that they take the world very much as they find it. Each lives in his own world, but he must deal in that world with others and with the worlds they live in. Organizations come into existence when we talk and act with others. We strive to communicate with these others, to touch them, to understand them and often to control them. Generalizations and metaphysical justifications that tell why things are as they are or how they might be different and better are totally irrelevant to them. As A. E. Houseman, the English poet, says,

Malt does more than Milton can
To justify God's ways to man.

People do what they have to do, what they can do, and what they want to do. They have opportunities to act, to remain silent, to maximize their pleasure or to forswear it, to prevail upon others or to submit to them. Concrete, specific action is the stuff organizations are made of. In both their doing and their not doing, people make themselves and they make the social realities we call organizations.

These ideas, linking life and organization, are existential realities beyond expression in purely logical forms, but they cry out to us continually in our day-to-day existence. Their cries, when we hear them, we call

53

experience. Organization is an imposed and often self-accepted order that brings regularity and routine to our lives. It may bring change and revolution or even chaos and oblivion. (Did Prometheus know what he was doing and what consequences his act would have?) Above all, organizations are patterns of living, ways of seeing the world. They are designs for existence forged in the fire of life. They are the rules we choose to live by; they are also the rules that others have chosen for us and that we accept. Organizations are the meanings we find in our lives, regardless of how those meanings came to be there. The self cannot escape organizations. Indeed, self *is* organization in a profound sense, though the self may behave and feel quite differently as it moves from organization to organization – from fragment to fragment of its personal world.

A FALSE DICHOTOMY BETWEEN ORGANIZATION AND INDIVIDUAL

When Boulding classified general systems according to their complexity, he separated individuals and placed them below social systems in the hierarchy.

> The unit of such systems is not perhaps the person – the individual human as such – but the 'role' – that part of the person which is concerned with the organization. . . . The inter-relations of the role and the person however can never be completely neglected – a square person in a round hole becomes a little rounder, but he also makes the hole squarer.[3]

A fundamental assumption holds that organizations serve essential functions and are in some sense real. This assumption is made by theorists who begin a study of organizations by looking first at society and finding that it manifests a necessary, natural, and largely beneficent order. The history of this idea may be traced back to Plato who saw justice as each man fulfilling his nature and thereby his obligation to others and to the state. So Socrates explains to Glaucon,

> After a hard struggle, we have, though with difficulty reached the land; and we are pretty well satisfied that there are corresponding divisions, equal in number, in a state, and in the soul of every individual.[4]

In modern times, Spencer and Durkheim provide the intellectual foundations of realist theories of organization. Spencer expressed his thinking with an analogy between society and an organism. For him society is characterized not only by 'the increasing dependence of parts', but also by an 'increasingly efficient regulating system'.[5] Thus we see the development of the argument that organizations are necessary, efficient, and subject to a centralized control working for the general good. While Durkheim recognizes that society is expressed only through individuals, he argues that

54

organizations are necessary because they serve needs that individuals cannot meet; they mediate between the individual and the state.

> It is on the mass of individuals that the whole weight of the society rests. It has no other support. . . . The primary duty is to work out something that can relieve us by degrees of a role for which the individual is not cast. To do this, our political action must be to establish these secondary organs which, as they take shape, will release the individual from the State and vice versa, and release the individual, too, from a task for which he is not fitted.[6]

It is organizations, of course, that must be 'worked out'; these are at once independent of individuals and necessary to them. The obligation placed on individuals by this line of reasoning requires them to serve organizations so that the wider society – and thereby individuals as well – may benefit. Organizations are thus universal forms, lying behind immediate social reality and serving human needs. In theorists' ultimate vision, organizations are symbolic systems, linking people together in moral, cooperative enterprises in which everyone has an interest.[7] The dynamics of organizations are therefore similar in all cases; what distinguishes different organizations is simply the goals to which they are directed.[8] Since these goals are unattainable without organizations, their moral order is seen not only as right but as effective as well.

An alternative conception of organizations rests on ideas about experience, about how we come to understand what we do and what is happening to us. It accepts that people are inherently part of organizations, that organizations themselves are expressions of how people believe they should relate to each other. We thus have good grounds to question an organization theory that assumes the universality of organizational forms and effects. The alternative view of organizations rejects the assumption, implicit in much of contemporary theory: organizations belong to a single species that behaves in predictable ways according to common laws. This view finds forceful expression in the work of Mayntz:

> Propositions which hold for such diverse phenomena as an army, a trade union, and a university, must necessarily be either trivial or so abstract as to tell hardly anything of interest about concrete reality. . . . In other words, explanation of concrete reality – historical individuals, as Max Weber would say – directs attention precisely to these factors which, in general propositions, fall under the '*ceteris paribus*' clause and remain unspecified.[9]

But what is an organization if it is not something separate from individuals? Organizations may be seen as pure process, as action where individuals change ideas into behaviour and possibilities into consequences. Our conceptions of organizations must be as complex as the reality we try to understand.

Organizations in environment

Administrative theory has long embraced the notion of the organization as a system responding promptly and purposefully to changes in its environment. The image evoked is the organism that adapts to its environment in order to survive in it. Changes in the environment – be they changes in ideology, technology, or human values – are felt within the organizations and responded to. This benign relationship between organizations and their environments is one congenial to the liberal, freedom-loving thought that prevails among the nations of the West. It implies that the institutions of society can generally be left alone to work out their own salvation; any limitation upon them only ensures better flows of information so that adaptation and mutual adjustment may move unimpeded to their natural end – achievement of human purposes in their best and most effective forms. Human intention, to say nothing of passion, scarcely enters this process. Notions of greed, duplicity, love and commitment, or sheer frailty, aging, and mortality have no place in this vision of the organization.

Stafford Beer, who speaks of cybernetics as 'the science of effective organization' and who is described as an international consultant in the application of that science, denies that organizations are simply 'entities'.[10] They are instead,

> Dynamic viable systems, and their characteristics are in fact outputs of their organizational behavior. The variety that is pumped into them is absorbed by regulating variety, through an arrangement of amplifiers and attenuators. A system that, through this kind of exercise in requisite variety, achieves stability against *all* perturbations, is called a homeostat.[11]

Recognizing that there are a few facts that fly in the face of a theory that defines organization as being by its own nature well-adapted to its environment, Beer goes on to note that there are indeed some organizations that do not adapt to their environments and may more likely resist adaptation. He thereupon immediately adds an *ad hoc* proposition that runs directly counter to the main body of this theory. As Feyerabend notes, this is the kind of solution that Newton adopted when empirical observations ran counter to his theory of light.[12]

Beer's solution to the nonadapting organization is to identify a part of it that perversely and against all reason will not play the adaptation game. And who is it that lets the theory down in this disappointing fashion? Bureaucrats, of course.

> Yet buried inside the institution is a nucleus which retains its homeostasis by ignoring not only external change but the primary function of the institution itself. This nucleus is the special kind of homeostat that produces itself. And it is this nucleus that I call the bureaucracy.

By this term I am not simply referring to paper-pushing but to an institution within the institution that exists – narcissus-like – in self-regard.[13]

So there we have it again. The data – this time in human form – have betrayed the theory. Therefore, the behaviour of bureaucrats has to be identified as a special case quite distinct from the rest of us whose behaviour can then still be seen as fulfilling the requirements of the main theory.

Contrary to Beer and other systems thinkers, Weick takes a different approach to organization and environment in his largely misunderstood *Social Psychology of Organizing*.[14] In Pondy's helpful phrase, what Weick does is 'bring mind back in'.[15] He conceives organization in terms of how people see it and its environment. There is no necessary connection between organization and a benign environment except as ideas, intentions and motives are held in the human mind and given reality through recognizable actions. Weick ignores the standard questions in organizational research: 'What is real?' and 'What must organization pay attention to?' In 1869 and with deliberate emphasis in his text, William James asked, '*Under what circumstances do we think things are real?*' and answered, 'Each world *whilst it is attended to* is real.' In drawing attention to James's classic essay, Goffman points out that it gives a 'subversive phenomenological twist' to the reality questions.[16] Weick asks a similar question about organizational realities and grounds his answer in George Herbert Mead's social psychology.

> Man notices those stimuli which permit him to do what he wants to do. . . . The predominant model of man adopted by organization theory is one in which the human is essentially reactive to the environment contingencies that occur. The environment can be inside or outside the organization, but in either case the actor essentially reacts to it as given. However, instead of adapting to a ready-made environment, it is entirely possible that the actors *themselves* create the environment to which they adapt.[17]

No studies in education begin with the premise that in some measure people control their environment and adapt it to their ends. The idea abounds in other fields, however. The behaviour of the oil cartel in 1973 is one obvious example. Someone decided that oil was in short supply and that there was no reason why those who depended on it should not pay through the nose for it. The result shifted vast wealth from one part of the world to another and had profound effects on world economies, some still staggering to adjust to this simple idea. In his book on the Vietnam War, Halbertsam gives another poignant example:

> The American military and propaganda machine uncritically passed on the lies of a dying regime. . . . As the war effort began to fall apart

in late 1962 and early 1963, the Military Assistance Command in Saigon set out to crush its own best officers in the field on behalf of its superiors in Washington. It was a major institutional crisis, but Washington civilians were unaware of it. It was not as if two different and conflicting kinds of military reporting were being sent to Washington, with the White House able to study the two and arbitrate the difference. The Saigon command systematically crushed all dissent from the field; the military channels did not brook dissent or negativism.[18]

Organizations are images of what we think of as real in the social order we see around us. Both Weber and Durkheim reject a superstructure of objective reality and elemental human characteristics adapted to it. Instead they point out that the meaning of such psychological elements and social 'laws' cannot be deduced without invoking meanings already existing in the social context.[19] Similarly, Douglas points out that Durkheim's functional variables (intention, suicide) rest on common-sense meanings he derided as valid sociological data.

> The man who rejected intention as too subjective for any scientific consideration based his whole work on disembodied numbers (suicide rates) which may look object-like but are actually the outcome of necessarily commonsensical evaluations of the 'intentions' of individuals by unseen coroners, police, priests, medical examiners, and other officials.[20]

For Weber the beginning unit for analyzing society is the individual human being. Though life itself is filled with contending ideologies, the quality of organization theory should clarify the process of contention – the rules and consequences of the battle. It should not constitute another position in the battle and should not present the view of its winning general as good, 'functional', or inevitable. In this argument it should be clear beyond doubt that giving up one position in theory, abandoning one side of the ideological battle between the organization and the individual, does not require advocating the contrary. The error of asserting the system as a universal reality is not corrected by asserting the primacy of the individual. The individual is the building block of organization, not the building. To begin, the individual is limited by existential reality, our changing and temporary bodies. Equally the individual is limited by other people, by their purposes and intentions, by their hopes and fears. Where theory asserted the system as the reality overwhelming the individual, we must not assume the individual opposed to the organization as inherently right in the struggle observed by the theorist. Such a view is a dead end, for it leaves unanswered the question, 'Which individual?' If there is truth in social theory, it will be found in understanding what links individual and organization, not simply in espousing one side or the other. This Weberian rationale for an interpretative sociology has important implications for the question of whether a value-free social science is possible.

METHODOLOGY AS AN END IN ITSELF

Weber's view of organizations is often misunderstood. Too often he is seen as the advocate of efficiency, when his position was rather that the growing technical rationalism of our time is so advanced that it can displace human capacity to make value choices. As he saw it, ours is the century that hoped to *calculate* the answers to all its problems, and in doing so confused value issues for technical procedures. This fundamental error pervades contemporary organization theory. If these observations seem extreme, I invite the sceptics to review the empirical research in educational administration. At the 1977 Conference of the American Educational Research Association, (AERA), a symposium on research examined leadership, organizational climate, bureaucracy, supervision, and change in school districts.[21] Could any array better represent major concerns of the current field?

As critic for the session, I noticed first the heavy reliance on quantitative analysis. The sophistication of the researchers' techniques are not in question. Indeed, the researchers used a formidable array of weapons from the statistician's armamentarium to bring order into arrays of data; in doing so they place the meaning and validity of their studies in question. I was struck secondly that their findings never served to shake or reshape the initial theory, whether the research hypotheses were confirmed or not. The observer dropping in would leave the session convinced that the theoretical study of administration was making immense strides and that it could only be some kind of unusual perversity that delays the application of such knowledge for the amelioration of problems that beset the educational enterprise. But then it is entirely typical of such studies that the data do not serve, as one might expect, to test the theory; instead it is the data that are to be judged by accepting the theory a priori as the standard of validity.

Readily accessible computer technology combined with faith in the unique explanatory power of experimental design has placed advanced statistical techniques at the command of all would-be social researchers and schooled them to believe that these are not just *some* methods of inquiry into social reality, but *the* methods. To unlock the secrets of the social system, researchers need only take time to follow the instructions in a manual with a name like 'Data Analysis Package for Social Sciences' and listen to the advice of a helpful expert on computer software. Eigenvalues, factor scores, Wilks's ω^2, discriminant functions, obliquimax rotations, multiple linear regressions, and a host of other bizarre but puissant servants are placed immediately at the command of the researcher: Pandora's box and the sorcerer's apprentice. Do we know what these servants are doing for us? If not, it is certain that the techniques themselves will not bring meaning where none before existed. The sophistication of data analysis cannot make up for the emptiness of the concepts to which they apply.

We must remind ourselves of elemental lessons on methodology. Reliability is not validity. Correlation does not imply causality, even if the correlation is large and reliable. The question we must continually ask is whether the view of the world we get from our current highly quantified technology squares with the view of persons whose actions we are trying to explain. Explaining variance in an array of data is not the same as explaining behaviour as an actor in a social situation sees it. Do people see leadership as a set of bipolar factors set orthogonally in twelve dimensional space? Do they think bureaucracies come in two dimensions representing hierarchy and expertise?[22] They may, but it is an obligation of researchers to show that they do. Otherwise the realities of the researchers' world are confined to their minds and to the workings of their computers. Their logic can have no force unless it conforms to a logic that people use in everyday life. Unless there is a close match between the world as researchers construct it and the world as people perceive it and act in it, the researchers' efforts to establish social truths will be a self-contained and ultimately self-deluding pastime.

VALIDATING THEORY[23]

In the standard view, research tests the adequacy of theory. A well-accepted logic requires researchers first to have a theoretical view of the world and then to test it stringently against reality by collecting empirical data through operationally defined procedures. In contrast, Kuhn and Feyerabend argue that theory is never disconfirmed by empirical research. If findings are inconsistent with the theory, we are likely to disbelieve them or to search for other data that fit better with the theory.[24] Or more commonly and subtly, the researchers' theories and methodologies themselves ensure that the findings will be consistent with the researchers' initial assumptions.

By a conventional criterion, the AERA studies are useful, because they begin with a clear notion of what they expect to find. Our logic teaches us that observation without theory is blind. But observation within theory and prescriptive methodology predisposes us to see what theory knows to be true. In this regard I have strong reservations about the use of factor analysis and multiple regression as methodological devices for testing theory. My reservations stem from the latitude that these methods give researchers for interpreting their results. For example, factor analysis rarely yields unique results. What a factor is depends on what the researcher is satisfied with. Researchers keep rotating their factors until something interpretable emerges; the criterion for interpretation comes sibyl-like from the theory the researcher began with. A researcher explained how this process works: 'The number of factors retained for rotation was determined by *balancing* three criteria: Kaiser's criterion, Cattell's scree, and interpretability' [emphasis added].

Another caveat arises when researchers claim to have 'explained' the variance they report. Standard practice in reporting results deals only with common variance. As a result, researchers claim that their factors explain a large part of variance. The proportion explained would certainly drop sharply if the factors were compared to total rather than to common variance. Again the assumption is that the world looks the way the researcher's theoretical and methodological assumptions say it looks, and if it doesn't it should. Noncommon variance, after all, contains error. In excluding noncommon variance, researchers say that the error is attributable to the world, not to the researchers' assumptions about it.

The tendency of researchers to ignore error variance has been noted in scholarly circles. In an article published over a decade ago, Schutz drew attention to the failure to consider error variance in assessing the meaning and practicality of experimental research. Researchers subordinate error variance to an incidental role, while at the same time elevating the final test of the hypothesis as the ultimate criterion for judging the research. According to Schutz, this practice has had 'an unfortunate effect on the behavior of educational researchers', in that it leads them to mistake statistical significance for substantive and practical meaning. He also deplored the situation in which 'even our most highly respected research journals fail to report the magnitude of the error term or any data that would permit its computation'.[25] This cavalier dismissal of information that does not fit the hypothesis helps to create the widening gulf between commonsense understandings of social reality and the increasingly obscure rituals of researcher-statisticians. In this situation, researchers sense a crisis of confidence and call on the laity in priest-like fashion to trust them. For example, Benjamin reflected on training British civil servants to use the statistical methods of social science and advised the nonstatistician as follows:

> The good administrator must be prepared to trust his statistical advisers provided that he can be sure that they are technically competent and professional in their approach just as a good administrator entrusts his subordinates with authority.[26]

The major point here is that far from being tested, statistical theory passes as social theory, and is used as the standard for interpreting the world. Data become meaningful when they fulfil the predictions of the statistical theory. Is that theory adequate? Even when the data let the theory down, as they often do, researchers say, as they often do, that what we need is more research, more variables, more data. After all, the theory can't be wrong, can it?

In case anyone believes the thinking I criticize is limited to scholarly gatherings, let us look at policy research carried out with the purpose of bringing rigorous economics to bear on issues that educators had been too soft-minded to look at under the hard light of scientific analysis. The question Summers and Wolfe set out to solve is an important one: What is the effect of school resources on educational achievement? After proclaiming 'Educational achievement, like shoes, canned tuna, and clean streets can be regarded as the output of a production process', these economists set out to resolve the class-size question by correlating every quantifiable variable in sight and submitting the whole thing to multiple regression analysis.[27] The results are illuminating, but not in the way the authors conceive them:

> Library books: As one more book per pupil is added to the library, pupil achievement growth declines by .5 months.

> Class size: Being in a class of 34 or more reduces achievement growth by 2.1 months. Being in a class of 28 to 33 rather than a class of less than 28 has no effect on students who scored at grade level in third grade, a negative effect on low achievers, and a positive effect on high achievers.

> Sixth grade Teacher's [sic] Experience: Teacher's experience has a positive effect on average and above average students. A student who is at grade level in the third grade (= 3.8) will increase achievement growth by .6 months for each three additional years of teacher's experience (to 11 years). A student scoring 5.0 will increase by 1.3 months per three additional years experience. Below grade level, down to 2.0, additional experience has no effect. Below that, it reduces growth.[28]

Surely even a convinced supporter of scientific analysis would not advocate removing library books to increase pupil achievement. If the teacher effects claimed are to be understood at all against the complexities of the interactions, they suggest the conclusion that some students learn better than others whatever the size of the class and the experience of the teacher. Such an outcome is hardly a new finding or a revelation to policy makers. Although their findings can be of little use for policy making, it seems unlikely that the researchers will alter their belief in educational achievement as the product of an ordered and well-understood production process.[29] Theory helps us to see and not to see.

IMAGE, REALITY AND METHOD

What we see depends in large measure on what we believe we are going to see. It may be argued indeed that we see, hear, and feel nothing without first having ideas that give meaning to our experience. Knowledge and learning, therefore, have to do with acquiring new ideas – new categories for perceiving reality. In trying to understand reality, we require concepts or categories that enable us to make sense of that which William James called 'the blooming welter' of phenomena around us. As aids for understanding, we use larger models – theories, if you like – that provide us with reservoirs of ideas. These models are images of reality; we carry them in our minds and use them as templates to stamp meaning into the world around us.

This argument rests on propositions that were established in the earliest era of Western thought. The philosophers of ancient Greece and Asia Minor argued long over image and reality and often made their points through analysis of everyday experience. For example, travellers approach a tower they see first from a distance. From this perspective, the tower appears round. At close quarters, however, they see that the tower is square. With this truth in mind, the travellers continue on their journey. On looking back at the tower from a distance once more, they find that it again looks round, though they now 'know' that it is square.

That we require ideas to understand our experience and to perceive reality is generally accepted as a principle of epistemology. What is in dispute is where the ideas come from and whether they represent – although possibly in flawed form – the ultimate reality of the world. In many cases, the ideas we use to understand the world run quite contrary to direct observation and common experience. Zeno's paradoxes prove that motion from point A to point B will never be accomplished in a world based on the notion of a continuum consisting of isolated elements. Feyerabend argues that this line of reasoning supports Parmenides' theory of 'the unchanging and homogeneous one which is contradicted by almost everything we know and experience'. Feyerabend goes on to show how this odd notion plays a role even today in the theory of general relativity and in Heisenberg's insight that 'the basic elements of the universe cannot obey the same laws as the visible elements'.[30] For Plato and philosophers of the naturalistic school, the images or forms we need to understand the world lie behind that which we immediately perceive as reality. In his allegory of the cave, Plato saw people as being chained in darkness so that they could see only shadows cast on the wall in front of them. In this allegory, reality lies outside of the cave – outside of man's immediate experience. Ordinary mortals therefore require help, if they are to see things as they really are. For Plato, it was the philosopher who could provide such help. In our time, we are likely to believe that it is scientists who give us access to knowledge. As Lord Rutherford said of his study, 'All of science is physics or stamp collecting.' In these views, knowledge is not easily come by; it rests on the assumption that scientists' theories are built only by painstaking, stringent research. Once tested, scientific theories tell us what *is* and how it works. But David Hilbert, a German mathematician of Rutherford's generation, gives us the warning: 'Physics is far too difficult for physicists.'[31]

The images we use to understand the world are man-made and socially maintained. This view rejects the naturalistic assumptions that suffuse much of research on organization theory.[32] Under naturalistic assumptions, theory is something that scientists build, largely from the armchair, by thinking up ultimate explanations for the phenomena observed. Contrary to accepted opinion, Kuhn argues that such theory is never open to disproof; it serves instead as a consensual agreement among scientists about what procedures constitute scientific activity and hence which explanations will count as scientific explanations.[33] Does the sun go around the earth or the earth around the sun? The Ptolemaic astronomers had no difficulty in fitting all kinds of facts into a system that saw the sun revolving about the earth. Copernicus did not batter down the old theory with new scientific observations. Instead, he showed that the old facts could be fitted into a different theory, if we believed that the earth were revolving around the sun. In both cases, the image of what scientists believed determined what they saw. Scientific enquiry too often confirms that we see what theory says should be there. It fails to test whether the original belief is true.

Feyerabend demonstrates how both reason and empirical observation supported the Aristotelian and Ptolemaic view of the structure of the heavens and the mechanics by which they moved.[34] A stone dropped from a tall tower fell at the base of the tower, not some distance from it, as it would surely do if the earth were hurtling through space at the rate of many miles per second. Ergo, the earth stands still. And ergo the whole social system that supports such reasoning is also right. Feyerabend also shows why the telescope that Galileo constructed to demonstrate the truth of a heliocentric cosmos failed to convince the scholars of the day.[35] Galileo could see that it proved Copernicus right, but *they* couldn't. It failed to convince the sceptics partly because of physical limitations in the telescope, but mostly because the viewers of that time had not yet learned to see what Galileo was convinced was there to be seen. Both the theory and the experience to understand and interpret the evidence from telescopic observations were lacking. Only faith in a new order of things, in a new method of inquiry, and in a new cosmology could bring one to see the rightness of the heliocentric view.

> For Copernicus now stands for progress in other areas as well; he is a symbol for the ideals of a new class that looks back to the classical times of Plato and Cicero and forward to a free and pluralistic society. . . .
>
> The ideas survived and they can *now* be said to be in agreement with reason. They survived because prejudice, passion, conceit, errors, sheer pig-headedness, in short because all the elements that characterize the context of discovery, *opposed* the dictates of reason *and because these irrational elements were permitted to have their way.* To express it differently: *Copernicanism and other 'rational' views exist today only because reason was overruled at some time in their past.* (The opposite is

also true: witchcraft and other 'irrational' views have *ceased* to be influential only because reason was overruled at some time in *their* past.)[36]

CAN THERE BE ONE BEST THEORY OF EXPERIENCE?

The power of the image to shape what we see is even more potent in social affairs than in the natural world. Strangely, this truth has largely been ignored in organization theory, where research has become more and more technically sophisticated, while attention to the validity of its concepts dwindles. Kuhn points, for example, to research by Bruner and Postman in which subjects were asked to identify cards, for instance, a red six of spades and a black four of hearts.[37] When subjects were shown the cards briefly and asked to say what they were, they would first transform the anomalous cards into normal ones and then, with longer exposure, begin to say things like, 'that's the six of spades, but there's something wrong with it – the black has a red border'. Some subjects never could see the anomalous cards for what they were. One of them exclaimed, 'I can't make the suit out, whatever it is. It didn't even look like a card that time. I don't know what color it is or whether it's a spade or a heart. I'm not even sure now what a spade looks like. My God.'

In naturalistic science, there is usually only one theory accepted at a given time as the best explanation of phenomena in the field to which it applies. Whereas the consequences of this one-theory-at-a-time approach are certainly important in the physical sciences, the limitations of their theoretical assumption are of immense importance in the social sciences. As Weber noted some time ago, atoms do not care whether physicists' theories are accurate. People, on the other hand, have a stake in social theory. The theory is about them, and someone is going to take action on the basis of the theory as though it were true. If, as Weber argues, there are various perspectives for seeking and understanding social phenomena, social scientists are making moral judgements at the same time they are selecting a model or theory from which to view social organization.[38] And if, as Kuhn and Feyerabend argue, theories are overthrown through intellectual revolutions, not through 'the findings of research', social scientists may readily deceive themselves and fail to note the imperial role their theories play in imposing meaning on reality.

There is a strong tendency in modern science to deal with new theories and hypotheses according to what Feyerabend calls the 'consistency principle'.[39] The consistency principle arises from the belief that things are what they are and cannot be otherwise. So that is why we must accept the version of them that best conforms to our reasoning and to observation within such reasoning. The consistency principle eliminates new theories, hypotheses, and methodologies, not because they are inconsistent with the facts, but because they are inconsistent with previously established theories. To combat the consistency principle, Feyerabend recommends testing hypotheses that run at variance to or directly against well-established theories, because such an approach provides 'evidence which cannot be obtained in any other way. Proliferation of theories is beneficial for science, while uniformity impairs its critical powers.'[40] And he goes further:

> Unanimity of opinion may be fitting for a Church, for the frightened, for greedy victims of some (ancient or modern) myth, or for the weak and willing followers of some tyrant. Variety of opinion is necessary for objective knowledge. And a method that encourages variety is also the only method that is compatible with a humanitarian outlook.[41]

The basic problem in the physical sciences is how to understand a world beyond our direct experience. This problem is solved by imposing meanings on observed behaviour and reasoning whether the behaviour is consistent with the explanation. In social reality, it is experience that is the unknown. And the problem is how we come to understand our experience and to communicate it to others. Laing echoes Max Weber when he says,

> Natural science knows nothing of the relation between behaviour and experience. The nature of this relation is mysterious. . . . That is to say, it is not an objective problem. There is no traditional logic to express it. There is no developed method of understanding its nature. But this relation is the copula of our science – if science means *a form of knowledge adequate to its subject*. The relation between experience and behaviour is the stone that the builders will reject at their peril. Without it the whole structure of our theory and practice must collapse.[42]

If we regard learning and experience purely as behaviour, we are likely to misconstrue its meaning and to distort seriously our understanding of it. Atoms cannot speak for themselves, even if we find reason to believe they exist. Neither can amoebas speak, although we can see them moving, if we learn how to see with a microscope. But people can talk, and they can say what they experience and how they came to understand that experience. No one can experience another's experience, but we may come to understand it. People can speak. They can speak with words, with silence, with the look on a face, the movement of an arm, the posture of the body. The events we see in social reality can speak. Social data can speak. They can speak for themselves, although it is not altogether clear how we are to understand them. Laing hammers home this point, and it is one that has been made often and often ignored in administrative and organizational studies:

> Natural scientific investigations are conducted on objects, or things, or the patterns of relations between things. . . . Persons are distin-

guished from things in that persons experience the world, whereas things behave in the world. Thing-events do not experience. Personal events are experiential. Natural scientism is the error of turning persons into things by a process of reification that is not itself part of true natural scientific method. Results derived in this way have to be reassimilated into the realm of human discourse.[43]

The physical world does not care what hypotheses we hold about it. Or, if it does, it never says so. But people care, and they go through elaborate exercises to prove that their beliefs are right. If observation and the facts fail to support our beliefs, we are likely to fall back on what we call reason. Neither the physical scientist nor the social scientist can afford to ignore this reasoning, because it is the process by which we come to understand the world. Feyerabend gives several examples of how scientists behave when they are confronted with facts that conflict with their theories. Newton shored up such discrepancies by *ad hoc* hypotheses and explanations. In a more usual response, scientists simply retain the theory and forget its shortcomings.[44] When confronted with discrepancies between data and theory, Barrow, Newton's teacher and predecessor at Cambridge, chose to believe the theory and then reflected on his decision: 'All of which does seem repugnant to our principles. But for me neither this nor any other difficulty shall have so great an influence on me, as to make me renounce that which I know be manifestly agreeable to reason.'[45]

Our ideas and our experiences are subject to human intervention. One generation trains another and it is these patterns and processes of institutional reality-making that we must come to understand, as Laing makes clear in speaking of the confrontation between the stone-age baby and the twentieth-century mother.[46]

OTHER IMAGES, OTHER THEORIES

What are the implications of this critique for inquiry? First we need to take our theories more seriously in one sense and less seriously in another. We need to be more serious about our theories, because they represent not just possible views of reality, but views that people believe in and believe to be true. We need to take them less seriously when it comes to proving or testing them. They are given meaningful and stringent tests when people attempt to act in accordance with them. When people engage in meaningful acts of leadership or when they act out a set of values, theore- ticians may glimpse the world as other people see it rather then as their own assumptions and methods of observation allows them to see it.

For example, leadership is acknowledged to be a dynamic phenomenon. Yet LBDQ-based research has been content to explain it in procedures that are unusually restrictive and static.[47] At best, the LBDQ gives us a Brownie camera snapshot of a complex and obscure process. We know that much went on before we took the photograph; we know that much will go on after it. We know that our fuzzy LBDQ snapshot represents only a tiny part of what was going on at the time it was taken. None of these limitations shake our faith in a concept of leadership whose chief virtue may be that it offers immediate and quantitative data we know how to handle. We know too that the future is incredibly hard to predict in any meaningful way. Yet we are willing to delude ourselves that Delphic techniques show the future rather than our own reflected images – through a glass, darkly.

Something of this deception and its futility is caught by Van Veen, Nabokov's mime of time, who muses on the connections between past, present, and future realities:

> What we do at best (at worst we perform trivial tricks) when postulating the future, is to expand enormously the specious present causing it to permeate an amount of time with all manner of information, anticipation, and precognition. At best, the 'future' is the ideas of a hypothetical present based on our experience of succession, on our faith in logic and habit. Actually, of course, our hopes can no more bring it into existence than our regrets can change the past. The latter has at least the taste, the tinge, the tang, of our individual being.[48]

The essential point turns on the images we have of ourselves, of social reality, and of our future. Is leadership better conceived as twelve kinds of behaviours described in terms like 'consideration', 'initiating structure', and 'tolerance for ambiguity', or is it better seen, as Cohen and March see it, as a man sitting at the wheel of a skidding car: what he does at the moment is of marginal importance compared to other forces that got him into the situation in the first place and which will largely determine its outcome.[49] These images of leadership are very different, and no amount of research is likely to prove either one. What we should pay attention to is the kind of questions we can ask and explore with the different models.

Researchers should pay attention to how their theories and assumptions generate knowledge. Researchers need theories to understand at all but they also need to spend more time looking at their theories as theories. What are the implications of seeing social reality one way as opposed to seeing it another? What are the moral consequences if we believe in one theory rather than other possible ones? How do different people at different places or times regard the same phenomena?

Answering such questions can make us more aware of what it means to work within a theory; it may make us more tolerant of the existence of other perspectives. I argue for research that looks at social reality from a variety of perspectives, particularly from the perspective of different actors in a given social situation. In this approach, researchers become interpreters of social reality, whose task is to explain the human condition. How that condition can change, or how it ought to be changed, are larger and more difficult questions to answer. It is to these questions that researchers should turn if their work is truly to extend our knowledge.

CHANCE AS TRUTH

Do these arguments doom us to an unending study of specific people in specific situations? Perhaps they do, but some basis for generalization still remains. The loss of sweeping generalizations about organizations is no great defeat, for we may well be better off as theorists and human beings with piece-meal explanations than with large explanations that mean little or nothing. The smaller explanations at least have the virtue of connecting with something we recognize as reality.

Why are we afraid of the specific? Many of the seminal ideas in contemporary social science come from someone thinking about small parts of reality in ways that later make sense to others as they deal with their realities. Freud studied himself and his dreams. Piaget watched his children growing up and asked them a few simple questions about numbers and quantity. Skinner contented himself with working with a few pigeons – some say perhaps only one.

Some of us are more concerned with chance and unique events, while others look for the regularities and overriding patterns of human affairs. Modern social science prefers to deal with reality in terms of generalizations and what it assumes to be universalities. Indeed, the principles of statistics, upon which much of the science in contemporary social science rests, relegates unique and chance events to 'error'. Whether an individual thinks of events involving him as an error might depend, for example, on whether he has just drawn the winning ticket on a million dollar lottery. For Steve Biko in South Africa, it might depend on the unique reality that he has just bumped his head while in the hands of the police. Yet the logical order that the Western scientific mind invariably sees in all phenomena rests on an assumption, as Wittgenstein makes clear:

> That the sun will rise tomorrow is a hypothesis; this means, we do not *know* whether it will rise.

> There is no force to make one thing happen because something else has already occurred. There is only a *logical* necessity for it.[50]

We learn to see order in reality; what one sees depends on the culture one lives in. Jung makes this point in a helpful introduction to the ancient Chinese writings of the *I Ching*. He begins with the assumption that much of life is irrational, unique, and determined largely by chance. In attempting to fit such phenomena into preconceived rational patterns, he argues that we simply prevent ourselves from understanding and experiencing 'what nature does when left to herself undisturbed by the meddlesomeness of man'.[51] If events are formed largely by chance, they must be understood for themselves, in and of that time, and by the people involved. Self-knowledge becomes more important than abstract principles. What Jung sees in the *I Ching* is the mind that prefers to understand reality from the specific rather than the general case and that prefers to infer the meaning of life from the living body rather than the cadaver.

> The Chinese mind, as I see it at work in the *I Ching*, seems to be exclusively preoccupied with the chance aspect of events. What we call coincidence seems to be the chief concern of this peculiar mind, and what we worship as causality passes almost unnoticed. . . . Theoretical considerations of cause and effect often look pale and dusty in comparison to the practical results of chance. It is all very well to say that the crystal of quartz is a hexagonal prism. The statement is quite true in so far as an ideal crystal is envisaged. But in nature one finds no two crystals exactly alike, although all are unmistakably hexagonal. The actual form, however, seems to appeal more to the Chinese sage than the ideal one. The jumble of natural laws constituting empirical reality holds more significance for him than a causal explanation of events that, moreover, must usually be separated from one another in order to be properly dealt with.[52]

What for example, does it have to do with the *theory* of organizations that Rosa Luxemburg thought the proletariat could and should participate in the central direction of the Communist Party? As it happened, Lenin opposed this notion. Such questions are pondered by those who wonder whether political parties as organization are *by their nature* under the control of the élite rather then under the direction of the masses whom they purport to represent.[53] The Lenin–Luxemburg battle probably adds little or nothing to the theory of organizations simply because one can readily find similar cases that suggest opposing principles. Thus we are left to look at the Lenin–Luxemburg battle as an event rather than as a theory about organizations in general. In winning, Lenin changed the course of modern history and the lives of millions of people. The consequences of this event must surely outweigh speculations about what abstract principle of organization was at work in the case.

CONCLUSION

If we accept the argument that reality is experienced subjectively, what are the implications for organization theory? For identifying this question and for providing a persuasive answer to it, theorists are indebted to Max Weber. Unfortunately Weber is usually quoted in the introductions to texts on organizations and ignored thereafter in framing their critical assumptions. What sets Weber apart from many contemporary theorists is his concern for science when what we perceive as truth in our subjectively defined worlds depends on assumptions in our methods of enquiry. Salomon explains these Weberian ideas as follows:

> Weber assumed at the outset that no individual science is capable of furnishing an authentic 'copy' of reality. The utmost that can be accomplished by such sciences, either in the historical or the social disciplines, is, through reasoned thought, to bring order into the world of reality, which is in a state of ceaseless flux. The principles of classification by which this order is to be achieved, cannot, however, draw upon reality, but must be imposed by the scientist himself.[54]

Weber requires of social scientists that they be aware of their own values, their own assumptions. As Bendix notes, 'These are minimal demands against self-deception and the deception of others.[55] Weber's method is to create images of reality as actors in social settings understand it and to show how action consistent with these images has consequences – expected and unexpected. Understanding comes from setting the images against each other. In this way Weber strives to build explanations that are both 'meaningfully' and 'causally' adequate. The explanations have both meaning for the actors and consistency in a logical, causal sense.

And of course it is not only scientists who can interpret social reality. Artists, poets, saints, and philosophers have always done so. Ingmar Bergman's films explore his own psyche and experience, yet the images he finds to express his insight are compelling to others who find meaning in them for own lives. They have a quality that illuminates something about themselves and their relations with others. All this argument for subjectivity does not compromise the sociological generalization out of existence. The argument means we have to learn to live with contending and even inconsistent generalizations about social reality and in what we perceive as organizations. It moves us towards accepting heretofore non-approved methods and rules for establishing reality and truths about it. Controlled experimentation in its real or ersatz forms will have to yield its monopoly as the only road to knowledge of power and validity.

In the face of a multi-faceted, ambiguous 'reality', one needs a conception, an idea of it, if one is to speak of organizations. The idea inevitably stands between us and what we think is reality; it links our experience and our sense of an outside world and others' behaviour in it. It is this mysterious void between behaviour and experience that the image must fill. What is needed are images and methods of enquiry that will illuminate what we understand by organizations. In such a quest, it should be recognized that experimental social science has largely failed us and so also has theory building that forgets that theories themselves are as much inventions about reality as they are explanations of it. All scientists face the task of determining what is. In interpreting the interwoven world of fact and value, the social scientist also bears – crucially so – the burden of determining what ought to be. Weber argued that the task for the social scientist could be framed within fact, at least within what we call historical fact, but he knew such inquiry inevitably stands on a value base. To determine what is in the social world, we must begin from a base that knows what ought to be in it.

NOTES

1 This is a revised and expanded version of the paper first published in *Die Psychologie Des 20. Jahrhundersts: Lewin Jund die Golgen*, Band VII in 1979.
2 *Tractatus Logico–Philosophicus* (London: Routledge & Kegan Paul, 1961), propositions 1, 2.1, 5.621, 5.633, 5.634, and 6.373. Trans. T.B.G.
3 Kenneth E. Boulding, 'General Systems Theory – A Skeleton of a Science', in *Modern Systems Research for the Behavioral Scientist*, ed. W. Buckley (Chicago: Aldine, 1968), 8.
4 Plato, *The Republic*, trans. by J. L.Davies and D. J. Vaughan (London: Macmillan, 1935), 146.
5 Herbert Spencer, *Principles of Sociology* (New York: D. Appleton, 1916), 526.
6 Emile Durkheim, *Professional Ethics and Civic Morals* (Glencoe, IL: Free Press, 1958), 108–109.
7 Chester Barnard, *The Functions of the Executive.* (Cambridge, MA: Harvard University Press, 1938).
8 Talcott Parsons, *The Social System* (Glencoe, IL, Free Press, 1951).
9 Renate Mayntz, 'The Study of Organizations', *Current Sociology*, XIII, 3 (1964), 113.
10 Stafford Beer, *Designing Freedom* (Toronto: Canadian Broadcasting Corporation, 1974), 13.
11 Ibid., 77.
12 Feyerabend, P., *Against Method: Outline of an Anarchistic Theory of Knowledge* (London: Newleft Books, 1975) 59.
13 Beer, *Designing Freedom*, 78.
14 Karl E. Weick, *The Social Psychology of Organizing* (Reading, MA: Addison-Wesley, 1969).
15 Louis R. Pondy and David M. Boje, 'Bringing Mind Back In: Paradigm Development as a Frontier Problem in Organization Theory'. (Department of Business Administration, University of Illinois, 1976.)
16 Erving Goffman, *Frame Analysis: An Essay on the Organization of Experience* (New York: Harper and Row, 1974), 2ff. Goffman shows the similarity between James's thinking on perception and that of later phenomenologists and interactionists.
17 Weick, *Social Psychology of Organizing*, 26–27.
18 David Halbertsam, *The Best and the Brightest* (New York: Random House, 1972), 248.
19 J. E. T. Eldridge, ed., *Max Weber: The Interpretation of Social Reality* (London: Thomas Nelson, 1971), 17–18.
20 Jack E. Douglas, ed., *Understanding Everyday Life: Towards the Re-Construction of Sociological Knowledge* (London: Routledge & Kegan Paul, 1971), ix–x.

21 American Educational Research Association, Session 20.06, 'Questionnaires in the Study of Administration' (New York, April 1977).

22 See Session 20.06 of AERA, 1977.

23 See Thomas B. Greenfield, 'Reflections on Organization Theory and the Truths of Irreconcilable Realities', *Educational Administration Quarterly* 14, 2 (1978): 1–23; idem, 'Ideas vs: Data: How Can The Data Speak for Themselves?' in *Problem-Finding in Educational Administration*, eds G. L. Immegart and W. L. Boyd (Lexington, MA: D. C. Heath, 1979), 167–190.

24 Thomas Kuhn, *The Structure of Scientific Revolutions* (Chicago: University of Chicago Press, 1962); and Paul Feyerabend, *Against Method: An Outline of an Anarchistic Theory of Knowledge* (London: New Left Books, 1975).

25 Richard E. Schutz, 'The Control of "Error" in Educational Experimentation', *School Review* 74, 2 (1966): 152–153. See also the discussion of ω^2 in James F. McNamara, 'Practical Significance and Mathematical Models in Administrative Research', in *Problem-Finding in Educational Administration*, eds G. L. Immegart and W. L. Boyd (Lexington, MA: D. C. Heath, 1979), 194–199.

26 Bernard Benjamin 'Teaching Statistics and Operational Research to Civil Servants', *The American Statistician*, 26, 4 (1972): 23.

27 Anita A. Summers and Barbara L. Wolfe, 'Which School Resources Help Learning Efficiency and Equity in Philadelphia Public School?' *Federal Reserve Bank of Philadelphia Business Review*, February 1976, 6.

28 Ibid., 24–27.

29 See Doris Ryan and Thomas B. Greenfield, *The Class Size Question* (Toronto: Ontario Ministry of Education, 1975), 232–285.

30 Paul Feyerabend, *Against Method: Outline of an Anarchistic Theory of Knowledge* (London: New Left Books, 1975), 58.

31 'Physics for Physicists' *Globe and Mail* (Toronto), 21 December 1991, D7.

32 Thomas B. Greenfield, 'Theory about Organizations: A New Perspective and Its Implications for Schools', in M. Hughes, ed., *Administering Education: International Challenge* (London: Athlone, 1975), 71–99; idem, 'Organization Theory as Ideology', *Curriculum Inquiry* 9, 2 (1979): 97–112.

33 Kuhn, *Structure of Scientific Revolutions*.

34 Feyerabend, *Against Method*, 69–161.

35 Ibid., 124–125.

36 Ibid., 154–155.

37 Kuhn, *Structure of Scientific Revolutions*, 63–64.

38 J. E. T. Eldridge, ed., *Max Weber: The Interpretation of Social Reality* (London: Michael Joseph, 1971), 11–19.

39 Feyerabend, *Against Method*, 35.

40 Ibid.

41 Ibid., 46.

42 R. D. Laing, *The Politics of Experience* (New York: Pantheon, 1967), 17. See Weber's statement that the individual is the 'basic unit' of social action in H. H. Gerth and C. Wright Mills, *From Max Weber: Essays in Sociology* (New York: Oxford, 1958), 55.

43 Laing, *Politics of Experience*, 53.

44 Feyerabend, *Against Method*, 59.

45 Ibid.

46 See p. 83.

47 Thomas B. Greenfield, 'Research on the Behaviour of Leaders: Critique of a Tradition', *Alberta Journal of Educational Research* 14, 1 (1968): 55–76.

48 In Aaron Wildavsky, 'Does Planning Work?', *The Public Interest* 24 (Summer 1971): 104.

49 Michael D. Cohen and James G. March, *Leadership and Ambiguity: The American College President* (New York: McGraw-Hill, 1974).
50 Wittgenstein, *Tractatus*, propositions 6.36311 and 6.37. Trans. TBG.
51 Carl Jung, 'Foreword', in *The I Ching or Book of Changes*, trans. Cary F. Baynes (Princeton: Princeton University, 1950), xxix.
52 Ibid., xii–xiii.
53 J. E. T. Eldridge and A. D. Crombie, *A Sociology of Organisations* (London: George Allen & Unwin, 1974), 139–143, 159–164.
54 A. Salomon, 'Max Weber's Methodology', *Social Research*, 1 (1934), 157, in Eldridge, *Max Weber*, 12.
55 Reinhard Bendix and Guenther Roth, *Scholarship and Partisanship: Essays on Max Weber* (Berkeley: University of California, 1971), 71.

4

ORGANIZATION THEORY AS IDEOLOGY[1]

Experience is mysterious, for it is not entirely clear how we come to understand what we do and what is happening to us. The placing of meaning upon experience is therefore an act of enormous importance. This argument recognizes the interpretation of human experience as the bedrock upon which human life is built and upon which organization theory should stand. Organization theory, however, usually ignores such mysteries in human life, and it does so at the cost of impoverishing its own insight into people's lives and social reality. In the name of comprehensiveness and precision, theory oversimplifies the variety and complexity of human experience within organizations. In a fundamental sense, organization *is* experience. The quality of experience within organizations, of course, varies greatly from person to person, from time to time, and from place to place.

Some people invent ideas that give shape and meaning to their experience; others borrow ideas to understand themselves. And many have little or no choice as others' ideas are forced upon them in the same way that the air surrounds them. They must breathe the air or suffocate; so must they accept others' ideas or break through them to a new atmosphere, to other ideas, to a new reality. This context of ideas by which we understand our experience is what I mean by organization. In this sense, organization exists whenever people accept sets of ideas as fit and proper guides for their own behaviour and for that of others. Even though these ideas may be internally inconsistent and do not always allow us to predict what will happen when we act in accordance with them, we remain dependent upon ideas for ordering our experience and for building an understanding of the world around us.

Artists have long understood the relationship between experience and ideas, between symbol and reality. My dissatisfaction with much of contemporary organization theory – or at least with that form of it which prevails in administrative studies – is that people who call themselves social scientists have forgotten the experiential basis of the ideas they use to interpret reality. Instead they are advocates of a particular vision of reality that holds no greater truth than a number of alternate views. And I would go further: systems theory and structural–functionalist thinking – which I see as the ideological hegemony in administrative studies – is demonstrably bad theory and leads to sterile research.

It is bad theory because organizations are, in Pondy's (1978) term, 'multicephalous', i.e. they have many brains that sustain mind, meaning, values, and culture. Despite this recognized complexity in organizations, theorists are often content to speak about them in terms of primitive models that seldom advance beyond images more complex than the cata-logue, the clock, or the gyroscope. Boulding (1968) noted that the 'advance in the level of theoretical analysis' provided by systems theory as 'a new discipline' had hardly carried the field beyond an understanding of mechanistic and naturally existing systems. And, he added, 'a mild word of warning even to Management Science . . . that in dealing with human personalities and organizations we are dealing with systems in the empirical world far beyond our ability to formulate'. He went on to conclude that 'we should not be wholly surprised, therefore, if our simpler systems, for all their importance and validity, occasionally let us down' (p. 10). Few theorists over the ensuing years seem to have noted, let alone heeded, Boulding's warning, for Pondy (1978) concludes over twenty years later that the 'dominating' concern of organization theorists has been 'explain-ing why organizations work well and do good'.

I will return to these points again, but let us listen first to what some artists have said about experience and reality. William Blake (1931, 230) asks,

> What is the price of Experience? do men buy it for a song?
> Or wisdom for a dance in the street? No, it is bought with the price
> Of all that a man hath, his house, his wife, his children.[2]

And one of Pirandello's (1954, 17) six characters tells the theatre producer who wants to redirect his life,

> Each one of us has a whole world of things inside him. . . . And each
> of us has his own particular world. How can we understand each other
> if into the words which I speak I put the sense and the value of things
> as I understand them myself. . . . While at the same time whoever is
> listening to them inevitably assumes them to have the sense and value
> that they have for him. . . . The sense and value that they have in the
> world that he has within him? We think we understand one
> another. . . . But we never really do understand![3]

These questions posed by Blake and Pirandello are inevitable and neces-sary questions for anyone who wants to understand himself and others, as indeed they are for the social scientist who wants to understand abstractly and in theoretical terms what social organization is and what it means to people within it.

Let me say something about myself for a moment and about some experiences that now seem enormously significant to me, though they did not at the time of their occurrence. I was born into a farm family in Saskatchewan, Canada, and began formal learning in a school where a single teacher taught many children in eight grades. We used to watch the hands of the clock on the teacher's desk move slowly to four. At that hour, if one were old enough and had no younger brothers or sisters to transport home by buggy or cutter, one might ride home on horseback through an open, unspoiled, tranquil landscape to a homestead that, short years before, was virgin prairie. At a point of crisis in my family, I went to live in the city. The farm part of my family has never shared my city life, though I can, or could, shift fairly easily back to farm ways. My farm family does not understand what I do as a professor. They would be incredulous but impressed if told that I had presented this paper at a large conference in New York and that people who had travelled far were willing to sit still for twenty minutes while I spoke to them. The shift between these separate realities is one that I am coming to understand in Blake's terms: understanding experience exacts its price and comes only from shifting perspectives, from the juxtaposing of one perspective against another.

I speak in these personal terms to make a point about experience, organizations, and ideology – three words whose meanings, in my view, are closely intertwined. The self that lives by one set of values, by one ideology, within one social organization, is not the self that lives by other values, within other ideas, or other organizations, though the same consciousness may connect the two realities. Under these assumptions, the prime task of the social scientist and the theorist of organizations is to understand those realities if they are to make generalized and abstract statements about them. The ideological or symbolic 'explanation' links the experience of individuals and the realities they perceive as social structure.

Poets, saints, charismatic leaders, ideologues, social philosophers, and yes, even organization theorists are important and powerful people because their thoughts can provide the link between experience and reality. The theorist and the symbol-maker are, therefore, linked to those whose lives they explain by a bond that is at once existential and moral. How do we see our life? What place do organizations play in it? What are schools? Can we or our organizations be different? Can we be better too? How? These are questions that organization theory should speak to and, indeed, does speak to. But it should do so by opening up the interpretation of social reality, not by attempting to fix it or control it. It should make clear the process by which we create our social and organizational world; it should not argue for a single interpretation of that reality. It should leave the persons theorized about with a greater understanding of themselves than before the theorists began their work. These are stringent conditions to lay upon social theorizing, and I am unsure whether much or any of it now lives up to them.

THE INDIVIDUAL AND SOCIAL REALITY

Recent writings, some by participants in this symposium, have sharply defined the theoretical issue facing those who conduct organizational studies in educational administration.[4] I do not propose now to relive old battles or to become nostalgic about them. In this spirit we might consider the words of Iris Murdoch when she asks disputants in education to 'use clear ordinary language, not obscure jargon or brutal rhetoric, and keep in mind that while theories are fighting individual children are growing up' (Cox and Boyson, 1975, 7).

So what is the issue we are talking about here? One cannot go far in organization theory without confronting a basic question: Why do we behave as we do in social organizations? Answering this question seems to me the main justification for organization theory, since it deals with the individual and social reality. I would like therefore to examine the implications of a view that sees organizations as ideological inventions of the human mind – as invented social reality. From this point of view, much of received organization theory appears blind to ideology in organizations and in theories about them. It is blind, too, to the experiential base of ideology and to the struggle of the deviant notion, the radical view, and the charismatic vision against a social reality that is routine, patterned, accepted, and considered right and proper. Organizational theory has too frequently defended conventional social realities and ignored the process whereby sets of people and ideas are in contention over what is reality and how one should behave in it.

Goffman gives us a sense of ideological control of the individual when he notes Grayson Kirk's reaction when students occupied and despoiled his presidential office at Columbia University. 'My God', said Kirk, 'how could human beings do a thing like this?' But as Goffman points out, the great sociological question is rather, 'How is it that human beings do this sort of thing so rarely? How come persons in authority have been so overwhelmingly successful in conning those beneath them into keeping the hell out of their offices?' (Goffman, 1971, 288; Manning, 1976). Social order is maintained, therefore, not because of necessary roles and functions operating in some well-working system, but because of ideas in people's minds about how they should treat each other. And the social system now appears, not as an objective reality, but as an ideological social order accepted by individuals or forced upon them. As Goffman (1967, 90–91) says, 'The rules of conduct which bind the actor and the recipient together are the bindings of society. . . . Others who are present constantly remind the individual that he must keep himself together as a well-demeaned person and affirm the sacred quality of these others.'

What we see in the social order depends upon the unit of analysis we choose. A major choice occurs when we choose the individual or the system for this purpose. Parsonians and other functionalists begin with the social system. Some years ago, C. Wright Mills wrote *The Sociological Imagination* (1959). I read it as a student in doctoral studies, but soon discarded what it had to say because it appeared too easy to read and too sensible compared with my usual texts. One of the services Mills performs in this book is to translate Talcott Parsons, whose work *The Social System* (1951) has had an enormous influence on studies of organization and administration. This *magnum opus* has formed not only the rhetoric of later theorists, but has also shaped the categories of thought by which they see organizational realities. What language Parsons was writing in Mills never says, but he makes it clear that the whole book can be rendered into four paragraphs of plain English. Part of his translation runs as follows:

> There are 'social regularities', which we may observe and which are often quite durable. Such enduring and stable regularities I shall call 'structural'. It is possible to think of all these regularities within the social system as a great and intricate balance. That this is a metaphor I am now going to forget, because I want you to take as very real my Concept: The social equilibrium. . . .
>
> One point does puzzle me a little: given this social equilibrium, and all the socialization and control that maintain it, how is it possible that anyone should ever get out of line? This I cannot explain very well, that is, in the terms of my Systematic and General Theory of the social system. And there is another point that is not as clear as I should like it to be: how should I account for social change – that is for history? About these two problems, I recommend that whenever you come upon them you undertake empirical investigations. (pp. 32–33)

Along with the notion of equilibrium in social systems goes the idea of a common core of values. This concept has long appealed to social theorists since Hobbes saw the social contract as the only solution to the 'war of all against all'. As Zeitlin (1973, 42) points out, functionalists who see society as being in equilibrium around a central core of values face some disconcertingly contradictory evidence: 'Are we to believe that in pre-Nazi Germany Junkers, peasants, industrial workers, Catholics, Protestants, Communists, Social Democrats, and Nazis all shared a common value system?' Indeed, can we look at any contemporary society where change and conflict have been so much the order of the day for more than a decade and retain belief in a society ordered around common values?

SOCIAL STRUCTURE IN TERMS OF HUMAN MEANINGS

If we reject a superstructure of objective social reality to which individuals must accommodate themselves, what are we left with as an explanation of human personality and group action? The psychological reductionists would offer a set of elemental personal characteristics that our genes or Fortune herself distributes to each of us through some inscrutable design. From these elements, one might then extrapolate the individual personality and ultimately the quality of social institutions. Both Weber and Durkheim reject such arguments by pointing to the fact that the meaning of such presumed psychological elements or 'laws' based upon them cannot be deduced without invoking meanings already existing in the social context (Eldridge, 1970, 17–18). For example, while some psychologists might claim that intelligence is operationally and independently defined in the Binet scale, the human sociologist points out that Binet's first step in building the scale was to ask teachers in a Paris school near his laboratory what they thought intelligence was and which of their pupils had it.

For Weber (1947, 88–100) the necessary unit for analyzing self and society is the individual human being. All explanations of social and personal phenomena must rest upon subjective meanings that appear 'adequate' to the individual. The task of those who would explain human action and social forms therefore becomes the 'interpretation' of human meanings. Weber also recognizes that interpretation of meanings alone will not suffice if we are to understand social phenomena in 'causally adequate' terms. The theorist must show how people typically construe social situations and how these constructions have consequences for themselves and for others.

> Interpretive sociology considers the individual and his action as the basic unit, as its 'atom'.... In this approach, the individual is also the upper limit and the sole carrier of meaningful conduct. . . . In general, for sociology such concepts as 'state,' 'association', 'feudalism', and the like, designate certain categories of human interaction. Hence it is the task of sociology to reduce these concepts to 'understandable' action, that is, without exception, to the actions of participating individual men. (Weber, 1958a, 55)

This Weberian rationale for an interpretative sociology has important implications for the question of whether a value-free social science is possible, and it also raises a number of methodological questions. But the point to emphasize is that organization theorists are cognitively and epistemologically bound by the same rules, possibilities, and limitations as the persons whose actions they are trying to explain. If we see theorists as trying to make sense of the social world by reducing it to generalities, rules, and abstractions, the Weberian assumptions force us to recognize that this process is the same one that goes on as Everyman attempts to make sense of his world in ideational terms. If Everyman's ideas, beliefs, hopes, and fears are his ideology, so also are those intellectual artifacts we call organization theories the ideology of the theorists. Human sociologists and theorists working under the assumptions of a Weberian interpretative sociology ask only that the theorists' explanations of human behaviour make sense in terms of a 'real' – if subjective – world in which people live and find their being. Though life itself and life in organizations is filled with contending ideologies, the quality of organization theory should clarify the process of contention – the rules and consequences of the battle. It should not constitute another position in the battle, and it should not present the view of its winning general as good, 'functional', or inevitable. Too frequently in the past, organization and administrative theory has – wittingly or not – taken sides in the ideological battles of social process and presented as 'theory' the views of a dominating set of values, the views of rulers, élites, and their administrators (Riffel, 1977). The same criticism can be made about curriculum theory and the decision-makers who define what is to be accepted as knowledge by the schools (Young, 1971).

The assumptions of interpretative social theory do not deny the biological and physical circumstances of the human condition. They merely require that we attempt to understand such conditions as people themselves do. As Goffman points out, physical and biological 'facts' mean little compared to the social rituals we weave around them: 'A person with carcinoma of the bladder can, if he wants, die with more social grace and propriety, more apparent inner social normalcy, than a man with a harelip can order a piece of apple pie' (Goffman, 1971, 353).

And for those who still resist accepting individuals and their ideas as both the focal point of social reality and its limit, George Herbert Mead's (1934) social psychology provides a rationale in which thinking becomes an internal dialectic whereby the human organism adapts to its environment. Thinking and being are thereby adaptive responses to environment, and primacy for explanation rests with the internal dialectic rather than with objective conditions. Mead's concepts of the 'generalized other' thus becomes an explanation of how society exists in the human mind. We now need not see man in society, but only society in man. The generalized other is thus the part of 'me' that expresses others' norms, values, and beliefs, though individuals see them as their own acts (Berlak and Berlak, 1975, 11).

VALUES AND METHODOLOGY

It is abundantly clear that Weber regarded value-free social science as an impossibility (Zeitlin, 1973, 58; Eldridge, 1970, 11–14). So Bendix points out, 'In fact, Weber made it clear that "no science is absolutely free from presuppositions, and no science can prove its fundamental value to the man who rejects these presuppositions'" (Bendix and Roth, 1971, 71). This is the position argued here. Or in the words of one of Pirandello's (1954, 24) six characters, 'But a fact is like a sack ... When it's empty it won't stand up. And in order to make it stand up you must first of all pour into it all the reasons and all the feelings which have caused it to exist.'

Weber requires social scientists to be aware of their own values, their own assumptions. As Bendix notes, 'These are minimal demands against self-deception and the deception of others' (Bendix and Roth, 1971, 71). This view sets Weber apart from Marx who thought that correct scientific inquiry could reveal an objective social structure against which individuals' subjective meanings might be seen as 'false consciousness'. In this belief, Marx is joined by many contemporary social scientists who regard theory as super-reality, which only the enlightened may be expected to understand.

Weber's method is to create images of reality as actors in social settings understand it and to show how action consistent with these images has consequences – expected or unexpected. Understanding comes from setting images against each other. The images portray different people at one point in time and take different vantage points over time. In this way Weber strives to build explanations that are both 'meaningfully' and 'causally' adequate. The explanations have both meaning for the actors and consistency in a logical, causal sense. The method is akin to cinematography where discrete images on film create a point of view and show why events in the action turn out as they do. But is the point of view that of the actors or of the photographer? In Antonioni's film *Blow-up* a photographer, accustomed to using his subjects as objects for his own purposes and profit, sneaks up to take pictures of a couple in a park. They walk in conversation, appear to embrace briefly, and then move on. When they spot the photographer, they object to his picture-taking. He returns to his dark-room and develops the prints. What has he seen? Was it innocent love or was he witnessing a murder in progress? He 'blows up' the pictures themselves, then enlarges parts of them again and again hoping that the larger prints will answer the question of what was going on. Ultimately the images must speak for themselves despite any theory that the photographer or we as different observers can hypothetically place upon them.

Nisbet (1967, 259–260) highlights the strength of this method in the hands of a scholar such as Weber. In explaining the relationship between Calvinism and the capitalist temper, Weber contrasts the 'paradox of the presences of a manifest capitalist spirit' in the 'backwoods circumstances of eighteenth-century America, and conversely, the lack of such a spirit in affluent, bourgeois Florence'. He quotes from Weber:

Now, how could activity, which was at best ethically tolerated, turn into a calling in the sense of Benjamin Franklin? The fact to be explained historically is that the most highly capitalistic center of that time, in Florence of the fourteenth and fifteenth centuries, the money and capital market of all the great political Powers, this attitude was considered ethically unjustifiable, or at best to be tolerated. But in the backwoods small bourgeois circumstances of Pennsylvania in the eighteenth century, where business threatened for simple lack of money to fall back into barter, where there was hardly a sign of large enterprise, where only the earliest beginnings of banking were to be found, the same thing was considered the essence of moral conduct, even commanded in the name of duty. To speak here of a reflection of material conditions in the ideal superstructure would be patent nonsense. (Weber, 1958b, 180)

In the study of organizations in general and of schools in particular, Weber is usually quoted in the section on 'theoretical framework' and ignored thereafter in the methodology of the study. Some empirical work on schools using other than social systems or reductionist theories are beginning to come forward (Magoon, 1977). Part of our difficulty in this respect comes from an ideological blind spot in recognizing research. We have so schooled ourselves to see statistically but – in Weber's terms – meaningless studies as research that we are willing, and even eager, to accept their tiny but neatly packaged 'findings' as knowledge.

We should now begin to look at wholly new kinds of routes to knowledge about schools and organizations. The 'controlled', highly empirical study is not the only road to truth about organizations. Reading – or better still seeing, – Pirandello's *Six Characters in Search of an Author* (1954) and *The Balcony* by Genet (1966) may make us think of new roads to truth, as reflection upon our own life and experience might do. We should be experiencing Miss White's second-grade class with Miriam Wasserman (1974, 52–58) and listening to the Schoolboys of Barbiana explain to their teacher what school is like to them (Rossi and Cole, 1970). And we might ask with James Herndon (1971) why his six-year-old son going to 'this good school' burst into inconsolable tears when he once forgot his homework (pp. 77–85). Or we might discover with Herndon what happens when some teachers behave as though everyone in the 'dumb class' can and must read (pp. 134–155).

LOGIC, WILL, SUBMISSION AND IMAGES OF REALITY

There is a logic that leads, as Wittgenstein (1961, 151) shows us, to a perception of reality and an understanding of our lives from which there is no retreat.

My propositions serve as elucidations in the following way: anyone who understands me eventually recognizes them as nonsensical, when he has used them – as steps – to climb up beyond them. (He must, so to speak, throw away the ladder after he has climbed up it.)

He must transcend these propositions, and then he will see the world aright.

Wittgenstein's logic takes him ultimately to a point where logic has no meaning, to a vision of the universe akin to that found in the contemplative religions of the East. In the *Bhagavad-Gita*, Arjuna, the man of action, the administrator and warrior, lays down his weapons on the field of battle saying he can no longer do what is required of him. When rational arguments and social pressure fail to persuade Arjuna of the error in such thinking, the Lord Krishna convinces him to resume his role as leader by revealing himself in 'divine manifestations', which ordinarily go unnoticed behind the 'form and disguise' of everyday life (Prabhavananda and Isherwood, 1971, 88). From this transcendental experience, Arjuna sees that living in the world is synonymous with action. The individual cannot escape doing; no more can the leader escape decisions or the agony that often goes with making them. As part of a long and beautiful invocation of life in which he enumerates the varieties of being and doing, Krishna – as the symbol of existence and action – says to Arjuna:

I am death that snatches all: I, also, am the source of all that shall be born: I am glory, prosperity, beautiful speech, memory, intelligence, steadfastness, and forgiveness. . . .

I am the dice-play of the cunning: I am the strength of the strong: I am triumph and perseverance: I am the purity of the good. . . .

I am the sceptre and mastery of those who rule, the policy of those who seek to conquer: I am the silence of things secret: I am the knowledge of the knower.

O Arjuna, I am the divine seed of all lives. (p. 90)

Krishna's message to leaders calls upon them to renounce the world while accepting it and acting within it. The leader, 'full of compassion', must engage in action 'for duty's sake only', not out of 'desire for its fruits' (p. 120). So Arjuna recognizes that escape from action is impossible, except as contemplation of this truth provides it. He then picks up his arrows and his bow, saying to Krishna, 'I will do your bidding' (p. 130).

Wittgenstein and the *Bhagavad-Gita* show us a vision of the world and action within it. They offer metaphors and artistic images as keys to understanding. These images are of the same kind as those hidden in the theories or models that social scientists build to explain human action. Both the images and the theories provide reservoirs of meaning for interpreting our experience. The difference between an image and a theory of reality does not lie in the claim that theory alone is open to verification by powerful and objective observation. Despite such claims, it may be doubted that social scientists ever place their theories and models in jeopardy when they appear to 'test' them with the methods of positivistic, experimental science (Kuhn, 1962; Feyerabend, 1975). In contrast, the symbols of nonrational discourse are not intended to be tested by methods of proof and, paradoxically, this independence of normal scientific truth-making gives them their interpretative power. This power comes, not through the methods of objective science, but from insight into the meaning of the symbols. Their validity comes when individuals recognize the truth that they contain. It comes when individuals accept them as giving meaning and form to their own experience. The relevance of such images to administration is simply that they may evoke the realities of being an administrator better than the rational knowledge upon which a supposed science of administration rests. These nonrational views of life and action in it will not yield to analysis by quadratic equations, much less to solution by social scientists' multivariate models that speciously compile the 'facts' of existence into a benign order. There is a flaw in its thinking, which the *science* of administration must consider: the possibility that the tidy order, that its theory sees in organizations, arises simply from the view of reality that administrators find convenient to hold from their vantage points somewhere near the locus of control in a particular social system.

The question that administrative theory ignores is why individuals, living far from any point of control in organizations, accept and willingly fulfil the ordered lives that tradition, their jobs, and the organization prescribe for them. The individual criminal or tyrant is an understandable figure. But how can we understand those who willingly set about to design and coolly execute a Holocaust that obliterated millions of Jews, homosexuals, and many other outcasts from a society that otherwise manifested a tradition of artistic accomplishment, humane learning, and sensitivity? How can ordinary individuals push the bomb release buttons that, in one evening, would burn Dresden and all its inhabitants to a crisp in an act of destruction unparalleled by any other single event in the brutal history of war? How can a person do any job? How can one be a teacher and make the decisions that strike deeply into the lives of children and their parents? How can one administer a school system or any other large enterprise knowing that they inevitably contain conflicts and dilemmas and – worse – knowing that a ruthless, imperial force must be used to resolve them?

When we now consider genocide and untrammeled war upon civilians we can readily see, in retrospect, that such deeds and all similar atrocities are wrong. The question remains, nevertheless, of why they were ever possible in the first place. From the perspective of this article, the answer comes in a somewhat surprising form. They are possible because organizations work, not in the sense of accomplishing overall objectives, but rather in the sense that organizations are nothing other than people doing and acting for whatever reasons seem adequate or desirable to them. Organizations are possible because people do, in the course of a day's work, simple acts that fulfil the will and intention of others whose vision of what should be – terrible or beautiful though that vision be – is thus made reality. Lacking their own independent visions of what to do or what to be, most individuals become what others now, or before them, have created for them. Administration thus involves an act of creation and compulsion. From all that might be, the administrator seeks to cause certain actions and events to prevail over others. The administrative act has force when people become and fulfill an ideological vision of what should be in the world. The vision acted out may be well established and noncontentious. It may stem from an ancient tradition, long venerated. Representing birth and creation, it may rest on a charismatic insight into the possibility of new social relationships among people.

Though I risk being misunderstood and may give offence as well in saying it, I must assert that there is a profound sense in which to be a teacher or principal is to become a force as violent as those at play in being a guard in a concentration camp or being a pilot of an aircraft in a fire-bombing raid. The violence in being a teacher or principal is not usually overt, though as instruments of punishment they may inflict physical pain as well. Rather, their violence is found in the quality of their relationships with others; it is personal and it is existential. Teachers and principals stand for an organization, for society – social forms that require order and regularity. They represent patterns of thinking and values that have spanned many centuries. They are symbols of knowledge and rationality. They must impose a way of being and believe that it is better than the impulsive, undisciplined, and often, unruly actions of the young. This shaping of a person's behaviour according to patterns desired by another is not unique to schools; it is part of the human condition, as Laing (1967, 50) makes clear:

> From the moment of birth, when the stone-age baby confronts the twentieth-century mother, the baby is subjected to these forces of violence, called love, as its mother and father have been, and their parents and their parents before them. . . . This enterprise is on the whole successful. By the time the new human being is fifteen or so, we are left with a being like ourselves. A half-crazed creature, more or less adjusted to a mad world.

This shaping and creation of the individual within intense relationships is precisely the process that occurs in organizations as people learn to bend to the will of others. For a glimpse of how this process works largely unseen in 'normal' organizations, one can hardly do better than to look at organizations where the exercise of will and unquestioned submission to it are pushed to what must be points close to the limits of human tolerance.

The Dead Sea Scrolls suggest that the vision of the world that those in today's cloistered, monastic orders act out extends back 2,000 years to that strand of Judaic thought lived by the Essenes and the monks of the Qumran community. In the contemporary Christian orders, which still exemplify the values of asceticism and rejection of the secular world, the religious spend a lifetime learning acceptance of, and devotion to, 'the Rule'. McGrath (1978) provides a moving description of this process at work among nuns of an order that still lives this vision of extreme asceticism. The entrant to the convent spends three years learning to be a nun under the exacting scrutiny of one woman, the Mistress of Novices.

> She it was who regulated all the neophyte's steps: how she should lift up her feet and not put them down noisily, how she should not walk on her heels, how she should not swing her arms, how she should keep her hands hidden under the folds of her dress, how she should not hold her head up too high. She it was who regulated the neophyte's words: when she should speak, to whom she should speak, about what she should speak; how quickly, how loudly, with what intonation. The neophyte learned quickly enough that she had no right of reply! 'Mother', the term which predictably had to be used by the neophyte in addressing the Novice Mistress, could never be challenged, because 'Mother' in this new world was in effect God. (p. 197)

Every detail of behaviour is carefully observed and controlled: '[The Scapular] is to be folded lengthwise; the crease in the centre is to be made on the wrong side, that is, when folding, the right side [is] to be turned in. It can then be folded in two parts, not more' (p. 202). The price of failing to live the Rule is loss of self. Such failure means that the novice will be 'condemned, denounced, and punished' while the 'Others', who were always there 'alongside everywhere', were still there, '*but differently*: Frightened eyes, averted gazes, lowered veils, and quickened steps told their own tale of desperate retreat' (p. 211). Punishment of the novice who fails the Rule is fearsome to those who still strive to keep it faithfully. They will see her 'banished from the public table to eat in disgrace off the floor, from the public prie-dieu to lie prostrate in shame at the chapel door, from the public lecture bench to kneel discredited at the back of the room' (p. 212).

After some period of time spent living this Rule, it is not surprising that the nuns no longer feel that their lives require submission to it; instead their lives embody the Rule. They themselves have become the Rule. Inevitably, not all novices succeed in making the transformation required of them, and the questioning of authority, which characterizes much contemporary religious thought, has weakened the ideological foundations upon which such orders rest. The example may be helpful, however, if we think how other organizations embody, in sometimes reduced intensity, the same controlling forces. What we need to understand more of in administrative studies are the power of command, on the one hand, and the responses of obedience or rebellion on the other. What we need to know more of in studies of schools as organizations are the realities of being a teacher or administrator and their consequences in the lives of children.

We live in separate realities. But we live with each other. The line of reasoning in this paper implies that we need to engage in a continuing process of discovery aimed at gaining an understanding of ourselves and of others – a process aimed at understanding social reality and its artefacts, which we call organizations. We need to move from the conviction that there is only one social reality to a recognition of the possibility that many exist. How we are to understand and appreciate these alternate perspectives as theorists and as human beings is not altogether clear. I have suggested the juxtaposition of meaning-laden, but disparate, images as a method that is both powerful and promising.

What, for example, do the Schoolboys of Barbiana tell us when they object to a teacher's complaint that their past instruction contained no 'Physical Education'?

> Anyone of us could climb an oak tree. Once up there we could let go with both hands and chop off a two-hundred pound branch with a hatchet. Then we could drag it through the snow to our mother's doorstep.

> I heard of a gentleman in Florence who rides upstairs in his house in an elevator. But then he has bought himself an expensive gadget and pretends to row in it. You would give him an A in Physical Education.
> (Rossi and Cole, 1970, 23)

Few, if any, of the ideas in this article are new. But some of them are new to me. By my standards, then, that puts them into Eleanor Duckworth's category of 'wonderful ideas' that have to do with insight and experience. The importance of such ideas is simply that we have them and can use them. Piaget recounts the experience of a mathematician. As a child, he put ten pebbles in a row. He counted them left to right. Ten. He counted them right to left. Ten. 'He kept rearranging and counting them until he decided that, no matter what the arrangement, he was always going to find that there were ten. Number is independent of the order of counting' (Duckworth, 1973, 263). That this theorem is not new makes no difference to the person discovering it. What matters, in this context, is the intellectual development of the child and his freedom to have such 'wonderful ideas'. My concern in organization theory is that we are restricting one another's thinking by insisting on searching for universal truths that fit within a framework that is narrower than the reality it is trying to represent.

We have been caught in trap that requires us, in the name of theory to hold a single image up to reality and test whether it is true – or at least whether it is a 'better' and more accurate representation of reality than any other image. But what is truth and falsity in social reality? If we are to understand organizations as containing multiple meanings, we must abandon the search for a single best image of them. An examination of great theorists' images of society reveals that the study of organizations can best advance by admitting multiple realities and different means of expressing them (Zeitlin 1968). A number of contemporary scholars now accept this position and argue that such a shift requires us to abandon the attempt to construct a value-free theory of social reality. Instead, we must recognize social and organizational theories as expressions of ideology and as moral judgements about the world. Then various theoretical insights might all coexist simultaneously, since theories would no longer be 'competing for the single prize of being the most-nearly-true' (Pondy and Boje, n.d., 2). In judging theories, as we would no doubt continue to do, we would therefore recognize that we were involved in a truth-making and essentially moral task within a disciplined process of enquiry into social reality.

NOTES

1 A revision and extension of a paper given to the symposium, 'Contemporary Theory Development and Educational Research', American Educational Research Association, New York, April 1977.
2 To explore the implications of Blake's vision for education, see Inglis (1975).
3 The ellipses shown in this and the subsequent quotation from Pirandello appear in the translated text and presumably indicate rhythm in speech rather than omission of words.
4 The following works were among the basic writings that were available at the time of the symposium: Greenfield (1975, 1976), Griffiths (1975), Crane and Walker (1976), and Hughes (1976). Some later writings that significantly extended the debate are also worth noting: Griffiths (1977), Kendell and Byrne (1977), Greenfield (1977–1978, forthcoming), and Hobbs and Bruce (1977–1978).

REFERENCES

Bendix, R. and Roth, G. 1971. *Scholarship and Partisanship: Essays on Max Weber.* Berkeley, CA: University of California.
Berlak, A. C., and Berlak, H. 1975. 'Towards a Political and Social Psychological Theory of Schooling: An Analysis of English Informal Primary Schools'. *Interchange* 6, 3: 11–22.
Blake, W. 1931. 'The Song of Enion'. In *Poems of Blake*, ed. L. Binion. London: Macmillan.
Boulding, K. E. 1968. 'General Systems Theory – A Skeleton of a Science'. In *Modern Systems Research for the Behavioral Scientist*, ed. W. Buckley, 1–10. Chicago: Aldine.
Cox, C. B. and Boyson, R. eds 1975. *Black Papers: The Fight for Education.* London: J. M. Dent.
Crane, A. R. and Walker, W. G. 1976. 'Theory in the Real World of the Educational Administrator'. *UCEA Review* 17 (May): 1–2, 37–38.

Duckworth, E. 1973. 'The Having of Wonderful Ideas'. In *Piaget in the Classroom*, eds M. Schwebel and J. Raph. New York: Basic Books.

Eldridge, J. E. T., ed. 1970. *Max Weber: The Interpretation of Social Reality*. London: Michael Joseph.

Feyerabend, P. 1975. *Against Method: Outline of an Anarchistic Theory of Knowledge*. London: New Left Books.

Genet, J. 1966. *The Balcony*. Trans. B. Frechtman. New York: Grove.

Goffman, E. 1967. *Interaction Ritual: Essays on Face-to-Face Behavior*. New York: Anchor.

—— 1971. *Relations in Public*. New York: Basic Books.

Greenfield, T. B. 1975. 'Theory About Organization: A New Perspective and its Implications for Schools'. In *Administering Education: International Challenge*, ed. M. Hughes, 71–99. London: Athlone.

—— 1976. 'Theory About What? Some More Thoughts about Theory in Educational Administration'. *UCEA Review* 17 (February): 4–9.

—— 1977–1978. 'Where Does Self Belong in the Study of Organization? Response to a Symposium'. *Educational Administration* 6, 1: 81–101.

—— 1979. 'Ideas Versus Data or How Can the Data Speak for Themselves?' In *Problem-Finding in Educational Administration: Trends in Research and Theory*, eds G. L. Immegart and W. L. Boyd, 167–190. Lexington, MA: D. C. Heath.

Griffiths, D. E. 1975. 'Some Thoughts About Theory in Educational Administration – 1975'. *UCEA Review* 17 (October): 12–18.

—— 1977. 'The Individual in the Organization: A Theoretical Perspective'. *Educational Administration Quarterly* 13, 2: 1–18.

Herndon, J. 1971. *How to Survive in Your Native Land*. New York: Bantam Books.

Hobbs, R. and Dennis, B. 1977–1978. 'The Phenomenology Debate'. *Educational Administration* 6, 1: 112–117.

Hughes, M., ed. 1976. 'Barr Greenfield and Organisational Theory: A Symposium'. *Educational Administration* 5, 1: 1–13.

Inglis, F. 1975. *Ideology and the Imagination*. London: Cambridge.

Kendell, R. R. and Byrne, D. R. 1977. 'Thinking About the Greenfield-Griffiths Debate'. *UCEA Review* 19 (October): 6–16.

Kuhn, T. 1962. *The Structure of Scientific Revolutions*. Chicago: University of Chicago.

Laing, R. D. 1967. *The Politics of Experience*. Harmondsworth: Penguin.

McGrath, H. 1978. 'A New Paradigm for Policy Research?' Ph.D. dissertation, University of New England, Australia.

Magoon, A. J. 1977. 'Constructivist Approaches in Educational Research'. *Review of Educational Research* 47, 4: 651–693.

Manning, P. K. 1976. 'The Decline of Civility: A Comment on Erving Goffman's Sociology'. *Canadian Review of Sociology and Anthropology* 13, 1: 13–25.

Mead, G. H. 1934. *Social Psychology: Selected Papers*, ed. Anselm Strauss. Chicago: University of Chicago.

Mills, C. Wright. 1959. *The Sociological Imagination*. New York: Oxford.

Nisbet, R. A. 1967. *The Sociological Tradition*. London: Heinemann.

Parsons, T. 1951. *The Social System*. Glencoe, IL: Free Press.

Pirandello, L. 1954. *Six Characters in Search of an Author*. Trans. Frederick May. London: Heinemann.

Pondy, L. R. 1978. 'Beyond Open Systems Models'. In *Research in Organizational Behaviour*, ed. B. N. Staw and L. L. Cummings Greenwich, CT: JAI Press.

Pondy, L. R. and Boje, D. M. n.d. 'Bringing Mind Back' In: 'Paradigm Development as a Frontier Problem in Organization Theory'. Unpublished paper, Department of Business Administration, University of Illinois.

Prabhavananda, S. and Isherwood, C., trans. 1971. *The Song of God: Bhagavad-Gita.* New York: Mentor.

Riffel, J. A. 1977. 'The Theory Problem in Educational Administration'. Un- published paper, University of Manitoba.

Rossi, N. and Cole, T., trans. 1970. *Letter to a Teacher.* New York: Random House.

Wasserman, M. 1974. *Demystifying School: Writings and Experiences.* New York: Praeger.

Weber, M. 1947. *The Theory of Social and Economic Organizations.* Trans. A. M. Henderson and T. Parsons, New York: Free Press

—— 1958a. *From Max Weber: Essays in Sociology.* Trans. H. H. Gerth and C. W. Mills, New York: Oxford.

—— 1958b. *The Protestant Ethic and the Spirit of Capitalism.* Trans. T. Parsons, New York: Charles Scribner.

Wittgenstein, L. 1961. *Tractatus Logico–Philosophicus.* Trans. D. B. Pears and B. F. McGuiness, introd. Bertrand Russell. London: Routledge & Kegan Paul.

Young, M. F. D., ed. 1971. *Knowledge and Control: New Directions for the Sociology of Education.* London: Collier-Macmillan.

Zeitlin, I. M. 1968. *Ideology and the Development of Sociological Theory.* Englewood Cliffs, NJ: Prentice Hall.

—— 1973. *Rethinking Sociology.* Englewood Cliffs, NJ: Prentice Hall.

5

THE MAN WHO COMES BACK THROUGH THE DOOR IN THE WALL

Discovering truth, discovering self, discovering organizations

We are much beholden to Machiavel and others, that write what men do, and not what they ought to do.

Francis Bacon

But men must know, that in this theater of man's life, it is reserved only for God and angels to be lookers-on.

Francis Bacon

Two things fill my mind with ever-increasing wonder and awe, the more often and the more intensely the reflection dwells on them: the starry heavens above me and the moral law within me.

Immanuel Kant

A role is a hole, an organization is related and orderly set of holes, and one sometimes catches a fleeting and slightly nightmarish vision of scientific universe as a set of holes bounded and defined by other holes.

Kenneth E. Boulding

The basic problem in the study of organizations is understanding human intention and meaning. Part of the complexity in this problem is found in the observation that people can act purposefully and yet bring about consequences that are wholly unintended for themselves and for others. We live. And in living we believe, assert self, establish order around us, dominate others, or are dominated by them. Action flowing from meaning and intention weaves the fabric of social reality. It is true that organizations appear to be solid, real entities that act independently of human control and are difficult to change. Yet the paradox is that the vital spark, the dynamic of organization is made from nothing more substantial than people doing and thinking. Organizations are limited by and defined by human action. In their deepest reality – that is, in their subjective reality – they are simply manifestations of mind and will. While this conception of organizations does not make them easy to control or to change, it does locate organizational reality in the concreteness of individual action.

The root problems of organization thus dissolve into questions about what people do, why they do it, and whether what they do is right. Ultimately such problems become the individual's search for identity and for truth. The questions generated by these problems remain fortunately unresolved, though the human mind has posed them repeatedly and striven continually to answer them. Such questions retain their power over time. Men and women ask them in ever-new forms and then fashion answers to them yet again. The purpose of this paper is not to argue for a particular set of answers, but rather to show that the study of organizations provides a rich source of ideas and experience for those who explore human action and would ask how we might best understand it and learn from it.

The epigraphs that open this chapter foreshadow its themes, providing a framework that defines the ground to be worked. Much can be said within that framework. Much has already been said within it. Indeed, readers will see how heavily the ideas I expound are dependent upon other voices, upon a long-standing tradition of scholarship and philosophy. They are the voices – some contemporary, some historic, and some ancient – of those who are the foundational thinkers in subjectivist philosophy and interpretative social science. These voices speak to us of ideas that have been largely ignored in the pursuit of a set of universal, objective, and 'scientific' truths about organizations. The consequence of this exclusion has led to a science of organizations that is no science, to a definition of organizations that excludes much of what we want to study in them, and to a failure of methodology and technique in the face of the moral and existential questions that are imbedded in organizational life.

The reason for my writing once more on these themes is found in recent articles by Hills[1] and Willower[2] who seek to reassure their readers that a singular substantive body of theory about organizations exists and that the power and truth of this knowledge can be demonstrated by the techniques of an objective science. What is needed now is a statement speaking to the many issues they raise and that yet advances a general argument. For several years such an argument has troubled my mind: how can organizations best be conceived and how can inquiry into them proceed most fruitfully.[3] When it comes to saying something about the realities of organizations, Hills and Willower live in one world while I inhabit another. We argue from different premises, see different facts in the world, and build different interpretations of them. Weber makes the same point in arguing that

> No science is absolutely free from presupposition, and no science can prove its fundamental value to the man who rejects these presuppositions.[4]

Both Hills and Willower live in a world where facts stand separate and independent from theories about the facts. In their world, it is possible to explain facts by theories and thereby to gain control over them. If they advance false ideas about the facts, the facts will destroy their theories and science will have made another step in its inevitable advance towards truth. In my world, the line between fact and value is at best blurred and what we see as facts is in large measure determined by ideas in our heads. Although I recognize some kind of dialectic between what we construe as fact and what we recognize as idea, it is not obvious to me that we can validate truth by means that are independent of the person seeking the truth. In a world where the thing to be known and the person knowing it are quite different from each other, it is possible to talk about an objective standard of truth that all observers can agree on. In a world where the observer and the 'object of knowledge' are in some sense one, how can we distinguish between them? If the knower and the known blend together, where shall we look for an objective criterion of truth? Both Hills and Willower assert (and assume) that ideas are a different sort of thing than facts. I cheerfully admit that my generalizations about organizations constitute a kind of theory about them. What I am pointing to, however, is the difficulty of finding 'empirical facts' that would objectively and incontrovertibly support or deny the theory. If our theories create the facts that are relevant to them, we can only explore truth within a framework that defines what it is.

The great advantage of positivist science is its objectivity; it provides a standard of truth that has nothing to do with the scientist or any other human agency. The scientist's statements about the world have no personal element in them other then the fortuitous circumstances that cause the scientist to focus on one set of facts rather than another. There is no recognition that a statement about the world is also a declaration of interest, intention, and will emanating from the observer. Such a notion would be totally alien in this depersonalized conception of reality that sees science as an immaculate standard for truth-making. So it is that Fred Kerlinger outlines alternative methods of knowing for readers of his respected and widely used text. Following the ideas of Charles Peirce, he defines four such methods of knowing – four ways of 'fixing belief'. The first three have in common a reference to human opinion whether such belief is held out of conviction, deference to others, or pure reasoning. The flaw that Peirce and Kerlinger see in such methods of determining truth is that they offer no means of adjudicating among competing claims about reality that different individuals may advance. What is needed, therefore, is a standard for truth-making that rests beyond human control, beyond the power of individuals to colour or distort it. What could such a standard possibly be? Where should necessarily fallible human beings look for it? Kerlinger and Peirce find such a standard in the *method of science*, a method that they claim gives us the only means of glimpsing reality, the reality that lies 'outside the scientist and his personal beliefs, perceptions, biases, values, attitudes, and emotions'.[5] Peirce describes this method and its criterion of truth:

> To satisfy our doubts . . . therefore, it is necessary that a method should be found by which our beliefs may be determined by nothing human, but by some external permanency – by something upon which our thinking has no effect. . . . The method must be such that the ultimate conclusion of every man shall be the same. Such is the method of science. Its fundamental hypothesis . . . is this: There are real things, whose characters are entirely independent of our opinions about them.[6]

It remains to be seen how men may perceive a criterion of truth that lies outside the workings of their minds and how they might express it without colouring and distorting it as they do everything else they perceive. It remains to be seen, as well, whether they would accept such a standard even if they were convinced it existed. Faced with these difficulties and the appalling prospect of a non-human standard for determining the truth of human affairs, I find it both reasonable and humane to assert the imposs- ibility of conceiving empirical facts or generalizing ideas that the human mind had not worked upon in some way. Even God reserves His judgement on day-to-day affairs in the world; only Science presumes to tell us the ultimate reality of things short of the day of the final judgement. For similar reasons, I find it easy to recognize the impracticality of getting all men to agree upon ultimate truths.

The necessary question for all scientists is what objective truth means in a world that can be perceived only subjectively. This is the world of Emmanuel Kant and of the long line of philosophers and social scientists who have followed his thought, for it is they who have confronted the difficulties of interpreting human action in a subjectively-construed reality. The thinkers in this tradition include Dilthey, Hegel, Marx, Weber, Croce, Heidegger, and Schutz, among many others.[7] They work from Kant's basic propositions that the 'object of reality' and the 'object of knowledge' are essentially distinct and that our knowledge is human knowledge created by agents engaged in active inquiry. The impact of the knower can, therefore, never be 'cleansed' from that which is known. As Bauman points out, from the time of Kant onward the knower was

> promoted from a distorting and unwanted factor of the cognitive act to a role as an indispensable condition of all knowledge. Subjectivity was shown to be inseparable from cognition; an objective knowledge, therefore, could be reached, if at all, only through this subjectivity.[8]

Common sense tells us that we know what facts are, but as Hodgkinson points out, philosophers have been hard pressed to define what they are;

they usually simply accept them as a priori givens. More importantly, Hodg-kinson demonstrates how facts blur into values: This, he says, is a pencil in my hand, a fact that can be defined as a set of atomic wavicles in space-time flux; it is gold; it has been around in my life for a long time; it was given to me by a lady-love. . . . And so 'on and on until the factual object which *in essence is valueless* is imbued with any amount of value or worth'.[9] What is science, then, if fact and value cannot be distinguished and if most of what we want to know about in a world of action is suffused with value? Even if we grant science a domain that deals in facts, that science is neutered, rendered immobile, and confined to self-delusion if it cannot relate those facts to values and deal with the questions of how one ought to behave in the world.

In what follows, I begin by outlining a set of themes that recur in interpretive social science and that are relevant to the analysis of organizations from the subjectivist perspective. These themes provide the basis for some propositions that I believe offer a 'new' and useful framework for the study of organizations. I write 'new' to warn readers that there is complexity here. Hills (p. 43) used my acknowledgement of this complexity to suggest that what I had to say could be safely ignored because (a) others had said it before and (b) what was said could all be comfortably fitted into conventional theory and into a methodology long since fixed by organizational science. I grant that the ideas are not new, but deny that this admission means that those who espouse standard theory and methodology in the science of organization can therefore rest easy. What is new is that old ideas when applied to the normal science of organization call the achievements of that science seriously into question. Such science can not be adequately defended simply by saying that the ideas that threaten it are old, not new. Secondly I will identify a number of continuing problems that anyone attempting to build a substantive theory of organizations within a subjectivist framework must cope with. I identify these problems not to resolve them, but merely to indicate what they are and to suggest the kinds of answers that some thinkers have advanced to clarify them and understand them. If I am successful in achieving these purposes, I hope it will be seen that I have acknowledged and dealt with the major points argued by Hills and Willower. In conclusion, I will deal with points in their critiques that warrant specific comment because they define in particularly vivid and concrete terms what this argument is about.

INTERPRETING SOCIAL REALITY: REASONING WITH ANGELS AND OTHERS

We want to know what is in the world, but our very act of inquiry into it denies us that knowledge. Bacon was right in pointing out that one cannot discover what is by arguing over what ought to be. But he and Machiavelli are wrong in thinking that what is can be detached from what we think ought to be. In separating ends, and means, Machiavelli brought down upon himself later generations' judgement of him as immoral. We might better call him (and Bacon, too) poor scientists for failing to note that *is* and *ought* are intimately joined in human action. At least in explorations of social reality, one can look exclusively at *is* in action only by holding the *ought* constant. That is to say that the social scientist or political philosopher who considers only what is in social reality must exclude from consideration what else might be under different value assumptions. Such an analyst becomes either an ideologue who denies the possibility of different values or an apologist for the values that undergird a particular manifestation of social reality. Should we rejoice or despair in this dilemma? Those who think there is (or ought to be?) only one interpretation of social reality will despair. These ideas destroy the notion of a single social reality that can be explained and controlled by piecing together the truth about it through science. Others who see man's freedom and creativity as necessarily linked to the possibility of new interpretations of reality will rejoice in the notion of an ever-evolving truth and in man's central role in its evolution.

We want to know what is in the world, but we cannot discover it without acting and bringing to bear upon the inquiry our own interests, attitudes, and values. As Bacon says, it is reserved only for God and angels to be lookers-on in the theatre of man's life. The rest of us are human, fallible interested, and biased. Nor can we escape these limitations to look at reality unfiltered by human perspective; we can only shift our perspectives and develop the humility that is appropriate to a condition that limits human knowledge and prevents it from ever comprehending ultimate reality and from gaining complete understanding. It was Robert Burns who prayed that some power would give us the gift to see ourselves as others see us. As Aldous Huxley points out, this power would be a 'salutary gift', but there is another that should be of at least equal interest both to the mature personality and to the social scientist. That is the capacity to see others as they see themselves. It is not clear, Huxley argues, how we can gain such a perspective, especially if those we seek to understand 'inhabit a radically alien universe'. Huxley confines his interest largely to questions of how we might approach such alien universes – how, for example, can the sane know what it feels like to be mad and 'how can we ever visit the worlds which, to Blake, to Swedenborg, to Johann Sebastian Bach, were home?'[10] The theorist, however, will recognize that the same problem occurs in everyday life: how are we to understand ourselves and each other given that none of use is free from self or from action that seeks to realize the interests of self?

It was Karl Marx who first brought to the forefront what Anthony Giddens calls 'the transformative capacity of human action'.[11] This is the power of the individual to obtain outcomes through action and thereby to create some part of the social world that is recognized as real. Not everyone, of course, has equal powers of transformation, but all action is launched out of individual interest. Although Marx begins with general questions of how people construct the social world around them and of how these constructions depend upon the interests of certain individuals and their power, Giddens argues that Marx abandoned these general questions in his later and narrower focus upon class interests and the place of labour in maintaining the capitalist economy.[12] We should avoid, however, the error of Willower who confuses the ideology of present-day Marxist political systems with the insights of Marx. It was Marx who drew attention to *Homo faber*, to man the producer, who creates not only things but the social world in which he lives and who shapes that world out of personal interests in it.[13] Marx also pointed out that social reality reflects the interests of certain people while it often oppresses those of other people at the same time. What we see as a necessary reality can, therefore, be re-shaped by further action that reflects other interests. In the Marxian analysis, social truth is created by the active knower; it depends on self.

The moral order lies within us. It is built into us by our experience and by the actions of others. In the subjectivist perspective, the moral order is not an 'order of nature' to which the individual must adapt or suffer the consequences. The moral order is not out there in the same way that nature is out there. There is no moral parallel to the law of gravity that binds all matter in its grasp. (Indeed, how could one *ever* break the law of gravity? And what would the consequences of breaking it be?) The subjectivist perspective argues, instead, that the moral order is man-made and socially maintained.[14] Individuals who break the laws of the moral order are punished not by nature, but by other human beings and often by conscience as well. It is always clear how to break such an order and it is usually quite plain what the consequences of doing so are. At least others will make such consequences plain after the breaking of the order occurs. Because it lies within people, the moral order is not everywhere the same, and people will disagree as to what it is and as to what it ought to be. These disjunctures lead to further action in which people attempt to shape the moral order as they would have it. They attempt to make others act according to the moral order that is within themselves, or they act to make those suffer who fail to embody the order that they feel within themselves.

The moral order within may be experienced as a natural order without. Given the subjectivist assumptions about self and the moral order, the social order that links people together in loosely-connected common action is simply a reflection of the moral order. One cannot study the social order, therefore, without studying also the self, its values, conditions of creativity and power, and considerations of what ought to be. How is it possible, then, to scientize the study of organizations that are but the reflection of an inner order? One may treat them as the starry skies, as an external objective order. But Kant and the long tradition of thought following him will argue that such science can never distinguish reflection from reality. Only by turning towards the source of light we know, towards man himself, can science begin to understand the complexity and the ambiguity that forms that reality. Can we ever split ends and means, subject and object? If not, we must turn back in studying organizations, we must turn back to *Homo faber*, back to the mind of man that creates, wills, and acts.

The closer one looks at the social universe, the less substantial it looks. Organizations are made by people doing and, in that sense, are insubstantial. They are based on ideas, values, and individual action. Or, as Kenneth Boulding says, they are a collection of holes bounded and defined by other holes.[15] But people are not holes. They are actors, they do things – *for* themselves and *to* each other. People simply make the holes, put them together, and call the result life, or society, or organization. Having spun a web of meaning to make sense of the world, man is caught in it, as Weber said. The world makes no sense without the web. Man must make it, yet the web both constrains his action and makes it possible. So we can never control the web, never control life, society, or organizations, for to do so would be to control individuality and to obliterate that which distinguishes self from other, person from person. We can only seek to understand ourselves through actions that define self, existence, and something of the history of human consciousness.

Hills and Willower take to task both me and those now mostly-silent other voices that I try to speak for. Our error, in their eyes, lies in a failure to see the world in scientifically objective terms, and in our denial of the utility of science as a method for understanding and controlling organizations. My reply is that they have not been paying attention to what the voices have been saying. At least if they receive the message, they reject it. That lies within their prerogative to do. One may ask for reasons for the rejection, but ultimately the judgement rests on an act of belief, an act of faith in objective science as opposed to the placement of faith in human ability to create social reality and to interpret meaning. In this present exchange of views, Hills and Willower claim to have on their side not only theory and empirical facts, but also the power of science to determine objective truth. For the other side, I claim insight, perception, and unruly humanity that will not be slotted into arbitrary categories or controlled by speciously validated theories. They would overlay action in the world with a scientific and objective explanation that has universal applicability. I would seek to understand social action by working from the perspective of those involved in it and would find explanation only in the juxtaposition of those understandings and in the interpretation of them. They see science as moving us closer and closer to general truths about social reality and toward control of social action; I see science – if I may still use the term – as argument where the one who wants to make a point looks for those ideas, facts, and meanings that will increase the completeness, intensity, and

99

persuasiveness of the initial insight. We can only move from insight to insight and argue whether we are moving in the right direction. Short of the Last Judgment, we cannot hope to escape through a door in the wall of reality and thereby gain a lasting and complete view of all that is. We must be satisfied with less, but of what does that less consist?

Two approaches are open to us. We can reason logically about what lies behind the wall of reality and infer from 'facts' in this world what ultimate reality is. This method applies not only to questions about the meaning of existence, but also to more mundane matters such as the nature of organizations and how they work. This is the method of science in so far as it combines logic with 'empirical facts' and hopes thereby to build accurate pictures of ultimate realities of the mechanisms that control events in the everyday world. This is also the logic of Plato, whose parable of the cave still speaks powerfully to the dilemma of knowledge that we face. He argues that we can never see things as they are, but only their shadows, for we are chained in a cave and can look only into the darkness at the flickering images cast by the true form of things as they move between the cave and the bright sun. Plato's answer to this dilemma was to place his faith in reason and logic and in those who could reason and be logical, namely, in philosophers. This is the answer also of objective science which adds only that the 'empirical facts' must agree with the logic – that is, that the theory must be supported by independent data. I do not deny this method works in dealing with the physical world. Whether this method brings ultimate knowledge and whether this method is appropriate for the interpretation of the social world are other questions.

The second approach to the problem of getting behind the wall is to stop trying to get behind it and to deal only with what is on this side of it. This approach embraces those who, in Huxley's words, would transform aspects of our experience of this world into 'Artificial Paradises'.[16] That is, it includes those who seek transcendence – escape through a door in the wall – by art, religion, saturnalia, drugs both artificial and natural, liquor, and tobacco. The limitation of all these doors in the wall is that they are temporary and often leave nasty side effects like hangovers and lung cancer. The person who uses such doors in the wall must always return through them unless, of course, the passage was so risky as to be fatal. What is of lasting value in this approach lies in the realization that one must still act after the artificial paradise is gone, after one has returned through the door in the wall to everyday life. While these escape hatches never lead to ultimate truth and freedom, the better of them may provide lasting insight into life on this side of the wall, or perhaps only the courage to go on with it. From temporary suspension of will, by momentary disengagement from the force of life and through liberating reflection on these drives, help arrives that somehow improves the individual and enables him to do better that which has to be done. We are dealing here with nonrational ways of knowing – ways that Peirce and Kerlinger do not even recognize as ways of knowing. They are not alone in taking this attitude. Plato shared it and for this reason excluded poets and artists from the Republic. Since their knowledge was based on something other than reason and pure logic, it was suspect in that it misleads the credulous who fail to realize that poets and artists deal only in images, not in realities. But what happens if we do not reject these images and instead deal with what is around us and its relation to our ideas? In this way, we begin to direct our attention to what is. Can we be satisfied with knowing what is from reflection about it, or must it have some larger explanation that connects it to ultimate truth and transcendental realities?

Huxley is satisfied with the *is*, a concept that can be expressed in German as *Istigkeit* ('Is-ness'). He recalls his experience with the drug mescalin, commonly known as peyote, when he saw 'what Adam had seen on the morning of his creation – the miracle, moment by moment, of naked existence'. Asked if this perception was agreeable, Huxley still under the influence of the drug replied, 'Neither agreeable nor disagreeable. It just is.'[17] Such a perception could never have satisfied Plato, who would have had to look for the explanation that lies hidden behind such an experience. Plato, so Huxley argues, could never

> have seen a bunch of flowers shining with their inner light and all but quivering under the pressure of the significance with which they were charged; could never have perceived that what rose and iris and carnation so intensely signified was nothing more, and nothing less, than what they were – a transience that was yet eternal life, a perpetual perishing that was at the same time pure Being, a bundle of minute, unique particulars in which, by some unspeakable and yet self-evident paradox, was to be seen the divine source of all existence.[18]

The choice we face is whether to interpret reality and all that we recognize as an empirical world by rational methods alone or whether to seek elements of truth also from insight, image, art, religion, and all the ways of knowing that rely upon intuitive, self-oriented, and nonrational perception. In his exploration of what he calls 'direct perception', Huxley quotes from Blake:

> I have always found that Angels have the vanity to speak of themselves as the only wise. This they do with a confident insolence sprouting from systematic reasoning.[19]

It is not, says Huxley, that we can do without systematic reasoning, but only that it in itself is not adequate for understanding the world. In order to remain sane, we need to revert to direct perception of the is-ness of things and to the unsystematic exploration of reality. In this way, we may bring together the inner and outer worlds into which we were born and make some sense out of life.

Are these notions consistent with a belief in science? Huxley implies that they are by bracketing the systematic reasoning of Blake's Angels with the unsystematic exploration of reality by direct perception. In taking this position he is supported by both Feyerabend and Kuhn.[20] Both of these philosophers of science agree that science moves not only on systematic reasoning but also by creative upheavals in thought where advance depends not on systematic reasoning but upon 'a mixture of subterfuge, rhetoric and propaganda'[21] or, in other words, upon unsystematic reasoning. Feyerabend advances this position with particular vigour. He makes it plain that he opposes 'scientism, the faith in the existence of a unique method whose application leads to exclusive "truths" about the world'.[22] In taking this position, Feyerabend can find support in no less a figure than Bridgman, who remarked that the scientific method, as far as it is a method, is nothing more than doing one's damndest with one's mind, no holds barred. Kaplan, too, finds that we can no more define 'scientific method' than we can speak of 'the method of baseball'. He points to conformism covered by high-sounding language and to norms of scientific inquiry based on what 'everybody's doing'. He, therefore, denies the methodologist any role 'as baseball commissioner writing the rules' or as 'umpire with power to thumb an offending player out of the game'.[23] Feyerabend, however, goes further and says: 'There may come a time when it will be necessary to give reason a temporary advantage and when it will be wise to defend its rules to the exclusion of everything else. I do not think we are living in such a time today.'[24]

To many of my colleagues in administration, these ideas will surely appear wild, exotic, and possibly dangerous. I would recommend to them that they read a tract Christopher Isherwood has written on yoga as a method of understanding reality. I recommend it, not as an answer to substantive questions in the study of organizations – though it may provide such insight as well – but, rather, it should be read to appreciate an attitude that may ease our acceptance of non-objective knowledge and help to break the lock that a tradition of Western, technical, means-oriented thought has used to bind our perception of the world. As James March also argued, we have focused almost exclusively on what now works in social organizations and ignored beauty and justice as criteria for judging our models of organization.[25] 'Can-we-make-the-facts-fit-our-explanation?' has been our only criterion of scientific knowledge, and so we forget the assumptions of this approach and make truth rest solely on the power of our models to predict observable, depersonalized behaviour. Within such limitations, organization theorists working in seventeenth-century Salem would have focused on the readily observable behaviours of witches and striven to construct a model that defined their characteristics and sustained reliable and valid methods for identifying them. Indeed, the more advanced theorists might have recommended against the punishment or killing of witches on the grounds that such 'treatments' did nothing to eradicate witchcraft as a problem. But only those theorists who rejected the prediction of witch-driven behaviour as a criterion for truth in organizational reality would be led to question whether witches existed at all.

In his exploration of yogic thought Isherwood explains the mantra, prayers of constant repetition that contain 'seed words' or elements of God's essence. The efficacy that Isherwood sees in such prayers acts to transform individual consciousness, not to work miracles or to satisfy personal desires. To the reader who doubts the efficacy of such prayers, he says simply, 'try it', for

> no amount of mockery, or argument, will ever prove anything to him, either way. It is like the symbolic pump handle in Tolstoy's *A Confession*. If you move it up and down, you may get water. If you deny that it is a pump handle and refuse even to try it, then you most certainly never will.[26]

For those who wish to try it, the following propositions may make the pump handle for an alternative approach to the study of organizations appear more substantial and practical.

PROLEGOMENON FOR A NEW STUDY OF ORGANIZATION

These observations are offered as prefatory comments for a yet-to-be-written treatise on organizations as invented social reality. They arise from subjectivist assumptions that see knowledge as constructed by men and women in a world they did not make. The observations are stated as propositions, and they summarize much that has already been presented in this article. They try to forge a coherent but necessarily incomplete argument about the nature of organizations and the possibility of inquiry into them. They should be regarded as insights that are possibly helpful in speculation about organizations. As heuristic devices, they may be counted successful in the degree to which they stimulate argument, effort towards clarification of meaning, and reflection on experience. They should not be regarded as a blueprint of organizational reality or as hypotheses that can be confirmed or disconfirmed by empirical facts alone. The claim for them is only that they weave together what some people have defined as the limits of knowledge with what others have experienced as the reality of organizations.

Proposition 1: That organizations are accomplished by people and people are responsible for what goes on in them

Organizations are not written into the natural order of things. They are the consequences of human action – now, in the past, and in the future. Let us begin, then, not with a statement about organizations but with a statement about people. Let us begin with the simple proposition that people can do many things and that one thing can be built upon another. People are by and large creative and talented, but some can do things that others cannot. The result of this creativity, this amassing of achievement and this differentiation of interest and ability, is a world of variegated textures. People do different things and live different lives. There are those who conceive the pyramids, those who are buried in them, those who drive workers to their tasks, and those who are driven to haul the blocks of stone into place. People can do many things or can be made to do them. So we have *Homo faber*, man who does many things and who in doing them creates the social world and organizations around himself. An organization is a set of people caught within a definition of how they shall relate to each other. People live large parts of their lives in organizations; they do things there because they want to or because they have to. From time to time a creative new definition of the encompassing social reality arises to change the organization – by force, persuasion, or charismatic will. By constantly doing, man not only creates but also re-creates. For some the organization descends and constrains like an iron cage; for others it never descends, for they are designers of a new cage that they call not constraint but opportunity. *Homo faber*: man who makes the Parthenon, the Mona Lisa, $e = mc^2$, recombinant DNA, games of chance, laws, prisons, schools, prayers, tightrope-walking, books for learning, instruments for torture or destruction, and everything that lies between these manifestations of creativity. In making these objects and ideas, man expresses self and makes his life, social order, and organizations.

Proposition 2: That organizations are expressions of will, intention, and value

They are manifestations of people doing what they want to do or what they think they must do. Organizations are modes of being that provide frameworks for action; they are sets of instructions for living one's life. The instructions are made by people and are directed both at others and at self. One organization may be distinguished from another by asking how the modes of being vary from setting to setting. We may come to understand organizations by recognizing that they are instructions for living acted out by people who repeatedly come together and work in concert or in opposition to each other. The power of organizations lies in the transformative capacity of human action. In thinking, being, and acting, people do things to themselves and to others. To understand organization requires that we understand how intention becomes action and how one person's intention and action triggers intention and action in others. Organizations are not something that controls people, but something that people control. The traditional science of organization has sought to locate and understand the mechanism of control in organizations with the hope that such understanding would enable people to control the mechanism of control. Such mechanisms are seen as separate from people; they are seen as devices whereby an independent, organizational will can be forced upon human intention. But it is individuals who intend, not organizations. There is no external mechanism out there to control people. There is no group mind that thinks for the rest of us and will have its way. It is we who must have our way or who acquiesce. The ways in which people exert will and intention and in which they restrain them are complex indeed. Learning to be in an organization is a matter of bending others to one's will and of being bent by others' wills.

Proposition 3: That organizations express becoming, not being

There is no ultimate reality about organizations, only a state of constant flux. Organizations are at once both the products of action and its cause. We act out of past circumstances and drive towards those we intend for the future. Social realities are constantly created and re-shaped, as what was becomes what is and both form what will be. In yogic thought, the Sanskrit word *Karma* also expresses the idea, as Isherwood explains:

A Karma is a mental or physical act. It is also the consequences of that act; good, bad or mixed. . . . The Law of Karma is the natural law by which our present condition is simply the product of our past thoughts and actions, and by which we are always currently engaged in creating our own future.[27]

This notion places the responsibility for action upon self. Given that action is inescapable, there is only the choice of what to do and how to do it. And if the moral order lies within, we must act out of it and take responsibility for that action. Again, Isherwood explains how this consequence arises:

We cannot run away from our actions because we carry the condition with us. On the highest mountain, in the darkest cave, we must turn at last and accept the consequences of being ourselves. Only through this acceptance can we begin to evolve further. We may choose the battleground. We cannot permanently avoid the battle.[28]

Proposition 4: That facts do not exist except as they are called into existence by human action and interest

There are levels of reality that correspond to the hard objects of the physical world at one extreme and to the subjective experience of the unique, human individual at the other.[29] As Schumacher argues from classic knowledge, the Great Chain of Being pervades all of nature; its commonplace hierarchy both links and differentiates four 'levels of being':

minerals, plants, animals, and man.[30] What separates man from other, lower levels of being is self-awareness. Man not only knows; he knows he knows and he reflects upon his knowledge and his action. Since the time of Newton man has been able to hope for a perfect knowledge of the world. Newton let us hope, in the words of Sir Karl Popper, that all reality could be understood as a clock, as a perfectly predictable mechanism with all its facts contained within a single explanation.

> Most open-minded men, and especially most scientists, thought that in the end [the new theory] would explain everything, including not only electricity and magnetism, but also clouds, and even living organisms. Thus physical determinism – the doctrine that all clouds are clocks – became the ruling faith among enlightened men; and everybody who did not embrace this new faith was held to be an obscurantist or a reactionary.[31]

In the study of organizations and administration this hope was kept alive – at least until recently – in the search for a theory that would express and explain human action in the same way that Newton's laws of dynamics explain the motion of the planets, thereby giving us entrée into the controlling mechanism of social behaviour. If the action of human beings in organizations could be grasped within such a theory, then it would be possible to predict and ultimately to control human action in much the same way that we can predict and control the motion of objects in the physical world. Those who believe in human freedom and rejoice in an indeterminate world can feel only relief that such understanding and control have not been possible in human affairs. We should not forget, however, that the belief in an objective social world that closely paralleled the physical world once led us to posit the same structure in organizations – and the same possibility of understanding it through logical empiricism – as was apparent in the motion of the planets. Griffiths explains what such theory would be like and how it would enable organizational scientists to understand and control human behaviour:

> A theory of administrative behavior will make it possible to relate what now appear to be discrete acts to one another so as to make a unified concept. The great task of science has been to impose an *order* upon the universe. Kepler's Laws, for instance, impose a set of relationships upon the planets of the solar system. . . . This is the great task of theory in the field of educational administration. Within a set of principles, yet to be formulated, it will be possible to recognize interrelationships among apparently discrete acts, it will be possible to predict the behavior of individuals within the organizational framework, and it will be possible to make decisions that will result in a more efficient and effective enterprise.[32]

But we now know, says Popper in an essay entitled 'Of Clouds and Clocks', that even the most precise of clocks have their cloudy aspects – that is, they rest on realities that are 'irregular, disorderly, and more or less unpredictable'.[33] If man cannot hope for a perfect, unclouded knowledge of the physical world, how can it ever be possible in the social world where the facts arise not only from what is out there but also from what is inside the subjective reality? Physical reality is difficult enough to understand. But as one moves through the levels of the Great Chain of Being one encounters increasing complexity and variety until one reaches the level of self-consciousness where what exists is dependent upon the mind that knows it. It is at this point that fact and value become so blurred that claims of scientific knowledge of them dissolve into speculation and error. Such ideas establish their truth not by empirical validation but by philosophical analysis.

Proposition 5: That man acts and then will judge the action

Facts, whatever they are, are less important to us than our judgement of them. Most of us know, for example, that smoking causes lung cancer and yet in smoking deny that this particular 'fact' applies to the existential realities of our own particular cases. To the rationalist, such behaviour in the face of facts is incomprehensible. The rationalist has difficulty in *understanding* such behaviour – that is, in seeing it as smokers do who regard the everyday rituals with cigarettes as a normal, natural, and even necessary part of life. What the rationalist fails to appreciate is that facts decide nothing; it is people who decide about the facts. Any administrator who foolishly sets out to base his action on facts alone will find himself swept away in the maelstrom of action created by those who will not yield their human capacity and – as they see it – their right to decide, to choose, to impose value on the world, and to assert self and will. The basic consideration in this matter is simply that *ought* cannot be derived from *is*. Facts are, but they cannot tell us what to do. As Huxley says, this realization comes as no surprise to historians who by necessity of their trade must deal with what men do, not with what reason would have them do.

> A firm conviction of the material reality of Hell never prevented medi-
> aeval Christians from doing what their ambition, lust, or covetousness
> suggested. Lung cancer, traffic accidents and the millions of miserable
> and misery-creating alcoholics are facts even more certain than was, in
> Dante's day, the fact of the Inferno. But all such facts are remote and
> unsubstantial compared with the near, felt fact of a craving here and
> now, for release or sedation, for a drink or for a smoke.[34]

Or, one might add, for another spin by hurtling automobile through mad streets and highways to the release of a day at the office or a weekend in the country.

In education, we see this same failure of fact in the face of values when, for example, someone raises the question of what the optimum class size is. The 'facts' of the matter are well known, are they not? Unfortunately for the rationalist thinker, in this realm there is enormous disagreement even as to what the facts are and even more contention in regard to their meaning.[35] Such examples abound in education, for the basic problem on which they turn arises from the possibility of choice, decision, and action. All of these are human behaviours, however much we might wish to objectify them and scientize them. Hodgkinson points to Litchfield's classic article in the founding issue of the *Administration Science Quarterly*, where Litchfield outlines a general theory of administration. This theory rests on a 'cycle of action' triggered by decision-making that may be 'rational, deliberative, discretionary, purposive' or 'irrational, habitual, obligatory, random', or 'any combination thereof'.[36] But how can the administrator *be* logical and rational in decision-making? How can he make his decision flow from the facts rather than from an attitude towards the facts or from personal values? Litchfield's answer and that of most planners and policy analysts requires the rational administrator to follow the familiar cycle that includes the steps: (1) Definition of the issue, (2) Analysis of the existing situation, (3) Calculation and delineation of alternatives, (4) Deliberation, and finally, (5) Choice. But as Hodgkinson points out, there are 'depths of ambiguity' in this way of being logical. How does one deliberate, for example? Or, for that matter, how does one choose? 'For to choose *is* to decide and the act of decision-making is that of deciding to choose among alternatives.'[37]

In the social world, facts are called into existence by an active interest, or at least they are brought into focus by an active interest and are organized by actors to make a point or to demonstrate a 'truth'. So it is that facts can be continually recombined, refocused, seen from new angles, and thereby made to demonstrate new truths. This process is precisely analogous to that in which history is created. It is historians who write history, not the past and not the facts that we may see as contained in the past. The past itself is silence purely. So it is that Collingwood says, 'Every new generation must rewrite history in its own way.' Franchini says, 'There is no history in itself, history of facts. . . . Facts are brought into focus solely by present life interests, and are constructed and reconstructed by them.' And Croce says, 'The past fact does not answer to a past interest, but to a present interest.'[38] What these historians have to say about the creation of ever new histories, each one better and 'more final' than the last, corresponds exactly to the process of interpretation and social truth-making that goes on in organizations. The facts of social life are subservient to what we want to say about them.

Proposition 6: That organizations are essentially arbitrary definitions of reality woven in symbols and expressed in language

They are a statement to the individual of how to be; they are a context defined by others for the individual and a context that individuals may define for themselves. The struggle in the stream of life is to determine which definitions are to prevail over others. The notion of organization as context can perhaps be understood by analogy with language. Such an analogy is not simply a convenient example to illustrate meaning, for it is apparent that language is at the heart of the process by which we understand reality and by which we exert control over ourselves, others, and the physical world. But language is an abstraction; it does not exist as a concrete entity. One cannot meet the English language – or any other language – face to face. It exists as a context, as a framework of meaning that makes speech possible. The same relationship exists between organization and action. Organization is the context and the possibility; action is the concrete and the specific. So we can say that language is to talk as organization is to action. And the same may be said of action that is directed at others and that requires a context of meaning and understanding to make it possible. What we refer to as structure in organization is something that is made by action and by talk and that is necessary for action and talk to occur at all. Structure exists only in concrete action and talk, but a context for this talk and for this action is necessary to permit the concreteness to exist. What people must assume as context for their action *is* the organization.[39]

Proposition 7: That organizations expressed as contexts for human action can be resolved into meaning, moral order, and power

This trinity of organizational reality should not be understood as independent variables in a model, but rather as faces or aspects of the entity itself. Meaning – or a sense of being in a social setting and belonging to it – is fundamental to the understanding of organization. If one person asks another, 'Do you want a game of tennis?' and the second replies, 'I have work to do,' this transaction can only be understood 'by implication', that is, by knowing what 'games' and 'work' are and why one should take precedence over another.[40] Meaning may also be manifest in the existential realities of those who wield power in organizations and those who suffer its application. 'We can find out about such meanings most readily by reflection and intuition – either our own or others.' We can perceive them in a nun's struggle to keep the Rule,[41] and in Thomas Gradgrind's confrontation with Sissy Jupe, who has grown up with horses but knows them not as Gradgrind would have her know them: '"Girl number twenty unable to define a horse"! said Mr. Gradgrind, for the general behoof of all the little pitchers. "Girl number twenty possessed of no facts, in reference to one of the commonest of animals!'"[42]

Moral order and power are no less important faces of the organization. Describing them need not be laboured further other than to observe that these aspects of organization are deeply imbedded in life itself. Those who forget this truth will be reminded of it, as was the researcher who thought a two-week course could advance administrators through the stages that Kohlberg defined as moral development.[43] The treatment failed and not even the most powerful of statistical massage applied to the data could sustain so much as a part of the initial hypotheses. 'Fortunately so', we may think after reflection on the implications of moral development that depended on technology. If moral development can be advanced, could it not also be stayed or reversed? What the theorists who launch such studies fail to realize is that the treatment that generates the moral order is life itself and life is something we have difficulty in manipulating. What we can do is describe such order and strive to understand our own part in maintaining it or in subverting it. Power is, of course, of great consequence in organizations since it has to do with the question of who holds the whip handle and who suffers the strokes of the lash or, as social scientists are wont to speak of these things, power has to do with the control of resources in the pursuit of interests. The resources so controlled may include not only money, material, technology, and symbolic honours, but also other people and their talents.

In the production of organizations, we should be aware of what Giddens calls 'asymmetries' in meaning and morality and in the power of certain people to force their meanings and moralities upon others.[44] The study of organization should be directed at mapping these asymmetries and at understanding the meanings of people whose actions create the very entity that enables them to act.

Proposition 8: That there is no technology for achieving the purposes organizations are to serve

People can act, but what can organizations do? The individual can paint a picture, write a poem, add a column of figures, solve a quadratic equation, cook a soufflé, say prayers and sing the national anthem at the opening of school, or give orders that others accept as reason to drop napalm on civilians and defoliate forests. But do these actions achieve the goal of an organization? They cannot in so far as organizations are expressions of value and instructions for existence. Values and existence are lived, not achieved, though in our action we may try to achieve them in many ways. So, March argues that

> like truth and beauty, justice is an ideal rather than a state of existence. We do not achieve it: we pursue it. In that pursuit we accept

responsibility for the social myths by which we live. As critics of modern social science have easily demonstrated, models are not neutral.[45]

Actions are one thing and organizations are something else. They are instructions to people about how to be or to act; they are announcements as to what moral order is best, and they are designs that distribute power among people in asymmetrical patterns. These instructions, announcements, and schemes are, of course, man-made, but they are set within a context, a model *for* action that permits people to deal with each other and to carry out their intentions in some fashion or other. Within organizations, people are busy with all kinds of activity directed at expressing themselves or at controlling others. When individuals come to determine how their ultimate organizational purposes are to be achieved, they are left to argue into the night, because they are discussing not what to do, but how to be. Perhaps the only option open to us in the face of this impasse is to accept responsibility for the activities we pursue, for the direction we think we are following, and for the social dreams and myths we live by.

Proposition 9: *That there is no way of training administrators other than by giving them some apocalyptic or transcendental vision of the universe and of their life on earth*

If there is no science that explains human action within organizations as Newton's laws explain the motion of the planets and if there is no technology for determining what values are best or how they can be achieved, how then can administrators be trained and made to serve their organizations beneficially? Those who have followed the argument of this paper with sympathy may see the futility of setting out to achieve such a purpose, for we have here simply another example of a complex, value-saturated organizational goal that we simply do not know how to achieve. We can, of course, make administrators read books, attend courses, gain graduate degrees, and obtain certificates. Does any of this do any good? Few, I hope, are brave enough to argue flatly that we already know how to train administrators, for it ought to be clear enough by now that both a science and a technology of value accomplishment are lacking. What, then, should we do for administrators if, as I think we must, we set aside most of what now passes as administrative training?

Plato's answer, as Hodgkinson points out, was to appoint philosophers as our Guardians – that is, as our leaders or administrators. Plato's case for philosophers as administrators rested on his assumption that they have some insight into the nature of truth and into the 'Form of the Good'. Recognizing that philosophers have a poor track record as administrators (certainly Plato's experiment with the idea failed miserably at Syracuse),

111

Hodgkinson argues that we may be able to make administrators into philosophers, or at least move them in a direction towards philosophical understanding. 'Administrative pathology', he says, 'is the disease of which philosophy can be the cure.'[46] But even if one accepts this goal, we are faced again with the problem of how we may achieve it.

My solution to the problem of training administrators is to recognize that administrative training is training for life and that only those who have some insight into life – its ironies, joys, and tragedies – are fit to be administrators. Again we are left with the problem: how can such insight be acted upon? Pushed to be a technologist in the face of values, I would urge what might be called the monastery solution. In this approach it would be recognized that it is life that must be understood and that life and the human spirit can take many forms and express itself in many realities. The aim, therefore, would be to place administrators-in-training in total environments that are alien to all they regard as normal and natural. We might begin the learning process by placing the novitiate in an actual monastery, preferably one carved into cliffs of a Greek mountain where the monks are sworn to vows of total silence. Then they might spend time as bartender, bouncer, or manager of a disco, followed by service as an orderly in a mental institution, or indeed as a patient in such an institution. Enough of these 'monasteries' would have to be experienced to give the would-be controller of other people's lives a sense of terror – that is, of the varied organizational realities in which people live their lives. The jolts and disorientation of this experience would be directed at making administrators take a few journeys through the doors in the wall of reality in hopes that on their return they would see life in more complex, ambiguous, and humane terms.

I cannot do better in concluding the major arguments of this article than to quote once again from Huxley:

> Under a more realistic, a less exclusively verbal system of education than ours, every Angel (in Blake's sense of that word) would be permitted as a sabbatical treat, would be urged and even, if necessary, compelled to take an occasional trip through some chemical Door in the Wall into the world of transcendental experience. If it terrified him, it would be unfortunate but probably salutary. . . .

> Near the end of his life Aquinas experienced Infused Contemplation. Thereafter he refused to go back to work on his unfinished book. Compared with this, everything he had read and argued about and written – Aristotle and the Sentences, the Questions, the Propositions, the majestic Summas – was no better than chaff or straw. For most intellectuals such a sit-down strike would be inadvisable, even morally wrong. . . . For Angels of a lower order and with better prospects of longevity, there must be a return to the straw. But the

112

man who comes back through the Door in the Wall will never be quite the same as the man who went out. He will be wiser but less cocksure, happier but less self-satisfied, humbler in acknowledging his ignorance yet better equipped to understand the relationship of words to things, of systematic reasoning to the unfathomable Mystery which it tries, forever vainly to comprehend.[47]

PROBLEMATICS

I am approaching what ought to be the end of this chapter with the sense that I have not addressed many issues that Hills and Willower raised in their articles. I have chosen instead to address broader themes in the hope that they encompass many of the specific points these critics have raised. The aim of this chapter is therefore to elaborate and clarify a position about organizations and about approaches to the study of them. I have chosen to try to strengthen that position rather than to argue exclusively on grounds chosen by the critics. In doing so, I recognize that the position is incomplete and leaves many problems unresolved. Before closing I would like to identify some of these problems and to sketch out a solution, or at least a stand, with respect to them.

The problem of self and others

If we are confined to subjective realities, how can we ever understand others? With Schutz,[48] I would simply assume that others do exist and that they live with meanings and intentions that seem sensible to them and give purpose to their lives. The problem then is to understand such meanings and intentions. With Giddens and others,[49] I believe that it is possible to mediate between frames of subjective meaning in somewhat the same way that we translate from one language to another. It *is* done, it *is* accomplished, though it is hard to lay down the rules for doing so. The method is that of hermeneutical analysis that demands as perhaps its only unequivocal rule 'a respect for the authenticity of the mediated frames of meaning',[50] that is, respect for other minds and meanings.

The problem of order

Shall we believe with Durkheim and Parsons in the *consensus universel* (a common core of human values) and in the *conscience collective* (individual's awareness of and acceptance of those values) or shall we believe that there are different values and interests distributed among groups of people?[51] If we take the position based in common values, conflict occurs between the individual and the larger moral order. In this case, the administrator acts on behalf of that larger order against aberrant individuals who are to be coaxed or coerced into aligning themselves with it. In this case, the administrator slips easily and understandably into a mode of thought where he need no longer regard his ideas, his beliefs, his decisions, his actions as uniquely his; they represent instead the larger moral order of which he is simply the chosen instrument. If we take the position that order is negotiated by powerful interests, and if it is achieved by the subjugation of one interest to another, then no uncontroverted basis exists for determining what moral order ought to prevail. The authentic administrator then becomes acutely aware of his decisions, choices, values and power – of the value choices *he* must make. Volition, interest, and intention enter the picture. Responsibility too. I can now no longer say that my finger moved, but that *I* moved my finger.[52] It is not that my mind thinks and perceives the natural order of things, but that I think, conceive what is, and move to act upon it. Conflict, in other words, occurs between equals though their powers may be different.

The problem of truth and mind

The problem here is whether we should think that our minds can ever perceive the truth. Bauman evokes an ancient debate with Heidegger's modern image; he reminds us that we may choose between seeing the mind as a mirror or as a lamp.[53] Platonic thought sees the mind as a mirror that can reflect truth from the light outside the cave. If this is the case, then the problem of arriving at the truth is one of polishing up the mirror so that its images become clearer and more truthful. On the other hand, if the mind is 'a lamp, a radiant projector' snatched, as Heidegger saw it, from the eternal darkness, then the human mind is not a recorder of the world but the instrument of its 'existential condition'. It is logico–deductive, empirical science that sees the mind as a mirror and interpretative science that sees it as a lamp.

The problem of meaning and self

Should meaning be discovered or imposed? Weber made the distinction between knowledge that came from acts of *Verstehen* and those which came from acts of *Erklären*. The former rest on understanding, the latter on explanation. For Weber understanding arises from the viewpoint of the actor, whereas explanation arises from the viewpoint of the observer. In the natural sciences, he argues, we can do nothing else but explain behaviour from an external vantage-point. If we seek knowledge about a falling body, a cell, or an animal, we can do nothing but impose the meaning. But in those fields that in German are called the cultural sciences (*Geisteswissenschaften*), Weber points out that 'we can accomplish something which is never attainable in the natural sciences, namely the subjective understanding of the action of component individuals'.[54] Natural scientists can do nothing but impose their meaning on atoms, cells, and pigeons since these entities cannot (or do not) speak for themselves. Indeed, much of the success of physical science has rested on the imposition of arbitrary meanings that accurately predict behaviour. Moreover, much of the success of the natural sciences has been achieved by avoiding common-sense meanings and, as Francis Bacon said, by eschewing words that designate ideas 'most obvious to the vulgar'.[55] For Weber it is clearly possible to treat human action as behaviour – that is, to treat it as though it has no meaning in itself and could not speak for itself. We might even be able to predict such behaviour accurately, but we should not think that this knowledge gives us an understanding of meaningful action. The difference is that which lies between treating a child as a child and treating it as a highly complex wind-up doll. Or, as Bauman says in commenting on the work of Dilthey, it is possible to treat all reality as nature; it is possible, for example, to treat individuals as though they were trees, but trees cannot play the role of people. 'Understanding is re-discovery of myself in thou; I cannot discover myself in a tree, much less can I re-discover myself there, as there was nothing to establish our kinship in the past.'[56] The implication of this argument is that the social sciences differ fundamentally from the natural sciences; their methods and basic logic of enquiry must, therefore, also differ.

The problem of language

The question here is whether science can help us to get around the ambiguities that are bound into common language, as Bacon, and later many physical scientists, would have us do. They aspire for the certainty of mathematics and the purity of logic and find these aspirations blocked by the inconstancy of meaning in language and its dependence upon constantly shifting contexts. The opposing view holds that language is not an obstacle to understanding but our only means for reaching it. Wittgenstein makes the case for language in propositions scattered throughout his famous *Tractatus*:

> The world is all that is the case.
> We picture facts to ourselves.
> *The limits of my language* mean the limits of my world.
> I am my world.
> The world of the happy man is a different one from that of the unhappy man.
> What we cannot speak about we must pass over in silence.[57]

Given that language both limits our realities and creates them, the student of organizations has little choice but to use language as people do in all its ambiguity, inconstancy, and richness, as they try to understand organizations. Language in some sense lets us understand organization and organization lets us understand language. Or, as Wittgenstein again said, 'An expression has meaning only in the rivers of life.'[58]

CONCLUSION

I will conclude by speaking briefly to certain points raised by Hills and Willower. I have not chosen these because they represent their most fundamental points. (I hope I have spoken to those already, at least indirectly). Rather, I have chosen these points because they in some way epitomize the gulf that separates their approach to the study of organizations that I am advocating.

Willower rests his case on the claim that science is superior to all other ways of 'fixing belief' because its claims are open to disproof. In making this claim, Willower is advocating scientism, not science. Seen against Feyera- bend's argument it appears that Willower has unwisely and unnecessarily restricted his view of what constitutes the logic of science and the methods of inquiry appropriate to it. I will not repeat the arguments against scientism, but only point out that Willower has taken Sir Karl Popper's position that the superiority of scientific reasoning lies in the fact that its claims are open to falsification. In his famous example, Popper argued that it may never be possible to know whether it is true to state, 'All swans are white', but we may at least know such a claim is false if we find one black swan.[59] But falsification turns out to be at least as complex a question as proof. As Giddens says, if we dyed a swan black, would that falsify the claim? And if we crossed a swan with another bird and got a black swan-like creature, would that falsify the claim?[60] Not likely, because we already have in our minds notions of what constitutes swanness, and we use these ideas to rule out certain 'empirical facts' as irrelevant or invalid. It is in this way that 'normal science' arises, as both Popper and Kuhn agree. And normal science does nothing to increase our understanding; it only moves in circles to re-discover what it already knows to be true and calls the result objective knowledge. Such, I argue, is the condition we have reached in much of our scientific study of organizations.

Both Hills and Willower believe there is a clear dichotomy between the 'scientific' study of organizations and any other study of them. They are prepared to take, therefore, any weakness in the argument for the other side as evidence that the scientific study of organizations can proceed in the well-established pattern of normal science and continue to make substantial progress. Hills in particular singled out my admission that much of what I have argued is not 'new' and used this statement to claim that 'cognitive psychologists, anthropologists, sociologists, and even political scientists' have for years all been engaged in the 'attempt to construct a

116

model of the human mind that will explain regularities in human behavior'.[61] If we are to understand this statement as meaning more than the observation that social scientists take humanity as their province of study, it must imply that they are all agreed on a unified approach to that study. Not so, as I hope this article makes plain. Willower takes the same stand when he says, 'I don't expect much substantive theory from the critics and I don't expect much research that will be very different from the qualitative research we already have. . . . However, some of them are quite earnest about the idea that they are bringing us a new paradigm, in the Kuhnian sense of the term.'[62] Again we find the insistence that there *is* only one kind of theory, one kind of science.

In making what he calls a 'crucial' point, Willower groups all enquiry ('empirical, naturalistic, pragmatic, or positivistic') that rests on 'scientific conception of knowledge' and sets it against 'intuition, faith, or authority as final arbiters of truth'.[63] But, like most critics working in the paradigm of hypothetico–deductive theory, he sees qualitative analysis as essentially a lower order of knowledge that must be validated through later quantitatively oriented theory and inquiry. He allows a role for qualitative methods and their 'obvious strength' only 'in the production of new concepts, ideas, and hypotheses, and in the immediate and holistic character of the information presented'.[64] He jokingly reports that he conducted telephone interviews with 50 school superintendents and only 'barely resisted' the urge to announce a 'phenomenological breakthrough'. Phenomenologists would likely only smile politely at the suggestion that superintendents' 'finest hours and bitterest regrets' could be gathered by a methodology totally dependent on long-distance contact, but the astonishing aspect of Willower's claim is that the two reports he contemplated making on his investigation would inevitably yield the same findings.[65] Clearly they would, if they were conducted by someone convinced that the findings *ought to be the same,* given that science cannot tolerate two separate and possibly contradictory truths about the same reality. Is there no ideology, therefore, in science? Are those who practice it free from commitment?

Hills claims that the value of my writings lies in their 'discussion-stimulating qualities',[66] and Willower largely concurs with this judgement. I agree that the controversy has generated useful discussion, but I will continue to disagree that the controversy can now be regarded as settled and that all of us can now go back to normal science in the study of organizations and administration. Both Hills and Willower refer to qualitative research such as that by Waller, Walcott, and Cusick, but they see it all as fitting within a single paradigm of unified science. This is not the opinion of researchers such as Becker[67] nor of the many theorists and philosophers I have cited in this chapter. Willower limits qualitative research to the role of 'furnishing

117

striking illustrations of what life is like to particular people in school organizations'.[68] He thus reserves for higher-order research the role of explanation and truth-making.

The point to be made here is that much qualitative or constructivist research stands on its own and cannot, without distorting its meaning and implications, be fitted within larger explanatory theories that see organizations as well-ordered entities that can be fitted within a single conceptual scheme or model. The work of Cicourel and Kitsuse,[69] for example, examines the role of guidance counsellors in high schools with a finely focused lens and finds that what they do in sorting students into groups by academic ability runs quite counter to Durkheimian and Parsonian notions of the *consensus universel*. We are not dealing here with 'illustrations of life in school' built around a presumed common core of values, but with insights into schools that can only be gained by shifting radically one's perspective on them. Similarly, Cusick's work can be neatly categorized as a 'study of the school organization' with all the assumptions thereby involved, or one may see it as a study of the separate realities that coexist in a given social context. Why was Mrs J. who got students deeply involved in intellectual tasks fired from her job? 'Was she fired because she encouraged the kids to "say all kinds of good little things", as the teacher said, because she "talked over the heads of the less sharp kids," as the principal said, or because she failed to thank the vice-principal when he did her a favor?'[70] We may conclude that all these reasons were true, but we should also note that those who held power in the school interpreted them as meaning Mrs J. was 'unable to relate to students' and, therefore, fired her. Cusick also points out that when we look closely at what people do in schools, we find many of them 'admit with apparent honesty' that their activities are massively disengaged from the overt concerns of those who run the organization.[71] If we come to recognize such truths, we need theory more potent than is provided by notions about formal and informal organization joined within a common experience of an overarching structure. To abandon our comforting theories and to accept alternative perspectives is to move towards a terrifying plunge into uncertainty and away from the non-political, single-criterion truth of a confident and objective social science. It is to move towards a view of organizations as a set of holes bounded and defined by other holes.

Ricoeur suggests that there is a 'plurivocity' in social reality; it speaks to us with many voices. That 'social phenomena may be *construed* in several different ways is well known by all experts in the human sciences'.[72] The problem, therefore, that both theorists and men of practical action must consider is how we can arbitrate between the different truths claimed by the voices. In the face of these constructions of reality, validation in the sense of logical grounding in empirical facts is not open to us. We may, however, validate interpretations by way of argument – by hermeneutical interpretation, if you wish – and thereby find that the truths of science are like those established in law and judicial action.

> Juridical reasoning clearly shows that the procedures of validation have a polemical character. In front of the court, the plurivocity common to texts and to actions is exhibited in the form of a conflict of interpretations, and the final interpretation appears as a verdict to which it is possible to make appeal. Like legal utterances, all interpretations in the field of literary criticism and in the social sciences may be challenged, and the question 'what can defeat a claim' is common to all argumentative situations. Only in the tribunal is there a moment when the procedures of appeal are exhausted. . . . Neither in literary criticism, nor in the social sciences, is there such a last word. Or if there is any, we call that violence.[73]

The paradigm I argue for in the exploration of social realities is certainly against overarching (Parsonian) systems of unilateral explanation; it is one that admits the many voices of truth and recognizes them as attached to self, to individuals. I do not know why Hills objects so strongly in his critique (pp. 26–30, 43) to my use of the term 'Harvard functionalists'. It is not my term and I used it only in a footnote to my paper. His point is that I misread Parsons or, perhaps, that I don't read Parsons. On the substantive issue I agree with Eldridge, who argues that the misreading lies with Parsons and the functionalists. He shows that Parsons tried to correct Weberian methodology and its assumptions because Weber was 'not enough of a positivist' and because he drew 'too sharp a distinction between the natural sciences and the cultural sciences'.[74] My chief argument, however, is against those who would fit all truth about organizations into a single, objective, non-political, self-less truth called science.

NOTES

1 J. Hills, 'A Critique of Greenfield's "New Perspective"', *Educational Administration Quarterly* 16, 1 (1980): 20–44.

2 D. J. Willower, 'Contemporary Issues in Theory in Educational Administration', *Educational Administration Quarterly* 16, 3 (1980): 1–25. See also, Willower's 'Ideology and Science in Organization Theory', *Educational Administration Quarterly* 15, 3 (1979): 20–42.

3 Up to 1983, the best summary of the issues – including a critique and bibliography – is found in Peter Gronn, *Rethinking Educational Administration: T. B. Greenfield and his Critics* (Victoria, Australia: Deakin, 1983), pp. 8–43.

4 Max Weber in R. Bendix and G. Roth, *Scholarship and Partisanship: Essays on Max Weber* (Berkeley: University of California, 1971), p. 71.

5 F. N. Kerlinger, *Foundations of Behavioral Research: Educational and Psychological Inquiry* (New York: Holt Rinehart and Winston, 1964), pp. 6–8.

6 Charles Peirce quoted in Kerlinger, *Foundations*, p. 7.

7 Z. Bauman, *Hermeneutics and Social Science: Approaches to Understanding* (London: Hutchinson, 1978).

8 Ibid., p. 48.
9 Christopher Hodgkinson, *Towards a Philosophy of Administration* (Oxford: Basil Blackwell, 1978), p. 104.
10 A. Huxley, *The Doors of Perception* (Frogmore: Triad/Panther, 1960), p. 12.
11 A. Giddens, *New Rules of Sociological Method* (London: Hutchinson, 1977), p. 110.
12 Ibid., pp. 99–111.
13 See Willower, 'Ideology and Science', p. 26 where he declares not only that Marxist theory is an ideology but that 'those who employ it are usually adherents of the political persuasion'. He continues to confuse this issue (Willower, 'Contemporary Issues in Theory', p. 18) where he refers to Marxists as 'true believers' who are 'antithetical to free inquiry and the free invention and testing of ideas'. Such polemics serve only to blur the basic Marxist questions and to retard the exploration of how interests and power are manifested in man's construction of social reality.
14 See Giddens, *New Rules*, p. 98 for a discussion of how Weber stands in opposition to Durkheim and Parsons on this point.
15 K. Boulding, 'Some Questions on the Measurement and Evaluation of Organization', in *The Dilemma of Organizational Society*, ed. H. M. Ruitenbeek (New York: E. P. Dutton, 1963), pp. 113–134.
16 Huxley, *Doors of Perception*, p. 50.
17 Ibid., p. 15.
18 Ibid., pp. 15–16.
19 Wm. Blake, quoted in Huxley, *Doors of Perception*, p. 62.
20 P. Feyerabend, *Against Method: Outline of an Anarchistic Theory of Knowledge* (London: New Left Books, 1975); T. Kuhn, *The Structure of Scientific Revolutions* (Chicago: University of Chicago, 1962).
21 W. J. Broad, 'Paul Feyerabend: Science and the Anarchist', *Science* 206 (2 November, 1979): pp. 34–37.
22 Ibid., p. 36.
23 A. Kaplan, *The Conduct of Inquiry: Methodology for Behavioral Science* (San Francisco: Chandler, 1964), pp. 25–27.
24 Quoted in Broad, 'Science and the Anarchist', p. 37.
25 J. G. March, 'Model Bias in Social Action', *Review of Educational Research* 42 (1972): 413–429.
26 C. Isherwood, *An Approach to Vedanta* (Hollywood: Vedanta Press, 1963), p. 43.
27 Ibid., p. 58.
28 Ibid., p. 59.
29 Hodgkinson, *Towards a Philosophy of Administration*, pp. 200–201.
30 E. F. Schumacher, *A Guide for the Perplexed* (New York: Harper Colophon, 1977), pp. 15–38.
31 K. R. Popper, *Objective Knowledge* (London: Oxford, 1972), p. 212.
32 D. E. Griffiths, 'Toward a Theory of Administrative Behavior', in *Administrative Behavior in Education*, eds R. F. Campbell and R. T. Gregg (New York: Harper, 1957), p. 388. Further comment on this remarkable passage occurs at p. 192 where the passage is given in full.
33 Popper, *Objective Knowledge*, p. 207.
34 Huxley, *Doors of Perception*, pp. 51–52.
35 D. W. Ryan and T. B. Greenfield, *The Class Size Question* (Toronto: Ministry of Education, Ontario, 1975).
36 E. H. Litchfield, 'Notes on a General Theory of Administration', *Administrative Science Quarterly* 1, 1 (1956): 12–14.
37 Hodgkinson, *Towards a Philosophy of Administration*, pp. 48–49.

38 These historians are quoted in Bauman, *Hermeneutics and Social Science*, pp. 42–43.
39 Giddens, *New Rules*, pp. 121–122.
40 The example is from P. Ziff, 'What is Said', quoted in Giddens, p. 107.
41 See page 80.
42 Charles Dickens, *Hard Times*, with an introduction by G. B. Shaw (London: Waverly, 1912), p. 4. Shaw points out in his introduction that Dickens is here joining Marx, Carlyle, and Ruskin to rise up against our social organizations and declare 'that it is not our disorder but our order that is horrible'.
43 G. W. Sinclair, 'The Development of a Program in Moral Reasoning for Educational Administrators' (Ph.D. diss., University of Alberta, 1978).
44 Giddens, *New Rules*, pp. 129, 157.
45 March, 'Model Bias', p. 414.
46 Hodgkinson, *Towards a Philosophy of Administration*, pp. 152, 170.
47 Huxley, *Doors of Perception*, pp. 63–64.
48 A. Schutz, *The Phenomenology of the Social World* (London: Heinemann, 1972).
49 See Giddens, *New Rules of Sociological Method*, pp. 144–148; cf. the rich reviews of interpretative social science in Bauman, *Hermeneutics and Social Science*.
50 Giddens, *New Rules*, p. 145.
51 Ibid., pp. 92–98.
52 Ibid., p. 74.
53 Bauman, *Hermeneutics and Social Science*, p. 153.
54 M. Weber, *The Theory of Social and Economic Organizations*, trans. A. M. Henderson and T. Parsons (New York: Free Press, 1947), p. 103.
55 Quoted in R. Bendix, *Embattled Reason: Essays in Social Knowledge* (New York: Oxford, 1970), p. 18.
56 Bauman, *Hermeneutics and Social Science*, p. 36.
57 Wittgenstein, *Tractatus Logico–Philosophicus* (London: Routledge & Kegan Paul, 1961), propositions 1, 2.1, 5.6, 5.63, 6.43 and 7.
58 Quoted in Giddens, *New Rules*, p. 42.
59 K. R. Popper, *The Logic of Scientific Discovery* (Toronto: University of Toronto, 1959).
60 Giddens, *New Rules*, pp. 140–141.
61 Hills, 'A Critique', p. 43.
62 Willower, 'Contemporary Issues', p. 17.
63 Ibid., p. 8.
64 Ibid., p. 11.
65 Ibid., p. 17.
66 Hills, 'A Critique', p. 42.
67 H. S. Becker, *Sociological Work: Method and Substance* (Chicago: Aldine, 1970).
68 Willower, 'Contemporary Issues', p. 16.
69 A. V. Cicourel and J. I. Kitsuse, *The Educational Decision Makers* (Indianapolis: Bobbs-Merrill, 1963).
70 P. A. Cusick, *Inside High School: The Student's World* (New York: Holt, Rinehart and Winston, 1973), 37.
71 Ibid., p. 176.
72 P. Ricoeur, 'The Model of the Text: Meaningful Action Considered as a Text', in *Interpretive Social Science*, P. Rabinow and W. M. Sullivan, eds (Berkeley: University of California, 1979), p. 91.
73 Ibid., pp. 93–94.
74 J. E. T. Eldridge, ed., *Max Weber: The Interpretation of Social Reality* (London: Thomas Nelson, 1971), p. 15.

6

AGAINST GROUP MIND

An anarchistic theory of organization[1]

> *There are no classes for beginners in life.*
> Rainer Maria Rilke

> *In solitude you can do what you will.*
> Robert Musil

An anarchistic theory of organization recognizes the individual as the ultimate building-block in social reality. Whatever it is that joins man and mankind exists in people. Whatever allows speech, understanding, sympathy, dominance, submission, rejection, inflicted trauma, and whatever allows social intercourse finds expression through the individual. Within the limits set by nature and our ephemeral life, we make the world we live through. We make it out of the self that reflects, chooses, wills and imposes order on itself and on others.

I offer not a philosophy of anarchism applied to organizations, but a glimpse of the anarchy that inheres in all thought and that tyrannizes (and humanizes) us under the guise of Logic and Social Order.[2] In Lewis Carroll's little fable, Achilles gives the Tortoise a lesson in Logic. When Achilles says we must all accept conclusions derived by Logic, the Tortoise answers simply, 'But *why* must I?' When Achilles fails by Logic alone to demonstrate the truth of Logic, he then reveals the real and only force of Logic by saying the Tortoise *must* draw the necessary inference, for otherwise Logic will take him by the throat and compel his acceptance. Of course, it is not logic that will so assail us, but rather other people who attack us when we reject the Logic that is in their minds.[3] The significance of Dodgson's deceptively casual victory over Logic is seen in Winch (1958, 57) who 'points to the moral' that the heart of logic cannot be represented logically.

Organizations hold the power of life and death over us as, for example, in the questions of whether the foetus has a right to life and whether Karen Ann Quinlan has a right to die. But these questions and all that lie between them are answered not by abstractions, but by other people. As Sartre said, 'Hell has no need of brimstone and turning on the spit. Hell is other people. It exists here and now. We ourselves, make it. Once made, we call the resulting order organization.'

An anarchistic theory of organizations may be summed up in two statements: first, a statement that rejects group mind and denies an over-arching social reality thought to lie beyond human control and outside the will, intention and action of the individual;[4] second, a statement that acknowledges the tumult and irrationality of thought itself.[5] Acting, willing, passionate, fearful, hoping, mortal, fallible individuals and the events that join them are therefore always more complex, interesting and real than the ideas we use, forever vainly, to explain them. As someone infected with anarchistic thought, I should stop at this point and possibly leave also. But as we all know, we must go on – for politeness's sake if for no other reason. And for the most part, we do go on. What we go on with is life in all its ambiguity, possibility, promise, apparent victories and defeats, its pleasure and pain. Let me offer twelve short observations that may helpfully elaborate what I have said to this point.

1 It is the individual that lives and acts, not the organization. It is, therefore, the experience of individuals that we must seek to understand. Huxley (1977, 11–12) says it clearly:

> We live together . . . but always in all circumstances we are by ourselves. The martyrs go hand in hand into the arena; they are crucified alone. Embraced, the lovers desperately try to fuse their insulated ecstasies into a single self-transcendence; in vain. . . . We can pool information about experiences, but never the experiences themselves. From family to nation, every human group is a society of island universes.

The world we know is created by our perception of it. We learn to see and we build what we see. As Kant said, we do not make our world, but we do create it.[6] This observation is true about the world in general, but has its greatest force and importance in the interpretation of social reality. Clearly, there is something 'out there' that contains forces man does not control. The individual does not give birth to herself or himself; nor can the individual by will withstand death. But within these limits the individual has enormous creative scope. As Wittgenstein (1961) makes us see, the ideas in our heads are not so much models *of* the world as models *for* it.[7] We believe in the ideas in our heads, we trust our models for the world so deeply that we make them true. We will them to be true.

2 Take the only road that runs a distance westward along the Strait of Juan de Fuca on the coast of British Columbia. Before you reach the

place Spanish explorers called Jordan River and as the road weaves between the ocean and trackless forest and mountain, you will pass Point No Point. There a no-point has become a geographical fact, as may be *seen* both on the ground and on topographical maps. Does its name describe reality or does it represent illusion, oversight, technical error, or the wrong thinking of idiosyncratic metaphor?

An intellectual no-point is now occurring in this discourse, too. But this grasping at meaning carries a number like the other points and so hides a gap that would otherwise be apparent in my flight from 1 to 12 in search of convincing academic argument.[8] In this way I, too, do my bit to keep anarchy at bay and to preserve a necessary, if not natural, order. (Does the anarchist betray himself, even if the organizational structure he creates is only a tiny cell?) By thus numbering the unnumberable, I hope to reassure those who might be troubled by the question of whether a nothingness can exist and whether, if it does, it is best represented by a real number or by an imaginary one.

The dangers of thinking too much about the relationship of number to reality are apparent in Robert Musil's novel, *Young Törless*, which is set in an Austrian military school at the turn of the century.[9] The title in German is *Die Verwirrungen des Zöglings Törless*. '*Verwirrungen*' means 'perplexities', and words of confusion, bewilderment and amazement ring through the novel to describe Törless's state of mind as he examines the complex ambiguities that lie beneath the surface of apparently uncomplicated reality. His difficulties often arise, however, because he takes words as meaning what they say. For example, he wonders during mathematics period, 'If this is really supposed to be preparation for life, as they say, it must surely contain some clue to what I am Looking for, too.' Such naïveté is bound to lead to trouble, especially if one is pondering the stated aims of an established educational institution and trying to understand them. The boys who attend the school come from 'the best families' of the dead Imperial glory and are assured of places in its society. But in the midst of an ordered and secure world, Törless finds 'manifold amazement and bewilderment in the encounter with life'. Among other things, he is perplexed by his reflections on imaginary and irrational numbers. He shares his concerns with a friend, but is met only with the attitude that asks, 'Why bother your head about something of no practical consequence?' The imaginary factors must cancel themselves out, his friend argues, so they can never make any difference in the real world. Törless tries again to explain to his friend:

> Look, think of it like this: in a calculation like that you begin with ordinary solid numbers, representing measures of length or weight or something else that's quite tangible – or at any rate

they're real numbers. And at the end you have real numbers. But these lots of real numbers are connected by something that simply doesn't exist. Isn't that like a bridge where the piles are there only at the beginning and at the end, with none in the middle, and yet one crosses it just as surely and safely as if the whole of it were there?

When he takes his difficulties to his teacher, the mathematics master tells him that the quantities that bother him have 'no real existence whatsoever' and that they are simply 'concepts inherent in the nature of purely mathematical thought'. He explains that Törless is not old enough to grasp the answer to the problem he has identified.

> Fortunately, very few boys at your stage feel this, but if one does really come along, as you have today – and of course, as I said before, I am delighted – really all one can say is: My dear young friend, you must simply take it on trust.

To cap his argument, the mathematics master points to a book of Kant's philosophy lying on his desk. He says it deals with the grounds that determine our actions.

> And if you could fathom this, if you could feel your way into the depths of this, you would come up against nothing but just principles, which are inherent in the nature of thought and do in fact determine everything, although they themselves cannot be understood immediately and without more ado. It is very similar to the case with mathematics. And nevertheless we continually act on these principles.

Thereafter Törless learns rapidly that there are many other things in the world that he must accept on trust as well. He watches as a bystander as fellow students brutalize and exploit another student who is singled out as different from the rest. Basini is also poorer than the rest and is easily trapped as the person who stole money from a student's locker. So Basini comes under the power of two students who systematically expand their hold over him and then share their secret with Törless. Away from others' eyes and often in the dead of night, his two tormentors use Basini to gratify their need to feel strong, powerful and better than he is. Hoping to be allowed to pay back the money he felt he had only borrowed, Basini is forced to act out the fears and homosexual fantasies of his two student masters, so that they can assert their own superiority and manliness. Törless is repelled by what he sees and yet does nothing to stop it. He seeks out Basini alone and finally shares tenderness and understanding with him. The others become fearful and perhaps envious of Törless when he tries to intervene on Basini's behalf; they begin to suspect his intimacy with Basini. They threaten to punish Törless even as they begin new humiliations of Basini by beating him naked in front of the whole class. Törless warns Basini that, after a final whipping with foils, his two tormentors plan to turn him over to the school authorities. Wishing only to end his torment in whatever way possible, Basini goes to the school authorities. As the school starts an investigation into these events, Törless disappears for two days and draws suspicion to himself. In their defence, Basini's tormentors explain that they were simply giving 'benevolent guidance' to a thief before reporting his base crime to the school. Basini is silent on what has happened to him, as his humiliation has removed all hope of explaining the realities and motivations of his world. Seeing the events only as students punishing one of their own for theft, the school authorities complete the stigmatization of Basini and expel him from the school.

The only question that remains is whether by silence Törless is somehow involved in Basini's shame. At a meeting of the school authorities convened to decide Törless's fate, the mathematics master recounts – almost as an accusation – Törless's questioning of mathematical theory. But Törless has suffered a 'great shock to the soul' and wonders about 'these older men who seemed to know so little about the inner life of a human being'. Yet he manages to step back from the abyss and to deny the attitudes and feelings that would destroy him. He expresses an uncertain but growing acceptance of social reality and its necessities even as he has struggled to overcome his perplexity about the validity of mathematics and the reality of numbers. To his accusers and judges, he explains,

> 'Now it's all over. I know now I was wrong after all. I'm not afraid of anything anymore. I know that things are just things and will probably always be so. And I shall probably go on for ever seeing them sometimes with the eyes of reason, and sometimes with those other eyes. . . . And I shan't ever try again to compare one with the other. . . .'

> He fell silent. He took it quite as a matter of course that now he could go, and nobody tried to stop him.

The principal resolves Törless's case by recommending to his parents that he be educated privately on the grounds that 'what he needs is a more thorough supervision of his intellectual diet than we are in a position to provide'. In abandoning Basini, Törless learns to see things as they are: That is, as they must be, since others see them that way. Those who reject social reality and accepted explanations of it will always be subject to special treatment until they accept the reality they have questioned and demonstrate their commitment to it.

3 We live in separate realities. What is true for one person is not for another. In that sense, we live in different worlds. Each of us, Huxley says, is an island universe. There is no action – however terrible or appalling it may appear to some of us – that is not sensible and rational to others. When news reports first appeared about them, I found it virtually impossible to read accounts describing certain events in Bihar, India's most feudal state. There police had sought to deter local bandits by giving them living proof of the swift and terrible justice that awaited them. To this end, they routinely thrust acid-tipped needles into eyes of those they caught and identified as brigands or 'dacoits'. And so about 30 young men living in the same town in northern India have 'the queerest and eeriest faces'. Reacting to these events, Prime Minister Indira Gandhi said news of the blindings 'made me physically sick'. She asked, 'How can anybody do this to their fellow men?' and suspended the policeman involved.

I have seen only one account that in some measure makes the events of Bihar understandable and that with compassion reveals the multiple realities in the situation through clear-eyed observation.[10] When Ian Jack, a reporter for *The Sunday Times*, and an Indian colleague reached Bhagalpur where the horrors were done, they found the town full of angry people. 'Trains had been stopped in their tracks; the town's lawyers had passed a motion of severe reproof; students marched in the streets and traders planned to shut their shops in protest the next day.' These protests were directed, however, not against the police but against Mrs Gandhi. The practice in rural India is to safeguard personal wealth in gold, and this is often kept in bands tightly wound around fingers or arms. To remove their victims' life savings more conveniently, the bandits lopped off hands or arms. The townspeople never heard from Mrs Gandhi when such things happened. 'When has she ever given money to a woman raped by dacoits, or to the widow of a man the dacoits chopped up and threw into the Ganges? Does she not know the policemen she suspended have made this town safe? Dacoits chop off arms to steal bangles. What, then, is a little acid in the eyes?' The Indian newsman may have spoken for his British colleagues too when he said, 'I am deeply ashamed of their savagery, but I understand it. To take the road to Bhagalpur is to stand on the edge of the abyss.'

4 Individuals act out of will and intention. If we are to understand organizations we must understand what moves people to act and we must suspend, if we can, our own judgement of their action. This task is difficult because our judgement of acts clouds our observation of them. It is difficult also because people usually hide their wilfulness – certainly from others and often from themselves as well. Yet the study of intention is the key to understanding organizations.

5 Facts and values are closely interwoven. Positivistic science insists on splitting them and disregarding the values. It thus ignores the most important part of our lives and falls into the error of thinking that values can be derived from facts. Facts decide nothing. It is we who decide about the facts. Hodgkinson (1978b, 220) sums up the conundrum of facts and values in the following aphorisms:

> The world of fact is given, the world of value made.

> We discover facts and impose values.

> Facts must go undefined.

> Values are special kinds of facts; but never true or false.

6 Modern science and ancient philosophy have taught us to think that a universal logic and rationality governs the world. And we are taught to hope as well that those who master the logic and the rationality may also govern the world. But ideas both ancient and modern give a glimpse of the chaos that inheres in our supposedly universal logic and rationality. Zen sets out to 'break the mind of logic' (Suzuki, 1955), and that perhaps is what we must do as well if we are to see past it to other realities. It is a delicious irony that Charles Dodgson, the Oxford logician and photographer of nude young girls, could write *Alice in Wonderland* and then turn his hand to a parable that uses Logic to unhorse Logic itself. He shows that at the heart of Logic is something illogical. As Winch (1958, 57) points out, 'inferring a conclusion from a set of premises is to *see* that the conclusion does in fact follow' [emphasis added]. There is therefore also an intentionality in logic, mathematics, and apparently objective science. For Wittgenstein, it is we who are inexorable, not mathematics. And he says, 'that is why it is inexorably insisted that we shall all say "two" after "one", "three" after "two" and so on'.[11] For Bertrand Russell, $1 + 1 = 2$ was not only a proposition of symbolic logic and mathematics, but also a declaration of intent meaning *'Know that'* or *'Know that I am aware that'* $1 + 1 = 2$.

7 Individuals are responsible for what they do. Organizations and our habit of thinking in categories ease this sense of responsibility. As Hodgkinson (1978b, 173) points out, the required allegiance to the organization removes notions of right and wrong. The organization is not only reified, but also deified. The individual is thereby no longer author of his act, but agent for a larger reality. Absolutist Christians often speak – usually through clenched teeth – of loving the sinner and hating the sin. This schizophrenia of thought serves both to sanctify the Christians and to justify what they are about to do to the sinner.

8 Hodgkinson (1978b, 208) says, 'We are all either administered or administering', while William Blake says, 'I must Create a System, or be

enslav'd by another Man's.' And G. B. Shaw's (1964, 169) Don Juan argues that it is better 'to be able to choose the line of greatest advantage instead of yielding in the direction of the least resistance. . . . To be in Hell is to drift: to be in Heaven is to steer.' This leads us to think that it is better to run organizations than to be run by them. And so we slip into seeing the force of the Machiavellian position: the 'reasonableness of evil', the wisdom of 'rejecting kindness and love for self-interest; trust for fear' (Segal, 1971, 158).

9 The alternative to action and probable evil is disengagement. Orwell uses the metaphor of Jonah inside the whale to express the individual's best approach to forces that are totally beyond his control:

> The whale's belly is simply a womb big enough for an adult. There you are, in the dark, cushioned space that exactly fits you, with yards of blubber between yourself and reality, able to keep up an attitude of the completest indifference, no matter what happens. A storm that would sink all the battleships in the world can hardly reach you as an echo.

The image here is of security attained by personal detachment from the maelstrom that swirls around the individual. But detachment from events does not mean non-awareness of them. As Orwell says, we should think of the whale as transparent. In this circumstance, Jonah becomes an observer who can see what others locked in the struggle are oblivious to. Because his detachment and security let him see things that remain hidden to others, Jonah as observer bears the obligation to describe what is happening and to make us aware of it. This task also becomes the obligation of the social scientist who sets out to understand and explain organization.

10 History and law should be our models for studying organizations, for these branches of knowledge know of no completion and recognize the interests of the writer and the advocate as crucial to what is declared to be true and right. So it is that Feyerabend (1975, 17), quoting the historian Butterfield, finds that history provides a model for understanding knowledge generally and not least for that knowledge we call scientific:

> History is full of 'accidents and conjunctures and curious juxtapositions of events' and it demonstrates to us the 'complexity of human change and the unpredictable character of the ultimate consequences of any given act or decision of men'.

In the study of organizations, the analysis of language and the flat description of what happens appear as our best approaches and methodological tools.

11 Language is power. It literally makes reality appear and disappear. Those who control language control thought, and thereby themselves

and others. We build categories to dominate the world and its organizations. The anarchist wants to let the reality of people within the categories shatter them and thereby to reduce the control. In the words of Thomas Szasz (1976, 46):

> the less a person understands another, the greater is his urge to classify him – in terms of nationality, religion, occupation, or psychiatric status. . . . In short, classifying another person renders intimate acquaintance with him quite unnecessary – and impossible.

And he adds (p. 42), 'The human larynx and tongue are actually used as claws and fangs, and words as venom.' Organizations are sets of categories arrayed for the linguistic and other wars that people wage among themselves. Or we may think here of the quip that runs: a language is a dialect that has its own army and navy. So an organization is a set of meanings that people act out, talk out, and back up with their own armamentarium of forces – psychological, moral and physical.

12 As Wittgenstein pointed out, propositions are not merely models *of* the world: they are models *for* the world. They offer ways of under-standing the world and also of creating it. We should pay closer attention, therefore, to the study of reality and social forms through propositions. Here are some propositions from Wittgenstein (1961, 15) in which he reverses common sense understanding and makes the world depend upon our proposition or models of it.

> We picture facts to ourselves.

> A picture is a model of reality.

> A picture is a fact.

> That is how a picture is attached to reality; it reaches out to it.

Propositions are thus pictures of the world. Their truth lies in our understanding them and in their power to make us believe in them and act in accord with them. Here are some propositions from Hodgkinson (1978b, 202 ff.):

> Language is the basic administrative tool.

> Language cloaks power and *has* power.

> Policy goes beyond logic.

> Administration secures services *from* men *for* organizations.

> To *advise* can be to *command.*

> Administrative power is a function of the will. The contest of wills is the pragmatic test of power.

There is such a thing as the judicious rage, the calculated loss of control.

Beware of friendliness in the realms of power. There is no need to beware of friendship. It does not exist.

AN ANARCHISTIC CONCLUSION

Anarchy does not fit neatly into a box. Neither does reality. This non-fit says it all. We press a few pieces of multi-faceted reality into our minds and live as though we were omniscient gods. That is why we must needs learn to unloosen our minds and let them run freely. If we are to understand what we ourselves and others see as reality, we should follow R. D. Laing's dictum when he says, 'I have made an arrangement with my mind: I let it do anything it wants to.' And that is the nub of anarchism in the study of organizations: while we ourselves are bound, we may yet free our minds.

NOTES

1 This chapter is a revision of a paper first presented to the symposium, 'Researching Educational Organizations – Three Perspectives: Marxist, Anarchist, Phenomenological' at the American Educational Research Association, Los Angeles, April 1981.
2 Most of what I offer in this vein has been written over the past decade in various articles, some of which are cited below. I do not claim the ideas advanced in these articles as uniquely mine. I just say the assembly of them is my own and that I have been trying to organize and advance them with enough clarity to encourage exploration of them in a field where a prevailing regime of 'normal science' yields little for the mind or imagination.
3 The difference between Logic and logic is that the first is held to be holy, unassailable and universal. In Szasz's (1976, 37–38) terms, Logic is a metaphor used for strategic purposes. The humbler logic is man-made, fallible and open to correction. Kaplan (1964, 6–11) argues for qualitatively different logics with 'logic-in-use' being a natural logic and 'reconstructed logic' an artificial logic. He perhaps best evokes the distinction by quoting John Locke: 'God has not been so sparing to men to make them barely two-legged creatures and left it to Aristotle to make them rational'.
4 Arrow's General Impossibility Theorem points to the problem of ordering preferences rationally, especially in groups. The Theorem shows that a forced choice, if not force itself, is essential to resolve conflicting orders of preference. This insight, as Hodgkinson (1978a, 272), argues, 'blows a lot of administrative battleships out of the water'. For further comment on Arrow's Theorem, see p. 45.
5 I acknowledge here Feyerabend's (1975) crusade against method and his outline of an anarchistic theory of knowledge. The idea echoes as well the mysticism in Wittgenstein's (1961) thought.
6 This paradox should give us pause to think about the differences in meaning between 'make' and 'create'. In the language of Kant, the subtle distinctions, overlaps and ambiguities in these words are even more apparent in *machen* and

schaffen. In German, *machen* carries the force of 'cause to happen' or 'bring into existence', as in the working of a first cause independent of human action, while *schaffen* evokes 'bring forth to life' or 'give form or shape to', as in the realization of a role or piece of art by talent, imagination and human effort. This reading of the words brings us to conclude that the existence of the world is God's handiwork or responsibility, perhaps, but the form, shape and reality of the world we see and experience are all our own doing.

7 Wittgenstein's ideas are terse but often expressed with beauty and clarity. He is a philosopher whose life and ideas bear examination together. See Malcolm's (1958) *Memoir* and the accompanying poignant biographical sketch by von Wright.

8 See point no. 6 for an 'inexorable' logic to explain why this no-point is called '2' and why we deny – especially in the presence of children – that there is any alternative to social reality or to our preferred modes of thinking and speaking about it.

9 It is worth noting that both Musil and Rainer Maria Rilke attended the same military school in Austria – one much like that described in *Young Törless*. The narrative given here and the quotations passages quoted are from pages 105–113, 145–163, and 198–214 of the 1955 edition of this short but remarkable book.

10 Ian Jacks, 'The Atrocities of Bhagalpur', *The Sunday Times*, 7 December 1980, p. 10.

11 For the sources of these ideas from Wittgenstein and Russell, see Greenfield (1979, 177–178) and Hodgkinson (1978b, 83).

REFERENCES

Feyerabend, P. 1975. *Against Method: Outline of an Anarchistic Theory of Knowledge.* London: New Left Books.

Greenfield, T. B. 1975. 'Theory about Organizations: A New Perspective'. In *Administering Education: International Challenge*, ed. M. Hughes, 71–99. London: Athlone.

—— 1979. 'Ideas Versus Data: How Can the Data Speak for Themselves?' In *Problem-Finding in Educational Administration*, eds G. L. Immegart and W. L. Boyd, 167–190. Lexington, MA: D. C. Heath.

—— 1980. 'The Man Who Comes Back Through the Door in the Wall: Discovering Truth, Discovering Self, Discovering Organizations', *Educational Administration Quarterly* 16, 3: 26–59.

Hodgkinson, C. 1978a. 'The Failure of Organizational and Adminis- trative Theory'. *McGill Journal of Education* 13, 3: 271–278.

—— 1978b. *Towards a Philosophy of Administration.* Oxford: Basil Blackwell.

Huxley, A. 1977. *The Doors of Perception.* Frogmore, England: Triad/Panther.

Kaplan, A. 1964. *The Conduct of Inquiry: Methodology for Behavioral Science.* San Francisco: Chandler.

Malcolm, N. 1958. *Ludwig Wittgenstein: A Memoir* (with a biographical sketch by G. H. von Wright). London: Oxford.

Musil, R. 1955. *Young Törless.* Trans. E. Wilkins and E. Kaiser, London: Secker and Warburg.

Orwell, G. 1957. *Inside the Whale and Other Essays.* Harmondsworth: Penguin.

Segal, R. 1971. *The Struggle Against History.* Harmondsworth: Penguin.

Shaw, G. B. 1946. *Man and Superman: A Comedy and a Philosophy.* Harmondsworth: Penguin.

Suzuki, D. T. 1955. *Studies in Zen.* New York: Dell.

Szasz, T. 1976. *Heresies.* Garden City, NY: Anchor.

Winch, P. 1958. *The Idea of a Social Science and its Relation to Philosophy.* London: Routledge & Kegan Paul.

Wittgenstein, L. 1961. *Tractatus Logico–Philosophicus.* London: Routledge & Kegan Paul.

7

THE DECLINE AND FALL OF SCIENCE IN EDUCATIONAL ADMINISTRATION

The study of educational administration is cast in a narrow mould. Its appeal stems from a science of administration whose experts claim that an objective view of the social world enables them to conduct value-free inquiry. They claim to possess knowledge that enables them to control organizations and to improve them. But such large claims appear increasingly unsound, for the science that justifies them rests on methods and assumptions that dismiss the central realities of administration as irrelevant. Those realities are values in human action. If administrative science deals with them at all, it does so only in a weakened or spuriously objective form. For this reason, scholars in educational administration are now called to consider whether the way forward is still to be defined, as it has been for a generation or more, by a single path called 'the way of science'. The alternative path would seek to understand administrative realities within a broader conception of science – a conception recognizing that values bespeak the human condition and serve as springs to action both in everyday life and in administration. But values are subjective realities, and people bind them inextricably to the facts in their worlds. Thus, an adequate new science may no longer be content to split facts from values, and deal only with the facts.

Promoters of the science of administration claim to have found a rational basis for human decision-making and a value-free technology for increasing the effectiveness and efficiency of organizations. Within a critical perspective, I will examine the basis of those claims and their mobilization on behalf of what Halpin (1970) called the 'New Movement' in educational administration. My aim is, first, to describe the intellectual and ideological development of this once revolutionary movement. Second, I will examine the consequences and offer a critique of the scientific approach to understanding the problems of administration. Third, I will suggest an alternative to New Movement science in educational administration. And finally, I will speak about the problems of administrative studies in education today and suggest how those who are concerned to improve such studies might approach them in the future.

THE RISE OF SCIENCE IN ADMINISTRATION

Self-conscious science entered administrative studies through the work of Herbert Simon. Published in 1945, *Administrative Behavior* constituted a wholly new approach to the understanding and study of administration.[1] His thinking transformed the field. Simon offered a totally new conception of the nature of administration, and, more importantly, a new set of rules for enquiry into administrative realities. From that time forward, his vision, his *Weltanschauung* of the world of administration, has dominated the field.

What Simon offered was a method of value-free enquiry into decision-making and administrative rationality. This method severely limited what could be considered as 'administration' or 'administrative decision-making', but its great advantage was that it brought the force of science to buttress any claims that might be made about the nature of administration or about the best means for improving organizations and life within them. Thus, the unfortunate consequence of Simon's work has been to shift attention from questions about the nature of administration to an obsessive concern for the methods of enquiry into it. Simon's critique of older knowledge in administration was that it offered little more than practitioners' prescriptive judgements on their experience. Simon's vision called for a knowledge of administrative realities founded on and validated by the power, objectivity, and utility of science. This transformation in administrative thought is perhaps worthy of being called a 'Revolution', for it stands for the belief that only the methods of science can yield reliable insights into the realities of administration.

With the publication of Simon's seminal work in 1945, the methods of positivistic science were established as the only ones by which scholars might gain reliable knowledge of administrative realities. Following this bias, scholars of contemporary thought in administration, like March (1965, x–xii), have classified as 'old' any knowledge created before 1950. This presentist bias stems from the ahistorical outlook of positivism and is seen in March's designation of his own and Simon's work as 'adult' and 'most fashionable'. But for March and other advocates of the science of administration, what most powerfully distinguishes old knowledge from new – and useless knowledge from useful – is that new and reliable knowledge can stand only on a foundation of empirical science.

Simon's achievement was to overthrow the past wisdom of the field – a wisdom that derived from the experience, observation, and reflection of writers who were administrators, not scientists. While practitioner-scholars, such as Taylor, Urwick, and Fayol, regarded their knowledge as scientific, their wisdom was expressed as 'principles', and the truth of what they

135

claimed rested more upon insight and assertion than upon science. Noting that the principles of administration occurred only in pairs, Simon (1957, 20) damned them as nothing more than mutually contradictory proverbs. Such knowledge suffered, he said (1957, 38), from 'superficiality, over-simplification, lack of realism'. To correct these errors, Simon set out to build a theory of administration on scientific knowledge, and his lasting contribution was to convince both scholars and practitioners that he had realized his vision. What is striking is how easily he appeared to have won the battle.

The work of Chester Barnard (1938), another of the scholar-practitioners, stands in dramatic contrast to Simon's. Barnard was essenti-ally a moralist, and for him the heart of administration lay in the leader's creation of co-operative effort among members of an organization and their commitment to institutional purpose. Yet Barnard was apparently dazzled by Simon's claim to have science on his side. He wrote a preface to *Administrative Behavior* in which he acknowledged Simon's 'important con-tribution [to be] a set of tools . . . suitable for describing an organization and the way an administrative organization works' (Simon, 1957, xli). But he also expressed confidence that these tools would simply confirm his belief in the abstract 'principles of general organization' and the import-ance of experience (such as his own), in understanding administration. Instead, Simon's science undermined the interpretation of experience as a means for understanding organizations, and it deflected attention from the moral questions about purpose and commitment highlighted by Barnard.

Unlike the scholar-practitioners, Simon did not attempt to provide a prescription for administrative action. Instead, he made minimal assump-tions about the nature of administration and narrowed the limits of inquiry. Simon set out to build a 'vocabulary of administrative theory', a vocabulary that would say nothing that could not be expressed in 'opera-tional definitions' (1957, xlvi, 37). Such theory and its vocabulary would then be open to validation according to the norms of truth recognized by positivistic science. Simon's starting point for a scientific theory of administration was a single proposition: 'Decision-making is the heart of administration.' From this vantage point, he set out to explore 'the logic and psychology of human choice' (1957, xlvi). The flaw in this definition is not so much its narrowness, for choice is certainly a fundamental and unavoidable dynamic in the making of organizational and administrative realities. Rather, the weakness stems from Simon's own choice to explore only the *factual basis of choice* and to ignore value and sentiment as springs of human action. Because science could not speak to the 'ethical content' of decisions, Simon eliminated values from his putative science of adminis-tration. Thereafter he was content with his struggle to predict and control decisions purely from their 'factual content':

The question of whether decisions can be correct and incorrect resolves itself, then, into the question of whether ethical terms like 'ought', 'good', and 'preferable' have a purely empirical meaning. It is a fundamental premise of this study that ethical terms are not completely reducible to factual terms. . . . Factual propositions cannot be derived from ethical ones by any process of reasoning, nor can ethical propositions be compared directly with the facts – since they assert 'oughts' rather than the facts. . . . Since decisions involve valuations of this kind, they too cannot be objectively described as correct or incorrect. (Simon, 1957, 38)

Simon's great contribution was his recognition that making decisions is the essence of administration. In a way not found in previous studies, he saw that decisions are taken by human beings, not by boxes drawn on an organization chart. He knew that 'principles' founded on such abstractions would be impotent.

To many persons, organization means something that is drawn on charts or recorded in elaborate manuals of job descriptions, to be duly noted and filed. Even when it is discussed by some of its most perceptive students – for example, Colonel Urwick – it takes on more the aspect of a series of orderly cubicles contrived according to an abstract architectural logic, than of a house designed to be inhabited by human beings. (Simon, 1957, xvi)

Simon's great failure was his own decision to focus exclusively on the factual basis of decisions and to regard as irrelevant all the other forces that shaped them, but which his science could not predict or control. And so the science of administration defined by Simon retreated in the face of the intractable powers and imponderable choices that make up the realities of life.

SIMON AND POSITIVISM IN ADMINISTRATIVE SCIENCE

Since positivism dominates Simon's conception of science, it seems fair to use 'science' in this discussion to mean positivistic enquiry. As Phillips (1983), Eisener (1983), and Culbertson (1983) suggest, positivism is both a philosophy of empiricism and a set of rules for determining what constitutes truth. The force of the assumptions of this method of enquiry dispenses with any knowledge not based upon objective and empirical observation. Such enquiry must therefore deny the world of value. It must abjure as proper subjects for scientific study all of what Halpin (1958, xii) called 'social philosophy' and all questions pertaining to 'right human conduct'. The positivist argument is, however, a powerful one. It reduces all internal states, all perceptions, feelings, and values to epiphenomena, to an unspeakable affect, to an externality that, as Hodgkinson (1983, 43) points

137

out, 'one can only rebut . . . by referring to one's own phenomenological and, therefore, unverifiable experience . . . and by taking a position outside the limits of positivist discourse'.

There is, of course, a broader conception of science in which the scientist is not only an observer but also an interpreter of reality. This view acknowledges that human interest and its possible biases are inextricably interwoven in what we call scientific truth (Bauman, 1978; Giddens, 1976; Rabinow and Sullivan, 1979; Toulmin, 1983). Such broader conceptions of science should, I believe, be accommodated within the study of educational administration, and, indeed, they are beginning to be expressed there – at least by the minority voices in the field who are advocates of alternative approaches. Fortunately these can now be found in the increasingly comprehensive and powerful statements of scholars such as Hodgkinson (1978b; 1983), Bates (1983a and b; 1985), Foster (1985), Gronn (1983; 1985; 1986a and b; 1987), Lakomski (1984; 1985; 1987a; 1987b) and Macpherson (1987).

Simon's conception of administration as decision-making and his dedication to the belief that the methods of positivistic science could be used to understand and improve the rationality of administrators' decisions have powerfully shaped the modern field of study. From these theoretical points of departure, he constructed a model of rationality – the limited, sufficing rationality of 'administrative man' who makes only decisions that are 'good enough'. Simon's administrative man 'satisficed', as opposed to omniscient 'economic man' who maximized and made the best possible decisions. Simon's view of administration thus retained the assumptions of the economic model, but modified them to accommodate a less than perfect rationality. What is perhaps not so readily apparent is that he also retained the assumptions so dear to systems theorists – that administration is a function in a productive system and that this function is open to manipulation in the same way as other independent and objective conditions. For Simon, administration was simply an element or function in a productive system; as such, it could be regarded as operating in precisely the same manner as all other technical variables of a productive system.

THE FAILURE OF ADMINISTRATIVE SCIENCE

My aim here is not so much to demonstrate the failure of administrative science in education, for I have been over that ground before (Greenfield, 1975, 1978, 1980; 1985a; 1985b). Over the last decade or more, the continuing 'turmoil' in the field has been well chronicled elsewhere (Griffiths, 1979). And the implications of the furore have been drawn so fully and so clearly that only the obtuse or the uninformed could claim to be unaware of them (Gronn, 1983; 1985). I have argued that administrative science has failed in education, but I believe its failure is equally apparent in the other sub-fields of administration as well. The difference in the sub-fields is perhaps best seen in the contrast between the journals, *Administrative Science Quarterly* and *Educational Administration Quarterly*. The former recognizes the Revolution may be in trouble, and its articles reflect a radically expanded view of administrative theory and empirical enquiry; the latter denies, or seems to, that there are any problems in the unfolding of the Revolution.[2] The predominating opinion in that journal continues to recommend more and larger doses of science largely in the form of improved methodologies, but still within the restrictive notions of theory and method that have pervaded the field since Simon blazed the revolutionary path.

The revolutionary goals that Modern Organization Theory set for administration generally were echoed in Halpin's New Movement in educational administration (Greenfield, 1985b). Although the ideology of these movements still reigns supreme as a kind of Doctrine of the Revolution of Science in Administration, the Revolution has failed; it has been unable to answer why the science that Simon stipulated to solve administrative problems has notably failed to do so. Mainstream thought in educational administration stands, though perhaps now with weakened conviction, on Simon's restrictive definition of administrative realities, embracing, *a fortiori*, his view of appropriate enquiry. For the most part, modern administrative theorists have heeded Simon's argument that the science of administration can be concerned only with means, not ends. The spirit of positivism, which is now pervasive, discourages historical enquiry, and so puts to flight any notion that scholars of administration should know their intellectual origins and the assumptions on which their field rests. But placed in the history of ideas, the belief that administration is (or can be) a science appears as a phenomenon of the mid-twentieth century. As we near the end of the century, this belief is beginning to appear as a misplaced faith. It is also becoming clear why it is an enormous error to conceive of administration as a science rather than as a moral act or as a political event.

Because positivistic science cannot derive a value from a fact or even recognize values as real, we have a science of administration which can deal only with facts and which does so by eliminating from its consideration all human passion, weakness, strength, conviction, hope, will, pity, frailty, altruism, courage, vice, and virtue. Simon led the science of administration down a narrow road which in its own impotence is inward-looking, self-deluding, self-defeating, and unnecessarily boring. These shortcomings are created by the blinkered view of choice and administrative action afforded by a narrowly empiricist science which lets us see but a pale and reduced reflection of the human will to achieve a purpose, to mobilize resources, to influence others – to do all that people in fact do as they make choices and strive to transform their values into realities.

The current overwhelming acceptance of positivistic science in administration has led theory and research to emphasize the epiphenomena of reality rather than the phenomenological force of that reality itself. This approach yields 'hard', but often impotent, irrelevant, or misleading data that are the only reality recognized by the hypothetico–deductive models favoured in such science. In this science, only that which is quantifiable and calculable is real, for that is the only kind of reality consistent with the limited rationality that finds its ultimate expression in the linear workings of computers. What is lost in such approaches is human intention, value, commitment – human passion and potential. What is lost is human will and choice, the sheer power of people pursuing their purposes, a pursuit that brings what some may call good and others evil. Hodgkinson (1978b, 18) has shown, moreover, that administrative science has led us to focus upon the personality traits of administrators – upon the mere characteristics of administrators rather than upon their character. In consequence, the empirical study of administrators has elided their *moral* dimensions and virtually all that lends significance to what they do.

If this selective focusing is noticed in contemporary critiques of research, it appears only in Haller and Knapp's (1985) terms. Their response to the futility of research on the superficial characteristics of administrators is not to look more deeply, but to remove entirely the individual as a focus in administrative research. For them, a focus on the individual confuses 'the *questions* that are studied with the *subjects* . . . of the studies'. They recommend examining only the organizational production functions that administrators oversee. This position highlights the ultimate concern of administrative science – the effectiveness and efficiency of the organization which is, of course, conceived as an entity independent of human will, purpose, and values.

WHAT SIMON OMITTED: RIGHT, RESPONSIBILITY, REFLECTION

Simon's aim and hope were sweeping and daring: to enhance organizational efficiency and effectiveness by ensuring that administrators chose – within the limits of the rationality open to them – the best possible means to achieve a given end. But to fulfil the promise of the new science of productive rationality, administrative man had to disappear as a value-bearer and wilful and un-predictable choice-maker. Thus Simon's administrative man emerged in a devalued, dehumanized, and technologized form.

> Once the system of values which is to govern an administrative choice has been specified, there is one and only one 'best' decision, and this decision is determined by the organizational values and situation, and not by the personal motives of the member of the organization who makes the decision. Within the area of discretion, once an individual has decided, on the basis of his personal motives to recognize the

SCIENCE AND EDUCATIONAL ADMINISTRATION

organizational objectives, his further behavior is determined not by personal motives, but by the demands of efficiency. (Simon, 1957, 204)

So, if this view defines the limits of a science of administrative decision-making, it must be noted that some vital questions of administration lie beyond them. All that governs the choice of the values for the system are beyond it, as is the question of what objective reality could exist to keep the personal motives, character, or ideology of individual members from impinging upon the choices they make in pursuing the values of the organization.

The horror of Simon's neutered science appears only with the realization that it conforms, almost perfectly, to the view that administrators seem to want to have of themselves: that they are instruments of an objective, selfless, rationality. Administrative science, as Simon conceived it, has done much to establish the belief that de-valued, but rational decision-making is desirable, attainable, and scientifically verifiable. This belief relieves the anxiety of decision-making and removes the administrator's sense of responsibility for his decisions. Scott and Hart (1979, 46–47) show how a devalued rationality can help administrators deal with practical problems, but only at the price of desensitizing them to the values that must be engaged in making a difficult decision:

> The management of organizations is a practical and mundane effort. Implicit within the pragmatic rule is a warning against philosophizing. . . . Organizations are run by managers who must make decisions about goals, policies, and strategies of action that influence human values and behaviour, both within and outside the organization. . . . The vice-president for personnel of a large company that must lay off five hundred employees is certainly not encouraged to consider the impact of this action on their lives. Instead, consideration is given to the health of the company.

A commitment to science in organizational affairs is not simply a commitment to rationality; it is, rather, a commitment to a restricted framework of rationality. Such a framework, called science, eases the sense of responsibility for powerful actors in organizational and administrative settings. It denies both responsibility and personal choice in the making of everyday decisions and in the making of decisions in the powerful world of organized reality. Such science takes sides in conflicts about the rightness of organizational purpose and about appropriate means for achieving them, but it denies it takes sides, and claims to look dispassionately at such reality. As Hodgkinson (1978b, 163) says, 'Obedience or compliance can be construed as a way of abdicating responsibility.' In our society with its reverence for science and technique, obedience to a truncated concept of rationality has become a cover for the powerful administrator: science and rationality provide the ultimately persuasive and irrefutable excuse for the abdication of personal choice and responsibility.

To choose and to acknowledge responsibility for one's choice is often a risky way of living. It may require standing with those who are defined as heretics by a powerful and possibly vengeful authority. The safe course for administrators is suggested by Szasz's rueful observation:

> The Platonic maxim that 'It is better to suffer wrong than to commit it' is fine for those to whom life is a spectator sport; the players, however, need something that gives them a little more protection in the clinches. (Szasz, 1976, 33)

The moral dilemma of the administrator whose best judgement leads him to stand on the wrong side of authority was noted nearly fifteen centuries ago by Boethius, 'the last of the Romans'. A scholar turned administrator, he tried to serve both the emperor and – as it turned out – the wrong pope. His reward for acting according to conscience was death at the hands of his master, Theodoric the Ostrogoth. The emperor, however, first placed Boethius under house arrest and thereby gave him time to reflect on his actions and to write *The Consolation of Philosophy*. There he makes the case that philosophy is the only consolation for a miscalculated risk. In his meditation, the figure of Philosophy appears to Boethius (1969, 53) and points out the high price of choosing to serve truth rather than sovereign power.

> If you desire
> To look on truth
> And follow the path
> With unswerving course
> Rid yourself
> Of joy and fear,
> Put hope to flight,
> And banish grief.
> The mind is clouded
> And bound in chains
> Where these hold sway.

In organizational politics and administrative affairs, the acknowledgement of clearly chosen values can be dangerous. But as Boethius's life makes clear, acknowledgement enables us – both leaders and followers – to reflect upon our values. And in thinking about our lives, we may come to recognize that our decisions represent something beyond the decisions themselves; they bespeak a value and perhaps a commitment. As Hodgkinson (1978b, 172) points out, such commitment

> is, of course, subject to critique from other philosophical positions, but all that the proponents of these contending positions can do is to

142

seek to persuade their audience by reason and rhetoric and all the powers at their disposal that they have the better values. In the end the act of choice is individual; and if free and conscious, then moral.

THE INFUSION OF SCIENCE INTO EDUCATIONAL ADMINISTRATION

Science emerged in public administration in 1945 with Simon's work and has dominated all parts of the field since then. The spirit of positivism spread to educational administration in the 1950s in a form Halpin (1970) called the 'New Movement'. This revolution began with a small band of social scientists who set out to redeem the older studies through science (Halpin, 1958; Campbell and Lipham, 1960). Halpin (1970, 161) describes the shock of the scholar-practitioners when advocates of the new science-based administration confronted them with the news that their knowledge was 'atheoretical and sloppy'. He also reports that the reception the practitioners gave this news was 'less than cordial'. But, by 1957, the New Movement scientists were in command, and they announced to a seminar held at the Midwest Administration Center of the University of Chicago the arrival of the scientific millennium in educational administration.

From that point onwards there began a remarkably rapid transformation of the theory, research, and graduate instruction in educational administration. Deaf to critical voices who warned against the founding of enquiry on a flawed and narrow foundation, scientists of the New Movement did not waver in their conviction. They justified their new understanding of administration with the claim that it brought research into line with the requirements of science and of rationality itself (Culbertson, 1983). Seeing the strategic advantage of having Science on their side, practitioners soon began to endorse New Movement assumptions and ideology. Under the banner, 'Administrative Theory as a Guide to Action', the Midwest Administration Center of the University of Chicago sponsored a second conference on theory, one that brought together social scientists and practitioners in the special mix that now marks so much of scholarly and professional endeavour in the field. Although Campbell warned the Conference that the millennium was not yet at hand, and though he cautioned that 'scientific knowledge offers maps, not prescriptions', he also discouraged stragglers from the way by expressing the view that 'social science is principally the description of an intelligent, rational person in action' (Campbell and Lipham, 1960, 175–176).

Halpin, however, was later torn by doubts concerning his role in promulgating a science that promised to enable the administrator to 'make wiser decisions' (Halpin, 1966, 285). He acknowledged that the ringing title of the conference invited administrators to believe in theory as a guide for action, when in fact there was 'no theory worthy of the name available to report' (Halpin, 1970, 157). But scholars and practitioners of the time were prepared to testify that the emperor called Science had clothes. Indeed, Marland, one of the superintendents at the 1959 conference (Campbell and Lipham, 1960, 34), told how practitioners awaited with interest the 'science of administration' and how they 'listen[ed] attentively to the counsel of social scientists'.[3]

What has been called 'modern organization theory' (Haire, 1959; March, 1965) was created in close parallel with Halpin's 'New Movement' in educational administration. Both may be seen as movements reflecting Simon's pioneering attempt to establish the study of organizations and administration on an objective scientific basis. Both began with a conscious break from previous studies that were viewed as mired in 'social philosophy' (Halpin, 1958, xii). Both advocated that science, cast in an objective, positivistic mould, could save the field from the philosophers, moralists, and other subjectivists. Together they represented the deliberate founding of a new science of organizations which aimed to establish the experimental verification of 'hypothetico–deductive theory' – an abstract, mathematically expressed theory that was held by its proponents to be the highest form of scientific knowledge. That there was no such theory of this kind in existence did not deter advocates from seeking it, indeed, from launching research into organizations to test it. Such theory, it was held, would produce control over organizations in the same way that it permitted control over the physical world. The aim of the New Movement in educational administration was to generate such theory about schools, to place it in the hands of administrators, and to train them in its use. And so began the effort to train educational administrators in the science of organizations.

Convinced by a similar logic, Haller and Knapp (1985, 161) have more recently urged researchers not to focus on administrators, but rather to study relationships within organizations. They define educational administration as 'the study of the patterned relationships . . . with particular attention to the effects of those relationships on the transmission of subject matter to learners'. The image of organizations assumed here is that of a productive unit staffed by human beings who are subsidiary to the unit and largely independent of it. In this conception, it is relationships and structures that are important, not people themselves.

The scientific view of educational administration continues to recommend systems theory, a conception which sees the organization as a productive unit striving under conditions of limited rationality to increase its output to a constraining environment. This view also continues to see the failure of science-based theories of administration as remediable by better and more powerful methodology. Such opinion thus reflects Simon's empiricism and his hope for improving the effectiveness and efficiency of the organization through rational decision-making. In these circumstances, it is not surprising to find that discussion of the failure of science-based theory and research soon reduces to technical issues – skewed distributions, outliers, Tukey's test, and box and whisker plots.[4]

THE CONSEQUENCES OF THE NEW SCIENCE OF ORGANIZATIONS

Despite the promise that the science of organization and administration was to be objective, quantitative, and value-free, the *images* of organization found in the theory-based research of the New Movement carry important values and philosophical assumptions. Taking these values and assumptions into consideration, four consequences of the movement should be noted.

The growing belief in administration as science

The New Movement gave social validation to the belief that an objective science for guiding organizations had indeed been invented. With this belief widely accepted, so too was the idea that administrators should be trained in the science through programmes of study in universities. Oftentimes, these programmes have been state-mandated and tied to certification. Such programmes teach the science of organization to administrators in the conviction it will enable them to do what they are supposed to do: direct organizations to achieve their goals in the most effective and efficient manner open to them. In this connection, the dominating metaphors of the science of administration are worth noting. Belief in the rationality of decision-making is prime among them, though this notion is closely tied to the systems concept that the organization is 'real' and exists in a natural balance with its environment. In the systems view, to study an organization scientifically means to study an aspect of natural reality – a reality that can be explored objectively and explained in the law-like, universal languages of mathematics and logic. Individuals disappear – and with them human agency, responsibility, and morality – and natural forces take over the conduct of human affairs. And so we have the language of abstraction – so common in the literature – that, for example, speaks of 'accommodating the organization to the reality demands of the environment and transforming the external situation' (Boyd and Crowson, 1981, 331).

To establish this science, it was necessary, as Hodgkinson pointed out to commit the biological fallacy of endowing the organization with an ontological reality. The organization is conceived not only as real, but as more important than the people within it:

and worse; the organization is not only reified, but deified. And the agent is not personally or morally responsible for the acts which are under the authority or authorship of the collectivity. . . . And

145

outwardly benevolent organizations can become latent collective forces for evil. (Hodgkinson, 1978b, 173)

And so another anomaly of scientific administration becomes apparent. Its emphasis falls not upon the phenomenological reality of administrators – neither upon the realities of those who wield power nor upon the perceptions of those who suffer its consequences. Such science chooses to study a greater reality, one that lies beyond the awareness of individuals: the reality of the organization itself. Even if we can assume the reality of the organization, and even if we assume that knowledge of that reality is in some way useful, we must still ask why administrative science has failed to explore the second of Simon's concerns: 'the logic and psychology of human choice'. The answer, as Hodgkinson (1978a, 272) suggests is 'perhaps for the basic and stupefyingly simple reason that the central questions of administration are not scientific at all. They are philosophical'. Here Hodgkinson is using 'science' to mean an objective, imperial Science that is presumed to live only within the limits that positivism has placed upon it: a limit that reduces values to epiphenomena and that precludes Science from speaking about values at all.[5] If such limits are accepted, then Science cannot presume to tell any of us that we should go to work today, let alone what we should do when we get there. But there is another and larger sense of science that sees it simply as truth, as reliable knowledge, and not as a particular method for arriving at knowledge (Schumacher, 1977). But what knowledge is reliable? Perhaps in the end we must be content simply with knowledge that lets us get through the day, preferably happily (Greenfield, 1983).

The devaluation of administrative studies

The scientific movement is closely connected to the notion that a value-free science of administration is not merely possible, but at hand. With the elimination of values, consideration of the conduct of organizations is reduced to technicalities. The substance of decisions is not important – only the manner of the making of them. As Bates (1983a, 8) points out, this approach brings with it a separation of problems in administration from problems in education. It also brings, as Tipton (1985) argues, the isolation of theory in educational administration from other academic studies that bear powerfully on its professed concerns and interests. Many texts in the field bear the unimaginative title, *Educational Administration*,[6] and from this emphasis one would expect that they should address uniquely educational issues. Not so. Readers look in vain for any substantive educational discussion. They may be told how to lead, motivate, communicate, develop morale, and maintain the organization in dynamic equilibrium, but they will find no discussion of an issue to which they must bring judgement. Radical and conservative critiques of school structure and curriculum, disputes over religion and language of instruction, the virtues of private versus public schools, class and cultural bias, unions, women, discipline, dress codes – of all these and the many other issues that beset education, there is no murmur of comment. Not even the major controversies about the meaning and reliability of administrative science are discussed in these texts.[7]

Hidden values of administrative science

Despite its claim to objectivity, the science of administration is usually to be found on the side of the status quo. It starts from a standpoint of things as they are, and then asks why they are so. It does not question whether that which is ought to be. The argument here is not that conventional society or the status quo are necessarily wrong, but that positivist science cannot and *should not* attempt to validate social reality without revealing the weakness of its credentials for doing so. But despite its claims to neutrality, Science cannot seem to resist taking on the role of social validator, and, in fact, is often well paid for its neutered conscience. This criticism has been launched against positivist social science generally, but in administration it has particular potency, for the state is the ultimate organization; it has almost unrestricted power over the individual – even the power that can ask and get an individual's life. But if Science conceives the state (and all organizations of lesser puissance) as an objectified reality that is beyond question by the science of organization, then its students have no recourse but to serve their organizations with all the skill and devotion of which they are capable. In Hobbesian terms, the administrative scientist becomes a servant of the General Will – of the Sovereign. The General Will is, of course, to be interpreted by the Sovereign, not by the scientist whose role is limited to that of a technician skilled in applying a kind of physics of sociation – the impersonal and objective science of social organization and administration.[8]

A science of administration limited by the assumptions of positivism can produce experts in technique, not experts in value. If, however, the positivists are right, and values are merely an illusion or an affect that registers only in the psyche of individuals, then no real problem exists, for there is no objective way of expressing or arbitrating between competing claims of perceived value. The physics of sociation would then suffice as a basis for understanding and evaluating social reality. But if values are real, and if they are beyond the scope of positivist science, then a science of social order that claims to be value-free must remain silent in the face of the central issues of organizational and administrative life. But remain silent it does not. The mantle of objectivity permits scientists to intervene on the behalf of values without seeming to do so, and to move readily from commenting on the way things are to advocating the way they should be. In the contemporary field, such scientists are everywhere: for example,

147

administrators who, following Hoy and Miskel (1982, vii), want to make their practice 'less of an art and more of a science', the agent of educational change and implementation, the consultant on organization development who promises to improve the 'health' of the organization, and now the purveyors of excellence in organization and designs for effective schools. Indeed, all *experts* in organization theory who claim their prescriptions stand on objective Science are open to challenge, for their values, not their Science, constitute the real foundation of their knowledge.

The difficulty that arises from a belief in the possibility of a devalued notion of rationality and decision-making is well illustrated with a metaphor from Hodgkinson: the sandwich of rationality. Closely following his explication of three levels of reality and three types of values, Hodgkinson (1983, 38, 78; 1985; 1988, 24) draws attention to *levels* of reality and value in rationality itself. In this view, any human choice is made up of three elements. One is cognitive and limitedly rational in Simon's sense of the calculation of the factual relationship between ends and means. This calculation constitutes the 'meat' of the sandwich, but it is held in place by two slices of bread made up of subrational effect on the one hand and another slice made up of super-rational ideology and transrational value. The sandwich metaphor thus recognizes that human beings are driven by their desires and fears, by their hopes and ideals, as much as by their rational calculations. And who is to say that such drives are not also a kind of rationality?

Angels and other rationalists say it. For as William Blake said,

> I have always found that Angels have the vanity to speak of themselves as the only wise. This they do with a confident insolence sprouting from systematic reasoning.

This point urges not that we dispense with systematic reasoning, but only that we recognize it as compact with an individual's ideology, ideals, commitment, and preference. What the angels of systematic reasoning and administrative science must comprehend is that issues great and small – whether to die for love of one's country, whether to close a school in the face of falling enrolments, whether to stop smoking today – are decided by people who bring all their belief, passion, habit, frailty, or nobility to the choice that faces them. Whatever the choice before them, they are unlikely to make it on the basis of a calculated, fact-driven rationality alone. Or as I have argued, facts *are*, but they do not tell us what to do (Greenfield, 1980, 43). Indeed, the facts alone decide nothing; it is we who decide about the facts. This realization comes as no surprise to historians and artists who deal with what men and women do, not with what the 'angels of reason' (Huxley, 1977) would have them do. But scientists of administration continue to be surprised, and spend much effort pointing out how the world would be better if people only behaved 'rationally'. This then is the failure of administrative science. Instead of providing, as it claims, an objective description of the world and of human choice, administrative science offers merely another value-driven prescription. Apparently despairing over the irrationality of the world, many otherwise encouraging critiques of administrative science offer expressions of hope that stronger research methodologies will yet plumb the depths of its mystery and find Simon's fact-only rationality at the bottom (see Haller and Knapp, 1985; Hoy, 1982).

Science-validated training programmes

New Movement science fosters and legitimates programmes for training and certifying administrators. During the 1950s, a foundation-supported drive began in the United States to transform the old-style training programmes into new ones based upon the assumptions of modern organization theory and administrative science (Tope *et al.*, 1965). These programmes were designed to bring New Movement administrative science to bear upon the practical problems of education. Such programmes have since spread through the proselytizing efforts of university-based advocates to other countries, notably the English-speaking Commonwealth countries, but increasingly to Third World countries as well.[9] To criticize the spread of such programmes is not to suggest that the training of administrators is futile and unnecessary; rather, it is to argue that many university-based training programmes, captured by a narrowly defined concept of administration, restrict the possibility of productive enquiry into administration.

Sovereign powers, in the form of state departments of education and other public and private authorities, have long had a role in the choice and validation of administrators for educational institutions. As Gronn (1986a) has shown, the selection of administrators is driven by a rationality that sweeps far beyond the logic of fact-driven choice. How could it be otherwise? Administrators are essentially value-carriers in organizations; they are both arbiters of values and representatives of them. Those who select and evaluate administrators are not so naïve as to ignore their surface characteristics. Indeed, they likely see all that meets the senses – dress, speech, custom – as expressions of the administrator's deeper values and commitments. But administrative science, holding up the ideal of the administrator as technician, is likely to argue otherwise. It offers the Sovereign the possibility of choosing the 'certified' decision-maker, the one who uses science to bring excellence, effectiveness, or efficiency – as though these conditions had no value content – to whatever organization employs him.

And so administrative science again plays into the hand of the social system. While the scientifically-based training programme claims to produce technicians skilled in decision-making and organization building, the Sovereign looks beyond such froth to the prospective administrator's values and character. But the froth is not irrelevant either; if for no other reason,

149

it is politically advantageous to be seen standing with Science. Therefore we see authorities increasingly turning to science-driven training programmes. The result is a happy one for both sides of the bargain. The Sovereign can claim a scientific validation of its decisions, and Science gets privileged access to the benefits the Sovereign can bestow.

Callahan (1964) has identified four stages in the historical development of administrative programmes for American school superintendents, and he shows how each stage was shaped by a characteristic ideal. In this development, we may also see the values that now generally pervade programmes for the training of educational administrators in the United States. And – thanks to the international network that promulgates science-based training in educational administration – we may see these same values in similar programmes in Canada and in many other countries as well. Callahan (in Khleif, 1975, p. 307) describes the stages through which belief in the value of science-based programmes for the training of educational administrators developed in the United States:

> The superintendent as scholarly educational leader, 1865–1910.
> The superintendent as business manager or school executive, 1910–1930.
> The superintendent as statesman in a democratic school system, 1930–1954.
> The superintendent as applied social scientist, 1954–present.

Khleif (1975) has reported an illuminating study of the socializing process and values of an exemplary programme for the training of an élite cadre of educational administrators in administrative science. He found that more of the effort of the programme was devoted to the inculcation of values than it was to the training of students in science. Indeed, he found that under the guise of training in social science, the neophyte administrators were offered a new persona and introduced to a set of values congenial to prospective employers. Students were carefully chosen for the programme and schooled at length in their roles. After an appropriate time, the neophytes were certified as experts in the social scientific knowledge needed to administer schools and were introduced to mentors who then recommended them for jobs in the power system of education. Thus, particular social values were advanced under the guise of a training programme dedicated to science. As Khleif (1975, 307) explains,

> The program is a high-speed course in social mobility. . . . The program is a school for statesmen or – if one is uncharitable – politicians. Candidates acquire an upper-middle class demeanor, dress, and presentability. Candidates become more socially polished, masters of small talk, alert politicians with – if necessary – a talent for

intrigue and little arts of popularity. They become adept at self-manipulations and manipulations of others.

With respect to the values in the four historical stages identified by Callahan, Khleif says the science-based programme

puts an emphasis on the three latter types of superintendency and definitely discourages or ignores the first type. Attention to school finances, a smooth facade of democratic leadership and pieties about it, and a realistic training in the ways of community power exemplify the historical heritage and current culture of this profession.

It is not likely that training programmes of the intensity and selectivity described by Khleif exist today. Such programmes have been the victims of both a new stringency in university budgets and of a diminishing faith in the ideology that inspired them. But many programmes of lesser purity and intensity undoubtedly remain, carrying on in the spirit noted by Khleif. Indeed, training programmes for educational administrators have surely increased in number and enrolment over the past twenty years. They have consolidated their presence and have gained even stronger acceptance by sovereign powers. Such programmes nurture Simon's conception of rational administration and decision-making. The pity of this situation is that such conceptions of administrative training block the development of programmes that might deal more openly and helpfully with the value problems that confront all those who manage organizations. For administration is not a science in Simon's terms. It is better conceived by Hodgkinson:

While it has at its disposal a managerial quasi-technology, it is essentially a philosophical endeavour, a kind of humanism. Its overriding mission is the civilization of power. (1978b, p. 100)

THE ALTERNATIVE

The criticisms I have made of the conventional practice of administrative science can be summed up in a few brief points. First, administrative science does not work as science; it has not brought us increased understanding and control of organizations. Yet proponents of the science of administration – both early and contemporary – claim such an outcome to be its whole justification. Administrative science was to provide useful and powerful knowledge. This was the very criterion by which the fledgling science of administration rejected all previous knowledge in the field. Second, administrative science has ignored power relationships and has been content to deal with administrative problems that ignore substantive problems in education. Third, administrative science has focused its efforts not upon the phenomenological realities of administration – upon the experience of wielding power and making decisions – but upon the organization. It has been content to regard organizations rather than people as the real actors in society. And finally, administrative science has devalued the study of human choice and rationality. It has insisted that decision-making be dealt with *as though it were* fully explainable in rational and logical terms. This has allowed administrative science to deal with values surreptitiously, behind a mask of objectivity and impartiality, while denying it is doing so.

For these reasons, I believe it a fair judgement to say that administrative science is in decline. Whether it has also fallen is a moot point. Some might argue that it does not matter whether the body of the science is dead or dying; it matters only that scholars and practitioners behave as though it were alive. Faith in administrative science certainly inspired the creation of the earliest models of science-based training programmes (Khleif, 1975) and a similar, if somewhat diminished faith surely continues to maintain them.

New directions are apparent in theory that again places value questions as central in administration (Hodgkinson, 1978b; Scott and Hart, 1979). What then is the alternative to a science- and fact-driven definition of the field? Though I have elaborated an answer elsewhere (Greenfield, 1983; 1985a), let me suggest again its dimensions.

1 Organizations are not things. They have no ontological reality, and there is no use studying them as though they did. They are an invented social reality of human creation. It is people who are responsible for organizations and people who change them. Organizations have reality only through human action, and it is that action (and the human will driving it) that we must come to understand. The alternative I am proposing rejects theory that explains human behaviour as though a depersonalized organization and its devalued, nonhuman environment *caused* it. The alternative theory grants a measure of free will to individuals, and so places a measure of responsibility upon them for their action. People do not exist in organizations. Organizations exist in and through individuals. The concept of organization should be understood as a moral order deeply imbedded in each of us – an order that is arbitrary, non-natural, and often backed by enormous power, even by violence. But that power may be redeemed by love, that is, by a dedication to better values.

2 Organizations are a nexus of freedom and compulsion. As invented social realities, they can not only be created but also manipulated. The creation and maintenance of this illusion is the root of what the world understands as leadership, although in less dramatic forms, it could as well be called administration. The metaphors of production and technical control, appropriate to systems, organisms, and other physical or biological unities, are not appropriate to understanding and

administering organizations. We need new metaphors to describe organizations and administration. Perhaps most important would be to rid ourselves of the concept of an equilibriating system responding to benevolent environmental control. I suggest the metaphor of the Bonsai tree. This image is particularly apt for education. The gardener does not let the young tree simply 'develop its full potential'. Instead, he acts upon his own view of what constitutes a proper expression of the tree's potential, and he keeps clipping and pruning until the tree manifests that form. Since in education the 'full potential' of a child (or of a teacher or administrator) could be anything from Charles Manson to Albert Schweitzer,[10] the gardener keeps pruning until the desired form is produced. The difference between the gardener's task and the task of the leader or administrator is that trees never learn. People do, and that is where organizations and human culture itself come from.

3 The world of will, intention, experience, and value is the world of organizations and administration. The building of a new science of administration will depend on our ability to understand these realities. It will require that we recognize their complexity (Hodgkinson, 1983, 57–91) and their personal and subjective dimensions (Greenfield, 1985a). Such a science will require methods and instruments that are adequate to these realities. As Schumacher (1977, 39–60) points out, the question of what constitutes adequate methods and instruments for understanding the world is essentially a philosophical one. And as Gronn (1982, 1984, 1986b, 1987) has shown, our assumptions about adequate methods and instruments for studying administrators will not only reflect what we think administration is, but will also shape powerfully how we see administrators and understand what they do.

4 Conflict is endemic in organizations. It arises when different individuals or groups hold opposing values or when they must choose between accepted but incompatible values. Administrators represent values, but they also impose them. Administrative science must come to understand these complexities if it is to speak meaningfully to the world of practice. Only then may it begin to help administrators understand and cope with the personal and existential stress of conflict. The texts of administrative science are suffused with metaphors that portray organizations in terms of equilibrium, stability, adjustment, and harmony. We need other metaphors to bespeak the reality of stress and conflict.

5 The ideas and insights of Barnard (1938), the scholar-practitioner, were largely swept aside in the rush to make the study of administration embrace the rationality of Simon's science. What Barnard focused upon was not rationality and the enhancement of it, but an essential value phenomenon in organizations: commitment. For him, the building of commitment was the fundamental task of administration. This view raises the question, 'How can administrators be moral?' rather than

Simon's question, 'How can they be rational?' Simon would make the administrator a technician; Barnard would have him be a moral leader. Barnard speaks of the moral complexity of the leader. If we return to Barnard's view, we need again his insights as well as new metaphors to ground the science of administration. To help us begin to think of leaders in moral terms, we should recognize that they are representatives of values: indeed, they are both creators of values and entrepreneurs for them.

6   The ethical dimensions of administration come constantly to the fore once we free ourselves from the metaphors of harmony, optimism, and rationality that administrative science imposes upon organizational reality. What amazes in all of this is to read the science-based texts and to mark how positive and optimistic they are about human nature and the human condition. Administrative science lives in a world of pristine goodness, and so its knowledge can be of little use to those who face the perplexities of the world – perplexities that come readily to those who do no more than reflect upon their own experience or who simply read the newspapers or literary portrayals of life in organizations. Those, like Hodgkinson, who observe life in organizations in a clear-eyed fashion find that things often go wrong in them; they are beset by conflict, self-interested action, and the debasement of value through compromise. He lets us see the power of commitment, the polestar quality of transcendent values, and the madness they may bring with them. He repeats Saul Bellow's simple but fundamental question: 'With everyone sold on the good, how does all the evil get done?' Of an earlier generation, Barnard speaks of the 'moral complexity' of the leader by which he seems to mean the leader's wisdom in knowing when to raise moral issues and when to defuse them. Reflecting on such questions and building answers to them must become an essential and pervasive purpose of administrative studies. If Science cannot answer questions of what constitutes right action in social contexts – if it cannot speak of praxis – then it is time to begin again with a conception that sees administration as a set of existential and ethical issues. If enquiries launched from this premise lead to an understanding of administration in moral terms, and if this knowledge helps administrators see themselves and their tasks more clearly and responsibly, we may then have reliable knowledge and a sound guide for action in the world. Although this is exactly the kind of knowledge that Simon found wanting and hoped to provide in a rational and control-oriented Science of Administration, could we not still call such knowledge 'science' in humbler form?

AN AGENDA FOR THE FUTURE

Scholarship in administration has been bound for more than a generation by the power of Simon's thought. While a weakening of this remarkable uniformity is now apparent in all branches of the field, orthodoxy still struggles tenaciously to maintain its grip. In educational administration, defenders such as Willower (1985) meet the challenge by repeating positions only slightly modified from Simon's philosophical assumptions about the nature of administration and the proper means for enquiry into it. Most scholars will surely continue in the path that Simon pioneered, but others are now beginning to question that direction. They seek an alternative way and, therefore, an alternative conception of science to guide them. They, too, may call theirs the way of science, though they will likely abandon the assumptions and methods that Simon espoused as proper for scientific enquiry into administrative and organizational realities.

What is needed now in the study of educational administration is, first, the honesty to face the intellectual disarray of the field and, then, the courage to begin enquiry in a new mode. To guide such enquiry, we need only turn to an existing tradition of interpretive science that recognizes both subjectivity in the construction of social reality and the inevitability of interpretation in science. Though this mode of enquiry is still largely unknown and unused in administrative studies, it is at hand; it offers the best alternative to the narrow and increasingly sterile path of rationalism and positivistic science.

Administration is about power and powerful people. The study of administration must stand therefore upon a resolute examination of people as they strive to realize their ends. Administrative Science has too often yielded to the temptation of power and desired to wield it, not just to study it. Those who stand close to sovereign powers readily find reason to assist them. An adequate science of administration, however, must study power while resisting its pull. The new science of administration must be free to talk about the values that power serves, but free it cannot be if it is closely dependent upon the Sovereign (Ramos, 1981). To escape that dependency, the new science should abjure those activities that are most likely to endear it to the Sovereign – recognizing that the Sovereign, like the Devil can take many forms. The certification of future administrators is one such endearing activity.

For more than a quarter of a century, a fact-driven model of decision-making and rationality has dominated training programmes for educational administrators. To the extent that these programmes embrace technically-oriented notions of administration, they offer less than they espouse. They miss the meaning of human action and most of what saves the study of administration from inducing a state of ennui in its students. They over- simplify administrative problems and overstate the claim that science can solve them. Yet such programmes recognize virtually no limit on what can be done through academic study to prepare candidates for administrative responsibility. Only by suffering through their perhaps intentionally boring training do students of science-based training come to glimpse the meaning of administrative power and its scope for good and evil (Greenfield, 1980, 47–48).

A more fruitful training may be achieved through approaches that work with practising administrators and aim to give them deeper insights into the nature of their craft – into its dilemmas and possibilities – through study of its realities and through reflection upon them. We must seek new models for administrative training – ones that acknowledge responsibility, right judgement, and reflection as legitimately and inevitably part of administrative action. Such programmes would lead the field of study toward what Scott (1985, 156) has called 'revolutionary moral discourse' and away, therefore, from instruction in a putative science or organization and administration.

When I first took up the study of educational administration, nothing I learned cast a scintilla of doubt upon the certainty and power of administrative science; its objectivity and probity were simply assumed as were the benefits that were supposed to flow from its application. Certainly I did not doubt these apparent truths. What then is to be said now? Would the world be the worse without an administrative science? Probably not. But the issue is not simply science versus something else – versus the humanities, philosophy, or doing nothing at all. The issue is rather 'What kind of science?' Toulmin (1983) has observed the progress of modern science and noted the transformation of the scientist from an observer of reality to a participant in its construction. Scientists who once worried only to do the measurement right, now find an even greater problem: to do the right measurement – that is, to make the right observation. Thus the inevitability of subjective choice and interpretation enters science, and the possibility of a value-free science disappears. We must seek a new definition of science in administration – one that can accommodate the view that values pervade the entire realm of administration and, indeed, constitute the proper focus of study. Toulmin explains how a demand for neutrality in scientific method and observation came to limit the very kinds of problems that scientists could think of as proper for study:

> This demand for value neutrality played two separate roles in the sciences. On the one hand, it required the modern scientist to approach all the intellectual problems that properly fell within the scope of his methods with a clear head and a cool heart. On the other hand, it served to demarcate those issues that were properly the subjects for 'scientific' investigation and discussion from those that were, rather, matters of human taste, choice, or decision. To begin

156

with, these two aspects were not always distinguished in people's mind. (1981, 81)

If nothing else, we must understand that the new science of administration will be a science with values and of values.

What is required now is a transformation of the administrative scientist's attitudes toward the reality he studies. Scientists inspired by positivism approach administrators with the conviction that their theories and methods enable them to know administration in a way mere practitioners never could. The reverse assumption now seems a better point of departure: administrators know administration; scientists don't. The point of such enquiry would be to enable scientists to come to know what administrators know and to bring a fresh and questioning perspective to it. To accomplish this purpose, we might well return to one of Simon's original starting points and seek to understand the logic and psychology of human choice. But that requires the study of decision, will, and intention in all their depth, perplexity, and subjective uncertainty. The new science will surely also require giving up the notion that decisions and organizations themselves can be controlled by science. Greater insight such science may offer, but greater control, no.

A possible research agenda of the new science is apparent:

1 How is the social reality of the organization built and maintained? What do administrators and others contribute to this process?
2 What is the role of language in the building of administrative reality? We might begin to answer this question by taking seriously Hodgkinson's propositions (1978b, 199–222): Two of these state, 'Language is the basic administrative tool' and 'Language *has* power and cloaks power'.
3 The character of administrators is clearly of great importance. We may study it through biography and history.
4 Law is built upon the arbitration of value conflict. Let us emulate its methods and learn from the substance of its knowledge.
5 We must consider more fully such philosophical issues as the nature of value and the question of right values. What constitutes good or right in administrative affairs and how can administrators gain knowledge of it?
6 Questions of what constitutes good and right action in administration must be answered not simply for themselves, but in context and with specific educational issues and policies.
7 We must understand more deeply the administrative career. Who administers our schools? What motivates them to climb the ladder of administration? What happens to them as they do? What routes lead upward? In the recent past, there was truth in the dictum: women teach and men administer. What made that dictum true? Is there a better truth and how may it be realized? What are the consequences of these truths

for women and for men, and how do they shape the organizations we understand as schools?

8 We need to understand the existential realities of leading and following in organizations. We need to understand the wielding of power and the making of decisions when much is on the line. And we need to appreciate what it is to suffer the decisions of such power.

This is a minimal agenda for research but it stands in contrast with much of what has gone before. If we could achieve it only partially, we would have some basis to say a valid and valuable science of administration is emerging.

NOTES

1 I will refer to the 1957 edition and use the valuable perspective that Simon's 'Introduction to the Second Edition' provides to *Administrative Behavior*. The year 1957 marks also the beginning of 'New Movement' science in educational administration and Campbell and Gregg's, *Administrative Behavior in Education* that does homage to Simon. See the discussion beginning at p. 196.

2 Perhaps seeing language itself as the problem, the editors of *EAQ* recently announced a prohibition on first person pronouns. Ironically they chose to begin their battle against the subjectivism of the world in a text dealing with *ethnographic intent.* So they extirpated 'I', 'me', and 'my' from Wolcott (1985) whose text thereby suffered a sea-change.

3 The attitude of the time is seen in Marland's deferential reference to 'scientist Halpin' (Campbell and Lipham, 1960, 34). For further comment from Superintendent Marland, see p. 154.

4 Among the many who call for better technique to shore up the sagging science of administration, see Willower (1979; 1980), Hoy (1982), Fields (1985), and Haller and Knapp (1985). Implicitly they defend the assumptions Simon made about appropriate theory and methods, though they never invoke his name.

5 I use 'Science' to denote the narrower, but imperial enquiry that claims objectivity and value-neutrality and that stands in contrast to the broader search for reliable knowledge that characterizes all enquiry (Schumacher, 1977).

6 For example, Hoy and Miskel (1982).

7 In a text devoted wholly to theory in educational administration, Silver (1983) devotes not even a footnote to the controversies that have shaken educational administration for over a decade.

8 These ideas are elaborated in Greenfield (1984, 147–151).

9 For further critique of this advocacy, see Riffel (1986) and Greenfield (1975; 1979/80).

10 Near one end of this continuum, there surely stands Jim Keegstra, the small-town Alberta teacher who until recently taught and examined his students on a history whose central 'facts' proved that Hitler's 'final solution' was purely a hoax perpetrated by Jewish conspiracy.

REFERENCES

Barnard, C. 1938. *The Functions of the Executive.* Cambridge: Harvard.

Bates, R. J. 1983a. *Educational Administration and the Management of Knowledge.* Victoria, Australia: Deakin University.

—— 1983b. 'Morale and Motivation: Myth and Morality in Educational Administration'. *Educational Administration Review* 3, 1.

—— 1985. 'Towards a Critical Practice of Educational Administration'. In *Leadership and Organizational Culture*, eds T. J. Sergiovanni and J. E. Corbally, 260–274. Urbana: University of Illinois.

Bauman, Z. 1978. *Hermeneutics and Social Science.* London: Hutchinson.

Boethius 1969. *The Consolation of Philosophy.* Trans. V. E. Watts, Harmondsworth: Penguin.

Boyd, W. L. and Crowson, R. L. 1981. 'The Changing Conception and Practice of Public School Administration'. In *Review of Research in Education*, ed. D. C. Berliner, 9: 311–373. Washington: AERA.

Callahan, R. E. 1964. 'Changing Conceptions of the Superintendency in Public Education: 1865–1964'. Fifth A. D. Simpson Lecture on Education. Cambridge, MA: New England School Development Council, Harvard Graduate School of Education.

Campbell, R. F. and Lipham, J. M., eds 1960. *Administrative Theory as a Guide to Action.* Chicago: Midwest Administration Center, University of Chicago.

Culbertson, J. 1983. 'Theory in Educational Administration: Echoes from Critical Thinkers'. *Educational Researcher* 12, 10: 15–22.

Eisener, E. W. 1983. 'Anastasia Might be Alive, but the Monarchy is Dead'. *Educational Researcher* 12, 5: 13–24.

Fields, M. W. 1985. 'Exploratory Data Analysis in Educational Administration: Tempering Methodological Advances with a Conservative Note'. *Educational Administration Quarterly* 21, 3: 247–262.

Foster, W. P. 1985. 'Towards a Critical Theory of Educational Administration'. In *Leadership and Organizational Culture*, eds T. J. Sergiovanni and J. E. Corbally, 240–259. Urbana: University of Illinois.

Giddens, A. 1976. *New Rules of Sociological Method: A Positive Critique of Interpretive Sociologies.* London: Hutchinson.

Greenfield, T. B. 1975. 'Theory about Organization: A New Perspective and Its Implications for Schools'. In *Administering Education: International Challenge*, ed. M. Hughes, 71–99. London: Athlone.

—— 1978. 'Reflections on Organization Theory and the Truths of Irreconcilable Realities'. *Educational Administration Quarterly* 14, 2: 1–23.

—— 1979/80. 'Research in Educational Administration in the United States and Canada: An Overview and Critique'. *Educational Administration* 8, 1: 207–245.

—— 1980. 'The Man Who Comes Back through the Door in the Wall: Discovering Truth, Discovering Self, Discovering Organizations'. *Educational Administration Quarterly* 16, 3: 26–59.

—— 1983. 'Against Group Mind: An Anarchistic Theory of Organization'. In *Reflective Readings in Educational Administration*, 293–301. Victoria, Australia: Deakin University.

—— 1984. 'Leaders and Schools: Willfulness and Nonnatural Order in Organizations. In *Leadership and Organizational Culture*, eds T. J. Sergiovanni and J. E. Corbally, 142-169. Urbana: University of Illinois.

—— 1985a. 'Organization Theory with a Human Face: The Search for Lost Values and the Disappeared Individual'. Paper presented to the Annual Conference of the Canadian Society for the Study of Education, Montreal.

—— 1985b. 'Theories of Educational Organization: A Critical Perspective'. In *International Encyclopedia of Education: Research and Studies*, eds T. Husén and T. N. Postlethwaite, 9: 5240–5251. Oxford: Pergamon.

Griffiths, D. E. 1979. 'Intellectual Turmoil in Educational Administration'. *Educational Administration Quarterly* 15, 3: 43–65.

Gronn, P. C. 1982. 'Neo-Taylorism in Educational Administration?' *Educational Administration Quarterly* 18, 4: 17–35.

—— 1983. *Rethinking Educational Administration: T. B. Greenfield and his Critics.* Victoria, Australia: Deakin University.

—— 1984. 'On Studying Administrators at Work'. *Educational Administration Quarterly* 20, 1: 115–129.

—— 1985. 'After T. B. Greenfield, Whither Educational Administration?' *Educational Management and Administration* 13: 55–61.

—— 1986a. 'Choosing a Deputy Head: The Rhetoric and the Reality of Administrative Selection'. *Australian Journal of Education* 30, 1: 1–22.

—— 1986b. *The Psycho-social Dynamics of Leading and Following.* Victoria, Australia: Deakin University.

—— 1987. 'Notes on Leader Watching'. In *Ways and Meanings of Research in Educational Administration*, ed. R. J. S. Macpherson, 99–114. Armidale, N.S.W.: University of New England.

Haire, M., ed. 1959. *Modern Organization Theory.* New York: Wiley.

Haller, E. J. and Knapp, T. R. 1985. 'Problems and Methodology in Educational Administration'. *Educational Administration Quarterly* 21, 3: 157–168.

Halpin, A. W., ed. 1958. *Administrative Theory in Education.* Chicago: Midwest Administration Center, University of Chicago.

Halpin, A. W. 1966. *Theory and Research in Administration.* New York: Macmillan.

—— 1970. 'Administrative Theory: The Fumbled Torch'. In *Issues in American Education*, ed. A. M. Kroll, 156–183. New York: Oxford.

Hodgkinson, C. 1978a. 'The Failure of Organizational and Administrative Theory'. *McGill Journal of Education* 13, 3: 271–278.

—— 1978b. *Towards a Philosophy of Administration.* Oxford: Basil Blackwell.

—— 1983. *The Philosophy of Leadership.* Oxford: Basil Blackwell.

—— 1985. 'Confucius, Wittgenstein, and the Perplexing World of Administration'. Lecture, Ontario Institute for Studies in Education, Toronto.

—— 1988. 'The Value Bases of Administrative Action'. *Journal of Educational Administration and Foundations* 3, 1: 20–30.

Hoy, Wayne K. 1982. 'Recent Developments in Theory and Research in Educational Administration'. *Educational Administration Quarterly*, 18, 3: 1–11.

Hoy, W. K. and Miskel, C. G. 1982. *Educational Administration: Theory, Research, and Practice,* 2nd edn New York: Random House.

Huxley, A. 1977 [1954]. *The Doors of Perception.* Frogmore, England: Triad/Panther.

Khleif, B. B. 1975. 'Professionalization of School Superintendents: A Sociocultural Study of an Elite Program'. *Human Organization* 34, 3: 301–308.

Lakomski, G. 1984. 'On Agency and Structure: Pierre Bourdieu and Jean-Claude Passeron's Theory of Symbolic Violence'. *Curriculum Inquiry* 14, 2: 151–163.

—— 1985. 'Theory, Value, and Relevance in Educational Administration'. In *Working Papers in Ethics and Educational Administration*, ed. Fazal Rizvi, 35–64. Victoria, Australia: Deakin University.

—— 1987a. 'Critical Theory and Educational Administration: Problems and Solutions'. *Journal of Educational Administration* 25, 1.

—— 1987b. 'The Cultural Perspective in Educational Administration'. In *Ways and Meanings of Research in Educational Administration*, ed. R. J. S. Macpherson, 115–138. Armidale, Australia: University of New England.

Macpherson, R. J. S., ed. 1987. *Ways and meanings of research in educational administration.* Teaching Monograph Series 5. Armidale, Australia: University of New England.

March, J. G., ed. 1965. *Handbook of Organizations.* Chicago: Rand McNally.

Phillips, D. C. 1983. 'After the Wake: Postpositivistic Educational Thought'. *Educational Researcher* 12, 5: 4–12.

Rabinow, P. and Sullivan, W. M. eds. 1979. *Interpretive Social Science: A Reader.* Berkeley: University of California.

Ramos, A. G. 1981. *The New Science of Organizations: A Reconstruction of the Wealth of Nations.* Toronto: University of Toronto.

Riffel, J. A. 1986. 'The Study of Educational Administration: A Developmental Point of View'. *Journal of Educational Administration* 24, 2: 152–172.

Schumacher, E. F. 1977. *A Guide for the Perplexed.* New York: Harper and Row.

Scott, W. G. 1985. 'Organizational Revolution: An end to Managerial Orthodoxy'. *Administration and Society* 17, 2: 149–170.

Scott, W. G. and Hart, D. 1979. *Organizational America.* Boston: Houghton Mifflin.

Silver, P. 1983. *Educational Administration: Theoretical Perspectives on Practice and Research.* New York: Harper and Row.

Simon, H. 1957 [1945]. *Administrative Behavior: A Study of Decision-making Process in Administrative Organization,* 2nd edn. New York: The Free Press.

Szasz, T. 1976. *Heresies.* Garden City, NY: Anchor/Doubleday.

Tipton, B. F. A. 1985. 'Educational Organizations as Workplaces'. *British Journal of Educational Sociology* 6, 1: 35–53.

Tope, D. E. *et al.* 1965. *The Social Sciences View Educational Administration.* Englewood-Cliffs, NJ: Prentice Hall.

Toulmin, S. 1981. 'The Emergence of Post-modern Science'. In *The Great Ideas Today,* eds R. M. Hutchins and M. J. Adler, 69–114. Chicago: Encyclopedia Britannica.

—— 1983. 'From Observer to Participant: The Transformation of Twentieth Century Science'. Lecture, University of Toronto.

Willower, D. J. 1979. 'Ideology and Science in Organization Theory'. *Educational Administration Quarterly* 15, 3: 20–42.

—— 1980. 'Contemporary Issues in Theory in Educational Administration'. *Educational Administration Quarterly* 16, 3: 1–25.

—— 1985. 'Philosophy and the Study of Educational Administration'. *Journal of Educational Administration* 23, 1: 7–22.

Wolcott, H. 1985. 'On Ethnographic Intent'. *Educational Administration Quarterly* 21, 3: 187–203.

8

ON HODGKINSON'S *MORAL ART*[1]

The distinguishing feature of the writings of Christopher Hodgkinson is that they place administration in a clear – even painfully sharp – focus. This book continues in the path pioneered in two earlier works. And so it takes up the old themes of what constitutes justice in the ordering of human affairs and what constitutes honour in administrative action: themes that scientific management of the modern era deliberately turned its back upon. Lest any think that the errors of scientific management are buried, consider that that movement is transformed in contemporary thought and continues to flourish under the more acceptable name, management science. This is the science of measured excellence with its obsessive fixation upon the technocratic and the spuriously rational – including the erroneously named 'bottom line' and the pervasive, but speciously precise rules for effectiveness, leadership, change, and implementation. The shallowness of these nostrums is revealed if one asks, 'Effectiveness for what, leadership towards what, change to what good purpose, and implementation of whose values, and with what justification?'

Hodgkinson's world turns on the fundamentals of administration: the application of power, the shaping of people and organizations, the search for better values, the making of choices, and the unending quest for and questioning of the justification of the administrator's power and choices. His work lets us see the administrator and the administrative act full and fair, and often warts and all. Not infrequently the insight he affords into the heart of administration – for that is where he leads the reader – is a glimpse into the heart of darkness. It lets us see administrators and administration in agonized or repelling conditions. To read Hodgkinson is to consider questions for which there are no easy answers. To read him is to work; it is to think hard thoughts and to look at things painful to bear. The strong and the compassionate, however, will see the relevance of this work, the truth of the realities described, and their force in everyday administrative affairs. They will acknowledge the need to face these issues frankly and without sentimentality or self-deception. Although Hodgkinson does not provide recipes for success, nor yet a prescription for 'effectiveness', he does show that administration can never become good in any meaningful moral sense until theorists and practitioners alike are willing to regard the depths of power-driven choice, the uncertainties inherent in them, and the ensuing responsibilities that fall upon themselves. Through his eyes, the reader sees administration in all its complexity, in its potential to thwart, injure, and destroy, but ultimately – and this is the justification for the difficult journey – in its power to attain the good, to redeem, improve, and fulfil.

To those who know the history and substance of science in the modern field – whose beginning is marked by the publication of Simon's *Administrative Behavior* in 1945 and by the emergence and early triumph of the 'theory movement' in educational administration a decade later,[2] it is apparent that Hodgkinson offers ideas that stand in sharp contrast to the accepted professional and academic wisdom. Where the thrust of the modern field offers science and certainty – and ultimately release from responsibility through technical correctness – Hodgkinson offers choice, responsibility, and the search for honour and rectitude; he offers art and morality in place of science and certainty.

His way is not for everyone. It runs profoundly against the intellectual temper of the times in administrative studies. And for this reason, some readers find his writing abstruse or perversely complex. Much of this apparent difficulty is a consequence of his reaching beyond and writing through the modern field to retrieve ancient ideas; he pierces to truths that challenge the received wisdom of the contemporary field. If there is difficulty in reading Hodgkinson, it arises from the unfamiliarity of his vision. The source of this alienation lies not in Hodgkinson, but in the contemporary field itself that happily and consciously turned its back on wisdom both ancient and modern to embrace an invention of recent times: the science of administration. So completely has the modern, pseudo-scientific approach – for that is what it is – denied its past that James March writing about organizations in 1965 could pronounce any idea of an origin earlier than 1950 to be 'old' and largely irrelevant to the newly promulgated science.[3] Such a judgement, reflecting the now widely accepted verdict of the field, shuts out the older wisdom that is the very essence of the matters explored by Hodgkinson. In contrast to this judgement, Hodgkinson deals with the simple, central, and appallingly plain Platonic questions, 'Who shall rule?' and 'With what justification?' It is this absence of the ancient but compelling questions in contemporary administrative thought that sets Hodgkinson's work apart. However authentically it comes finally to ring, his voice is often heard first as alien and difficult, though we may think it so only as long as we resist the fundamental questions he requires us to ask and only so long as we deny the truth of images he bids us regard.

The imaginations of those who propelled the 'Theory Movement' in educational administration to its current dominant position were fired by a potent and seductive promise: the promise that rigorous theory would take the guesswork out of administration and put it on a scientific foundation. Like an engineer approaching the draining of a swamp or the building of a bridge to span a river, the social scientist came to administration to set it right, to solve all its problems scientifically and rationally. It is not surprising therefore that after an initial resistance, administrators embraced the science, for it offered them certainty in their choices while absolving them of responsibility for them. Superintendent Marland, one of the early converts following the annunciation of a 'science of administration', records that he 'listen[ed] attentively to the counsel of social scientists'. Strengthened by this radical knowledge, he came to understand the newly science-supported administrators through the metaphor of the bush pilot who

> now finds himself in the pilot's chair of a monstrous flying machine of untold power and dimensions. The social scientist tells us that there are buttons to push, levers to adjust, gauges to watch, beacons to reckon, and codes to decipher. He tells us that one cannot fly this craft by the seat of the pants, but that certain buttons and levers, when actuated, produce specific and predictable results in the performance and posture of the craft.[4]

The early joy of Superintendent Marland finds a more sophisticated and restrained expression among administrators today, but they no doubt see even more clearly the advantage of taking shelter under the certainty and authority promised by administrative science. Anyone who doubts this spirit prevails in the contemporary field need only refer to the popular text whose authors have dedicated it in three editions over recent years to the conviction that administrative practice in education can be 'less of an art and more of a science'.[5]

Not for these social scientists and administrators the observation of Blaise Pascal: 'The heart has reasons, reason knows nothing of.' The error most theorists make in thinking about organizations and the administration of them is to conceive them as somehow separate from life, love, sex, growth, conflict, accomplishment, decay, death and chance. The exclusion of values from administrative science, the exclusion of both the human and the humane, the exclusion of passion and conviction in all their frailty and perseverance, in all their power and majesty does leave a residue for study – and one that is perhaps scientifically manageable. The most obvious consequence of this exclusion leaves a field that is regrettably and unnecessarily bland and boring. The difficult and divisive questions, the questions of purpose and morality, the questions arising from the necessary imposition of one person's will upon another, the questions that challenge the linking of ends and means – all these matters are set aside in a search for a pallid consensus and an illusory effectiveness. The great issues of the day in education are similarly set aside: how big the school, who should be in it, embracing what behaviours or convictions, reading and learning what, using what facilities, paid for by whom, to what ends and purposes? And so many familiar, but urgent, issues are elided: bussing, multiculturalism, bilingualism, streaming, equal opportunity, drugs, sexuality, allegiance, community and personal morality, excellence in any profound sense, prayer, religion, the state, and ultimately the economic wellbeing and survival of the culture.

Not that Hodgkinson addresses these issues directly or in detail, for his purpose is to make the case that these problems are valuational, educational, and administrative, and must be approached as such. Without applying them himself, he offers the tools by which these problems may be addressed and resolved, as in the following propositions from an earlier work:

> The [administrator] must know two things: where the values are and where the power lies.
>
> The lure of efficiency leads to the fallacy of quantification. Some costs and some ends are non-quantifiable. True accounting is always incomplete.
>
> Valuation precedes rationality. One can only be rational within the limits set by value.
>
> First order valuation is the identification and analysis of the values in a case.
>
> Second order valuation is the determination of the values to be used in trying the case.
>
> Motives are sources of value. They may be in the dark or in the light. In the first case they push us and we call them drives, in the second they pull us and we call them reasons.[6]

Thirty years ago Andrew Halpin warned that the social scientific portrait of administration is egregiously, if not fatally flawed. At its heart it is vacuous, jejune:

> There is indeed something missing. The fault is that the scientist's theoretical models of administration are too rational, too tidy, too aseptic. They remind us of the photographs in magazines devoted to home decorating – glossy pictures of dramatic and pristine living room interiors. . . . The superintendent distrusts such tidiness in administrative theory and senses intuitively that the theoretical–analytical approach has ignored much that is reality.[7]

Such science rests on illusory and therefore dangerous images. It cleanses what is impure only by denying the impurity, the very problem to be faced and resolved.

When his novels were criticized for their portrayal of darkness and immorality in human relationships – in today's parlance they would be called 'negative' – Thomas Hardy replied that 'to know the best, we must first regard the worst'. It is that unwillingness to look at the dark side of the human condition that prevents administrative science from dealing with the heart of administrative problems and also from ascending to the heights of human possibility and accomplishment. So Hodgkinson reminds us that values in all their possibility and accomplishment are to be contemplated and the better of them striven for. He reminds us – and requires us – to think there are choices to be made and responsibilities to be assumed.

Hodgkinson points to the errors of the putative science of administration: first that its focus of enquiry is organization theory, *not* administration, *not* 'administration *qua* administration' – the essence of administration, as the early proponents of the theory movement liked to put the matter. Organization theory is at best an analysis of the background factors that bear upon administrative choice, decision, and responsibility. It says nothing about the choice and the decision to be made, nor the responsibility to be assumed. Second, Hodgkinson points out that the reason the science of administration – or organizations – does not work is stupefyingly simple: the central problems of administrative theory are not scientific at all, but philosophical. That is, the central questions of administration deal not so much with what is, but with what ought to be; they deal with values and morality. As Hodgkinson points out, administrative science must be silent about the issues that lie at the heart of administrative action: 'No science, social or physical, can tell us what is right or wrong.'[8] To repair this deficiency, to regain necessary knowledge about administration, much needs doing. The task is difficult. To attempt it, some old, but underused tools turn out to be the most reliable and powerful: first, clear-eyed description, a mapping of the administrative world as it is, secondly, reflection upon that world, and finally, argument about what to do. These avenues to knowledge are restored to dialogue in the work that follows.

Hodgkinson restores a vision of administration. His title lays out the central issue. Administration is a *moral art*. He offers a vision of what administration is and of what it might become. It *is* a matter of will and power: of bending others to one's will and of being bent in turn by others. The overlap between education and administration is therefore substantial and unavoidable, if education is recognized as being the process of identifying the valuable, opening it to others and, yes, inculcating it into them. Moreover, the Hodgkinsonian vision of administration as a moral task redeems the notion of hierarchy and thereby of leadership. Everyone wants the good, at least for themselves, at best for others as well. Everyone therefore opposes evil – or what is less good – and supports the mobilization of power against it. A hierarchy of the good is therefore inevitable, as is the demand to ground it in an authority and to further it through leadership.

Hodgkinson's view of administration allows us to see in new directions, towards the world of the valuable, the right, the justified. The answers he offers are as much questions as answers. But there is a uniquely practical – or one might better say praxical quality to this work, for it considers not only the problems of administration in their general forms. He moves beyond theory into praxis, into the specific, into the politics of day-to-day living and their justification; he speaks to the mundane, but inevitable and *valuable* question of how to get through the day; ultimately he speaks also to the question of how to make one's way through a career, through a life.

There is a quality of transparency in this work. It evokes 'other voices, other rooms'. It leads to other realms of thought and experience. Asked what constituted the quality of great teachers, Northrop Frye replied, 'They are transparent', by which he said they give access to the subject and to the writers they teach. They evoke the idea itself and the person who advances it. The novelist, Margaret Atwood, recalls what happened as Frye taught, the power of his words, his vision: 'He said, "Let there be Milton, and there was Milton."' Hodgkinson's work too has this quality of greatness in its power to evoke greatness. When an interviewer nagged Frye to square his observation of the transparency of the teacher with the conventional view that great teachers are remembered as 'personalities', Frye pointed out it is the denial of ego that creates the true and memorable personality. This theme runs also though the Hodkinsonian vision of the nature of administration and of the great administrator. 'Desire', he observes, 'is satisfied by *its* extinction, the desirable by *my* extinction, that is, by loss of ego in the nomothetic domain.'[9] In such sharp and arresting paradoxes, he lets us hear the voices of the past, of those whose achievements bear so profoundly on a sound understanding of administration and of the dilemmas of the administrator today. Simon, Barnard, Machiavelli, Plato and the insights of the great religions are evoked through his pages. Recognizing the ancient Greek contribution to an understanding of morality in social and personal life, Erasmus, the great humanist, could pray, '*Sancte Socrate, ora pro nobis*'.[10] And so may we all, recognizing in '*St. Socrates, pray for us*' that the problems of life, politics, and administration are ancient and that human insight has already done much to see a way through them. Certainly it had done much before 1937, the arbitrary cut-off point March set as the date before which administrative science had nothing to learn from the past. Setting the clock of organization theory – the foundation of administrative science – in motion at 1937, March could call anything written before 1950 the 'old' literature. Yet even this literature he considered only through the filter of its 'fashionableness', its acceptability to the new breed of organization theorists.[11]

Hodgkinson redresses this reckless short-sightedness. Blended now with contemporary assertion, we hear again the ancient voices and their wisdom. And much does he add to those voices: first, the foundation of value in the personal and its extension into the interests of the organization, secondly insight into how one value can be better than another and where the conflicts among them lie, and finally a vision of what constitutes right action – honour – in administration and what might make it possible to attain. Hodgkinson's enormous contributions to the field of study can be discovered by any reader willing to reflect upon the experience of administering or being administered. But to follow the way he shows requires courage and resolution – more for the wayfarer than the reader – for it entails clear-eyed observation of the realities, dilemmas, difficulties, and defeats of life. Only along this path and by right action on it may a better life – and better organizations – be attained. In short, Hodgkinson is the antidote to scientism and specious science in the study of administration. His work is gateway to the world of values – its complexities, its dilemmas, and its unrelenting challenge to attain what is good, the challenge for us to be better administrators, to do better for our ourselves and for our organizations, to make ourselves better and to strive for a better world.

NOTES

1 Christopher Hodgkinson, *Educational Leadership: The Moral Art* (Albany: SUNY Press, 1991).
2 Jack Culbertson, 'Theory in Educational Administration: Echoes from Critical Thinkers', *Educational Researcher*, 12, 10 (1983): 15–22.
3 James G. March, ed., *Handbook of Organizations* (Chicago: Rand McNally, 1965), xii.
4 R. F. Campbell and J. M. Lipham, eds, *Administrative Theory as a Guide to Action* (Chicago: Midwest Administration Center, University of Chicago, 1960) 24.
5 W. K. Hoy and C. G. Miskel, *Educational Administration: Theory, Research, and Practice*, 3rd edn (New York: Random House, 1987) iii.
6 Christopher Hodgkinson, *Towards a Philosophy of Administration* (Oxford: Basil Blackwell, 1978), 203–221.
7 Andrew W. Halpin, 'Ways of Knowing' [1960], collected in *Theory and Research in Administration* (New York: Macmillan, 1966) 284.
8 Hodgkinson, *Towards a Philosophy of Administration*, 146.
9 Ibid., 215.
10 Marcello Craveri, *The Life of Christ* (New York: Ecco, 1966), 188.
11 March, *Handbook of Organizations*, xi.

9

RE-FORMING AND RE-VALUING EDUCATIONAL ADMINISTRATION

Whence and when cometh the phoenix?[1]

The fundamental problem in knowing and understanding social reality is what place values shall play in the enquiry. For nearly two decades this question has troubled the theory and knowledge promulgated in the field of educational administration. While some proponents (Pitner, 1988; Willower, 1988; Greene, Caracelli, and Graham, 1989) would by fiat or simplistic analogy declare the issue settled and dead, others (Bates, 1989; Hodgkinson, 1988, 1990; Smith and Blase, 1989) show that it continues – puissant, troubling, and profoundly revolutionary in its implications for the conduct of research and training in the field. The issue runs far wider than educational administration and calls into question, as Geertz (1980, 178) points out, the putative objectivity and universality of all the social sciences.

> A challenge is being mounted to some of the central assumptions of mainstream social science. The strict separation of theory and data, the 'brute fact' idea; the effort to create a formal vocabulary of analysis purged of all subjective reference, the 'ideal language' idea; and the claim to moral neutrality and the Olympian view, the 'God's truth' idea – none of these can prosper when explanation comes to be regarded as a matter of connecting action to its sense rather than behavior to its determinants.

Ultimately, of course, it is the science in social science that comes into question. Recognizing the value bases of administrative action utterly transforms the standard and previously accepted view of the field, as Hodgkinson (1978b, 59) has shown: 'The intrusion of values into the decision making process is not merely inevitable, it is the very substance of decision.'[2] Taking the value dimension meaningfully into account, as does Bates (1989, 16), leads to a view of the field that stands in sharp contrast to almost everything that has gone before in the modern era,[3] the era in which the field conceived itself as offering universal, objective, and theory-based science:

169

> The starting point for the analysis of educational administration is that it is a *socially constructed* system of behaviour which is the result of *contestation* between social groups of unequal power in terms of such matters as, for example, *class, race and gender.* The resulting *organizational structures* can be seen as facilitating the *agency* of certain groups and limiting that of others.

The present is a time of dialectical struggle in educational administration and indeed in much of social science generally. In Griffiths's (1979) memorable phrase, the field is in 'intellectual turmoil', and has been for nearly twenty years. To some the established empiricist highroad to truth, objectivity, and control in social organization is still plain, and as sound as centuries of Enlightenment science and rationalism can make it. To others the empiricist approach is a delusionist dream, a nightmare indeed that needs exorcism to liberate and restore the human and moral perspective before the irrationality of devalued science further misleads us, as we seek to understand ourselves and human affairs. In this view the time left for restorative action may be short. Indeed, the empiricist dream – or nightmare – ultimately threatens to obliterate the human and humane understanding of life in organizations, for it elides the moral complexity that flows inevitably through administrative action. It is now widely accepted in educational administration that some form of renewal or redirection of the field is overdue and necessary. What remains in dispute is how fundamental that rebuilding should be, whether a clear break with the empiricist past is needed or whether a reassertion and improvement of established approaches and assumptions is all that is required.[4]

What seems plain is that we have a choice in reading the entrails of the ambiguity and uncertainty that everywhere prevail in the field. Almost everyone calls for a rejuvenation, for something new. But fundamental differences remain about what that newness should consist of. There are those who find a newness in a return to the proper and stringent standards already established in the scientific foundations of the modern field; there are those who see the need to transform the field utterly. Thus there are those who desire a return to the standards and promise of 'normal science' – of science as defined by logical positivism and experimental inquiry. And there are those who see a departure from the assumptions of the modern field as not only necessary, but as the only hope for the field. The issue dividing us is where to find the form and substance of the new phoenix in administrative studies. On the question of newness and how it is to be attained, T. S. Eliot's comment to D. H. Lawrence says it all: 'One can hardly have the phoenix without the ashes, can one?' Some think they see the phoenix reconstituted and already risen intact from the past, from a reassertion and strengthening of old assumptions and approaches. In contrast there are those who say that to hold on to the errors of the past ensures that nothing new can arise. Until the old field lies in ashes, we cannot conceive nor receive the phoenix in its new form.

In these circumstances, we do well first to look back at what has constituted the crisis of knowing and acting in our field over the past two decades. Second we need to look ahead to ways that offer the best prospects to take us truly forward, to bring us to moral and valued ends, not just to a fallible and mendacious technical progress.

LOOKING BACK

The controversy that has risen in educational administration about the substance of its knowledge and the means for establishing it has been a paramount issue of discussion at least since 1974. That was the year of IIP–1974[5] where I presented a paper (Greenfield, 1975) calling into question empiricism, Parsonian functionalism, logical positivism, and an erroneously objective and control-oriented rationalism as a basis for knowledge and action in educational administration. The reaction to my paper was instant and negative: I discovered in existential and personal perspective that the dedication to rationality and empiricism in educational administration represented not an objective truth about the world, but a deeply held conviction and bias that could be challenged only by putting one's self in jeopardy.

Speaking of my critique offered at Bristol in 1974, Culbertson (1988, 20) says

> [Greenfield] fired a shot at the theory movement that was heard around the world. Striking hard at the key suppositions of the theory movement, he precipitated controversy which is not yet ended. [He] stressed that organizations cannot be equated with such objective phenomena as planets and stars. Rather, organizations are social inventions, which humans construe in diverse ways. Organizations do not think, choose, or act as theories claim; rather, individuals do. Nor are organizations regulated by scientific laws; rather they are guided by human intentions and decisions. Greenfield stressed that academicians, who assume that 'social-scientific secrets' can explain 'how organizations work or how policy should be made', indulge 'at best in a premature hope and at worst in a delusion'.

That quotation is certainly a fair and insightful summary of the position I argued at Bristol and that I have been at pains (Greenfield, 1986) to defend, elaborate, and extend since then.

Like Culbertson, Griffiths (1988, 30) assesses the Bristol paper as an attack upon the theory movement in educational administration, but he sees the significance and implications of the critique in sharply different terms:

171

> While the theory movement had been in decline for a number of years . . . the demise came at the 1974 meeting of the International Intervisitation Programme (IIP) in Bristol, England. The coup de grace was delivered by Greenfield who made an across-the-board denunciation of every aspect of the theory movement. . . . The major thrust of Greenfield's critique is . . . epistemological. The first sentence of the published version of Greenfield's Bristol speech is the basic theme of his critique: 'In common parlance we speak of organizations as if they were real'. He then attempts to demonstrate that such is not the case and contends that organizations are 'invented social reality'.

Griffiths (1988, 30–31) then goes on to make a point of special importance in the contemporary context.

> The Greenfield critique has been hailed in the British Commonwealth countries and largely ignored in the United States. Probably the major reason why Greenfield did not catch on in the United States is that his arguments are too extreme and too inclusive. Further, there is no consistent line of argument in his papers except an attack on the theory movement. In addition, his work has resulted in little, if any, empirical research. Ignoring the critique is unfortunate because what Greenfield did was to tell professors of educational administration that the social sciences are undergoing tremendous changes and that the philosophical and methodological bases on which the theory movement was founded (logical positivism) are now considered by most philosophers of science, and many social scientists, to be outmoded.

Griffiths thus reveals a profound ambivalence about the critique – deploring the consequences of ignoring it, but at the same time justifying the fact that as far as American theorists and researchers are concerned it 'did not catch on'. Indeed, my critique of educational administration is better known and more widely appreciated elsewhere than in the United States and Canada. For example Gronn (1983) saw what began at Bristol as a promise for 'rethinking educational administration'. These disparate reactions make a point in the sociology of knowledge: whatever value scholars elsewhere find in my work, the lens of appreciation used by many of my American and Canadian colleagues brings a 'sea change' to my critique – but not a change 'into something rich and strange'. Their lens does not so much change and transvalue what it sees, but rather obscures and obliterates it. Thus such 'foreign' comment as my work has drawn, for example Johnson (1990), hardly enters into the phenomenological reality of scholars in what I have come to call the 'Mother Church' of educational administration.

The phoenix and no ashes?

To understand what is at stake in allowing values a place in the study of organizations and administration, it is instructive to return to the claims of early theory in the field. In his review of the theoretical models developed by Jacob Getzels and others, Lipham (1988, 175) makes clear that these models constitute 'a landmark in the application of social-science theories to education'. In his view, the models provide a set of formulaic and law-like statements to describe, explain, and potentially control all of human behaviour in organizations.

> Behavior in a social system, therefore, results from the interaction between a given institutional role, defined by the expectations attached to it, and the personality of a particular role incumbent, defined by one's need-dispositions; it can be represented by the general equation $B = f(R \times P)$. (Lipham, 1988, 174)

But as Hodgkinson (1983) points out, the tensions between the nomothetic and the idiographic are the tensions between the demands of society and the actions of individuals. The working out of such tensions is the consequence of action by human agents, all of which is chosen, imposed, and existential. Thus it must be seen that the integration of nomothetic expectations and idiographic action requires a judgemental *resolution* of social and personal tensions, not a *calculation* of objective and independent forces. Such a resolution is created and mandated in a dramaturgical and political context where

> the task of the executive is thus revealed as one of reconciliation, reconciliation of organization to society and organization members towards organizational goals, reconciliation of individual and increasingly large collective interests, reconciliations which can, of course, be static or dynamic, creative or uninspired, divisive or harmonious, synergetic or degenerative. (Hodgkinson, 1983, 23)

> Lipham (1988, 181) rejects criticism that Getzels's models ignore 'the very stuff of the humanness of human beings . . ., [their] hates, loves, fears, aspirations, symbols, values, perceptions'. All this he argues is included in the models. What he fails to understand is that such realities make impos- sible the very calculation of behaviour by formula that is claimed as the models' great achievement. What the proponents of the models do to bring in 'the humanness of human beings' is to make value statements that are denied to be value statements. Instead they are introduced as merely fixed background conditions, as largely immutable contextual factors. This split- ting of values from facts permits a view of the organization as objectified and rational. Thus Getzels, Lipham, and Campbell (1968, 134) claim the

models make possible a technical superiority in administrators' decisions, for in their view the models express and mirror the putative rationality of the organization as a whole:

[The educational administrator's] dominance . . . is based on superior knowledge and technical competence in a particular element in the division of labor. The administrator's claim to obedience – or perhaps better here, to cooperation – ideally finds its root in . . . rationality. He has the technical training and the competence to allocate and integrate the roles, personnel, and facilities required for attaining the goals of the system.

That the force and function of values is *exogenous* to the dynamics dealt with in the model is seen in the understanding of values offered in a statement by Guba and Bidwell (1957, 75). Drawing on Talcott Parsons' 'suggestions for a sociological approach to the study of organization', they explain,

Parsons . . . suggests that a major function of the institutional value system is to provide an operating code for decision-making. Values, he suggests, form a structure for administrative and staff decision. In this case the institutional value system would seem to set the limits to the exercise of individual discretion in that the assignment of particular decision-making functions to a given role is itself determined in large part by the nature of the institutional values.

The disguised moral dimension of Getzels's models is made even more plain in a statement by Guba (1960, 126) about the dynamics of integration and equilibrium that the models assume. Following 'a brief review of the historical phases through which scientific administration passed' (p. 114) and after making the statement (p. 120) that 'the science of administration may . . . be viewed as a science of managing behaviour', Guba asserts that in an organization

the integrating forces are posited by logical necessity. . . . We note that in an organization we have a system in equilibrium – people fulfill their roles and continue in their appointed rounds. But there are alienating forces which militate against this equilibrium. Ergo, there must exist other integrating forces which tend to hold the system together. Their nature is no great mystery. After all the persons involved in any common enterprise would rarely be so different from one another or so uncommitted to the general goals of the enterprise that the only force keeping them involved in the organizational activities is the presence of such tangible rewards as the weekly pay envelope. Certainly this is true of the educational enterprise, where deep commitment and unselfish devotion have long been a part of the cultural image of the teaching profession, an image shared by teachers themselves. The administrator who can sense such common commitments and values, or who can develop them where none exist, thereby enlists a powerful ally without whose aid the task of maintaining an integrated organization is almost impossibly difficult.

Defenders of normal science make a noteworthy response to the news that the presence of incalculable values negate their putatively objective and calculable theory of organization. They offer a twofold answer to the difficulty. First they call for an expansion of the repertoire of the techniques of observation to include qualitative methods, thought to be the appropriate ones for dealing with values, and secondly they seek the incorporation of qualitative methods within the assumptions of quantitative and statistical analysis. For example, after reviewing powerful arguments against the mixing of methods from incompatible paradigms of enquiry, Greene, Caracelli, and Graham (1989, 257) set aside all such fundamental problems and argue for a pragmatic mix-and-match combination of methods that gets the job done. And so they conclude that

> The practical demands of the problem are primary: inquirer flexibility and adaptiveness are needed to determine what will work best for a given problem. Or, in the pragmatic view of Miles and Huberman, epistemological purity does not get the research done.

Nor, it may be presumed, does epistemological purity bring in the consulting fees and institutional funding.

In a similar approach, Pitner (1988) reviews methodologically diverse studies and finds it easy to incorporate them all into a linear model of 'administrator effects and effectiveness'. Pausing to consider whether such a combination of methods is theoretically sound, Pitner resolves any conflict by conceptualizing qualitative methods as a kind of lower level or approximate empiricism into which body of objective truth the softer methods can ultimately be fitted. Quoting a solution to the value problem appearing in the *Academy of Management Review*, Pitner (1988, 119) accepts the argument of Morey and Luthans:

> In brief, they call for objectifying subjective data and producing quantifiable data for traditional techniques of statistical analysis. Their position squares with the suggestion to move beyond either tolerance of or advocacy for qualitative methods in favor of support for the enhanced use of multiple design and analytic designs.

To those who think this solution may be unsatisfactory theoretically, Pitner closes her review by evoking the illusionist art of M. C. Escher. Pitner finds support for her position with an analogy to an Escher graphic that reveals a woodland pond as 'Three Worlds'. Thus she offers that work as evidence

175

that mixed methodologies can indeed meet the joint demands for factual objectivity and value freedom in social action. Referring to the graphic, Pitner argues that 'using the water's surface as a mirror, Escher creates a more complete view of the pond than direct observation might yield'. And so, she leaves us to think, pragmatically mixed methods subsumed within statistical assumptions can provide objective and scientific solutions to leadership problems that are deeply value driven. If only the answer were so easily found in an artistic image! Even if such an answer were readily available in this way, it is inconceivable that any such image should displace the force of values with statistical analysis.

That we have at hand a reborn phoenix of administration capable of dealing with all its epistemological and methodological problems without prior ashes is the position taken by Willower. Or rather what Willower asserts in his synthesis of the *Handbook of Research on Educational Administration* is that the old phoenix is still in good shape: it just needs polishing. In his concluding judgement, Willower (1988, 730) holds that the phoenix is intact without ashes, its inbuilt self-correcting mechanisms assuring us that empiricism is not only the best road to truth, it is the only way.

> The norms of enquiry stress the provisional character of ideas and results and the self-corrective nature of science. Hence, inquiry and change are close companions, for a field of study that values inquiry continually seeks new and perhaps better ways of conceiving its subject matter. . . . Now there is not only an applied social science called educational administration, but it has spawned a number of specializations and subspecializations. The *Handbook* is a splendid reflection of that situation.

That a field of scientific enquiry *committed* to an open truth seeking must rest on moral judgements upheld by human fiat, not by rationality or science, is a consideration inconsistent with and therefore ignored, as Willower declares his faith in a self-correcting applied social science of administration. His phoenix is simply the old bird, polished and reasserted.

Parsing the paradigms

The flaw that surely sinks Willower's summation and endorsement of administrative science is his rejection of the notion that paradigmatic boundaries define and separate sets of assumptions and that these modes of enquiry are quite inconsistent and incompatible with each other. This easy denial of conflicting modes of enquiry is a widely held position in the field. It is used to support a pragmatic eclecticism in methodology, an approach to enquiry that Griffiths (1988, 45) acknowledges and tacitly endorses, calling it 'paradigm diversity':

> The idea is emerging that research on organizations should not be restricted to a single paradigm; rather research should proceed in all four (more or less) paradigms.

The mischief worked by this view has already been argued above: it encourages the researcher not just to select a paradigm, but to make a patchwork melding of divergent methodologies and conflicting epistemological assumptions. Ultimately it reasserts, as is seen in Pitner's and Willower's arguments, the dominance of the empiricist paradigm of enquiry.

Those who see no fundamental conflicts among the paradigms take the strategic position that the challenge of alternative assumptions can best be met by denying they constitute anything different from that which has gone before in 'normal science'. According to Willower (1988, 743–744) the paradigms simply do not exist. Dismissing Kuhn's *The Structure of Scientific Revolutions*, he reports that Kuhn's use of the concept of paradigm is 'not without ambiguity'. He asserts that the real meaning of paradigm is found in its Greek roots, meaning simply 'pattern, example, or model'. This view leads him to conclude that the meaning of paradigm is adequately conveyed by the concept of theory: 'It does not seem appropriate to talk about paradigm shifts in the sense of a world view or in the sense of the fundamental redirection of a discipline by a new theory and its associated methodology.' Willower's appreciation of the power of paradigms as argued by Kuhn is not shared by Bernstein (1988, 52) who sees the ultimate fate of fundamental scientific ideas as socially determined.

> With elegant conciseness William James described 'the classic stages of a theory's career. First, you know, a new theory is attacked as absurd; then it is admitted to be true, but obvious and insignificant; finally it is seen to be so important that its adversaries claim that they themselves discovered it'. Something like this has already occurred with the theory advanced by Thomas Kuhn. . . . The reaction to the book by its critics was immediate and sharp; Kuhn's leading ideas were absurd, contradictory, and wrong. It was even suggested that they were immoral and irrational. His views were caricatured and ridiculed. After the first flurry of heated polemic, calmer voices came to his defense and argued that although not without difficulties and ambiguities, many of his theses were warranted – though some said that what was true in Kuhn was 'obvious and insignificant'.

In the field of administrative and organization studies, the concept of paradigm has been given some currency by Burrell and Morgan (1979), but their understanding of the concept is inserted with Procrustean force into the familiar 2 × 2 table of orthogonal Cartesian dimensions. The result places new and disturbing ideas within a framework congenial to empiricists who may thereby take comfort in the familiar form. But this fourfold conceptualization is otherwise unfortunate, for it diverts attention from the conceptual differences among the paradigms and places it upon a structure of simplistic and ambiguous dimensionality where complex and diverse notions are forced into an artificial and ill-fitting unity. Griffiths (1988, 42) is among those who work to give currency to Burrell and Morgan's presentation of the paradigms. But in an earlier writing where he referred to the 'intellectual turmoil' of the field, he does more to convey the notion of paradigm by quoting Perrow's insightful comment:

> Since I am still very much a mainstream theorist, the reader should bear with me in the quite painful process of trying to think oneself out of a paradigm one has lived with, even contributed to. It is difficult to think that one's work on, say, goals or technology, while not wrong in any normal sense, is largely irrelevant in the face of notions that were dimly recognized but put aside. (Perrow quoted in Griffiths, 1979, 44)

In his own exegesis of the intellectual turmoil in educational adminis- tration, Griffiths goes on to say that Perrow's phrase, 'think oneself out of', is 'central' to his own article. And thus he appreciates the force of the *moral* difference between normal and revolutionary paradigms. It is this force that others who would maintain the status quo in administrative studies resist.

This is not the occasion for extended comment on a better under- standing of the paradigms. It is worth noting, however, that in a compre- hensive, but concise statement that reflects widespread understandings in sociology and the philosophy of science, Ribbins (1985, 228) offers a notion of three paradigms and relates this understanding helpfully to research in educational administration. Noting that there is no absolute to mandate 'just these three epistemologies', he nevertheless goes on to argue that

> The conception of sociology as characterised by a number of compet- ing paradigms is both deeply rooted in contemporary thinking and may offer an illuminating way of tackling the task of exploring the contribution which the social sciences may make to the study of the school as an organisation. . . . A number of writers have used this approach to distinguish three sets of theories or competing para- digms: that which tends to assume consensus, that which tends to assume conflict, and that for which the resolution of conflict is an essentially empirical matter.

Although Ribbins does not name the paradigms other than by explicating their positions *vis-à-vis* conflict and consensus in social organization, it is not a large step to suggest that the basic paradigms are first, the systems– empiricist, second the subjective, and finally the critical or ethno–marxist. No doubt there are methodologies of enquiry and positions about the truths of social reality that do not fit within this typology. It is nevertheless a good working beginning for anyone trying to understand what characterizes and distinguishes the modes of enquiry in the field and what watersheds of assumption and world-view divide them.

Without attempting to explicate further the nature of the paradigms, I would make some observations on the general idea of paradigm that speak to misunderstandings and unfortunate misconstruals that are all too prevalent in the field and that diminish the value and meaningfulness of the term.

1 The systems–empiricist paradigm is, of course, the one that dominates the field and which some hold to be the best standard of rational and objective truth available to us. It is the view of the world that all those robed with power and authority prefer to take, for it lays claim to and confers certainty, rationality, and universality. Those theorists and researchers who support this view are more likely to be serving authority than describing objective reality. This is MacIntyre's point from *After Virtue*, and it profoundly touches the claims of *management science*, revealing them to be 'a moral fable' not an objective view of immutable reality. It is therefore in the interests of both established power and its servants in 'normal' science to disguise their value judgements as objective observations about the world and the conduct of social affairs. To fail to understand and acknowledge this point is not to defend reality, but to defend a view of reality and the prevailing power relations within it.

2 The preferred mode of enquiry in the systems–empiricist paradigm is, of course, the statistical and the quantitative. A common error is to appropriate the putative objectivity and rational force of quantitative analysis to the systems–empiricist paradigm, relegating all qualitative analysis – words, fuzzy meanings, interpretation, and subjectivity itself – to the other paradigms. There is nothing about numbers that appropriates them uniquely to the systems–empiricist paradigm.[6] As Weber (1971, 19) advised researchers, 'First get the facts', by which he meant all demographic and economic data relevant to the social situation under analysis; then attempt to describe and understand it from the internal perspective of *verstehen*. It is therefore a simplistic and unfortunate error to set qualitative and quantitative analyses in contrast and opposition to each other. Both quantitative and the qualitative analysis may be found in any of the paradigms of inquiry. In a recent writing, Guba (1992) controverts

> the mistaken idea that the relativist position, or any paradigm that depends on it, demands the use of *qualitative* methods. . . . Both qualitative *and* quantitative methods can be used in the service of *any* paradigm, whatever its presuppositions and assumptions may be. The only criterion that ought to constrain choice of methods is their *fit* to the axiomatic structure of the paradigm selected to guide the inquiry.

179

3 It is possible, as Bauman (1978, 36) points out, to treat people as though they were trees, but trees cannot play the role of people. 'Understanding is re-discovery of myself in thou; I cannot discover myself in a tree, much less can I *re*-discover myself there'. Or as Schumacher (1977, 39) shows, 'the understanding of the knower must be *adequate* to the thing to be known'. The systems–empiricist paradigm may be adequate for certain purposes, but for understanding the intentions, choices, meanings, and the causal links and consequences of people engaged in social action it is clearly inadequate. Speaking of the 'Cartesian anxiety' to reduce all reality to a set of coordinates in space, Guba (1992) recalls Archimedes' boast that if he had a lever long enough and a place whereon to stand, he could move the earth. This is also the hubris of the scientists of the systems–empiricist school who continue their search for ultimate control – for ultimate social control. Even as their failure feeds the anxiety that drives the search, these scientists are doomed to failure and disappointment, for as Guba says, 'the Archimedean point is an illusion'. Belief in and search for an Archimedean point of administrative control defines the spirit of the contemporary field in educational administration. Any who doubt this claim need only refer to the popular text whose authors (Hoy and Miskel, 1987, iii) have dedicated it in three editions over recent years to the conviction that administrative practice in education can be 'less of an art and more of a science'.

4 Smith and Blase (1989, 4) note that one of the concerns of empiricist science is to distinguish what 'is' from what 'seems' to be the case. And so it does, and appropriately and necessarily so, in the case of physical phenomena. To the commonsense observer, the sun rises in the east and moves to the west. But physics teaches us that this illusion is produced by the earth moving in precisely the opposite direction. As Weber knew, the progress of physical science requires the scientist's imposition of such an 'is' perspective, for the physical world has no voice to say otherwise. But the social world does have a voice, and it was one of Weber's great contributions to establish how this difference must transform the work of the social scientist and distinguish it from that of the physical scientist. The same issue of 'is' and 'seems' has its echo in the social sciences. While the interpretive social scientist is content to deal with the world of 'seems' in social action, the critical theorist (Carr and Kemmis, 1986) knows that what seems to be the case in social reality appears in the light of true, but external understanding to be false consciousness, ideological repression, and erroneous moral judgement.

For example, Hargreaves (1978, 11) highlights the assumptions that Sharp and Green (1975) made about social reality in their noteworthy study of 'progressive primary education' in an English inner city school. In exploring realities apparent to administrators and teachers in the school, Sharp and Green 'seek to go *beyond* subjective meanings and see an important difference between "things seeming to be the case to the actor and things *being* the case"'. Thus critical theory appears as concerned to determine the ultimate truth of social reality as does empiricist science. In this light, a further significant implication flows from the structure of the paradigms of inquiry posited by Ribbins (1985). In his typology the systems–empiricist paradigm stands at one end, critical theory at the other of a continuum arrayed from social order to social conflict. Where the systems–empiricist approach establishes what 'is' by eliminating values, critical theory sets out to establish the ought of values, by determining their appropriate 'is'. Thus pushing critical theory to its logical end reveals a continuum bent back upon itself. The critical theory perspective leads ultimately to a certainty as firm as that claimed in systems–empiricism, but now the certainty is not just about factual reality in a value context, but about the values themselves. This too is not science, or at least not an appropriate and adequate social science. It is rather another imposition of values in the name of science.

Splitting facts and values

As Hodgkinson (1978b, 220) says, 'Values are special kinds of facts; but never true or false.' They are good or bad, but never falsifiable. The question of the divisibility of facts and values continues to bedevil an understanding of the paradigms and issues of methodological adequacy. For example, Smith and Blase (1989, 4) make the common error of blaming Weber, the messenger, for the unhappy messages he bears. In their view, Weber 'firmly established the separation of facts and values in the social sciences'. This view reflects an unfortunate received truth about Weber that seriously distorts his position. To begin with Weber recognized that a fact-driven rationality (*Zweckrationalität*) increasingly drives the modern world. What is often called modernity and professionalism calls for such a separation. Thus Weber recognized that, though they are analytically separable, the social scientist faces a world in which facts and values are inevitably and intimately intertwined. Weber's great question was to ask what a value-free social science could mean in a world suffused with values. That he never gave up striving to answer that question should not – and does not – put him on the side of the rationalizers and those who split values from facts. But he clearly saw that much of the modern world is driven by a set of assumptions that does make such a split. Those who make the split are often those who set policy, and so a 'subjectively adequate' view of policy making must take into account the convictions of those who believe that facts can be and appropriately are split from values.

Eldridge (Weber, 1971, 18) points out that 'Like Durkheim, Weber argued that economic theory had a tendency to treat presuppositions as self-evident when they were nothing of the kind.' In his own words, Weber

(1978, 69–70) argues even more strongly that the whole question of the separation of facts and values 'cannot be discussed in scientific terms, since it is itself entirely dependent on practical value-judgements and so irresoluble'. He goes on to reject the view that

> it is desirable as far as possible to keep all practical value-questions in the background in one's teaching. . . . The attempt to do so merely serves to disguise the practical implication of the opinion being suggested to the audience. Finally the view that it is an essential feature of the academic approach that it should be 'dispassionate', and that consequently all questions which run the risk of stirring up 'heated' arguments should be excluded, would, once value-judgements in general became a feature of academic teaching, be a merely bureaucratic opinion, which every independent teacher would have to repudiate.

What Weber (1978, 76–78) does separate – and so should we all – is, first, the facts that we as researchers claim to generate and, second, our value judgements about them.

> I would rather not discuss any further whether it is 'difficult' to distinguish between statements of empirical fact and practical value-judgements. It is. . . . What is at issue, however, is exclusively the requirement, utterly trivial in itself, that anyone engaged in research or in presenting its results should keep two things absolutely separate, empirical facts (including facts established by him about the 'evaluative' behaviour of the empirical human beings whom he is studying); and secondly, his own practical value-position, that is, his judgement and, in this sense, 'evaluation' of these facts (including possible 'value-judgements' made by empirical human beings, which have themselves become an object of investigation) as satisfactory or unsatisfactory.

And, of course, Weber's acknowledgement of the analytic separability of facts and values should be set in context of his view that no science can provide an authentic 'copy' of reality and that all scientific visions of reality must be imposed by scientists themselves. Moreover, Weber saw a fundamental and unavoidable distinction between the natural and the 'cultural' sciences. Whereas the images of the natural world must be imposed by the scientist from external observation, those of the social world require 'understanding' and interpretation, which can and should involve the perspectives of the actors themselves.[7]

Values are asserted, chosen, imposed, not measured

Values lie beyond rationality. Rationality to *be* rationality must stand upon a value base. Values are asserted, chosen, imposed, or believed. They lie beyond quantification, beyond measurement. They are not 'variables', though they may be treated as such. Simply and clearly Hodgkinson (1978b, 220) puts the fundamental quality of values, the essence that distinguishes them from facts and lets us understand their force and meaning: 'The world of fact is given, the world of value made. We discover facts and impose values.'

Again it is Weber who helps us understand the relationship of values and rationality. As Weber argues, a technical or narrowly scientific rationality asks only what means best fosters an end. It assumes the end is un-questionable and clear and that the means to attain it rationally and efficiently are equally clear and available. Weber's insight into the mischief wrought by a devalued science is well represented in the conflict portrayed in Kubrick's *2001* where HAL, the super-rational and devalued computer comes into conflict with the valuing astronauts. In that scenario, it is the surviving astronaut who, when faced with the ultimate victory of the nonvaluing computer, decides that the reassertion of human control over the computer is *worth* the price of his own death. For Weber, the technical spirit of modernity exists in a disenchanted world, one bled of values. Brubaker (1984, 80, 98) demonstrates Weber's view that modern science

> 'disenchants' the world by construing it as a rationally calculable and manipulable causal mechanism. . . . It is intellect that rules the dis-enchanted world, a world in which 'one can, in principle, master all things by calculation'. The truly human life is one that is guided by reason. To live a life informed by reason, an individual must become a personality. To become a personality, he must commit himself to certain fundamental values. But this commitment . . . cannot itself be guided by reason, for in Weber's view there is no rational way of deciding among the plurality of conflicting possible value commitments. Every rational life, in short is founded on a non-rational choice.

The impossibility of the empiricist dream – or rather the impossibility of ever assuaging the empiricist anxiety for certainty and control – is mocked with trenchant irony in Julian Barnes's *Flaubert's Parrot*. Though the book is a novel, it is also a *tour de force* evoking Flaubert's moral vision, his despair over the technology propelled by 'democracy' that reshaped the nine-teenth century in the name of progress and transformed our own. In 1853 Flaubert watched the sun go down over the sea at Trouville and declared that it resembled a large disc of redcurrant jam. Laying a trap for the empiricists, Barnes (1984, 92) asks with apparent naïveté:

> Vivid enough. But was redcurrant jam the same colour in Normandy in 1853 as it is now? (Would any pots of it have survived, so that we could check? And how would we know the colour had remained the same in the intervening years?)

183

Barnes mocking science as it tries to verify ineffable meaning is but a side jest. The targets he aims at through Flaubert reveal a blind science that destroys people while insisting it is morally neutral, while insisting it is only helping people to live better, to achieve their goals more fully. Referring to Homais, the *pharmacien* and man of science in *Madam Bovary*, Barnes (1984, 84–85) puts the issue thus:

> The spirit of Homais: progress, rationalism, science, fraud. 'We must march with the century' are almost his first words; and he marches all the way to the *Légion d'honeur*. When Emma Bovary dies, her body is watched over by two people: the priest, and Homais, the *pharmacien*. Representing the old orthodoxy and the new. It's like some piece of nineteenth-century allegorical sculpture: Religion and Science Watching Together over the Body of Sin. . . . United at first only by philosophic error, they quickly establish the deeper unity of joint snorers.
>
> Flaubert didn't believe in progress: especially not in moral progress, which is all that matters. The age he lived in was stupid; the new age, brought in by the Franco–Prussian war, would be even stupider. . . . 'The whole dream of democracy', he wrote, 'is to raise the proletariat to the level of stupidity attained by the bourgeoisie'.

What does constitute progress? What is the good and how may it be attained? How does education contribute to the social good and to personal well being and happiness? How should schools be organized to achieve such goals? What are the moral choices that face educational administrators? Such questions are hardly asked any more. Instead the field seems bent upon implementing a uniform, but undefined 'effectiveness'. Decisions are obviated. Training in procedure, mouthing the accepted answers is all that is required. This will not do. But this mindless devotion to technicism could engulf us, sweeping the field away into a spuriously scientific irrelevancy, to a technology of claimed, but unexamined effectiveness, one that is easy for masses to accept and vastly profitable to those who exploit and merchandise it.

LOOKING FORWARD

In looking back at the events and issues that have moved and motivated the discussions and disagreements of the past twenty years, I have likely used up most of the space available to me for writing this statement and probably my readers' patience as well. I will conclude rapidly therefore with a shorter section in which I attempt to suggest what issues and problems will confront those who teach and research in educational administration in the coming years. The future is, of course, never cut off from the past, but is rather an extrapolation and extension of it, though the utterly new may sometimes confound the progression. The utterly new is, of course, unpredictable and before its advent unspeakable as well. In these circumstances, it seems likely that the issues that have divided and engaged us in the past will continue to do so in the future. It is this consideration that gives me hope that the extensive treatment I have given to the old will yet serve as a guide for understanding and dealing with the problems that still face us. In my view, we certainly need more ashes than are currently to be seen in the field if we are to conceive and shape study and practice in better forms. I can certainly not offer any blueprint for the new form of the field. That a reform of the field, that a re-forming of it is needed seems to me to lie beyond reasonable question. I will speak to this matter of reshaping under three topics, first on the openness of the field to enquiry, second on out-of-control organizations, and finally on the school as a crux of value. On hearing these points, I can imagine critics saying that they constitute little more than the reverse side of the coinage I have already argued and that has been the theme of my critique for nearly two decades. So be it, for whether these matters are *worth* discussing is a matter of human valuing and appreciation. I hope there are readers who share with me the values I advocate or who at least see the merit in discussing them.

The openness of enquiry

When they thought it possible and desirable to license the publication of truth, Milton addressed the Lords and Commons of England with the well known words, 'Give me the liberty to know, to utter, and to argue freely according to conscience, above all liberties.' But the great power of the argument in the *Areopagitica* is found as Milton addresses the question of how truth is to be known: 'Assuredly we bring not innocence into the world, we bring impurity much rather; that which purifies us is trial, and trial is by what is contrary.'[8] Milton spoke out against the truth makers who operate out of doctrinal and religious certainty. But as Flaubert knew, science may stand equally in error and in equal intolerance with religion. This is Kuhn's point too in his explication of scientific revolutions. Truth, to the extent we know it at all, comes out of the oppositional contention of ideas.

Looking over the development of educational administration from the time of its exciting early growth, one may well see how rapidly the field moved from its early phase of debate, discussion, and disagreement about theory and method into an era of established truth and orthodoxy. Much of the 'turmoil' of recent years, as Kelsey and Long (1983) have shown, is an attempt to restore and preserve orthodox opinion in the field from heterodox challenges. One of the most effective ways of defending orthodox opinion as incontestable truth is to see that heterodox opinion is not published, or that the rare heterodox opinion that does get published is

185

well countered with extended bulls of orthodox refutation. Above all, the calm surface of orthodox opinion must be seen to prevail in terms of extent of comment and ease of access to the publications of record and authority in the field.

In a survey of articles in *EAQ* and *JEA*, Miskel and Sandlin (1981, 18) reported that scholarly enquiry in educational administration rests upon a single method of enquiry – survey research. In a later critique of articles published in *JEA*, Lakomski (1989, 60) echoes Miskel and Sandlin's findings and their criticism that the quality of empiricist research dominating the field is generally low, giving inadequate attention to methodological issues. In an even more serious criticism of publications in *JEA*, Lakomski (1989, 61) finds that it 'maintains a relatively strong "mainstream" orientation' and that it does so

> *not* in the sense of furthering the development of theory which was the aim of the Theory Movement, but in the narrowness of research methods employed in its articles, its behavioural orientation, and the particular clusters of topics presented.

In her conclusion, Lakomski (1989, 62) emphasizes that the field of academic study in educational administration is characterized by an 'absence of some of the most debated developments in educational administration', by an absence of comment on 'problems of knowledge, values and practice'.

In response to such criticisms, Thomas (1982, 10), the editor of *JEA*, admits the facts of the charge and makes the defence that the emphasis in the journal is a consequence of pressures from school principals 'to reduce the methodological content . . . and to focus more on projects' findings and implications'. Administrators want facts and instructions for using them to improve their practice. As Lakomski argues, such an approach perpetrates and gives credence to the error Popper called 'the bucket theory of mind', the theory that if the mind can be filled with scientific facts, the road to truth, to purposeful and effective action will be plain. As Lakomski (1989, 64) observes, such an approach yields to a 'pernicious demand for immediacy' that short-circuits a necessary exploration of theory and method, ultimately obviating the very understanding that is sought.

The question now facing the field is whether it can tolerate trial by what is contrary in exploring and assessing the ideas needed to carry it into the future. The record of the past does not suggest so. But splendid exchanges of thought and argument such as that seen in the dialogue among Smith and Blase (1989), Allison (1990), and Schwandt (1990) are indeed hopeful portents for the future. That dialogue is characterized by deep disagreements, by reasoned, hard hitting argument, and by sound scholarship avoiding all comment *ad hominem*. All of this wonderful dialogue, all of it all too rare in the field, leaves the reader thoughtful, well informed and better able to think through the issues. The irony of this dialogue cannot be lost on the bemused, but perhaps pessimistic reader: it appears in what can without making an invidious comparison be called a fringe publication in the field. And in a further irony upon that, the dialogue was occasioned by *EAQ*'s rejection of a paper that would have discussed the very issues that lie at the heart of this illuminating and important dialogue.

Can the main journals of the field do better in the future? Can they allow honest and full examination of the issues to take place. Can they expand the range of ideas explored, the methods used to explore them? Can they allow more 'turmoil' in the belief that it is a necessary precursor to the ashes that might see the better and stronger shaping of the field? Can they permit trial of truth by what is contrary? I am hopeful, but not optimistic. Allison (1990, 5) dismisses *EAQ*'s rejection of Smith and Blase's manuscript with the sanguine view that truth will out, that if it does not find publication in one place it will in another.

> It is not unreasonable to expect some paradigmatic bias in such process and at times submissions which attack established values and assumptions may well be rejected because of their heretical flavor.... Yet although errors will inevitably be made from time to time, there can be no alternative to the traditional academic review and editorial process. In the long run the process is self-correcting and necessary criticisms and important ideas will be disseminated one way or another and take their place in the literature.

I very much doubt the 'self-correction' Allison relies upon. Having seen 'the traditional academic review and editorial process' from the inside, I know what illusions of subjectivity and bias the façade of objectivity and impartiality can hide. Or to put the matter somewhat more positively, the 'self-correction' lies ultimately in human hands; the judgements of acceptance or rejection arise purely from someone's choice and will, even if these workings of the mind are couched not in words that presume a personal responsibility in the matter, but in rating scales that deny it.

In my case, two papers have met *EAQ*'s review standards with the fortunate consequence that they were published in that widely read journal. But when I sent a third, the editor rejected it saying the editorial board felt that deans, academics, and practitioners were 'tired' of reading my critiques. I could better accept that judgement as marking my failure to add anything to older themes were it not for the consideration that voices of the orthodox mainstream not only fill the pages of that journal, they get to explain and interpret any critical writing that does appear in it. Heterodox writing in *EAQ* is thus well and firmly placed in its proper place and perspective: the space for argument is limited and the voices of orthodoxy write the last word – and it is usually the same word again and again.

The sensitivity of the field to clear, issue-driven language is that of the restless princess disturbed by a pea 'neath layers of mattresses. An editor preparing a set of papers for scholarly publication once suggested that my ideas might get a better hearing if I reduced the sharpness of my words. The words that concerned him came as I argued that the methods of atomistic enquiry favoured in the field missed many realities of life in organizations. To help convey this notion I quoted a line from Wordsworth: 'We murder to dissect'. The editor recommended deleting the line. No doubt the editor knew better than I the readership the book would reach, but I was appalled by the attitude of mind his judgement accepted as a commonplace of the field: a near anti-intellectualism at best. The theoretical and practical strength of the field must depend upon the strength of the ideas that are used to discuss and understand its issues. There are difficult, painful, distressing, and vital issues to be discussed in the field. If they are to be ruled out of discussion because of those qualities in them, we will make the field, as has been observed, 'unnecessarily boring'. More importantly the ruling out of subjects of enquiry will make what passes for knowledge in the field increasingly jejune, ultimately making it barren and irrelevant, though the industry that dispenses and claims to validate such ideas will no doubt continue.

Out-of-control organizations

The irony of control-oriented empiricism in social affairs is that its effects are exactly the opposite of what it claims. While it claims to bring organizations under rational control, the actual consequences of its pseudo-science and devalued technology are the reverse: it disguises where the control actually lies, placing it in the hands of a pseudo-democratic organizational élite who are freed from responsibility for their actions and decisions. The computer, HAL, in Kubrick's *2001* symbolizes the ultimate end of such a dynamic: there is no one in control and human beings are made victims and sacrifices to amoral science and technology. Once such a technology-based dynamic is created to guide and control organizations, it is difficult if not impossible to remove, as the astronauts of *2001* discovered. The fundamental error that allows this pernicious situation to develop is the belief that moral problems can be solved by technical and rational means. Szasz (1976) explicates this dilemma in the context of psychiatry, but his aphoristic insights deal ultimately with fundamental distinctions among natural science, the pseudo-science called social science, and morality.

'Evil', observed Flannery O'Connor, 'is not simply a problem to be solved, but a mystery to be endured'. Not until psychiatrists realize this and act accordingly, will the practice of psychiatry cease to be a moral affront, if not an obscenity. (p. 33)

The fundamental error of psychiatry is that it regards life as a problem to be solved, instead of as a purpose to be fulfilled. (p. 129)

In natural science, the task is to make new discoveries and to formulate novel theories, and to have the courage of propounding them in opposition to established knowledge; in moral science, it is to rediscover old observations and to rearticulate ancient principles and to have the courage to defend them in opposition to the pretensions of scientism. (p. 177)

Or as Flaubert speaking through Barnes says, the spirit of the times believes there is a science to solve moral dilemmas, and the consequence is 'progress, rationalism, science, fraud'.

In a recent issue of *Harper's*, Lewis Lapham, wrote an article entitled 'Democracy in America?' in which he questioned whether the country could still be called democratic. The response (Lapham, 1991) was a flood of letters, many saying he hadn't gone far enough and identifying the fundamental problem as one of organizations out of control. As one correspondent wrote,

The United States of America is composed of hundreds of smaller 'states' called corporations, many of them extraordinarily powerful, none of them democratic. ... Once I walked through the door of the corporation where I used to work I found myself somewhat compelled to forgo my right to free speech for eight hours each day. Sure, I could criticize national politicians until I was blue in the face. But call into question the firm's shareholders and I risked termination. From what I understood, this is the conventional wisdom that prevails among corporate employees in America, the land of the free and the home of the extremely rarely brave.

No voice in administrative studies has done more than William Scott (Scott and Hart, 1979) to place within a body of theory the notion of out-of-control organizations. These he sees as a product of a devalued and technocratic management science called 'managerialism'. As Scott (1985, 150–151) says, 'We should repudiate the orthodoxy of managerialism because it is a value system that encourages the treatment of humans in ways that deprive them of their humanness.' He identifies four 'contradictions' inherent in much of what passes as present day management science:

1 The exacerbation of the subculture of poverty . . .
2 The widening gap between classes . . .
3 Cultural boredom wherein people are encouraged to pursue debasing titillations supplied by organizations for economic reasons . . .
4 Intellectual dishonesty whereby individuals with public visibility in management teach, research, write, and speak in behalf of systemically corrupt beliefs.

Within our own administrative specialization, it is Hodgkinson (1990) who palpates and diagnoses the malady that besets our field. Hodgkinson (1990, 10) notes that 'faddism or trendyitis . . . is endemic to education and its administration'. He makes suggestions for re-introducing and strengthening the ancient notions about administration as a moral task:

> Consider the German concept of *Zivilcourage*. This is the power or quality of being able to express unpopular opinions, of speaking against the weight of apparent consensus, of doing what is politically dangerous or unpopular. How many of our educational leaders are imbued with *Zivilcourage*? How many would dare question the ecology movement, the use of computers, or bilingualism? . . . Talking about *Zivilcourage* is not the same as getting it. But it's a start. (p. 15)

Let me demonstrate a little of what I hope is a justified *Zivilcourage* and suggest that educational administration cannot address the moral problems that beset it without also considering the historical, cultural, and political problems that surround them. Canada too is coming to be governed by out-of-control organizations, as is evidenced by the corporations who bought the last federal election in order to implement a Free Trade Agreement in their interests, but arguably profoundly threatening to the wider Canadian cultural and economic fabric. The point is one already well established in Canadian historical, cultural, and educational critique, as may be seen in Frye's (1971, 14) insight:

> Historically a Canadian is an American who rejects the Revolution. Canada fought its civil war to establish its union first, and its wars of independence, which were fought against the United States and not Europe, came later. We should expect in Canada, therefore, a strong suspicion, not of the United States itself, but of the mercantilist Whiggery which won the Revolution and proceeded to squander the resources of a continent, being now engaged in squandering ours. . . . The Canadian point of view is at once more conservative and more radical than Whiggery, closer both to aristocracy and to democracy than to oligarchy.

What does all this have to do with educational administration? Two points may illustrate the relevance. First it may be noted that traditionally and increasingly in modern years the Canadian provincial and federal governments have pursued a policy aimed at equalizing resources both within the provinces and between them. Canadian educational systems have been important beneficiaries of this policy, building them in strength, size, and economic power. American policy reflecting user-pay assumptions largely leaves school systems to pay their way. As Susan Sontag (1988, 73) notes, this is 'the culture of self-interest, which is much of what is usually praised as "individualism"'. Thus school systems with the greatest problems often have the narrowest economic base from which to deal with them. Moving against past tradition, the present policy of the Canadian federal government reduces its assistance to the provinces and cuts sharply its spending on social and educational programmes. While this new direction may move in the spirit of free trade, it promises to weaken substantially the fabric of Canadian educational and cultural institutions.

Second, it is apparent that inadequate social programmes in the United States are the root of many of its educational programmes. That one of the wealthiest countries in the world has for all practical purposes no public broadcasting is a fundamental educational ill. That a third of its population has no ready access to adequate medical care cannot but have a pervasively negative impact upon the quality of its educational programs. No technocratic programme of educational evaluation can do anything to reverse these educational problems other than to continue, as they do, to record the seemingly inexorable decline of the measured educational standards. A recent article in the *Scientific American* (Aral and Holmes, 1991, 62) records some of the empirical facts of the social problems that face those who are responsible for programmes of health and education in the United States.

> In almost all of the industrialized countries the three classic venereal diseases – ghonorrhea, syphilis and chancroid – have nearly disappeared. . . . In shocking contrast, those three sexually transmitted diseases (STDs) have actually been increasing at epidemic rates among urban minority populations in the U.S. . . . The deteriorating STD situation of the U.S. urban underclass increasingly resembles that seen in the slums of the least developed countries, where acquired immunodeficiency syndrome (AIDS) . . . has been spreading at epidemic rates among heterosexuals.

Among the American poor, 'Preventable diseases such as measles, whooping cough and polio are increasing.'[9] Students of educational administration are unlikely to find that any of these social, historical, cultural, economic, and medical considerations – all of them essentially moral in their implications – have any place in their texts, though such considerations must profoundly influence education and the administration of it in schools.

Despite these horrors of Dickensian proportion, the most prominent and popular developments in the contemporary field continue to emphasize a technocratic approach to the solution of moral problems in education and administration. For example, Leithwood's work (Leithwood and Montgomery, 1986) addresses questions fundamentally moral in quality, but it does so by relying on the assumptions of systems–empiricist thinking. Inevitably then values are again relegated to the background and taken for granted. In consequence, the Leithwoodian prescriptions ignore vital questions of purpose in order to get on with mandated prescriptions for effectiveness, and these predictably are couched within the language of scientific objectivity. The product of such analysis is little more than a set of formulaic answers that lend themselves to ready inculcation by mass programs of training and certification. Thus the Leithwoodian evangelism for effectiveness and the emphasis in his training programmes upon proven means for problem-solving amount to little more than a set of enthusiastic exercises in indoctrination. Once again technocratic pseudo-science claims to have the answer to moral dilemmas. The proposals of the National Commission on Excellence in Educational Administration are similarly depressing. Its proposals offer at best a cautious extension of what is already established and familiar. Its endorsement of 'approved programs' of study and of the licensing of 'successful practice' (Griffiths, Stout, and Forsyth, 1988, 22) seem sure to retain the dead hand of a technocratic and blinkered approach.

The school as a crux of value

All that has gone before in this text makes the argument that the school *is* a crux of value and for value. It is the crux of value and of administrative value. Let me close this writing therefore by speaking directly to the theme. Schools are obviously a reflection of the culture they exist within, but they are also a prime instrument for shaping and developing that culture. Hodgkinson (1978b, 197) makes perhaps the most explicit argument on this matter, saying the administrator's task involves 'a major concern for value' requiring first an initial commitment to the role and its values, then a reflective disengagement from them, and finally a critique of the values and recommitment to them entailing a possible evolutionary or transformative change in them.

To understand the school as a crux of value is to look at it in cultural and historical perspective. David Halbertsam's *The Reckoning* (1986) offers a comparison of the organizational cultures and histories of Nissan in Japan and the Ford Motor Company in America. It chronicles the rise of Nissan from the ruin of the Japanese economic and political systems following the Second World War to the near economic collapse of major American automobile manufacturers in the 1980s, Ford among them. What Halbertsam sets out in lucid and near ethnographic detail is the contrast between the competing set of careers and cultures in the two corporations. The Japanese company is ultimately an expression of engineering excellence within a consciousness of both social and environmental constraints. It is a reflection of the Japanese dedication to knowledge, tradition, and education in its broadest sense. That American automotive companies came close to economic collapse – from which they were saved largely by government intervention – is a reflection of managerialism, of a management oriented to Wall Street and the dictates of the 'bottom line'. Ironically managerialism among the American car makers, their fixation upon the immediate, and their obsession with financial gain were the seeds that nearly destroyed their companies, and that still leaves them vulnerable to Japanese competition. What the Japanese knew from their deeply ingrained education system and culture was that quality is a matter of value and judgement, whereas the American companies were sure that their problems could be resolved by continued reliance on failing management strategies, on tighter financial control and larger advertising budgets. The success of Nissan is in many ways a reflection of the Japanese education system and its respect for knowledge and sound judgement; the near disaster at Ford is in many ways a reflection of the corporate managerial view that value has no meaning beyond cost accounting. In this view the nature of the product is irrelevant: the selling of it is the only responsibility of corporate managers. Any other knowledge, any other valuing is seen as worthless, irrelevant, and demonstrably non-productive.

Lasch (1985) looks at this 'bottom line' managerialism as applied to education and finds it disastrously inadequate. He points, for example, to the error of allowing the economically and rationally determined 'needs' of industry to govern the quality and amount of education provided as a public good. Even more pointedly, he shows that if the only requirements of industry are to determine the content and funding of education, society needs less of it, not more. The majority of jobs now offered by business and industry are defined by simple routine, and require little training and almost no education. In these circumstances, a small managerial and technical élite can do all the creative thinking for masses of people who need training only to know the colour of the buttons to push on the computerized devices they operate. Only if we believe in education as a desirable end itself and only if we see it as essential for the political and cultural development of masses of people is there any point in putting vast amounts of investment into education. Otherwise a small élite is all that needs education to higher levels; at relatively low cost the rest can be taught contentment with mind-numbing activities – the pacifying circuses of sport or the violently exploitative or jejune entertainment offered through the mass media.

In his critique of *A Nation at Risk: The Imperative for Educational Reform*, Lasch (1985, 2) has noted the timidity of the reforms advocated by the National Commission on Excellence in its prescriptions for American schools. Reviewing the list of reforms 'that have been advocated by reformers ever since the last wave of reformist enthusiasm in the fifties', Lasch concludes that 'the Commission on Excellence isn't very serious about excellence'. The answer to the burgeoning social and political problems of America – problems that in some degree are found in all Western societies – Lasch finds in education, in an education dedicated to the beneficent transformation of the individual.

> In the tradition of social thought stretching back to antiquity, education is not seen as a means to an end – personal advancement, social control, professional training, or even good citizenship. It is seen as an end in its own right, to which other activities are ancillary. The entire political order, in the ancient view, is an essentially educational enterprise. Its purpose is the training of character. . . . The political community unites men in a shared vision of the good. It frees them from biological and material necessity in order that they can submit voluntarily to the discipline of citizenship. (pp. 7-8)

I will close this already too long statement with a point that moves from education *qua* education towards administration qua administration, though the inevitable connection between the two is, I hope, plain.[10] Hodgkinson points to the errors of the putative science of administration and the missed dimensions of administration as a moral and educative task: the central questions of administration deal not so much with what is, but with what ought to be; they deal with values and morality. As Hodgkinson (1978b, 146) points out, administrative science must be silent about the issues that lie at the heart of administrative action: 'No science, social or physical, can tell us what is right or wrong.'

In his most recent writing, Hodgkinson (1991) restores a vision of administration. His title lays out the central issue: Administration is a *moral art*. He offers a vision of what administration is and of what it might become. It *is* a matter of will and power: of bending others to one's will and of being bent in turn by others. The overlap between education and administration is therefore substantial and unavoidable, if education is recognized as being the process of identifying the valuable, opening it to others and, yes, inculcating it into them. Moreover, the Hodgkinsonian vision of administration as a moral task redeems the notion of hierarchy and thereby of leadership. Everyone wants the good, at least for themselves, at best for others as well. Everyone therefore opposes evil – or what is less good – and supports the mobilization of power against it. A hierarchy of the good is therefore inevitable, as is the demand to ground it in authority and to further it through leadership.

Hodgkinson's view of administration allows us to see in new directions, towards the world of the valuable, the right, the justified. The answers he offers are as much questions as answers. But there is a uniquely practical – or one might better say a praxical quality to this work, for it considers not only the problems of administration in their general forms. He moves beyond theory into praxis, into the specific, into the politics of day-to-day living and their justification; he speaks to the mundane, but inevitable and *valuable* question of how to get through the day; ultimately he speaks also to the question of how to make one's way through a career, through a life.

Hodgkinson's work and that of all others who see the educative and moral task of administration are gateways to the world of value. Such contributions to the field of study can be discovered by any reader willing to reflect upon the experience of administering or being administered. But to follow the way of values requires courage and resolution – more for the wayfarer than the reader – for it entails clear-eyed observation of the realities, dilemmas, difficulties, and defeats of life. Only along this path and by right action on it may a better life – and better organizations – be attained.

The shape of its new phoenix is perhaps emerging from the ever more apparent and abundant ashes strewn across the old field.[11] That shape has education at its core and value: values in all their complexities, their dilemmas, and their unrelenting challenge to attain what is good, the challenge for us to be better administrators, to do better for our ourselves and for our organizations, to make ourselves better and to strive for a better world.

NOTES

1 Phoenix: 'A mythical bird, of gorgeous plumage, fabled to be the only one of its kind, and to live for five hundred years in the Arabian desert, after which it burnt itself to ashes on a funeral pile, and emerged from its ashes with renewed youth, to live through another cycle of years', *Shorter Oxford English Dictionary*. A revision of a text prepared for a meeting of the Organization Theory SIG (Special Interest Group) of the American Educational Research Association, Chicago, April 1991.
2 This issue is examined at greater length at p. 110.
3 In administrative studies generally, the modern era dawned with the publication in 1945 of Herbert Simon's *Administrative Behavior*; in educational administration the sun rose upon the new era with the publication in 1958 of *Administrative Theory in Education*, a collection of the 'New Movement' thinking edited by Andrew Halpin.
4 Among others, Smith and Blase (1989, 1–2) make the necessary distinction between 'empiricist' and 'empirical'. Empirical reality surrounds us all, and is too important to be abandoned to the empiricists who would limit its exploration to experimental methods. Empiricism thus invokes the methods of physical science and particularly the methods and assumptions of logical positivism, which is, of course, the spirit that drives Simon's administrative science and also all of 'New Movement' theory and research in educational administration. See Allison's (1990, 9) hesitant, but ultimate rejection of this distinction. See also Evers and Lakomski (1991) whose whole book strives to obliterate the distinction.
5 The International Intervisitation Programme, 1974 held in Bristol, England and other centres in the United Kingdom.
6 See discussions at pp. 129 and 54 by Russell and Hodgkinson of the erroneously factual mystique of numbers.
7 For a further explication of these points, see Eldridge's discussion of 'The Problem of Knowledge' (Weber 1972, 11–19).
8 Using as title Milton's phrase, 'trial by what is contrary', I have elsewhere looked more extensively at how opposing thought is our best assurance of truth. See Greenfield (1985).

195

9 Edward Lucas, 'Shock treatment for US health care', *The Independent* (London), Tuesday 25 June, 1991.

10 In his classic prolegomenon for true (positivist) science in the study of administration, Halpin (1957, 159) evokes the phrase that was a veritable mantram in the theory of the time: 'There is administration *qua* administration. . . . The characteristic ways in which administrators behave are essentially the same whether the administrator operates in industry, government, the military, or public education.'

11 A looming shape is seen in the stimulating work of Evers and Lakomski (1991). Claiming a 'coherentist epistemology' as basis for their truth claims, they offer new arguments for eliding facts and values into a single science. Had I seen their published text before finishing the body of this writing, I might have spoken to its challenges, admiring its depths of scholarship, and warning of and attempting to refute the false byways opened by their theory, which notably says much of epistemology and little of administration. That task of rejoinder must await more thought than I can now give.

REFERENCES

Allison, D. J. 1990. 'Empiricist Science under the New Regime: A Reply to Smith and Blase'. *Organizational Theory Dialogue*, April: 1–9.

Aral, S. O. and Holmes, K. K. 1991. 'Sexually Transmitted Diseases in the AIDS Era'. *Scientific American* 264(2): 62–69.

Barnes, J. 1984. *Flaubert's Parrot.* London: Pan Books.

Bates, R. 1989. 'Is there a New Paradigm in Educational Administration?' Deakin University, Victoria, Australia. Unpublished paper.

Bauman, Z. 1978. *Hermeneutics and Social Science: Approaches to Understanding.* London: Hutchinson.

Bernstein, R. 1988. *Beyond Objectivism and Relativism: Science, Hermeneutics, and Praxis.* Philadelphia: University of Pennsylvania.

Brubaker, R. 1984. *The Limits of Rationality: An Essay on the Social and Moral Thought of Max Weber.* London: George Allen & Unwin.

Burrell, G. and Morgan, G. 1979. *Sociological Paradigms and Organisational Analysis: Elements of the Sociology of Corporate Life.* London: Heinemann.

Carr, W. and Kemmis, S. 1986. *Becoming Critical: Education, Knowledge, and Action Research.* London: Falmer.

Culbertson, J. A. 1988. A Century's Quest for a Knowledge Base. In *Handbook of Research on Educational Administration*, ed. N. J. Boyan, 3–26. New York: Longman.

Evers, C. W. and Lakomski, G. 1991. *Knowing Educational Administration: Contemporary Methodological Controversies in Educational Administration Research.* Oxford: Pergamon.

Frye, N. 1971. *The Bush Garden: Essays on the Canadian Imagination.* Toronto: Anansi.

Geertz, C. 1980. 'Blurred Genres'. *The American Scholar* 99(2): 178.

Getzels, J. W., Lipham, M. and Campbell, R. F. 1968. *Educational Administration as a Social Process: Theory, Research, Practice.* New York: Harper & Row.

Greene, J. C., Caracelli, V. J. and Graham, W. F. 1989. 'Toward a Conceptual Framework for Mixed-method Evaluation Designs'. *Educational Evaluation and Policy Analysis* 11(3): 255–274.

Greenfield, T. B. 1975. 'Theory about Organization: A New Perspective and its Implications for Schools'. In *Administering education: International challenge*, ed. M. Hughes, 71–99. London: Athlone.

—— 1985. 'Trial by What is Contrary: I & II'. *Curriculum Inquiry* 15(1): 1–6; 15(2): 113–119.

—— 1986. 'The Decline and Fall of Science in Educational Administration'. *Interchange* 17(2): 57–80.

Griffiths, D. E. 1979. 'Intellectual Turmoil in Educational Administration'. *Educational Administration Quarterly* 15(3): 43–65.

—— 1988. 'Administrative Theory'. In *Handbook of research on educational administration*, ed. N. J. Boyan, 27–51. New York: Longman.

Griffiths, D. E., Stout, R. T. and Forsyth, P. B., eds. 1988. *Leaders for America's Schools.* The report and papers of the National Commission on Excellence in Educational Administration. Berkeley: McCutchan.

Gronn, P. 1983. *Rethinking Educational Administration: T. B. Greenfield and his Critics.* Victoria, Australia: Deakin University.

Guba, E. G. 1960. 'Research in Internal Administration – What do We Know?' In *Administrative Theory as a Guide to Action*, ed. R. Campbell and J. M. Lipham, 113–130. Chicago: Midwest Administration Center, University of Chicago.

—— 1992. 'Relativism'. In the symposium, 'Objectivity, Subjectivity, and Relativism in Qualitative Educational Research'. *Curriculum Inquiry* 22, 1 (forthcoming).

Guba, E. G. and Bidwell, C. E. 1957. *Administrative Relationships: Teacher Effectiveness, Teachers Satisfaction, and Administrative Behavior.* Chicago: Midwest Administration Center, University of Chicago.

Halbertsam, D. 1986. *The Reckoning.* New York: Morrow.

Halpin, A. 1957. 'A Paradigm for Research on Administrator Behavior'. In *Administrative Behavior in Education*, eds R. F. Campbell and R. T. Gregg, 155–199. New York: Harper.

Halpin, A. W., ed. 1958. *Administrative Theory in Education.* New York: Macmillan.

Hargreaves, D. 1978. 'What Ever Happened to Symbolic Interactionism?' In *Sociological Interpretations of Schooling and Classrooms: A Reappraisal*, eds L. Barton and R. Meighan, 7–22. Nafferton, England: Nafferton Books.

Hodgkinson, C. 1978a. 'The Failure of Organizational and Administrative Theory. *McGill Journal of Education* 13(3): 271–278.

—— 1978b. *Towards a Philosophy of Administration.* Oxford: Basil Blackwell.

—— 1983. *The Philosophy of Leadership.* Oxford: Basil Blackwell.

—— 1988. 'The Value Bases of Administrative Action'. *Journal of Educational Administration and Foundations* 3(1): 20–30.

—— 1990. 'Madness and Malady in Educational Administration'. Paper presented to the Canadian Association for the Study of Educational Administration. Victoria, Learned Societies of Canada Conference.

—— 1991. *Educational Leadership: The Moral Art.* Albany: SUNY Press.

Hoy, W. K. and Miskel, C. G. 1987. *Educational Administration: Theory, Research, and Practice*, 3rd edn. New York: Random House.

Johnson, N. 1990. 'Understanding and Administering Educational Organizations: The Contribution of Greenfield's "Alternative Theory"'. *Journal of Educational Thought* 24(1): 28–38.

Kelsey, J. G. T. and Long, J. C. 1983. 'Educational Administration, Orthodoxy (and Heterodoxy?)'. In *Education Studies: Foundations of Policy*, eds R. F. Lawson and R. L. Schnell, 407–447. Washington, D.C.: University Press of America.

Lakomski, G. 1989. 'The Journal of Educational Administration: Mainstream, Tributary, or Billabong'. *Review of Australian Research in Education* 1: 57–67.

Lapham, L. H. 1991. 'Notebook: Opening the Mail'. *Harper's* 282 (February): 4–16.

Lasch, C. 1985. '"Excellence" in Education: Old Refrain or New Departure?' *Issues in Education* 3(1): 1–12.

Leithwood, K. A. and Montgomery, D. J. 1986. *Improving Principal Effectiveness: The Principal Profile.* Toronto: OISE Press.

Lipham, J. M. 1988. 'Getzels's Models in Educational Administration'. In *Handbook of Research on Educational Administration,* ed. N. J. Boyan, 171–184. New York: Longman.

Miskel, C. and Sandlin, T. 1981. 'Survey Research in Educational Administration'. In *Educational Administration Quarterly* 17, 4: 1–20.

Pitner, N. 1988. 'The Study of Administrator Effects and Effectiveness'. In *Handbook of Research on Educational Administration,* ed. N. J. Boyan, 99–122. New York: Longman.

Ribbins, P. 1985. 'Organisation Theory and the Study of Educational Institutions'. In *Managing Education: The System and the Institution,* eds M. Hughes, P. Ribbins, and H. Thomas, 223–261. London: Holt, Rinehart and Winston.

Schumacher, E. F. 1977. *A Guide for the Perplexed.* New York: Harper Colophon.

Schwandt, T. A. 1990. 'On Methodology and Moral Inquiry *or* What's Going on Here? A Commentary on Smith & Blase and Allison'. *Organizational Theory Dialogue* July: 1–7.

Scott, W.G. 1985. 'Organizational Revolution: An End to Managerial Orthodoxy'. *Administration & Society* 17(2): 149–170.

Scott, W. G. and Hart, D. K. 1979. *Organizational America.* Boston: Houghton Mifflin.

Sharp, R. and Green, A. 1975. *Education and Social Control: A Study in Progressive Primary Education.* London: Routledge & Kegan Paul.

Simon, H. A. 1957 [1945]. *Administrative Behavior: A Study of Decision-making Process in Administrative Organizations,* 2nd edn. New York: The Free Press.

Smith, J. and Blase, J. 1989. 'You Can Run But You Cannot Hide: Hermeneutics and Its Challenge to the Field of Educational Leadership. *Organizational Theory Dialogue,* January: 1–7.

Sontag, S. 1988. *AIDS and Its Metaphors.* New York: Farrar, Straus and Giroux.

Szasz, T. 1976. *Heresies.* Garden City, NY: Anchor/Doubleday.

Thomas, R. 1982. Twenty Years of a Journal: An Anniversary Statement. *Journal of Educational Administration* 20(1): 23–33.

Weber, M. 1971. *Max Weber.* Ed. and introd. J. E. T. Eldridge. London: Thomas Nelson.

—— 1978. *Max Weber: Selections in Translation.* Ed. W. G. Runciman. Cambridge: Cambridge University.

Willower, D. J. 1988. Synthesis and Projection. In *Handbook of Research on Educational Administration,* ed. N. J. Boyan, 729–745. New York: Longman.

10

SCIENCE AND SERVICE

The making of the profession of educational administration[1]

The eagle in its flight does not leave a mark; the scientist does. Inquiring into this question of freedom there must be, not only the scientific observation, but also the flight of the eagle that does not leave a mark. . . . For the description is never the actuality that is described; the explanation is obviously never the thing that is explained; the word is never the thing.

Krishnamurti

A phrase from Mary Parker Follett captures the spirit that has driven both management studies as they developed through our century and educational administration as it followed that development: in her words, a profession must rest on 'a foundation of *science* and a motive of *service*'. In accepting this view of professional practice, Belisle and Sargent say it constitutes 'the essential meaning of "administration" and "management"'.[2] The occasion of the 35th Anniversary of the Department of Educational Administration at the University of Alberta provides reason and opportunity to return to this foundational thinking and to examine its meaning and implications. In what follows, I will argue that the marriage of science and service – or rather of science and values, for that is the essence of the union – has left us with a legacy of unresolved problems and of false hopes and illusions.

To explore this topic, I have turned to two bodies of literature, sources that set out the fundamental issues. The first is that fecund catalogue of new thinking for educational administration, the book that in many ways constitutes the Holy Writ of educational administration: Campbell and Gregg's *Administrative Behavior in Education*. The work is, of course, an edited collection containing fourteen articles, many by authors whose names are easily recognizable as the intellectual progenitors of the modern field. I do not propose to review the book as a whole, but I would note that it was commissioned in 1954, took two and a half years to produce, and was published in 1957 as the realization of a plan 'to synthesize research findings in administration and to suggest implications for preparation programs for educational administrators'.[3] The creation of this collection of the new administrative thinking and the establishment of the Department of Educational Administration at the University of Alberta occurred therefore as overlapping events. If one wishes to understand something of the assumptions and intellectual foundations of the Department, Campbell and Gregg provide a mirror that reflects the past to the present. I first encountered the book as a beginning Master's student in the Department, and I can assure you the copy I still possess shows evidence that it was studied virtually cover-to-cover. My copy is dated November 1959, and cost $5.70 at the University bookstore. This commentary and reflection thus take me back to a point near the origin of the field in its consciously modern form and to the early years of the Department as well.

The second source I will review is my own critique that I have developed over the past two decades. I will not review that critique in detail, for it is a matter of record,[4] but I will use it in a contrapuntal interweaving of its issues with the hopes, claims, problematics, and assumptions that are apparent in Campbell and Gregg. Joining these elements may offer a clearer understanding of the past and point to an inherent conflict between science and values in the foundations of the field, a conflict that continues to trouble it today. 'Trouble' is perhaps not the right word to use here. The conflict between science and values in the study of educational administration is one that troubles me, but the field itself appears to have overridden an earlier recognition of the difficulty. Thus it has declared a victory over the problem of science and values and has declared its success in establishing a fortunate and strategically advantageous union that undergirds the modern profession.

In addition to these formal sources of ideas, I have also looked to my own recollections of the early years of the Department. In doing so, I hope that insight from these reflections will add a dimension of personal understanding to the intellectual issues that the remainder of the article focuses upon. The sources cited below are largely contemporary therefore to the events reflected upon in the following section.

A TROUBLING FOUNDATION

In Campbell and Gregg's extensive collection, the article that most repays reading now is Belisle and Sargent's chapter, 'The Concept of Administration'. They make plain Follett's hope for a profession based on science and directed to service; but they also chronicle the whole drive from the early years of the century to create the science that was to inform both the management of American industry and the direction of the nation's public institutions. Although Belisle and Sargent do not mention it, Halbertsam in his ethnographically detailed comparison of the historical development of Ford and Nissan, shows that Taylor's scientific management was the spirit of the time. This spirit also drove the movement to make educational administration a profession. Thus is the science of educational administration connected to the development of Ford's assembly line at River Rouge.[5] The Rouge was of enormous significance, for as Halbertsam says, 'That was the birth of the assembly line, the very essence of what would become America's industrial revolution.'[6] Now is not the occasion to explore how the money-driven American industrial revolution has been overtaken by the culture- and value-driven revolution of Japan. 'The Rouge was Henry Ford's greatest triumph,'[7] but it stands now as a symbol of cruelly exploitative enterprise; it is the quintessential realization of science as the essential tool of management. As Halbertsam shows, when the standards of management 'science' supplant 'service' in the conduct of an enterprise, the resulting increased productivity comes at an enormous social cost, ultimately at the cost of productivity itself. For example, Ford's innovation of the $5 a day wage, pay that the *Wall Street Journal* called an 'economic crime', was in Ford's view only a way of safeguarding his investment and commanding better workers. Thus the Rouge was less a 'beacon to the genius of its founder' than a testament to the excesses of science-driven management; it was a place where the treatment of human beings was 'mean and violent', a place where the lasting legacy was a hostile antipathy, a 'distrust and hatred' between strong management and powerful unions.[8] This is the theme that deserves careful attention now: ultimately the science of management overwhelmed its dedication to service. Science became identified *as service* and the distinction between fact and value – a distinction that Belisle and Sargent were at pains to define and defend – was lost, even in Belisle and Sargent's own thesis.

'Is' and 'ought to be'

In chronicling the development of the concept of administration Belisle and Sargent spend little time on historical antecedents outside twentieth-century America. Their concern is the new science and its profession in the context where these matters were of greatest concern. Having carefully and cautiously argued that there is both a science and profession of management, they then turn their attention to the problem of the relationship between the science and the profession. This problem is certainly one they recognize clearly. Under the heading, 'Polar Orientations of Administration', they discuss 'the two major trends of outlook concerning administration', noting that these have given rise to 'differences in orientation' to theory. Using what they call 'figurative language', they set out two polar positions 'as assumed exponents of the respective views' might do. Two paragraphs suggest the essence of the opposing views:

All we know or can say about administration is something like this: Organizations are composed of persons. No organization exists corresponding to pure abstractions about continuing structure or patterns of relationship. No system of abstractions formulated out of the kind of terms predominating in 'scientific management' and much of the early associated 'public administration' conceptualization corresponds to anything found in the real world of human beings.

Individuals come and go. They die. Social organizations and institutions survive; individual lives have no meaning except in relation to them and the values they maintain and develop as the heritage of all that is best out of the purposes, thought, and labors of lives that came before them. But organizations survive only if individuals, or enough of them, are ready to do what may be needed in order for organization to survive.[9]

Belisle and Sargent call the first of the polarities human relations; they do not name the second, but it is easily recognized as the systems view. After describing these views, Belisle and Sargent make a major point about them:

Each [of these polar views] constitutes a unity of outlook and activity in which 'is' and 'ought to be' are inseparably combined. . . . What, then, is the situation when there is a rapidly increasing growth of information, presumably reflecting a value-free science devoted strictly to the making of statements concerning what 'is' and declaring that any statements concerning what 'ought to be' are, by their very nature, outside of the domain of science?[10]

Before answering this question, Belisle and Sargent expand at length upon the problem it poses for the administrator. In this expansion, they describe trends in society, trends in which people look to the 'is' of science to solve their 'ought' problems, their ethical dilemmas. The 'new conditions' described by Belisle and Sargent force administrative science into a basic fallacy, the fallacy that 'assume[s] an ultimate indivisibility between "is" and "ought" inherent in the notion of science in relation to human organization'.[11] They then proceed to ignore the problem they have just identified and move with the assumptions and social trends that would blend the roles of the administrator as determiner of fact and determiner of value. Near the end of their article, they turn over to the administrator both science and values, ignoring completely their earlier arguments and the arguments of the whole modern field that insisted upon the necessary separation of fact and value. As they end their article they endorse a concept of administration that sees it as justified in both fact and value. The vision of the administrator's role thereby defined and endorsed by Belisle and Sargent is breathtaking in its scope and power and in the presumed knowledge and certainty it claims to stand upon. Thus Belisle and Sargent

shift from accepting the injunction of positivist science that placed statements of what ought to be 'by their very nature outside the domain of
science'; by the end of their lengthy article they have moved to join 'is' and
'ought to be' in the administrator's role. In the end, they find the sole
remaining problem

> is to absorb and integrate the rich abundance of 'is' statements into
> an outlook and activity – administration – which cannot but influence
> values. . . . Some choice of value directions – whether toward one or
> the other of the polar orientations, or toward a purely adventitious
> adjustment to the administrator's own perceptions of 'is' factors . . . is
> inescapable in administration.

> Administration is, therefore, today forced to grapple with a major
> problem of modern thought, namely, the development of a satis-
> factory theory of values. All 'is' information from the purportedly
> value-free social science which come within the purview of adminis-
> tration will be selected, ordered, related, and interpreted in accord-
> ance with the value system operating within the administrator. His
> own awareness of and sense of justifiability of his values will even
> influence his search for and use of different kinds of 'is' statements.
> How, then, shall a model of values, defensible from the viewpoint of
> administration, as a profession, be formulated today?[12]

In answer to the question of how the administrator is to develop 'a satisfactory theory of values', Belisle and Sargent endorse a vision of the
administrative profession in which the administrator combines the facts of
science and the *administrator's view* of the values of society. In their final
arguments, they see the administrator as a co-ordinator, as a balancer of
science and values, though it is plain the administrator is to be understood
both as justified by science and as empowered by the values of society. By
their penultimate paragraph they have accomplished the union of science
and values. There they speak of administration as 'a necessary social invention', one in which the administrator takes on

> the task of trusteeship and responsibility for maintenance and advance
> of social values via the multiplicity of organizations and governing
> systems of the pluralistic society. It is the area of social values – as
> reflected in the organizations and relationships of society – toward
> which the science and service of administration are directed.[13]

The fount of values: system and society

If anyone is dissatisfied that Belisle and Sargent have defined a problem
and then departed the scene having hastily declared its resolution, the
following chapter of Campbell and Gregg takes up the theme and expands

upon it. Graff and Street's chapter is entitled 'Developing a Value Framework for Educational Administration'. Gone from this exposition is any concern that ought statements by their very nature lie outside the realm of science. Graff and Street's purpose is to define the framework of values within which the science-based profession of administration is to be practised. Calling the assumption 'obvious', they emphasize that 'the administration of the schools derives its specialized nature from the objectives, purposes, and methods of the institution being considered'.[14] That statement might indeed be accepted as obvious were it not that Graff and Street see no ambiguities, conflicts, and uncertainties in the value framework they recommend to administrators. To them the values of society are clear; reflecting the assumptions of the Parsonian social system, they find that 'cultural systems have been developed' to guide the administrator.[15] Nor do Graff and Street shrink from defining the values they find pervasive and clear in society. In what they call ideals of 'superior status' based upon 'pragmatic freedom [and] democracy', they catalogue a list of values that emphasize the 'worth of each individual' within a context of 'group responsibility'. They note as well that the solution of the problems of our age 'require the cooperative application of the scientific method'.[16] So there it is again, a happy combination of science and values, but now the values are laid out explicitly for the administrator who wishes to ply his science-based profession.

Graff and Street's view of the union of science and values is clearly reflected in subheadings under which they address the major topic, 'Differing Value Systems Operate in our Culture'. Their analysis of this theme is easily resolved under two headings, 'The Practical Value of Value Systems' and 'A Consistent Value System is Essential'.[17] Indeed, Graff and Street never do examine the differing values systems that impinge upon the administrator nor do they suggest how conflicts among them might be resolved. Their answer, cast in the true systems mould, is that *a* consistent value system is essential. Although they claim that they do not 'presume to prescribe values for others', they immediately add that every administrator requires 'an operational value system', arguing that three criteria, consistency, comprehensiveness, and workability, 'cannot be ignored in the development and justification of such a system'.[18] Controversies about curriculum and educational purpose find no echo in Graff and Street. Commentators contemporary to that time, but writing outside the developing faith in administrative science saw pervasive problems of educational purpose and value. Conant, for example, spoke of 'a caste system [that] finds its clearest manifestation in [the] educational system', a system that allows 'social dynamite to accumulate in our cities'.[19] In another work, Conant looked at 'the Anglo-Saxon Tradition' and questions of equality of educational opportunity. There he opposed increasing 'the number and scope of private schools', but he also argued that non-denominational, tax-supported schools can be deeply 'concerned with moral and spiritual values'.[20] In both statements, Conant bolsters his arguments with arrays of facts, but he makes no appeal to science to support the positions he takes.

In an insightful statement, William G. Carr, executive secretary of the [American] National Education Association, identifies pervasive conflicts that surround questions of curriculum. He begins his catalogue of problems by enumerating some of the groups that exert diverse and often conflicting pressures on the school administrator.

> Each of these groups is anxious to avoid overloading the curriculum. All any of them ask is that the nonessentials be dropped in order to get their material in. Most of them insist that they do not want a special course – they just want their ideas to permeate the entire daily program. Every one of them proclaims a firm belief in local control of education and an apprehensive hatred of national control.
>
> Nevertheless, if their national organization program in education is not adopted forthwith, many of them use the pressure of the press, the radiance of the radio, and all the props of propaganda to bypass their elected local school board.[21]

Nor does Carr suggest that management science can guide the administrator's hand in resolving such curricular dilemmas and conflicts.

From the earliest days of the theory movement in educational administration, it was apparent that two competing and antagonistic views were at work in the field. One force worked for the integration of science within a framework of values and looked for societal legitimation of the administrator. This was the optimistic view, the one that thought science could guide the administrator's hand and make his decisions. The other position was that of the New Movement, the new science-driven movement in educational administration that reflected the administrative theory of Herbert Simon and that echoed the assumptions and methods of logical positivism. The epistemology and methodology of positivism insisted, of course, that science could make no meaningful statement about values, for values themselves were not meaningful as scientifically knowable entities. In the contemporary field of educational administration we have managed to integrate the two positions so as to incorporate the worst of both worlds. The modern administrator looks to society for legitimation of the values he espouses and to science for their grounding in objective truth. One source of legitimation may thus be played off against the other, and the administrator's personal responsibility for his choices, for his interpretation of what he accepts as fact is attenuated, if not elided completely. Two rabbits disappear *into* the administrator's hat so quickly, we forget there were rabbits, or even a hat. Before looking further at this significant development and its unfortunate consequences, let us look first at the 'pure science' position in educational administration.

Two chapters in Campbell and Gregg deal extensively with value questions, but there is hardly a unity of view between them. Graff and Street give the joyous, systems-oriented view that since a unified set of values pervades society, the administrator is free to use science as it is available to pursue those values. Belisle and Sargent come to a somewhat similar conclusion, but not without warning of the philosophical chasm that yawns between value and fact, between the administrator's decision and truths of administrative science.

In subsequent chapters, the reader moves into the world of fact, theory, and research – the only entities that the New Movement science thought worth directing attention to. In his chapter, Halpin presents his famous 'Paradigm for Research on Administrative Behavior', a statement that is well worth reading today. Another chapter that should be read in conjunction with it is Griffiths's 'Toward a Theory of Administrative Behavior'. There Griffiths argues forcefully that the science of administration must be cast within the assumptions of positivist science generally and must call upon the stringent requirements of positivist science generally and of hypothetico–deductive statements cast in mathematical forms. One of the formulas Griffiths provides as an example of what is needed has the form,

$$\frac{dI}{dt} = b\,(t - \beta I).$$

For those who may have missed more rabbits disappearing into a hat, Griffiths explains: 'Translated, this means that friendliness will tend to increase if the amount of interaction is disproportionately large in relation to existing friendliness, or will tend to decrease if the amount of interaction is disproportionately small.'[22] Thus we see the early science doing what it often did: putting the obvious into complex, but arcane and powerful-appearing mathematical symbols. Reflecting injunctions from Simon and from positivist science generally, Griffiths asks, 'Does theory tell an administrator how he "ought" to administer?' He answers somewhat regretfully, 'the answer appears to be "no"'.[23]

Griffiths, like Belisle and Sargent, soon forgets this unfortunate limitation on the science of administration. By the end of his chapter he offers a ringing testament to the power of administrative science, one that aligns administrative science with the long line of achievements in physical and mathematical science. His confidence in the theory and research he offered was then virtually unlimited, as appears in one of the most memorable passages from the New Movement writing. Succinctly and powerfully it summarizes and symbolizes what the field thought it was doing and where it was going.

A theory of administrative behavior will make it possible to relate what now appear to be discrete acts to one another so as to make a unified concept. The great task of science has been to impose an *order* upon the universe. Kepler's Laws, for instance, impose a set of relationships upon the planets of the solar system. Within this framework of laws, the motions of the planets make sense, their positions can be predicted, and order is apparent to all who care to look for it. This is the great task of theory in the field of educational administration. Within a set of principles, yet to be formulated, it will be possible to predict the behavior of individuals within the organization framework, and it will be possible to make decisions that will result in a more efficient and effective enterprise. Research will have more meaning because it will be directed toward the solution of problems, have clear definitions, and will contribute to the whole concept of administration. It will be more easily understood because it will use concepts that have the same meaning to all in the profession.[24]

Griffiths doesn't say what the planets did before Kepler imposed order on them. Nor does he explain how a science of administration, parallel to Kepler's laws in form and power, could speak to value issues in the educational enterprise. He leaves aside the question of how such laws could solve problems and enable the administrator to make decisions. Thus here again is the error of understanding of the time. Though the proponents of administrative science recognized the need to separate the values of action from the facts of science, from its inception they called upon their science to serve values. Increasingly leaving philosophical caution behind, the rhetoric of the new science elided the separation of facts and values and came to advocate an administrative science that offered a union of science and values. In the first more cautious mode, technique supplants values, or more accurately the values of administrative technique become the values of the administrative system. In the second more active conception of science and values, they are seen as integrated, values blessing science, and science informing values. Both views are dangerously and pervasively in error. But at least we may now better understand where these errors come from. Halpin helps us to understand what went wrong as the New Movement science of administration embarked upon a crusade that would establish it as science and profession.

Halpin's paradigm is consistent with the tenets of positivistic inquiry that Griffiths sets out in his chapter. His acknowledgements are to Simon, Feigl, and Cassirer, thus establishing his work in the tradition of logical positivism, specifically in that branch of it that Simon introduced into administrative studies. At the outset, Halpin makes clear that apart from the specific varieties of administration in schools, hospitals, and etc., 'there is administration *qua* administration; and that this is a domain worthy of study'. At the same time he notes that research should be 'focused upon the *behavior of administrators* rather than upon . . . the totality referred to as "administration"'.[25] In these assumptions, he explicitly follows the injunctions of Simon. It was Simon, who set out to explore human choice but failed to look at why people choose their purposes and values, for science, he knew, could not speak to such an issue. As Simon saw it, the administrative scientist could not attend to notions of 'good' or 'bad', for then 'a science of administration would be impossible'. But admitted by the back door, 'good' and 'bad' do have a place in Simon's science. Cut off from a consideration of organizational purpose, means become good or bad as they lead to such a purpose. In such science there is no 'ethical sense', only a judgement of means as they are conducive to the attainment of whatever purposes the organization has set. Thus having eliminated ethical content from statements of good and bad, and having limited enquiry to factual means, not the valuational ends they serve, Simon concluded, 'It is this factual element which makes up the real substance of an administrative science.'[26] Such also was the devalued administrative science that Halpin imported into education.

The whole of Halpin's paradigm assumes that the purposes of the organization are clear and its outcomes measurable. It is for this reason that the purpose or context of administration is irrelevant to New Movement theory and research. It is only the administrator's behaviour as a variable intervening between purpose and product that is of interest to Halpin. The paradigm itself is familiar enough that it does not require explication here. But it should be emphasized that it rested on all the concepts of operationalism and hypothetico–deductive reasoning that Griffiths endorsed in his article on theory. Within these strategic assumptions and limitations, Halpin's model is complex and complete; it rests on the assumption that an organization is a productive entity, oriented to goals and directing its process to outcomes appropriate to them. The model Halpin offers contains four 'panels' and 29 'boxes', all of this process conceived as acting from $Time_A$ through $Time_B$ to $Time_N$. Although Halpin recognizes administration as a 'normative discipline', he places that quality below the study of it through 'descriptive science'. The two approaches to administration must certainly not be confused or combined. The normative aspect of administration is, for Halpin, an ideal, and there-fore not of the world of science.

> Administration as a normative discipline deals with how an administrator ought to behave and is predicated upon an ideal situation in which time is theoretically infinite and choices are not coercive; in studying administration as social scientists, the concern is with how administrators actually behave in the 'real' world where time is limited and choices must be made.[27]

The issues that concerned Carr and Conant are by virtue of Halpin's assumptions matters of indifference to him. Devoid of any ethical content, only the description of pure administrative process within the organization is of interest to him. In considering the panel of the model that recognizes normative statements of organizational purpose, Halpin dismisses its content as irrelevant to the scientist:

> The social scientist, *as a scientist,* does not have to evaluate these dimensions; his job is to identify and describe them. It is not for him to say that changes along Dimension Q are to be valued as more important than changes along Dimension K, but he must define the dimensions in operational terms and must devise reliable techniques for measuring whatever changes occur.[28]

As a true positivist separating ends and means, values and facts, Halpin was interested only in the administrator's behaviour and its 'effectiveness'. What end the behaviour served was a matter of indifference to Scientist Halpin.

> *Let it be emphasized again that if one fails to establish the relationship between the behavior of the administrator and syntalic measures of the organization's 'effectiveness', he evades the most fundamental research issue at stake.*[29]
> [Emphasis in the original]

'Balancing' science and values

A reading of the four articles identified in this review of Campbell and Gregg's collection defines a set of powerful and important ideas. These were the ideas that provided the intellectual foundations for the modern conception of educational administration; these were the ideas that established the expectation that science itself could provide the foundation of professional practice in the field. A new reading of these ideas points now to inherent conflicts among them, conflicts that serve to weaken, mislead, and impoverish educational administration. Some observers might examine these same foundations and fail to see the cracks, though my inspection finds these shortcomings both apparent and hostile to a sound development of the field. The failure to grasp the inherent conflicts built into the conception of the modern field can be seen in the article Fisk contributed to Campbell and Gregg's collection. Fisk sees neither cracks nor problems in the emerging profession. He is completely confident about the prospects for establishing a profession uniting science and service. He ends his article on the task of administration by concluding that 'the challenge to those who would prepare effective school administrators is that of narrowing the gap between . . . *observed actuality*, at least from the scholar's point of view, [so as to make it] congruent with the *socially desired* definition'.[30] In Fisk's view, 'the-man-on-the-job' as school administrator lacks both a sound understanding of what society needs and of what the scientific study of administration offers. To Fisk and many other contributors in Campbell and Gregg, the distinction between the needs of society and the scientific knowledge base of administration is first blurred and confused, and then eliminated: what the science of administration knew came to be understood as what society needed – and wanted.

A reading of the foundational writing in the field reveals three significant positions about the relationship of science and society, about the relationship the facts of science, theory, and research on the one hand and the values of an encompassing culture and society on the other. These may be summarized as follows:

1 Science can have nothing to do with values. Values are completely exogenous to science; it can make no statement about them. Administrative science, therefore, can only operate if it is given value limits and directions to work within. Administrative science and any profession based upon it must wait upon the specification of a set of socially determined purposes and values.
2 Because there is an agreed-upon and functional set of values that does indeed govern society, administrative science can take its direction from those values and work to assist society and its institutions, such as schools, in the attainment of their ends.
3 Facts and values can never be completely separated. The scientist and the professional administrator must always use judgement to 'balance' the knowledge they have as fact and the values they choose as leaders.

A significant observation to be made on these points is that they are *all* valuational in nature. Even the first position that insists that values are exogenous to science takes a value stance. This view that makes science independent of values is echoed in Halpin's paradigm and in Griffiths's argument that hypothetico–deductive theory is simply a 'logical organization of the facts'.[31] Commenting on Simon's conception of the administrator as value-free scientist, Hodgkinson calls this the view that holds the administrator to be a cipher or kind of moral eunuch.[32] Could there be a scientist – could there be a human being – who would simply do his job, as Simon advised, and be responsible for nothing? In discussing the meaning of responsibility – whether in general or administrative terms – Hodgkinson again puts the answer well:

> Responsibility is always *to* somebody *for* something. The subtlety is that the some*body* may be oneself and the some*thing* may be an internal phenomenological event.

It is readily apparent that some conception of the relationship between science and values informed an understanding of the nature of the new profession of educational administration. Each of the three positions identified above had its apologists and advocates in the emerging literature that celebrated educational administration as science and profession. What was less well understood was the fundamental tensions among the positions and how unresolved conflicts would impact upon the profession said to be emerging. Exploring this impact will be the theme of the remainder of this paper. But let me suggest now what those tensions and conflicts are.

1 Administrative science as pure science was an early favourite in the field. In Miklos's review of doctoral studies completed over three decades under the auspices of the Department of Educational Administration, the predominant type of study was what he called 'relational' or 'descriptive/relational'.[33] Science *qua* science was the criterion of excellence that many early researchers strove to realize in their work, as may be seen in an earlier analysis of the 'tradition' of leader behaviour studies that were a favourite and early focus of study in the Department. Nevertheless such studies did not escape criticism for 'their very large weaknesses', including their snapshot approach to a problem of great depth and complexity.[34] In any case, it is apparent that the 'pure science' approach to administration is now much less popular than it was in the early years of the theory movement in educational administration.

2 The systems view of society and of science within it often went hand-in-hand with the approach that saw administrative science as pure and independent. The union of the two appeared to offer a happy solution to the problem of the relationship of science to values: the system supplied the values, while science provided the facts. Among the writings reviewed here, this position is seen pre-eminently in the articles by Graff and Street and by Fisk. Other writings also make plain the relationship in which administrative science was to be handmaid to the values of a functional society. In these writings, the social sciences are likely to be portrayed as 'viewing' educational administration. Whatever their titles, the message was implicit and explicit: the social sciences offer a reservoir of fact, theory, and research, and all of this great body of scientific knowledge should be understood to lie open to the administrator who wishes to select the most effective means for attaining the value premises mandated to him. For example, Eidell and Kitchel introduce a set of reading they claim offer 'strategies for implementing the utilization of knowledge in the context of educational organizations'.[35] In retrospect the assumption of such a project seems both foolhardy and overweening: that bodies of knowledge are like unused tools that lie waiting the administrator's attention and application. In this view, the only problem considered is a want of 'strategies' for the 'utilization' of these tools. Similar assumptions are readily found in other literature of the time.[36]

3 Of the three positions outlined above, the most subtle – and perhaps the most defensible – view of how science might be integrated within a frame

of values is that which recognizes that only through the administrator's 'balanced' judgement can the facts of science be united within a framework of social and personal values. Before abandoning themselves to the view that science solves both moral and technical problems, Belisle and Sargent argue with urgent clarity the impossibility of making a union of science and values. If there is to be any such union, they show, there must be a resolution of competing values, and this resolution is the task of the administrator, a task that is human and humane, a task that must end in action open to question and dispute. The balancing of value against value, of fact against value certainly cannot yield scientific certainty. As Belisle and Sargent argue, any reduction of such conflicts

> does not imply their resolution in a complete synthesis or unity of administrative action; increasing expression and balance of the respective values within the organization itself emerges, however, as a function of the administrative effort to resolve the competing values.[37]

4 Writing as a social scientist of organization, George Strauss comes to virtually the same judgement. In a striking article he emphasizes the values that undergird much of what is called the science of organization. At the outset of his article he questions the 'universality of the desire for self-actualization', an assumption that pervades the human relations literature; it is, he says, a value judgement that 'the *job* should be the primary form of need satisfaction for everyone'.[38] After a lengthy examination of the limits that would have to be placed upon power-equalization as advocated in human relations, Strauss concludes that deciding how much power-equalization should prevail in an organization is 'a balancing job'.[39] The person making the balance in such situations will, of course, be the administrator, and it will be the administrator's judgement, not his science that draws the balance.

Thus it appears again that the ultimate questions facing the administrator, whether as academic or professional practitioner, are valuational and philosophic in nature.

REMEMBERING

An invitation implicit in this conference is to look back, to remember. Surely it is important that we do so, that we ask ourselves how we were and how we are, that we explore the relation between what was and what is. As I took up that invitation, the images that came first to my mind were of the culture of the '50s: The pervasiveness of cigarette smoking, the risqué jokes that every conference presentation opened with, the bottles of rye and men telling jokes about sex to each other after the sessions of the conference were ended, the separation of men and women at parties and in study. But those cultural rituals, I soon concluded, were ephemeral and not ultimately of great significance. Other memories, deeper ones and of a possible darker hue, came to mind. I offer the following thoughts therefore as representative of the dynamics of 'then'; yet they may also point to dynamics that have helped to shape our 'now' in educational administration, if only in a present-day rejection of them.

Reflections

To be in the Department of Educational Administration was to be in a select and separated group. In the beginning, we had all our classes in one room, and no one else used it. If we were not using it, the classroom stood empty. Later the whole Department moved to a floor at the top of the engineering building, and still there was a sense of separation, of encapsulation.

As students we learned early that our academic success and our later careers were of great importance. That success reflected not only upon ourselves, but even more importantly upon the Department. Anyone who took a course 'across campus' or in other departments of the Faculty of Education or who sought advice outside the walls of the Department was expected not just to do well; he was expected to excel.

In the beginning, the curriculum took philosophy and law as seriously as it did the new 'social science content'. The serious student was exposed to a wide and stimulating set of ideas. At least in my experience of those early years, the curriculum had a liberal focus and effect.

Ultimately one felt forced to choose, to take either the social science or the law, finance, and philosophy. And the hierarchy one encountered in making the choice was clear, though implicit; it put social science unmistakably at the top of the heap. Social science as applied to administration was generally recognized as the great hope of the field, as the means that offered – as no other kind of study did – the Great Leap Forward. If one wanted to move with the 'best and the brightest' one chose the way of social science.[40]

We were all expected to be experts and professionals in the science of administration and organization. How this transformation occurred was never clear – though it was generally regarded as having happened abruptly and completely. When we went into the world of practical affairs, we all had to carry a we-know attitude. What it was that we knew became clearer as we mastered the language of social science and the quantitative techniques of experimental design and methodology. On various public occasions we were called upon to dazzle practising administrators – and usually very senior ones – with a display of social science lingo and analysis. Such displays were a ritual at the various Banff conferences.

A foundation of science and a motive of service was the implicit motto we all served. We strove to expand our social scientific knowledge so we could be of use in the world. I recall two events that exemplify both the power of this implicit motto and the dangerous conflict and error that were inherent in it. Trips to the field were always an occasion where students and professors lowered the usually formal barriers between them and shared insights and human perspectives. On one such occasion I recall John Andrews speaking of why he left physics, the discipline that was his first field of study. One day as he was observing a 'cloud chamber' in a laboratory, he watched an ionized particle move through the atmosphere, and asked himself, 'What good was this knowledge in the larger world?' By analogy then we learned from this respected and knowledgeable professor that the socially valuable pursuit was to see the social system as a kind of cloud chamber and to master the forces that – ion-like – could be seen to be moving through the social atmosphere.

Second, I recall that John Andrews ran for trustee on the Edmonton school board. Running as a professor of educational administration, he was swept into power. The implication was that a little bit of administrative science would clear up the well known administrative problems of the board. The old war horses of the board now faced enlightened science, and Andrews was chosen to be chairman. One of the issues that arose early in his tenure concerned supplementary reading materials that were being used in the junior grades. The materials were American in origin and took the form of a news sheet that students could read after they had completed exercises in their regular readers. The sheets were emblazoned with flags and other symbols of American culture, and a protest arose that such materials were not appropriate in Edmonton schools. Speaking in a public board meeting and hoping to support the continued use of the materials, Andrews began his defence with the phrase, 'I'm as anti-American as anyone, but . . . ' He must surely have finished that sentence, but as far as the public and the media were concerned, he never did. He was understood to be saying, 'I am anti-American', and that issue swept the other out of public understanding. Over coffee in the cafeteria, we, the experts and professionals, smiled at this incident, failing to appreciate the depths of conflict it represented between rational and cultural values, failing to understand a conflict that science was helpless to resolve.

It was the science we saw ourselves practising that put service in jeopardy and that brought us to intervene with teachers and administrators in ways that were manipulative at best and possibly injurious to them at worst – certainly unethical in the context of today's values. One of our practices was to enlist schools from a district in a seminar on leadership, though leadership in this context meant a purported measurement of it using the LBDQ, the Leader Behavior Description Questionnaire.[41] The proposal to use the LBDQ in this way would be made first to a district superintendent. We

214

usually had little difficulty gaining access and participation, for what enlightened superintendent would turn down an in-service project on leadership for his principals? The principals were given the right to decline to participate. They understood that a survey of their leadership would be conducted in their schools by a questionnaire given to teachers. It was teachers therefore who were called upon to describe their principals' leader behaviour, but the seminars and the results of the survey were intended as in-service training for principals. The data from these questionnaires were collected before the seminar and placed in a comparative grid. The seminar itself consisted of a morning devoted to describing the LBDQ and its theory of leadership. After lunch the familiar 2×2 typology appeared with the results of the survey among the schools of the district. The principals were then given a code to identify themselves in the array. No cautions were given the principals about the limits of the LBDQ as an instrument for measuring leadership; on the contrary the LBDQ was presented as a new and powerful social science instrument. No one paused to reflect on the reliability and validity of such instruments, and no one raised the question of the ethics of disclosing such a measurement of leadership to the participants. In my recollection, the principals participated somewhat grudgingly, none of them willing to stand against university researchers, yet none of them reflecting a conviction that the event was a happy and helpful experience. Indeed, the tension throughout the whole day was palpable, and I always felt relief when the event was over and we headed back to Edmonton, to more study of the social science of administration devoid of any involvement with the practice of it. In such pursuits one did not have to think about the ethics of the science, only its effectiveness. Although we did very few such seminars, the practice persisted. In research conducted at the University of Calgary, researchers asked 'Who's a good principal?' and answered a moral question with measurements from the LBDQ. In that research the feedback to principals was somewhat attenuated, being given to them in a mode that was 'largely personal and interpretive'.[42]

Few studies in the early science of administration ever met the criteria of experimental design. One that did induced stress by manipulating it as a variable during supervision of teachers. This study was praised and repeatedly cited in the most theory- and research-oriented of the texts in educational administration. There indeed it was used as the basis for an extensive discussion of the Getzels–Guba model, a model that provided the foundational assumptions of the text.[43] When this same research was published in an early issue of *The Canadian Administrator*, a journal designed to communicate the results of the new science to practising administrators, it drew numerous letters and comments from administrators, all of them negative in tone and critical on ethical grounds of the technique that used random assignment of teachers to stressful supervision.[44] This negative reaction from the field surprised us at the time, for it came in articulate full voice. Could they not appreciate the need to understand administrative issues from a scientific perspective? At the time, I was associate editor of the *Canadian Administrator* and largely responsible for its content. In my memory of the matter, I thought the *Canadian Administrator* had published the letters of criticism and an editorial of reply. But as I went back to read the documents of record, I discovered that no such material was ever published, despite the fact that later articles spoke directly to issues in teacher supervision.

The question that needs attention in this looking back to the early days of the Movement lies not in the research itself. More important in this matter is the gulf of understanding – the contrast of values – that separated the researchers and their budding science on the one hand and practising administrators on the other. It was the researchers who were bedazzled and bewitched by the technical possibilities of the science they practised; it was the practitioners who saw its ethical implications and shortcomings. Milgram-like, we as practitioners of the new science-based profession were rather blindly obedient to the authority of that science. Indeed, we largely failed to see that an ethical issue of authority and responsibility was involved in the matter. Our attitude held that science was above such criticism. It was too important to be stopped. As professionally trained administrators we could see the science of our profession, but not the issues of ethics and responsibility that it entailed. All of this flowed from what we had been taught; ultimately we cast away the values portion of our curriculum and took up what we had learned to regard as pure science.

PROSPECTS FOR EDUCATIONAL ADMINISTRATION AS A FIELD OF STUDY

The Department of Educational Administration at the University of Alberta has reached its thirty-fifth anniversary: a notable event indeed, for it can hardly be doubted but that this institution is the largest and most notable enterprise of its kind. Thousands of students have graduated from its programmes and their influence has spread worldwide. The research and the researchers of the Department are widely known and cited. On such an occasion as this celebration, I might say with Mark Anthony, 'I come to bury Caesar, not to praise him' – with Caesar being the pseudo-science of administration, not the Department itself. I offer a weighing of the problems and prospects of the field in general and a reflection upon its past and possible future. In this assessment by sheer virtue of its position the Department cannot escape a deep involvement.

As springboard for this reflective assessment, I will use ideas from the critique of educational administration that I have struggled to formulate and defend over the past two decades.[45] From that critique, I will set ideas

216

in counterpoint against the foregoing analysis of the development of educational administration as a science and a profession. I will conclude by drawing implications and conclusions from all of this.

The following points from my critique of educational administration are germane to the arguments of this paper.

1 A theory is not merely, as Griffiths once said, a logical organization of facts. It is also a moral vision of the world. This observation has particular force when the theory is about social reality.

2 Organizations are not objects in nature; an organization is a moral order invented and maintained by human choice and will.

3 The 'pure' science of educational administration never worked as science. It suffered from what Sorokin called 'quantophrenia'. A fundamental reason for this failure lay in the banishment of values from the theoretical understanding of the administrative act.

4 To the extent that modern administrative theory has considered values, it has relegated them to the background or dealt with them as quantifiable variables in the foreground. Either way values are excised from consideration. The message from all this is that rationality stands on facts alone.

5 The systems view holds that society and its organizations are ordered around a coherent and consistent set of values. As one moves from this view towards an understanding of the individual, the more disordered and conflict-ridden life in organizations appears.

6 To claim that there *is* a science of effectiveness in organizational affairs is to misuse and misrepresent science. Such a misuse and misrepresentation can be both deliberate and profitable.

7 Values are made or chosen. To understand that making and that choosing requires not a calculation, but an insight into life and human affairs.

8 There is no science to determine what is good. To declare one value better than another requires a force, a choice, and ultimately the imposition of one person's will upon another's. If we are to escape, or at least justify, this imposition, we need to move administrative action beyond will, fact, and preference. We need to found it in a realm of higher values.

9 In the world of action, fact and value are inevitably intertwined. It is for this reason that science cannot guide the administrator's hand or make decisions for him.

10 Conceptually fact and values *are* separable. Both theorists and practitioners should make that separation, at least as they analyze the world of action. Otherwise they condemn themselves to a world without freedom, driven either by fact on the one hand or value on the other.

11 The business of committing people to values is the basic stuff of both education and administration. Much of the modern study of

administration has assumed that science obviated the task of selling values, defending them, and committing people to them.

12 A profession of administration cannot rest on facts and science alone, for it requires appreciation and judgement. Ultimately such a profession requires not simply an acquaintance with a body of fact, but an understanding of values and a commitment to them. Much of what has passed as training for administrators is irrelevant to their tasks, but it may be helpful to their careers.

13 Given that both education and administration are suffused with values, the way forward requires a critical examination of the great and significant choices before us, a fuller and more searching examination than either programmes of training or professional action has usually given them.

14 Law, history, and philosophy constitute promising but now largely neglected sources from which administration can be understood within a context of values.

15 The certification of administrators is inimical to their education.

Implications

The implications that flow from this statement of critique and reflection are varied and diverse. I will content myself with identifying only a few in hopes that they will summarize the weight of the arguments made to this point. These points may also set the arguments of the paper as a whole in a context clear enough to stimulate further discussion of the history and development of the field and of its prospects for the future.

1 The heart of the arguments advanced here turns on the relationship of fact and value. Positivist science decreed an unhappy and unfortunate split between fact and value; the ill consequences of that schism were imported into educational administration as it attempted to base professional practice upon a purely fact-driven science.

2 The appeal of New Movement science, as Halpin called it, was so strong that it drove out older knowledge and approaches that were of considerable value in themselves. In effect, the new science lobotomized the field, cutting off its roots in more liberal studies, law, history, and philosophy. Certainly the new science virtually removed any historical perspective the field had on itself. Even the issue of the relationship of fact and value could no longer be examined, as Belisle and Sargent explored it. The new science was ahistorical, quantified, and hostile to any knowledge that could not be expressed within its tenets and assumptions.

3 Despite its emphasis upon quantification, the new science was impatient with even the study of the fundamentals of statistics. Computer

supported 'statistical packages' shaped the design of research and the definition of problems for enquiry. All of this led to a kind of efficiency in programs of study in educational administration. The models of enquiry were clear; the means to implement them easily acquired. An instant, but palpably unsatisfactory, science of educational administration was attained.

4 The failure of positivist science as a foundation for administrative knowledge was tacitly, if not explicitly, recognized after the second decade of the Theory Movement in educational administration. In a turning point statement in 1979, Griffiths spoke of 'intellectual turmoil' in the field.[46] Miklos's survey documents the return of more varied research methods,[47] while Griffiths, finding virtue in alternative paths to knowledge, endorsed 'paradigm diversity' as a necessary and justified assumption for enquiry.[48]

5 The cost of the Theory Movement in educational administration was a loss of faith in humane studies – in their widest sense – as a proper study for administrators. In common practice, the enquiries of researchers became as means oriented as the science they studied. Though faith in the science ultimately diminished, the efficacy of a pseudo-science as a route to career advancement was apparent to many aspiring administrators.

6 If the essence of administration is appreciation, judgement, and balancing, it is apparent that the New Movement science of administration displaced the study of administration with the study of organizations. The fall of this science and its claims has yet to restore a focus upon the essence of the administrative function. Instead it appears to have legitimated the examination of virtually any administrative task. The cost of this development is that enquiry becomes disparate, disjointed, and noncumulative. Virtually any topic is good enough. The field as a field of study begins to disappear.

7 The promises and assumptions of the Theory Movement have certainly not disappeared from the contemporary scene in educational administration. They find new form, for example, in the excesses of the school effectiveness movement where indoctrination in procedures replaces reflection upon and judgement about ends and means in education. The popularization of the procedures of school effectiveness represents a recrudescence of pseudo-science.

8 The time to rethink the curriculum of administrative studies is at hand. The restoration of a programme of more liberal studies in law, history, and philosophy is called for. The social sciences will continue to contribute to our understanding of administration, but if they are to serve their most helpful function they must be liberated from the narrow vision imposed by the positivist blinkers that defined social science after the advent of the Theory Movement.

9 A consideration of the ends of education should command the administrator's attention as much as the means to them. Indeed the good administrator and the insightful one must needs reflect upon and analyse the interplay of ends and means. Thus administrative studies should become more generalist on the one hand and more issue-oriented on the other.

CONCLUSION

The management science founded by Simon and introduced to educational administration by Halpin, Griffiths, and other social scientists of thirty-five years ago aimed to establish control over decision making within the organization. Such science claimed to be indifferent towards the ends for which such control was used. The paradox of control-oriented science is that its consequences are exactly the opposite of those claimed: means supplant ends and become their own ends in the out-of-control organization.[49] As Bates points out, a management science focused upon control in the organization brings with it an unfortunate consequence in education: 'The separation of administrative and educational concerns.'[50] More fundamentally, as Kant warned, a control-oriented science aimed at the individual becomes an instrument of social repression and a threat to personal freedom.[51]

Two examples will serve to illustrate how ends and means, facts and values, are interwoven in the fundamental issues that educational administrators deal with – or ought to. First, we may note with Lasch that the contemporary drive to link education to the needs of industry is an argument for less education, not more. The demands that industry place upon education are relatively modest – a highly educated élite and a largely ignorant mass made adept in simple technical routines and kept quiescent by the anodynes of mass media and sports.[52] As Lasch argues, education that serves the deepest needs of society and the individual must serve ends that sweep far beyond the demands of industry. Paradoxically an education so conceived serves not only the individual and society generally, but also the needs of industries bent upon increasing their productivity and competitiveness. In this example, the line of argument finds that the administrator must override factual statements of needs in order to arrive at a right conception of education.

A second example of the complex interrelationship of fact and value in education is found in controversies surrounding different methodologies of reading instruction. The 'language experience' approach to reading is now widely used in school systems, and in some is virtually an article of faith. This approach claims to value the learner; it seeks to capitalize on the natural language abilities of the child and largely avoids a focus upon orthography and the phonemic structure of words in the acquisition of reading skills. A growing body of research, however, shows that the skilled reader must

> develop a strong sense of how to search deliberately and methodically for information in letter sequences, word sequences or meaning. . . . [This body of research points] toward the conclusion that skillful reading depends critically on the deep and thorough acquisition of spellings and spelling-sound relationships.[53]

In this example, it appears that professional judgement has overridden the facts of empirical enquiry. In both examples, the critical role of the administrator as mediator, agent of appreciation, and balancer of fact and value is apparent.

It should be apparent from all that has gone before that a central issue in the study of educational administration – and in management science generally – is the place that facts and values should have in the shaping of the administrator's action. On this question rides our concept of professional practice and perhaps the possibility of it. While people of practical affairs tend to ignore such questions, getting on instead with their science or their convictions, many who struggle in the arenas where theory is still debated can be divided in two camps: those who see the central administrative issue as being all fact and those who see it as all value. In this paper I have taken the middle ground, the position that argues the central questions of administration turn on an interweaving of fact and value. The ground on which such a position may be argued appears to be disappearing rapidly as the proponents of new forms of pure science define one camp and the advocates of pure value define another. In the camp of the pure value advocates are found amongst the critical theorists, the deconstuctors, postmodernists and radical feminists and phenomenologists who are convinced science and critique has led them to a final understanding of good and evil. Their error is to think that science can deal with values as it does with facts, establishing an ultimate truth about them. In a sense both camps offer a pure science, one focused on facts, the other on value.

'Coherentism' is the name that Evers and Lakomski give to their position.[54] A brief examination of this position must suffice for now, but it may serve to define the problem and to show the weakness of both camps, those that would drive science to consider only pure fact or pure value. The problem is succinctly defined by Lakomski:

> If attending to our values helps us to make *better* decisions, then we need specific criteria to help us decide *between* competing values. In other words, there has to be a way to determine if value X is better than value Y in some specified way. But if values are merely non-cognitive or affective and *subjectivist*, then we cannot determine rationally or finally, which of two conflicting values is better.[55]

The clue to the answer Lakomski will give to this problem lies in her phrase, 'if values are *merely* noncognitive'. The answer is to make values cognitive, to turn them into facts. She notes that even subjectivists will defend their values with argument. From this she concludes that

> actually defending or acting on personal preferences implies that *in practice* not all values are considered equally acceptable or worthy. When people actually defend their preferences, they admit a modicum of rationality and objectivity by admitting that some preferences or values *are* better than others.[56]

But what would convince one person of another's value position? Why *should* we be rational? What Lakomski fails to recognize is that an appeal to argument is an appeal to values. Rationality itself is ultimately a value position. As Brukaber, drawing on Weber, explains the issue,

> commitment . . . cannot itself be guided by reason, for in Weber's view there is no rational way of deciding among the plurality of conflicting possible value commitments. Every rational life, in short is founded on a non-rational choice.[57]

To be rational or to decide to look for the 'coherence' of evidence is to make a value choice. Such a choice may be one that many people make or that many scientists make, but consensus about a value does not transmute it from the value realm to the cognitive and rational. If we are to ask what values are *better* than others, we must look in a domain other than rationality or coherence.

The spirit of the times: encouraged by charters and codes of human rights the individual seeks maximum advantage for self, ignoring the consideration that one person's rights are enforced at the cost of another's loss of them. The furtherance of individual rights often comes at the cost of civility and social order. Can anyone look at contemporary life and not think we live in a dog-eat-dog world? As the symbols of authority in schools have been attacked and removed, the power of the institution to teach and educate has been denigrated and diminished. The spirit of the times encourages individuals to be irresponsible, calling it freedom.

To rectify this loss and to determine how we are to find and act upon *better* values requires a redemption of two closely associated notions that have all but fallen into disrepute in contemporary society: authority and hierarchy. Both of these notions assume that there *are* better values and that an organization can represent them. Indeed, this is how we should think of an organization: as a moral order in action. The administrator is a representative of a moral order and an entrepreneur for its values. Both ancient scripture and philosophy recognize that the notion of the good requires an insight into, if not a vision of, the nature of reality and into the ultimate purpose of the individual life. For example, the Book of Common

Prayer sets out two ethical obligations that are to bind believers in their relationship to God and to others; they are then to pray to God saying, 'Write both these laws in our hearts we beseech thee.'[58] This is a metaphor or as Frye says, 'a myth to live by'.[59] I hope I will not be misunderstood if I say that is the way better values are acquired: by beseeching God that we may understand them. Such an answer may not be very satisfactory, but it is the Way; the only way we have if we look for insight into what is good and reject the pseudo-sciences that either turn their back on ethical issues or insist they are matters of cognition and calculation. The dictum of the Jesuit educator bespeaks how values – and better values one hopes – are acquired by those in his charge: 'I don't care whether they believe what they do and say, for if they do it and say it long enough they will believe it.' Values are acquired within the structure and dynamics of an authoritative moral hierarchy. The repertory of means by which the administrator may build a moral order around values is limited indeed: invitation to the individual to accept other values, selection of individuals who already possess these values, or compulsion. The limits that bind administrators who would inculcate values bind the most radical collective of contemporary society as much as they do church and school. The only difference is that while we are likely to question the authority and hierarchy of church and school, we fail to recognize the authoritative and hierarchical processes in organizations that declare themselves dedicated to freedom and self-realization.

The Bible is full of injunctions cast in the form of invitations to accept better values:

> And these words which I command you this day shall be upon your heart; and you shall teach them diligently to your children and shall talk of them when you sit in your house, and when you walk by the way, and when you lie down, and when you rise.[60]

Those who find the religious basis of the foregoing arguments unacceptable might note a trend in contemporary society. Increasingly our society welcomes the thought and symbols of eastern religions – Sikhs wearing turbans and kirpans to school and police duty – even as that society is bent upon removing its own cultural symbols – and thereby its symbols of authority and hierarchy – from its public institutions, particularly schools. It is important to note therefore that support for concepts of legitimized authority and hierarchy exist in purely philosophical forms. While Frye was certainly a believer, he defended his belief in a higher order of the good in arguments from language and the proper understanding of reality. In particular he drew upon Plato and the Greek philosophers.

> With Plato we enter a different phase of language, one that is 'hieratic'. . . . Specifically, words are 'put for' thoughts, and are the

223

outward expressions of an inner reality. But this reality is not merely 'inside'. Thoughts indicate the existence of a transcendent order 'above', which only thinking can communicate with and which only words can express. Thus metonymic language is, or tends to become, analogical language, a verbal imitation of a reality beyond itself that can be conveyed most directly by words. . . .

One feels that some of the pre-Socratics and atomic philosophers, such as Anaxagoras or Democritus, were moving toward what we should think of as science, from gods to the operations of nature, and that Plato turns away from this direction, toward a transcendent world rather than an objective one. . . .

In the later Classical period Plato's sense of a superior order that only language, in both its verbal and mathematical forms, can approach merges with the conception generally identified as *logos*. . . . In metonymic language this unifying conception becomes a mono-theistic 'God', a transcendent reality or perfect being that all verbal analogy points to.[61]

We need to turn to a notion of *something higher* if we are to find in the school reason to respect it and to believe in it as a justified moral order.[62] The redemption of the hierarchy and authority of the school – or of any organization – requires its dedication to that something higher. This issue, the redemption of the moral order of the organization is a difficult and contentious one; it is value saturated and touches notions of the desirable that often stand deeply in conflict with each other. The point to be made here is that we will not escape hierarchy and authority in any organization; the fundamental question then is what justifies a moral order and makes it worthy of obedience and respect. If all values are of equal merit, no organization can claim legitimation for the order it seeks to impose on others, no legitimation other than that of power, personal preference of the administrator and the application of a self-interested *Realpolitik*.

Commitment requires more than this. What more is required is not easy to put into words. At this juncture another religious metaphor may help our understanding. St Paul is much criticized for the passage in which he says, 'Wives be subject to your husbands as to the Lord.' Modern critics then use Paul's admonition to condemn authority and hierarchy – especially in their patriarchal forms. Such critics usually do not attend to that statement in its context. There the passage opens with Paul addressing the general issue: 'Be subject to one another out of reverence for Christ.' He adds that being subject to one another must be accomplished with love. Towards the end of his meditation on being subject to one another and to a higher power, Paul recognizes the complexity and ambiguity of the matter. 'It is a great truth that is hidden here,' or in the words of the King James version, 'This is a great mystery.'[63]

In their essence schools are moral orders dedicated to a broad and significant set of values. These values range from the power to read to the sensibilities of the civilized and cultured person. Through the inculcation of these values the individual is transformed by the process of education. This is indeed a transformation more than a meeting of 'needs'. The school in its educative capacity builds new and desirable skills, attitudes, and talents in those who did not possess them previously. A 'bottom line' definition of the school can recognize only something called 'basic skills' or skills to strengthen the 'competitive' edge of industry reflects a value position too. The bottom line is an illusion, but nevertheless a value position, though one that foreshortens and ignores much of the potential of the school as an instrument of values. Similarly the view that sees the school as a place where children can be happy until such time as they naturally develop their own interests and capacities offers only a shrivelled and diminished view of the value potential of the school. We should recognize too that the means by which good values can be inculcated require varied programmes, including active *instructional* programmes in the arts and athletics. These varieties may offer escape and perhaps haven to those children who find a single and unavoidable programme of academic studies painful, and even unbearable. All of this is a mystery indeed and one that administration as study, practice, and profession should focus upon and come to grips with.

To comprehend freedom, says Krishnamurti, we need both the flight of the eagle that leaves no mark and the work of the scientist that leaves a heavy trail.[64] Science in educational administration has left a heavy mark, but has it comprehended the issues that matter most? The great issues that face us in education and administration cannot be understood from science alone; they require insight, appreciation, judgement, and commitment. These are the practices that 'leave no mark', for they arise uniquely and unforced from the human mind and spirit.

NOTES

1 A paper given to the Thirty-fifth Anniversary Conference of the Department of Educational Administration, University of Alberta, Edmonton, September 1991. This text is written in the inclusive language of tradition, as in Genesis, 1: 'So God created man . . . ; male and female created he them.' I wish to thank Professor Erwin Miklos for encouraging me to undertake this work when I was unsure about embarking on its risks and challenges.

2 Eugene L. Belisle and Cyril G. Sargent, 'The Concept of Administration', in *Administrative Behavior* in Education, eds R. F. Campbell and R. T. Gregg (New York: Harper, 1957), 96.

3 Roald F. Campbell and Russell T. Gregg, eds, *Administrative Behavior in Education* (New York: Harper, 1957), ix.

4 Thomas Greenfield, 'Re-forming and Re-valuing Educational Administration: Whence and When Cometh the Phoenix?', *Educational Management and Administration* 19, 4: (1991): 200–217.

5 David Halbertsam, *The Reckoning* (New York: William Morrow, 1986), 79.

6 Ibid., 80.

7 Ibid., 88.

8 Ibid., 104.

9 Belisle and Sargent, 'Concept of Administration', 110–112.

10 Ibid., 113.

11 Ibid., 114.

12 Ibid., 114–115.

13 Ibid., 117.

14 Orin B. Graff and Calvin M. Street, 'Developing a Value Framework for Educational Administration', in *Administrative Behavior in Education*, eds R. F. Campbell and R. T. Gregg (New York: Harper, 1957), 121.

15 Ibid., 136.

16 Ibid., 148–150.

17 Ibid., 135–141.

18 Ibid., 147.

19 James Bryant Conant, *Slums and Suburbs* (New York: McGraw-Hill, 1961), 11, 2.

20 James Bryant Conant, *Education and Liberty: The Role of the Schools in a Modern Democracy* (Cambridge: Harvard, 1958), 79–80.

21 Quoted in Robert K. Merton, *Social Theory and Social Structure* (Glencoe, IL: Free Press, 1957), 374.

22 Daniel E. Griffiths, 'Toward a Theory of Administrative Behavior', in *Administrative Behavior in Education*, eds R. F. Campbell and R. T. Gregg (New York: Harper, 1957), 378.

23 Ibid., 365.

24 Ibid., 388.

25 Andrew W. Halpin, 'A Paradigm for Research on Administrative Behavior', in *Administrative Behavior in Education*, eds R. F. Campbell and R. T. Gregg (New York: Harper, 1957), 159.

26 Herbert A. Simon, *Administrative Behavior: A Study of Decision-Making Processes in Administration Organization*, 2nd edn (New York: Free Press, 1957 [1945]), 249.

27 Halpin, 'Paradigm for Research', 198.

28 Ibid., 183.

29 Ibid., 185.

30 Robert S. Fisk, 'The Task of Educational Administration', in *Administrative Behavior in Education*, eds R. F. Campbell and R. T. Gregg (New York: Harper, 1957), 226.

31 Griffiths, 'Theory of Administrative Behavior', 358.

32 Christopher Hodgkinson, *Towards a Philosophy of Administration* (Oxford: Basil Blackwell, 1978), 20.

33 Erwin Miklos, *Evolution in Doctoral Research in Educational Administration at the University of Alberta, 1958–1990*, draft version (Edmonton: Department of Educational Administration, University of Alberta, 1990), nos. 2–12.

34 T. B. Greenfield, 'Research on the Behaviour of Educational Leaders: Critique of a Tradition', *Alberta Journal of Educational Research* 14, 1 (1968): 74.

35 Terry L. Eidell and Joanne M. Kitchel, *Knowledge Production and Utilization in Educational Administration* (Columbus: University Council for Educational Administration, 1968), vii.

36 Frederick Enns and Lawrence W. Downey, eds, *The Social Sciences and Educational Administration* (Edmonton: Division of Educational Administration,

University of Alberta, 1963; Donald E. Tope *et al.*, *The Social Sciences View School Administration* (Englewood Cliffs, NJ: Prentice Hall, 1965); Jack Culbertson *et al.* eds, *Social Science Content for Preparing Educational Leaders* (Columbus: Charles E. Merrill, 1973.)

37 Belisle and Sargent, 'Concept of Administration', 113.
38 George Strauss, 'Some Notes on Power-Equalization', in *The Social Science of Organizations*, ed. Harold J. Leavitt (Englewood Cliffs, NJ: Prentice Hall, 1963), 50–52.
39 Ibid., 80.
40 The texts and references of the day reflect this hierarchy in any knowledge that really counted, e.g. Tope *et al.*, *The Social Sciences View School Administration*. The best view of administration was obviously that of the social sciences.
41 R. M. Stogdill and A. E. Coons, eds, *Leader Behavior: Its Description and Measurement*, (Columbus: Bureau of Business Research, Ohio State University, 1957); Halpin, Andrew W., *Theory and Research in Administration* (New York: Macmillan, 1966), 81–130.
42 Barry D. Anderson and Alan F. Brown, 'Who's a Good Principal?', *Canadian Administrator* 6, 3 (1966): 10.
43 Jacob Getzels, James M. Lipham and Roald F. Campbell, *Educational Administration as a Social Process: Theory, Research and Practice* (New York: Harper and Row, 1968), 270–282.
44 Alan F. Brown, 'Teaching under Stress', *Canadian Administrator* 1, 6 (1962): 25–30.
45 Greenfield, 'Re-forming and Re-valuing', 200–217.
46 Daniel E. Griffiths 'Intellectual Turmoil in Educational Administration', *Educational Administration Quarterly* 15, 3 (1979): 43.
47 Miklos, 'Evolution in Doctoral Research', nos. 2–28 to nos. 2–31.
48 Daniel E. Griffiths, 'Administrative Theory', in *Handbook of Research on Educational Administration*, ed. N. J. Boyan, 27–51. (New York: Longman, 1988), 45.
49 Greenfield, 'Reforming and Revaluing', 211.
50 Richard Bates, *Educational Administration and the Management of Knowledge* (Victoria, Australia: Deakin University, 1983), 8.
51 Kant's warning is given renewed life by the contemporary philosopher, John Macmurray. See comment on the implications of this issue for educational administration in Thomas B. Greenfield, 'Leaders and Schools: Willfulness and Nonnatural Order in Organizations', in *Leadership and Organizational Culture*, eds T. J. Sergiovanni and J. E. Corbally (Urbana: University of Illinois, 1984), 149.
52 Christopher Lasch, '"Excellence" in Education: Old Refrain or New Departure?' *Issues in Education* 3, 1: (1985): 7–8.
53 Marilyn Jager Adams, *Beginning to Read: Thinking and Learning about Print* (Cambridge, MA: MIT Press, 1990), 421.
54 Colin W. Evers and Gabriele Lakomski, *Knowing Educational Administration: Contemporary Methodological Controversies in Educational Administration Research* (Oxford: Pergamon, 1991), 37.
55 Gabriele Lakomski, 'Values and Decision Making in Educational Administration', *Educational Administration Quarterly* 23, 3 (1987): 71.
56 Ibid., 80.
57 Rogers Brubaker, *The Limits of Rationality: An Essay on the Social and Moral Thought of Max Weber* (London: George Allen & Unwin, 1984), 98.
58 *Book of Common Prayer*, 'The Holy Communion'.
59 Northrop Frye, *The Double Vision: Language and Meaning in Religion* (Toronto: University of Toronto, 1991).

60 Deuteronomy, 6: 1–3.
61 Northrop Frye, *The Great Code: The Bible and Literature* (Toronto: Penguin, 1990 [1983]), 7–9.
62 Christopher Hodgkinson, *Educational Leadership: The Moral Art* (Albany, NY: SUNY Press, 1991), 97.
63 Ephesians 5: 21–32.
64 J. Krishnamurti, *The Flight of the Eagle* (New York: Harper & Row: 1971), 11.

11

EDUCATIONAL ADMINISTRATION AS A HUMANE SCIENCE

Conversations between Thomas Greenfield and Peter Ribbins

SCENE SETTING

For students of educational administration, 1974 was an exciting year. It was the year in which the third International Intervisitation Programme was held. At the conference Thomas Greenfield delivered a paper which changed the face of educational administration as a field of study. To understand why it is necessary to locate the paper in its historical context.

Since the 1950s educational administration had been dominated by positivist thought in the form of the 'Theory Movement.' This envisaged the development of a general theory of human behaviour, within which the theory of administrative behaviour in educational contexts would be a sub-set. In this paradigm the natural sciences, especially physics, would provide the model (Griffiths, 1957, 388).

By the late 1960s doubts were being voiced. But as Griffiths (1988, 30) acknowledges, its 'demise came at the 1974 meeting of the IIP in Bristol. . . . The coup de grace was delivered by Greenfield who made an across-the-board denunciation of every aspect of the theory movement'. Since then, Greenfield 'has broadened and deepened his critique. In an impressive series of papers . . . he has sought to develop a systematic view of social reality as a human invention, in opposition to the systems scientific perspective of social reality as a natural system. He has constructed strands of argument on the nature of knowledge, on administrative theory and research, on values, on the limits of science, and the importance of human subjectivity, truth and reality. . . . the magnitude of his undertaking and a corresponding elegance of argument make his work the most important theoretical development in recent educational administration' (Evers and Lakomski, 1991, 76).

Accordingly, his papers are eagerly sought in many parts of the world but are not always easy to get hold of individually or collectively. A solution is the publication of a collection and since 1990 we have been involved in producing one. We have done so in all the usual ways including spending several days together in Birmingham in June 1991. Some hard choices have had to be made in selecting ten papers to represent his thinking from among the sixty Greenfield has published since 1961 [Appendix 1]. Once this was done we have been involved in the equally demanding task of editing in a way that respected the integrity of individual papers but which minimized repetition in the text as a whole. With this under way two tasks remained – producing a foreword and writing a postscript. The former was straightforward – we had only to ask Christopher Hodgkinson.

The latter took more thought. We wished to enable the reader to locate the set of papers within the context of Greenfield's personal and professional history as he saw it. This led us to a 'novel' approach. During the five days of our meeting in Birmingham we conducted a series of wide ranging discussions. These were taped and transcribed. Since then we have refined, revised and elaborated the text of these talks. They represent an unusually sustained attempt to explore with a scholar how and why his thinking developed as it did.

BEFORE 1961: TOWARDS THE SCHOLAR'S LIFE

PR: Let us try and get some purchase on the development of your thinking over time. Partly by looking at your life, career and work. You were born in Saskatchewan?

TG: Into a farm family and I lived the first few years of my life on a farm.

PR: You didn't enjoy farming much?

TG: I didn't experience much of it but I remember from an early age having a longing for something else. That something else was the city. I can recall my mother telling me of cities and their various wonders.

PR: Most of your schooling was in city contexts?

TG: From the 'Second Grade' to my degree studies in English and German at the University of British Columbia.

PR: These studies were an influence you came back to later in your career and thinking?

TG: They certainly were. I fell into those choices of study, as many do, but it left a lasting impression on me. After finishing my degree I needed a job quickly and teaching seemed the easiest and most obvious thing, also my mother had been a teacher so perhaps there is that kind of influence. If I'd been more courageous or had more money I might have done other things.

PR: So you spent a number of years teaching in an elementary school?

TG: I was trained as a secondary school teacher and worked as one briefly and was quite happy at it. But I was offered the job in Vancouver and they put me in an elementary school because that was where there was a shortage of teachers. Initially I found that difficult.

PR: Presumably you became reasonably good at it because from '58 to '59 you had a year as a Vice-Principal?

TG: Yes that's right. I guess by the end of my teaching career I had some success. It was in an interesting school. Some of us were advanced and I was one of those.

PR: What were your responsibilities?

TG: Assistant to the head. That was my first insight into practical adminis-tration. The principal was the opposite of the previous one. He was very aggressive and direct whereas the other man had been in-competently *laissez-faire*. He was repressive with the children and indifferent to the teachers. I suppose that was when I first began to think about what administrators do.

PR: You had a year as a deputy principal?

TG: Then another happenstance from above. Someone in Edmonton contacted the BC Teacher's Union and asked if they knew of some-body to nominate for a scholarship in educational administration. The thought of getting away for a year from that principal was attractive.

PR: Did you also want to research?

TG: My plan was simply to go for the year. I realised that if I did go I would probably be launched into an administrative career.

1961–1971: OBJECTIVIST YEARS – FROM CERTAINTY TO DOUBT

PR: In Alberta you studied Teacher–Leader Behaviour and Its Relation-ship to Pupil Growth. Why?

TG: The Department was just establishing itself. It had been going for only two years and there were two kinds of staff. Older people who had come to an academic position from a background of senior positions in administration and those, like the professor I worked with. He had some experience of education and then had gone to study in the University of Chicago, which is where the thrust of the Theory Move-ment arose. When I started my studies, I had a sense that the diffi-culties and complexities I had been introduced to in my study of the arts could be answered. They could be calculated, they could be resolved – exactly. I had a sense of turning my back on what I had understood to be knowledge for many years.

PR: That in comparison what you had known hitherto was sloppy, im-practical, soft?

TG: That's right, there was clarity, answers and certainty. As I understood more of the New Movement theory I saw it could bring discipline and knowledge to thinking in the field, to make it more useful.

PR: Was your Doctoral research a development of your Masters work?

TG: It was. My masters' study focused on leadership, and I worked within a pre-existing instrument designed to measure leadership. The standard thing to do was to take such measures and relate these to other variables. I related these to measures of output, in particular to measures of pupil growth. For my doctoral studies I tried to understand more of how these measures of output were related to organisational variables.

PR: This was very much within the positivistic frame?

TG: Oh absolutely!

PR: It relied on a good deal of number crunching?

TG: I did a great deal of number crunching. This was offered to us as *the* methodology. All problems in education were thought to be ultimately resolvable in this way. Of course we were drawing on the whole school of thought that is described as 'Logical Positivism'.

PR: This was a time in which the Theory Movement and logical positivism were at the height of their influence.

TG: Logical positivism was powerful in the social sciences generally and predominant in philosophy. We were not aware of this. These things were simply offered to us as part of the method we should use. We were aware there were problems to be solved in education and this was the means for understanding and resolving them.

PR: At a fundamental level it was taken for granted that tackling such problems raised technical rather than philosophical considerations?

TG: That was reflected in our training program. There were two kinds of emphases, the first and most important, was on quantitative method, the second was on an understanding of the social sciences. The social sciences were seen as a great repository of knowledge that would give us ideas and theories on which we would use our methods of quantitative analysis. We learned the social science of empiricist realism, that is the methods of logical positivism. We were also involved in studies that from the new perspective were seen as rather useless. We did a course in educational philosophy, which was taught by one of the old line scholars who had grown up in the tradition of Dewey. He took us through thinking on education, from Spencer onwards. We looked at thought right back to the Greeks. We had wonderful discussions and debates and being in that class re-awakened ideas that entered our heads as undergraduates. They certainly interested and challenged me. But when you walked out of that class you realised it didn't really help at all.

PR: It was entertaining – but not really useful?

TG: It was simply self-indulgent, and didn't address the great social issues of the day. I'd grown up in an environment of protest, a generally left-wing ideology. I was raised by my mother. She had a vivid sense of social outrage at the social injustices she suffered. I also had a sense

232

of social mission, that there were great problems in the world that had to be set right.

PR: And that science was the way to do it?

TG: My first inclinations were towards the arts but I came to feel that was for nothing and one ought to devote oneself to studies that could be socially useful.

PR: The serious citizen is a scientist? You published three papers in 1961.

TG: From early in my studies I could write well enough to put things clearly and forcefully, to draw people's attention, to get good marks. Since then I've thought about my writing a great deal more. As Barnes says, 'Mystification is easy, clarity is the hardest thing of all.'

PR: Your early papers use an essentially quantitative approach?

TG: They do. Within the systems metaphor that orders the whole thing. The school is a productive unit, there are distinguishable outputs, they are caused by effective process, all under the control of the administrator.

PR: And such thinking informs your Ph.D. study: '*Systems Analysis in Education – A Factor Analysis and Analysis of Variance of Pupil Achievement*'?

TG: A terrible title – but it displays the things I was proud of at the time. I cringe to think of it, a blaring trumpet advertising method, and no substance at all.

PR: Ideas derived from systems theory backed up by great technical skills in manipulating the numbers.

TG: I had a sense I was a possessor of a kind of arcane knowledge and had to display that in the title.

PR: You were an insider?

TG: I was inside, I could do a factor analysis, I could do an analysis of variance.

PR: And you felt comfortable with that at that time?

TG: Oh yes.

PR: When you finished your Ph.D., you became Research Director at the Canadian Teacher's Federation?

TG: In Ottawa. I had gone to Alberta for a year, but had stayed four. I was too educated to return to the ordinary classroom. But there wasn't an academic position available at that time in Canada. So I took an opportunity to get into research administration.

PR: To what extent was this a research role?

TG: My main role was as an advocate for research. There were interests the Federation wanted pursued with regard to the interests of teachers. They wanted salary scales, benefits and things of that kind examined. It was low-level survey research. There was also interest at that time in classroom research. I published several papers advocating that role for the classroom teacher in research.

PR: Did you hope for a 'proper' academic appointment?

TG: I went there happily but before long I became less happy. I found the position was that of tame scientist, in which you were hired because you could add a certain cachet to the proper opinions that my employers wanted to highlight. We were very much on display as scientists of education.

PR: Paid to find things you were expected to find or at least to find evidence to support such expectations?

TG: You could say what you wanted as long as you didn't question certain sacred truths. I came to be very aware of that.

PR: So there were frustrations in working in that context and when the chance came to get a post at OISE [Ontario Institute for Studies in Education] in Toronto you were interested.

TG: I was very much imbued with the attitude that saw the typical role of the researcher as the creator of superior knowledge, so I did resent the political control that was put on me, even though it wasn't all that binding. So when the university system began to expand I remember thinking long and deeply about leaving the Federation. But I had the opportunity to join the newly formed OISE. What decided me to go was the knowledge that my former Professor, John Andrews, was going to the Institute. That was a strong attraction. Also the thought of moving to a big city was very attractive.

PR: Andrews was quickly promoted. In 1967 you became Head of the Department and held this post for the next four years. What was involved?

TG: The chief thing was managing its growth. The Institute was growing very fast, money seemed to be no object. Every year there was a competition among the departments for the increased resources given to the Institute. Growth was seen as good in itself.

PR: Presumably at that time you accepted this?

TG: Oh I did, and we were growing also in terms of students and of the depth and complexity of the programmes we were offering.

PR: How large was the Department by the time you completed your term?

TG: We were twenty or more by 1970.

PR: Good grief.

TG: Good grief yes!

PR: What was managing that growth like?

TG: Appalling.

PR: What kind of administrator were you?

TG: I was proactive. I saw things to do and I did them. I didn't feel badly about using my power, except sometimes, and I thought I was working for the greater good.

PR: Did you see yourself as a consultative manager?

TG: I didn't mind overriding a decision that I thought needed to be overridden. I didn't do that very often but I saw the need for it. I was keenly aware of the demands the Department was under, demands to expand both research and training. We had to meet our obligations, and this moved me to take risks. I pursued senior scholars, but not many of them came. So the salvation of the Department lay in recruiting new, untried talent. I appointed a woman to the faculty at the time when such an appointment was exceptional. I also took risks in the specializations I promoted and the greenness of the persons I recommended. I was pretty green myself.

PR: How did your four years experience as an administrator shape your thinking as a scholar?

TG: It shaped it a very great deal. When I finished my first term as Head, I was up for review for a second term and I felt that there was no question about it. To my surprise one of the senior people came to me and said he wanted the job. I was just completely dumbfounded. He said he would get it and that the best thing I could do was to step down.

That was my first encounter with the Realpolitik of organisations and, of course, it rubbed me the wrong way. I might have been persuaded to leave and go back to doing what I really preferred. I decided he was wrong, that he didn't have the power, and even if he did, I wasn't going to go that way. The ensuing months were sheer hell. He was a consummate political animal and he was able to find enough resentment about things I had done and exploit this. It came to a vote of the whole Department, staff, students, support staff – everybody. I could see that to win by a small margin, which I did, was not enough, so I quit.

PR: So you went back to being a professor and ceased being an administrator. That experience must have been one you learnt from?

TG: During that time I was aware again that we were expected to be tame scientists.

PR: Even at OISE?

TG: We were an instrument of provincial government policy, and one of the issues was the amalgamation of schools and school districts. There was a belief that bigger was better. I saw that I was being used as a kind of strategic lever against popular opinion. I could see the complexity of the issues. I could see these were to do with values. I was there to build the technical argument, to give it credibility. But on more than one occasion people would listen and then say, 'That may be true if you say it. We still don't want to do it.'

PR: So the doubts which have dominated much of your work since then can be traced back to this period? And these doubts were wide ranging and fundamental, relating even to your understanding of the methods that you were using? This takes us neatly to the first of the papers in which you begin to express these doubts in a published form. 'Critique of a Tradition', in 1968 raises doubts concerning the

235

ideas and methods of researching that had characterised your work in the past.

TG: My task was to review the research years at the University of Alberta, research using the instrument known as the Leadership Behaviour Description Questionnaire, the LBDQ. There had been much research of this kind. I looked at its outcomes and its implications.

As I did the paper, I came to realise the limitations of such theory and methodology. I said in a muted way that these methods were inadequate as a means for studying leadership.

PR: Were you also beginning to have doubts about the quantitative approach itself as a means of understanding things like educational leadership?

TG: I had to think things out, I had to understand them as deeply as I could. My arts training left me with the idea that the world was a mystery and that understanding of it was gained only with great difficulty, much scepticism and a lot of work. When I examined a body of findings based upon the LBQD, that scepticism returned.

PR: Unlike some who share your reservations about the quantitative approach you had a very good grasp of statistics. You spent a decade or more working with statistics. You were very comfortable with them but began to see their limitations?

TG: There are enormous subjective elements in these supposedly objective methods. I knew too that numbers opened up a whole arcane study which was immensely satisfying because of its apparent exactitude and closed logic. That such logic is comfortably abstruse and impervious to question by non-initiates is part of its attraction. It impresses by its apparent power while repelling questions, hiding the fact that it often has much less to say to the everyday world than it seems to. Numbers can be useless, but strongly addictive.

PR: What was it about the late '60s which began to make you doubt all this?

TG: I began to think through the nature of my science. Earlier I had become aware of the enormous subjective elements in these supposedly objective and quantitative analyses. There were problems with factor analysis, one of the prime tools, and also with multiple regression. With factor analysis, for example, there is no unique solution. Solutions are imposed by the researcher and what is interpretable becomes the decision of the researcher. In multiple regression, subjective decisions such as the order in which the variables are input significantly affects the result. In Coleman's study of equal opportunity, for example, the order of entering the variables shifts the value of in-school factors from virtually everything to almost nothing. On one occasion when members of a Senate committee asked about the meaning of the beta weights that powerfully shape his

236

findings, Coleman replied they were purely mathematical concepts which had no bearing on practical reality.

PR: Such an approach may manipulate quantitative data, see various pretty patterns and suddenly say 'This pattern represents truth, life and reality!'

TG: That's it exactly. Much later I came across a statement from Francis Bacon where he says, 'God forbid that we should mistake a dream of the imagination for a pattern in the world.' Many findings produced by the quantitative methods are dreams of the imagination asserted as truth.

For example, if statisticians find a relationship statistically significant, then all the variation in the display which does not reveal that pattern is called error.

PR: And is systematically set aside?

TG: You simply eliminate the error and everything looks better because you are dealing with it through a lens that draws you up close, and instead of seeing the whole of the aquarium you're looking at a tiny little droplet.

PR: And then extrapolate to the whole phenomenon.

TG: In this context an objection often made against the qualitative researcher is that he doesn't understand the relationship between the regularities observed and a larger world, that inference and representation is impossible. That is exactly the problem: the quantitative researcher creates in eliminating error.

PR: Concern for such issues is evident in your 1973 paper 'Social inventions'. When did you first begin to think in such terms?

1971–1974: TOWARDS AN ALTERNATIVE PARADIGM

TG: I saw these problems before the end of my formal studies. But I did not appreciate their full implications until I realised these matters touched upon the essence of the claim that science offered salvation for the social problems of the world.

This is first expressed in my 1968 paper, which ends with a series of questions, These questions and their wider implications were forming in my mind and between 1968–1972 they came to the fore. In 1971–72 they crystalised.

PR: Before we turn to this, let us first consider what you mean by 'empiricism and 'the empiricist approach'?

TG: It arises from applying logical positivism to the world. I first encountered this view in an aphorism from Spearman: 'Anything that exists, exists in some quantity, and anything that exists in a quantity can be measured.' This implies that anything immeasurable does not exist, not beauty, justice, or truth.

PR: Does Spearman's claim self reference? How do you measure a claim? What of the hypothetico–deductive method itself? It does not necessarily derive from logical positivism or empiricism?

TG: No it doesn't, except that there is an easy bridge between that view and mathematical physics.

PR: That reminds me of Griffiths's point, made many years ago, that properly conceived the study of educational administration could replicate Kepler's Laws of motion. It could produce general laws of human behaviour in social contexts.

TG: That's right, and there is an enormous leap of logic and faith in such a claim. It is only in retrospect that you realise that what is being advocated is a view of the social world that sees it as a version of the physical world. The methods which enabled understanding of the physical world are exactly the methods that will bring us to an understanding of the social world.

PR: The argument advanced was that the objectivist approach had brought vast leaps of knowledge in physics so why should it not do so in the social sciences? But let us try and clarify your own empistemological position. Evers and Lackomski seem to claim you doubt objectivity in the physical as well as the social world.

TG: I don't doubt the objectivity of the physical world. I do not question that, in their example, a door may be a better way of leaving a room than trying to go through the wall, floor or roof. I would say that it's not clear that the door is the only way out – there may be a window – even if it is forty floors up!

PR: As I understand it, what they want to do is to argue, following Quine and others, that there are ways of choosing between competing theories which are neither wholly positivist nor wholly subjectivist.

TG: They rely on something like an agreement among scientists.

PR: Perhaps a bit more than that – the criteria they propose are things like which of two or more competing theories is the more economic, which explains more, which leaves you with the fewest messy problems, which is related better to what we already know.

TG: Yes and that a significant group of people accept it – which to me puts it on a social basis. I think of the fate of Galileo and other heretics who were right but forced to say their theories were wrong. Evers and Lakomski's arguments may best apply to the interpretation of the physical world, although conundrums exist there too. It ends in mystery in that reality too. The limits of both macro- and micro-analysis are found in emptiness, darkness, the unexplained, the unfathomable. But Evers and Lakomski's argument becomes shaky indeed when it is applied to the social world. There truth is defined, as Szasz says, not by scientists looking into test tubes and telescopes, but by 'experts' who go not to their laboratories to observe, but to make judgement. As Szasz points out, whether schizophrenia is a disease, a sin, or an acknowledgement is a willful and moral choice.

PR: The paper in which you first began to voice the concerns which have dominated your subsequent writing was 'Social inventions' in 1973. Limitations of space have excluded it from our book. Why did it not cause the stir your 1974 paper did?

TG: Where it was known, it was as much a *cause célèbre* as the later one. I spent much of the year following my resignation doing very little, just teaching and licking my wounds, and then I had a leave. It turned out to be a very important year.

PR: What did you do with it?

TG: I went to the University of Alberta, then to the University of British Columbia and finally to Germany. I read and read, being drawn into the world of Max Weber. And I had to write a paper on change.

PR: That was for AERA? [American Educational Research Association]

TG: Yes. I tried to use the new understandings. After that I went to Germany. In going to Germany I was opening a door. I turned to things that had moved me as an undergraduate student.

PR: What kinds of things?

TG: Generally the arts – art, language and philosophy.

PR: How long did you spend in Germany?

TG: Only four months!

PR: You didn't go there to explore German thinking on the things which have characterised your later writing?

TG: No, I wanted to go through a door I had previously rejected. That turned out to be an important experience. I knew the fount of knowledge there. I encountered a body of thought that much of my critique rests upon. I lived in Germany in German, and that was difficult and stressful. We surround ourselves with our mother language, with the realities and assumptions of that language. To have that torn away and operate in a system that you suddenly don't understand is hard. You don't understand the social architecture.

PR: A hard existentialist experience.

TG: It is. That is a theme that comes back in my later writing, that we need that tearing away from our existing social reality to appreciate what it is.

PR: To see it in its strangeness and familiarity?

TG: And it's mutability. We think of it as inexorable, it's the water the goldfish never sees. I came to see German thought and history in a new context.

PR: It seems as if this experience confirmed rather than triggered your growing disenchantment with empiricism and your search for another way? What about the paper you wrote? What was the response to it?

TG: I don't think it was remarked on much. It was just one of thousands of papers at AERA.

PR: Can we now turn to something that did cause a major stir – your paper to IIP '74 in Bristol? How did you come to be asked to give the IIP paper?

TG: I knew George Baron. When he became the Coordinator of the IIP '74, he asked if I would do a paper on leadership. I said, 'I'd be happy to do that but I have to tell you that what I would say about leadership now would be rather different from what I said a few years ago.' I sent him a copy of the 1973 paper and he wrote back saying, 'Forget about leadership. Write some more of the new.' He referred to the work of contemporary British sociologists he thought I might find interesting. One was Filmer. It was from Filmer I picked up 'Phenomenology'.

PR: You must have known some of this work anyway?

TG: I did. I'd read Silverman and a good deal of German philosophy, sociology and history, centring in particular on Weber. Previously I'd used the 'action framework', a term Silverman draws from Weber. Filmer's book drew my attention to phenomenology in contemporary analysis. My critics thought it was a mistake. I remember writing the paper easily. It was all there. It was all sensible and apparent. It all came together. George gave me the title and I recall sitting down and the whole thing just seemed to flow out.

PR: In retrospect, what were you trying to say in the paper? Is it possible to pick out the main themes?

TG: I pointed to the inadequacy of social science as science and to organization theory as a foundation for management science.

PR: In Griffiths's memorable phrase, you were thinking yourself out of a paradigm? Was that painful?

TG: It was painful.

PR: How did you come to reject the paradigm? What objections were crucial for you? Were your objections essentially empistemological? Evers and Lakomski seem to think so and so also does Griffiths?

TG: I came to see there were complexities in the world other than those that the systems framework had led me to see. I was strongly aware of the existence of alternative realities. The systems perspective offers certainty and an ordered view, but I knew from my experience such a view of the world was only one. The more interesting questions often lay in the contestation between alternative perspectives, how some became dominant and others subordinate. Power was inadequately dealt with in the systems model.

PR: In so far as it was dealt with at all?

TG: This came to me with an absolute clarity. My year away solidified my views. It enabled me to return to my intellectual roots. I was returning to understandings I had been led away from.

PR: Into the more complex social world you discovered in the study of literature for example?

TG: Exactly.

PR: A world in which motive, interest and reason are important in shaping how people think and act. In your IIP paper you used words and made claims which some found difficult to cope with. Labels like subjectivist began to be attached to you and your views. Were you ready to accept such a label when you were writing the paper?

TG: Shortly thereafter I began to use the word subjectivist. I don't know why I didn't use it earlier, I can't imagine that it wasn't available to me.

PR: Subjectivism is implied in the paper but you don't use it.

TG: I had a sense of working alone. I was still groping to understand. When I was in England, British sociologists like Beryl Tipton wanted me to become 'structural', but I always resisted the ethno–marxist or critical perspective. The people I talked to were books, some old, others new. I think, perhaps, I was subject to the error the solitary scholar is apt to fall into. I was unable to check things out by talking to other people, I did it mostly by myself.

PR: Were you aware in writing the paper that you were presenting an essentially epistemological argument?

TG: I didn't set out to study epistemology. My key issue was 'How are we to understand the social world?' It is not known in the way the physical world is to be known. This was very clear to me. As was the notion that in some sense we construct the world around us.

PR: Which entails that it is different – in some cases significantly different – for each of us?

TG: And so science fails as a basis for rational social action. I saw the cultural differences between the world of educational administration as it then was and the things that I was reading, I saw the difference between those rules and the rules I had grown up with in under-graduate study. To an extent I saw this as part of a general split between European and North American modes of thinking and understanding. I acknowledged that in the paper, without wanting to drive it home too far. What I tried to emphasise was not the geo-graphical aspect of the cultural difference, though this seemed real enough, but the different sets of ideas which some people used to understand the world. I was most clear about the invalidity of a claimed universal science using the methods of logical positivism: I was sure that was wrong and said so.

PR: Evers and Lakomski seem to argue you're a subjectivist with regard to the physical and the social world. Is that a correct representation of your views?

TG: No. we are grounded in physical reality. That we do not escape, cannot escape, but there are other kinds of realities built on that.

241

Schumacher makes this point. He speaks of the great Chain of Being in which the world of self-consciousness is built first on consciousness, then both upon life, and ultimately all three on a fourth, the physical stuff of the world. Each of the links in the Chain is qualitatively different from, radically different from, the ones above and below it. The living body is not the dead one, though the physical reality of both may be virtually indistinguishable. Or as Lear says, carrying the dead Cordelia in his arms, 'I know when one is dead, and when one lives.' That is my position now: we exist in physical reality but we are not limited by it, much more we transcend it. After all, you can still enter the Lenin tomb in Moscow and see the body incarnate, as vividly as it was the day before Lenin died. This failure to recognise a hierarchical difference becomes a source of great error: a society congealed around a distorted and malevolent perception.

Evers uses the example that you exit by the door of your office. For the most part this may be true, but it is not the last word. I could exit by the window or I could refuse to go out at all. That I cannot walk through a wall is meagre knowledge compared with how I might construe it. Is it a Wall to be wept at and venerated? Is it a Wall men may weep and pray at, but not women? Or should I take a bazooka and blast it? The interesting questions about the physical world are how we construe it. *Où sont les neiges d'antan?* Auden writes of returning to a city

> where Euclid's geometry
> And Newton's mechanics would account for our experience,
> And the kitchen table exists because I scrub it.
> It seems to have shrunk during the holidays. The streets
> Are much narrower than we remembered; we had forgotten
> The office was as depressing as this.

Physical reality exists within a subjective reality. It's a slippery slope we live on.

PR: You could take some quite simple alternative cases to the one they use about a room. You could ask what a fine paintbrush means to me as opposed to somebody else? At a physical level it is the same for everybody. But someone seeing a paintbrush for the first time would not see it as I do. Nor, perhaps, would Michaelangelo.

TG: Exactly. There's a wonderful dialogue in *The Countesthorpe Experience*, which is a commentary upon Countesthorpe College and the many controversies which surrounded its development. The dialogue is between Armstrong the head of social studies at the school and Professor Bantock of the School of Education, University of Leicester. They talk about the different ways people construe the world. At one point Bantock argues that Thomas Aquinas and the mediaeval

242

peasant did not worship the same God, nor it might be added, did they worship in the same church. Quoting Blake, Bantock says, 'The fool sees not the same tree the wise man sees.' To me it is obvious that the realities we see are dependent upon what we think those realities are, and this includes our interpretation of the physical world.

PR: But the argument may be easier to make in the case of the social world than the physical world. Take the case of the roles people play. It is possible for two people to share similar roles but to interpret and enact them in very different ways. We make roles, we do not just take them. I suppose the issue we have to address as subjectivists is that if you push this argument too far it is hard to see what account one could give of the social world. Social life must at some minimal level be predicated on the idea that we can work together and share understandings about what we can expect of and from each other. The question becomes how do we work together if we see the world in different ways?

TG: You have slipped from talking about the physical world to the social. The two are quite different. One is a world of 'is' and the other of 'ought to be'. Consider the differences of will. We manipulate the physical world, not create it. We do not 'create' the social. We assert ourselves, we want to control others. The social dynamic has no counterpart in the physical world. It is uniquely human.

Attempts to control others' perceptions are never completely successful. They work, by and large, but there's always the possibility of the renegade and the rebellious. Patterns of social life are all ultimately controlled by the action, will and intention of individuals. We can try to organise and shape this and we spend a great deal of effort in doing so but are never more than partially successful. In thinking about this I find R. D. Laing's discussion of the confrontation between the twentieth-century mother and the Stone Age baby very telling; 'After fifteen years what you end up with is a half-crazed creature more or less adjusted to a mad world.'

PR: The IIP paper has been described as an 'across the board attack' on the kind of thinking that had dominated conventional theories about organisations and their management. Is this the way you saw the paper yourself and did you expect it to be seen by others in this way?

TG: I didn't go to Bristol to throw down a gauntlet. I went there having written out the dialogue that had been taking place in my own mind over the last few years. I went in the hope of inviting others to join the dialogue. I certainly saw the implications of the position I was adopting and I think I spelled these out clearly at the end of the paper.

PR: I am surprised to hear that? I've always read the paper as a kind of manifesto for a new paradigm. Has it not been interpreted by others in this way?

TG: I didn't think in paradigms at the time but perhaps I though what I had to say could be accepted as inquiry. I didn't go to Bristol to cross the Rubicon, but as soon as I arrived I began to get intimations others would see things differently. The paper had been sent to the conference and distributed to participants. When I arrived a couple of days after the conference began, there was a kind of electric tension that burst out at the session itself.

PR: When I first read it the paper made a great impression on me. I had encountered some of the ideas it contained and these had begun to make me think hard about my own position which up to then was largely that of a conventional positivist. My first thoughts were 'Great! Somebody has thrown down the gauntlet at last and has done so in an elegant forceful argument'. I thought it a crunching paper so I am surprised to hear you did not expect it to cause the stir it did.

TG: I think it was a kind of naïveté on my part. There were people there who were toweringly angry with me.

PR: Was there a respondent? What was his response?

TG: The respondent was Alan Crane. His response was largely to ignore the paper and to seek to repair the damage. Unfortunately his statement does not appear in the proceedings. As I remember it, his text affirmed the existing paradigm. He soon came to change his view.

PR: Who were the people who spoke forcibly for and against from the floor? What did they say?

TG: For the most part, the questions and comments were neither for nor against. They were exploratory, but the atmosphere again revealed the gulf, the audience behaving like schoolboys in an assembly where a visiting speaker has said all the wrong things, explored a forbidden topic, even under the eyes of the headmaster. Griffiths's brooding presence was very much apparent.

PR: He was present?

TG: He was indeed, he challenged me from the floor, but not before there was a forest of hands and questions after my presentation and Crane's response. I don't recall anything hostile from that response, only keen interest, if not support. It was clear something rather extraordinary was happening. Even before the session the atmosphere was electric. It was like a time-bomb waiting to go off, and I walked into the session with many doubts and uncertainties. As the paper had been circulated, I didn't read it or even summarize its main points. I don't remember what I said, I just wanted to get the ordeal over with. I'd presented my thing, said a few words, made a few points, and Alan Crane stood up, seemingly to calm the horses, and then there was an explosion. Everyone, it seemed, wanted to say something. I remember George Baron saying to me afterwards, 'Well, it had a slow start, but once you got wound up . . . ' He recalled an incident where Griffiths interrupted me as I answered a question. I had been saying that the dominating theorists of the field were systems thinkers – I may have added most were Americans. Later the whisper campaign against me claimed that the point of my critique was no more than a cover up for my administrative incompetence, a fight against my American nemesis in the struggle that deprived me of the Departmental headship. In any case, Griffiths interrupted at that point. 'Name one,' he demanded in his stentorian voice, 'Talcott Parsons,' I shot back. I might have added 'Daniel Griffiths.' Baron said he was in admiration of that exchange. Certainly from that point on the gloves were off, I have come to be deeply grateful to Daniel Griffiths for his latter day views, but it was another case in the beginning.

PR: I think I've met about 400 people who have told me they were there. What happened after the session?

TG: The room was full but it was a moderate sized classroom, with about sixty present. Immediately after the meeting people came to talk to me. Griffiths was seething with anger, telling me 'You are poorly informed' I remember those words. He then turned on his heel and left after advising me to read more. I tried to talk to him later, but it was difficult. I felt I had betrayed something, stabbed Caesar. I had always stood in admiration of him – in awe even. It was painful. I felt alone and isolated. There seemed no community of scholars, no camaraderie. If there was support, it came from individuals who didn't count, people from places on the periphery of the great world of theory and accepted thinking about it. Four years later when IIP '78 was held in Canada, my colleagues ensured there would be no echo of the Bristol error. I was not invited to attend or make a presentation. I watched the IIP caravanserai as it passed briefly through Toronto.

PR: What happened after the conference?

AFTER 1974: THE SUBJECTIVIST YEAR – FROM BRISTOL TO EDMONTON

TG: Things went quiet. I knew in UCEA [University Council for Central Administration] circles the thing would come back as a *cause célèbre*, I was aware Griffiths was speaking out. I began to get invitations to write, some of my later papers are a reflection of that.

PR: From North America as well as in Europe?

TG: There were exchanges in the UCEA *Review*. I remember by that time feeling almost paralysed by it all. I had not anticipated the bombshell that broke over my head. I began to understand the way it was seen. It was interpreted as deliberately challenging, threatening and hostile, I had not thought of it like this. I simply wasn't prepared to mount any platform in an adversarial way. It was just not me, I didn't want to go through some kind of trauma or intellectual combat, and for some time I felt paralysed. I felt I was not doing good work at that time, it took me a long time to overcome that fear. To accept a burden I didn't want, a kind of curse of insight. In those years I was unsure about my insights, unsure at least that I could invoke them again to defend the original vision. That's how I felt about it, as a vision whose source I was unsure of, and could not command. In each subsequent paper I had a sense of struggling to draw again from the deep well of insight that moved the 1974 paper. To reach the Muse, as it were, was uncertain, an undertaking fraught with risk. And in those days, the overthrow of reason and professorial authority that Allan Bloom describes so well in *The Closing of the American Mind* – all that made it hard to be a scholar of any kind other than one who upheld the new political orthodoxy. It dismays me to find how often my writings are seen by younger readers as support for academic fascism then and now, for that is what it is. I learned to listen to the depths, to alternative realities for inspiration. I began to feel like Winston Smith in *1984*, beset from both left and right. I learned to listen to the depths, to alternative realities for inspiration. Though argument helped I learned to tune into and hearken to the non-rational, to return to modes of knowing I knew from the arts and my other training.

PR: In Britain, *EMA* [Educational Management and Administration] published a series of papers which tried to take up the debate. 'Self' in 1977–78 was a response to that symposium. What were you trying to say in it?

TG: I knew the argument about the social construction of reality brings in very personal issues. I realised you couldn't just march into an assembly, as I did at Bristol, and present the intellectual arguments for a radically different view of social life and not see the personal dimensions it entailed. I've never seen my arguments as *ad hominem*. I aimed only at the intellectual issue, but of course you cannot advance such arguments without, as I say in my paper, cutting into something unexpectedly human.

PR: Were you not trying to insulate what you do as a scholar from the account you were giving of what social life is like?

TG: There was an element of the sorcerer's apprentice in what I was doing. It is one thing to get all those brooms moving and another to stop them. I soon realised once it had started there was no going back.

PR: Are you saying you assumed that the kind of social world you were depicting would not quite apply to you?

TG: I was quickly disabused of that – 'Self' begins the march towards that recognition.

PR: Can you elaborate on that?

TG: Where does the self belong in the study of organizations? That's the point. There are reflections of my struggle in that paper and it acknowledges that our ideas are very much connected to ourselves, to our personal constructions of the world, and to our values. That the assertion of one's own self and values is apt to bring one into conflict with stronger dominating expressions of self.

PR: To some you might be the dominating. . .

TG: I definitely wasn't then. The paper began to be talked about in unscholarly ways. I discovered something about my field: its pettiness, its calcified and limited vision, its conventionality, its hostility to dissenting opinion, its vituperativeness.

PR: The attack was personalised?

TG: The attack was personalised, it was by second-hand statement, innuendo – people who had not read the paper but claimed they knew what it was about.

PR: They attacked your motives not your arguments?

TG: Some put up the straw man 'phenomenology' saying I didn't understand it, this was evidence of the inadequacy of my argument. I was aware I was being attacked unfairly in an unscholarly fashion, that people sought to explain the paper in personalised terms. They began to circulate stories about my administrative competence and the business about losing the leadership of the Department started to come up. I felt beleaguered and alone.

PR: Several of the *EMA* contributors were sympathetic.

TG: That was in England. The first person who extended the personal hand of friendship and support to me here was Chris Hodgkinson.

PR: You have not formally collaborated? A case of two people sharing a similar view of the world and learning together and sharing ideas as they learn together?

TG: He came to me at a time I was very vulnerable. This was about the time his book *Towards A Philosophy Of Administration* came out. He had sought me out. Chris's style means there are no secrets with him, nothing you can't talk about. We talked of the whole intellectual furore, my changing personal circumstances, my marriage dissolving. He would talk about everything, intellectual and personal, everything others avoided in disdain, disagreement, or embarrassment. He offered the steel of intellectual argument and the hand of friendship. There were no others like him. Everything was on the table, no averted eyes, no sham, no shame, no pitying condescension. No rejection. Acceptance, but also no-holds-barred disagreements when it came to that. But always understanding and support. The first time I met him, he said something like, 'What's this I hear about your

247

taking up the vices of the ancient Greeks?' And I probably replied something like, 'I'm not just taking them up.' He was, as I say, a great, friendly, and supportive hand, and there weren't many then.

PR: Not even amongst your colleagues at OISE?

TG: Not in that way. There were not the people there that I could talk to intellectually or personally. I always felt my Canadian colleagues waited to see how the show would play New York or Chicago before committing themselves. Well the 'Phenomenology' show is still getting mixed reviews in New York and Chicago, though fringe voices like William Greenfield's *Organization Theory Dialogue* has invited my views, as is seen in 'Phoenix'. My Canadian colleagues have now come around, too, though often they would rather put me on some kind of honour role than ask my views on anything. At one time however some of the colleagues closest to me virtually averted their eyes when they saw the fuss and furore. There were friends but not in a way that Chris was. I never felt with Chris a personal rejection although I did feel this with other people; a sense of being beyond the pale.

PR: How, and in what way did you begin to affect each others thinking? Had this begun to happen when you started to write 'Truths' in 1978?

TG: I had begun to take in what he said about administration as an act of will and choice, as asserting self, as dramaturgy. In the next paper, 'Research in Educational Administration', I cite Sir Geoffrey Vickers, after writing to him at Hodgkinson's suggestion. Chris was in correspondence with Vickers, who was most generous with his time and thought, though he was old and ill. The correspondence between Vickers and Hodgkinson began after Vickers had written a critically appreciative review of *Towards a Philosophy of Administration*, a book that was admired everywhere but in educational administration, where it was ignored or misunderstood.

PR: So 'Reflections' in 1978 tries to work out some of the themes raised in the debates after 1974?

TG: I was trying to explain again what the 1974 paper was about, going over the same ground and speaking to the critics who had addressed it in print in the United States. I make reference to Hills, Griffiths, Kendell and Byrne.

PR: Who first criticised your use and understanding of phenomenology?

TG: Griffiths and Willower did, and much of 'The man who comes back', in 1980 speaks directly to them.

PR: How were you using 'phenomenology'?

TG: Not in the way some American phenomenologists were using it. I suppose you might say that I was using phenomenology with a small 'P', Griffiths and Willower were using it with a big one. And they insisted that if I was not using their way I must be using it incorrectly.

248

PR: This debate was conducted in the American context and with the American scholars who were key members of the ruling orthodoxy and who had been notable in defending it against you.

TG: For a long time that's what I did. I was invited to these events as an *enfant terrible* to come and say again and again those threatening and outrageous things.

PR: What of 'Ideology' in 1979? In it your concern begins to turn from epistemological to value issues.

TG: Here I was able to get away from the old platform. I was at last able to look ahead again, to resume the dialogue I had begun with the 1974 paper. I was able to set aside the debate and get on with the thinking.

PR: Let us turn briefly to 'Talk, Chance, Action and Experience' of 1979. What do you mean by experience and chance in this context?

TG: The world of chance is one the statistical view seeks to do away with. In stressing regularities, statistics leaves out irregularities even though they may explain a great deal about how the world actually functions. What is vivid, individual, living gets left out. In this paper and in 'Truths' I ask the question, 'Why are we afraid of the specific?' The argument for chance is to bring in the specific, the individual, the reality of contingency and circumstance and to recognise the importance these things can have in organizations. To take this view, is to move towards a historical view of social reality.

PR: How important is it to be clear about the notion of experience if we are to understand social life?

TG: The word 'experience' echoes through many of my papers after 1974. We all exist within our own phenomenological reality, that is our experience. It is a great resource, it is irreducible and it is not to be summed up in statistical and general propositions. The important point about experience is what we think we know about it and how we come to understand it. In one sense our experience is irreducible but in another it needs explanation or rather it needs understanding. It doesn't come ready-made to us.

PR: Some of the gurus of the Theory Movement have challenged the idea that the experiences of practitioners as seen and interpreted by the latter can be an important way of understanding organizations and their management.

TG: That puts the point well. In many ways natural science is a matter of building knowledge that goes against experience. Our experience tells us the sun rises in the east and sets in the west but natural science tells us this is false, that the sun doesn't rise at all. Just about all natural science is a supplanting of immediate experience with better knowledge. That is the approach taken in much of the social sciences and in the Theory Movement. It amounted in practice to a belief that administrators did not and could not know what was really going on. They thought they experienced something but this had little to do with the reality of what was happening.

PR: They had to have their experience explained to them to understand it. They needed a theorist to do this?

TG: Against this I would argue that while experience may not in and of itself be sufficient to understand reality, it is a crucial building block for such an understanding. Any worthwhile explanations of social reality must not contradict that experience. It may reinterpret it but it must not contradict it. This is the perspective of phenomonology, the perspective of the first hand, the perspective of the subjectivist.

PR: Natural science can explain but not understand?

TG: More and more I used images from literature and art. In 'Ideology' I quote from William Blake. He asked,

> What is the price of experience, do men buy it for a song?
> Or wisdom for a dance in the street? No, it is bought with the price
> Of all a man hath, his house, his wife, his children'.

One begins with the experience but there is more. You come to understanding through that bed-rock, through that thing that no-body can dispense with. We live in experience but what understanding are we to place upon it? A social science that assumes that experience must be obliterated or replaced is wrong.

PR: Can I have access to or learn from the experience of another?

TG: The only way we can gain access to another's experience is in symbols of one kind or another, frequently linguistic symbols. We struggle with language to put names on our own experience, to understand better and to understand others. As Schumacher says 'There must be an altruism, I must first of all believe that there is somebody else there who is sentient even as I am, whose experience is as valid as mine and which I ought to try and understand.' That's a moral principle.

PR: For what purpose should I do that?

TG: In the fundamental sense of respect for others, beyond the utilitarian sense of mutuality. In a deeper sense it has an ethical base: Love thy neighbour as thyself.

PR: 'Research in Educational Administration' of 1979 documents the continuing dominance of the positivistic, scientistic, empiricist paradigm in the study of educational administration in North America?

TG: I attempted to set out the credos of New Movement theory. Then I examine the research that flowed from it. I was trying to show its inadequacies in theory and research – attempting to lay out the altern- ative directions in which we might go.

PR: You talk a good deal of Andrew Halpin?

TG: I try to understand the genesis of the Theory Movement, and Halpin was very much involved in it. He was a founding father. I don't think anybody has more penetratingly used Simon's ideas – a brilliant mind. I find it interesting that in his earlier writings Halpin seems to have been clearly aware of the shortcomings of the idea of a Grand Theory. He was one of those who raised questions and did so right at the beginning. It has long surprised me why Halpin and others stopped asking them.

PR: I don't know of a more evocative set of titles than 'The Broken Icon', 'The Fumbled Torch' and 'A Foggy View From Olympus'. Is his concern in writing these papers the same concern he expressed at the beginning of the Theory Movement? Or rather is he arguing that it is the theorists who have failed the movement rather than the theory which has failed the theorists?

TG: What interests me are the doubts he expressed in some of his early papers, In 'Ways of Knowing' he ruminates on the idea that the way scientists know is not the way that administrators know. He recognises there are ways of knowing that are non-scientific. But later on, he put these doubts aside and becomes a committed convert to the New Movement. At the end he is saying that the Theory Movement failed because the following generation of researchers watered down and despoiled the pure and potent methodology, the vision the founding theorists handed down to them from Olympus. The methodology was not done the way it should be, the acolytes failed the priests. The rite became impure. So, I would question your statement that Halpin thought it was the theory the founders offered that was betrayed. Halpin was under no illusion that such theory existed. He complained bitterly about loss – the loss of the methodology. The rite – the methodology defined by Simon and in logical positivism generally – was no longer performed by knowledgeable and competent practitioners. Halpin went back to believing in pure positivist methodology, setting aside all his earlier doubts that it was adequate to the task set for it. It is those doubts I offer in this paper as foundation for a critique of the Movement.

PR: If this approach will not do, how and what should we research in educational administration? You begin to address these issues in the paper.

TG: I need to make an observation before I try to answer that question. We should ask ourselves why a flawed science persists. Why a science that does not work is still hailed as science. An answer can be found in the argument MacIntyre advances. There are strong reasons for believing in such a science, even if it doesn't work. It offers a world in which there are answers to all problems. You must have been at sessions where the science of effectiveness is preached. It is a world of cheerfulness and certainty. The alternative is conflict-ridden and uncertain, opening up the pain that comes with recognising the different realities we live in, of confronting the value chasms that separate us. The Canadian government hires conflict resolution 'experts' from America to ease the acceptance of its proposals for constitutional change. We want to believe such a technology exists and that it works to remove the value gaps separating Canadians. Welcome to the world of management science and the relief managers or politicians feel as their responsibility for value choice is devolved into a technical, non-responsible realm where choice is a product of scientific analysis, not personal judgement. Choosing responsibility leaves one in an exposed and vulnerable position, and so science comes to the administrator's rescue: science not the administrator makes the decision, thus absolving the administrator from responsibility, while giving strategic advantage over the choice.

To go back to your question, we should be studying decision-makers, how they make their decisions and what they decide. It is a conclusion I come to with assistance from Vickers and Hodgkinson: that a science of values is meaningless, that science cannot resolve value differences, though for strategic purposes we may wish to say it can. Without science the administrator simply makes choices. The choices made may be good or bad, but someone is responsible for them. This is a hard road and one reason why it is difficult to be a manager and why managers look for help from science. And finally I would note the paper argues that the proper role of research in the face of these dilemmas is description.

PR: How do you justify the existence of scholars of education administration given the assumptions you have outlined? How can we help?

TG: We can help by enabling administrators to understand their experience better. One of the implications I drew at the end of my 1974 paper said the study of educational administration should use the social sciences as windows of discovery, windows into alternative perceptions, windows into alternative values.

PR: In thinking about the way in which we construct reality, how do you see the balance between reality as individually and socially constructed?

TG: What the social researcher is doing is launching out upon an inquiry into other people's realities. I assume that the portrait can be of value not just to the researcher but to people within that social reality as well or to others who have interests in it.

I would also hope that enquiries into social reality make plain the contestation, the different visions of reality that people have, of how one prevails over another, of how power is used to sustain and propel certain views over others, and to ask what the consequences are. But

I do not see this yielding the technology of control that management research seeks. The research I have in mind offers the hope of achieving insight into social realities. It is overwhelmingly descriptive and historical. It looks for insight, but first it is descriptive. It records decisions and points to their implications.

PR: Can it help to improve things?

TG: Maybe it can but not in an instrumental way. We are not looking at physical reality but at a chancy, value-driven cultural enterprise. All we hope for is a better vision beyond the shadows in which people will somehow rise to what is good to what is better. It can bring us to argument, to better argument, to an appreciation of people and their values behind the argument. That is my position: description first, followed by argument and ultimately, of course, prescription. While positivistic management science wants to shut down argument by calculating the answer, I want to open it by standing at the gulf that separates us, by recognizing the chasm that must be overcome.

PR: I know 'The man who comes back' of 1980 gives you satisfaction, not least because of those marvellous quotes from Francis Bacon in the beginning. Why is it significant for you?

TG: It's a paper written after I had come to terms with my homosexuality, not that there are references to homosexual realities in it, as there are in some others, 'Anarchy' for example. But in this paper and for the first time I let a part of myself that I had earlier suppressed speak freely. This paper comes from the heart, not just from the head. Here I began to use strength out of gay realities to say something about the world. I drew strength from myself, from newly understood experience, to call upon the Muse, and to let myself speak the truth I saw. From that special reality I gained strength. The horrible uncertainty of the past, the doubt that I might have something to say to the world was largely assuaged, if not completely exorcised. 'The Man Who Comes Back' is a paper where I address my critics, but also advance the argument. I look at some of the deepest conundrums of understanding social reality. In doing so I don't think I ignore my critics. I am attentive to what they say, but at the same time, I speak past them, trying to build a framework of sound understanding.

PR: And it's built around nine propositions?

TG: It ends with those nine propositions saying how we might understand organisations. It seemed to have no impact in the central academic institutions of educational administration in North America. To this day it goes virtually uncited, as is apparent in the record of the major American citation index. Though *EAQ* [Educational Administration Quarterly] is sometimes reluctant to publish my papers, the editors know they represented good business. Issues in which they appeared were good sellers.

PR: Can't get a better quantitative test than that!

TG: I attribute this response to the interests of students and junior faculty who read my articles almost as a subversive activity. One colleague starting his academic career told me recently students were enthralled or profoundly troubled when examples of my writing were offered them.

PR: 'Anarchy' of 1983 sketches an anarchistic theory of organisations, but does not draw on traditional anarchistic notions.

TG: I am using anarchism here, in the sense of an awkwardness of things, of things that don't fit, of an unwillingness to participate, of a non-intended, but ultimately conscious rebelliousness. At the end I talk of the anarchy that adheres in all thought. It's a personal statement in many ways. I am no longer addressing critics, I am simply stating my position. I suppose in a lot of my work there is a theme of the individual versus the organisation. I am for the individual, I am for freedom, for independence.

PR: Some of these papers reflect a return to themes you touched upon at the beginning of your academic career. Themes to do with leadership. You appear to be trying, in part, to bring this up to date with your contemporary thinking?

TG: In 'Non-Natural Order' of 1984 I take up Halpin's ideas about ways of knowing. There are ways of understanding and expressing knowledge that are powerful, satisfying and important, but non-rational – ways that are essentially cast within an artistic, literary, historical, philo-sophical even journalistic mode. A mode that is descriptive, with-holding judgement, though moving towards it, moving to insight.

PR: You began to develop an approach to understanding leadership which entailed taking examples from literature which illustrates the analysis you want to make. In the paper there is a long section from *A House for Mr Biswas*. Why did you decide to use this?

TG: I found myself drawn to the book. It is powerful, evocative. Perhaps in it I saw something of my own experience. It tells us things about education which, narrowly conceived, the social sciences can't begin to approach. It helps you to understand what education means, and what a painful process it is, if it works in a deep and fundamental sense. I found it a tragic expression in one sense and hopeful in another.

PR: What does it tell you about leadership?

TG: That leadership is more than an individual phenomenon; it is a cultural thing, that it's embedded in whole lives, whole lives within cultures. The programme of education we see in *Biswas* is certainly not 'implemented'. We see elemental cultural dynamics at work. There is a kind of leadership in what Naipaul describes, and Biswas is a leader too – he leads himself. 'If you would be a leader,' said

254

Bethune, 'first lead yourself.' That's anti-leadership, and I admire it, as I do this sentiment from Mackay, a Canadian poet: 'Rend your heart and not your garments.' Whatever the power or restriction of the wider culture, the person within it who thinks right, believes right is of ultimate importance.

PR: The idea of knowing yourself as a route to understanding educational management is a recurrent theme in your work. Along with the belief that the kind of excessively task-orientated approach to leadership development advocated in much of the literature is not a promising way to hope to achieve this.

TG: Technocratic approaches to leadership and technocratic approaches to literacy are empty. A text like Naipaul's has more to say about illiteracy, say in the inner cities of England, than many of the technocratic studies that are talking about effective teaching. They do not begin to touch the power of insight Naipaul offers, insight into the importance of tradition. Mr Biswas moved from poverty in rural Trinidad to seeing his son embarking for Oxford. That is an awesome journey, but it is carried out within a tradition of knowledge, and reveals the dynamics that ultimately bring about change. These are not simple, technocratic variables, they are deep-seated attitudes towards knowledge. Biswas's life tells us that all education is in one sense invasive of individual experience. What Naipaul lets us see is the shaping of the individual in line with cultural values.

PR: Coming to grips with these things has been a kind of twenty year odyssey for you. Who have been your guides as you struggled to think through the enormously complex issues that you have been trying to come to terms with? And are the old ones like Weber or Laing being supplemented by a very different set including Naipaul and Shakespeare?

TG: First a methodological point in terms of a question: 'What represents the world and allows us to understand it?' The claim of empiricist social science of course is that we can know reality only through its restricted rules. This is dangerously wrong in that its representations of the world are both limited and impoverished. What I came to realise is that other modes of representing the world are not just a supplement, as some people would see it, to the stronger objective and powerful understandings of science, they are true alternatives to it. But of course, they do not lead to what science promises us – control. So we follow the narrow route of science because of the false promises it offers. It doesn't offer control, or if it does, in a very spurious mode. There are more fundamental and powerful insights into reality. These are descriptive; they do not yield control. You look at the life of Mr Biswas and it doesn't tell you what to do, it doesn't tell you which variables are to be manipulated, but it does give you an understanding and appreciation. It gives you what Sir Geoffery Vickers calls 'appreciation'. There is that value-oriented stance again. A novel like *Mr Biswas* allows you to appreciate what was involved in the building of literacy. It has powerful policy implications but they're not the kind that you deduce in the way that empirical scientists claim to do. The inference in empiricist science is supposed to be obvious and logical, I doubt they are. In 'appreciation' that obvious logic does not exist. One understands and comes to value. A look a*t Mr Biswas* would incline you to evaluate education as a desirable end in itself – you certainly wouldn't do it for a productive reason, you would do it for what it says about the maintenance of culture and what it offers the individual even though all individuals would not benefit from it. So the implications that I would draw there run against the kind of production-oriented, mechanistic, market-driven analyses that we have now. You invest in education in and of itself. But the power of that investment can be such as to transform the individual and – possibly, ultimately – the culture itself. That is how change comes about.

PR: I am trying to understand the way your thinking has developed, as opposed to where you are now. Can we consider this in three questions: First, 'What can I know?' Secondly, 'How can I achieve such knowledge?' and thirdly, 'Who can help me to know?' And in considering each of those questions, can you also say something about the sequence in which your ideas have developed? What came first, what next and what last?

TG: Initially, I was seduced by a methodology that, collapses the first two questions. The first becomes irrelevant and the second all-important. The argument I've been making is that logical positivism offers us a shrunken view of the world. It offers a methodology for manipulating reality so as to control it, a methodology that promises more than it actually delivers. It ends up hiding more than it reveals. In terms of the nature of knowledge, I've turned my back on the people who were my mentors in educational administration. I have found myself going back to ways of knowing and bodies of knowledge that I had encountered much earlier. On coming to educational administration I concluded that my earlier knowledge was useless, or more exactly, valueless. This paper recognises that those other bodies of knowledge are relevant and may be powerful. That they are not just supplements to what social science lets us understand, but are truly unique insights in their own right. Partly because they are not paralysed by the only way of knowing recognised in positivistic social science.

PR: How does art relate to social science?

TG: I don't think we should see art as another kind of social science, the two are quite different. There is a role for social science as social science. It's a very complex role, and it is not the social science that is

256

envisaged by logical positivism. The vital point is that the arts are not to be cast into the role of a lower level support to social science. Studies of the humanities and educational administration say, 'To illustrate the principles established in social science, to colour them in with the tones of fleshy reality, one draws on literature and the humanities.' You read *A Bell for Adano* or view *The Bridge on the River Kwai* to add weight and relevance to general principles, colouring in the laws of social science. Everything, including *King Lear*, can be brought into the service of social science. But for me the arts are not to be so easily dragooned to serve the propositions of social science by adding convincing evidence to support what such science has already established. Much more the arts speak to questions of how to live a life. People who make policy based on what social science tells them will need something more. They would do well to call on the humane vision that the arts can give.

In this view of the arts, they are not simply a parallel vision of scientific truth. Theirs is a starkly different vision, one in which moral questions are to the fore. Should Henry Kissinger weep at his desk before ordering the fire of napalm to be dropped on peasant villages, a question raised in Wallace Shawn's play, *Aunt Dan and Lemon?* Would such weeping make it impossible to do what has to be done? As Northrop Frye has said, 'We don't go to *Macbeth* to learn about the history of Scotland, but to understand what it's like to gain the world and lose your soul.' Somebody who understands that is a better person, certainly a better person to be in a leadership position.

PR: But how does it help you with the identification and education of such leaders?

TG: I have proposed that leaders require a period of withdrawal and contemplation, that is what I would see as the role for training. Certainly there is a role in training for the provision of information, concepts and theories. But I think the most valuable form of training begins in a setting of practice, where one has to balance values against constraints – in which one has to take action within a political context. I think only somebody who has acted in that way is ready for true training in leadership. In that context I would be Platonic, not striving to make philosophers kings, but kings philosophers, or artists maybe. To make them more humane in any case, more thoughtful of their power, more aware of the values it serves or denies.

PR: Aristotle and Plato were not all that successful when they actually tried their hands at leadership?

TG: Which takes us back to the idea that the practising administrator may know something the philosopher and the theorist do not know, and vice-versa. I think we have to bring those things together. The ultimate training of a leader would be a kind of philosophical withdrawal to look at the larger issues in fresh perspectives. Perhaps they will return and administer as they were doing it before but with an added insight. That's all I can see as a hope, that there is an added insight. A deeply clinical approach to the training of administrators is needed, as it is for teachers. Our training for both is disjointed, reflection is separated from action, thinking from doing, praxis from the practical. Why do we merely throw people at these jobs, expecting then to do well with almost no experience of them, offering them no *analysis* of their experience? The answer seems to lie in a virtually anti-intellectual bias, in the belief that experience alone, shored up by quick nostrums of science will turn the trick.

PR: There is a practical hope as well?, That they will be better leaders for it?

TG: I think there is. One of the things I have sensed in speaking to leaders in education, is how impoverished their real world is. They don't see beyond a narrow horizon. They don't see the problems of education, except in rather technological terms, or if they do see it, if they talk about it in larger terms, they are sentimental or platitudinous. We need leaders in education who can think about some larger issues, it's the only thing that's going to save it. It is interesting that the reports we get from Japan indicate that is the way they see administrative training. Junior officers entering government or business spend time just sitting and contemplating the beauty of the flowers. Senior people are expected to have a sense of history, of their own culture, of what is ultimately of value and they spend time on such things. Yet these things may seem non-productive, though of course the practical never escapes ultimate attention. It isn't just navel-gazing or New Ageism. Can we expect our educational executives to think of larger but seemingly non-productive matters? I hope so, but it will be an uphill struggle to bring them to such contemplation. Perhaps we need different kinds of executives in terms of character and vision.

PR: There are examples within western culture which have looked back at such folk, they can sometimes be very nasty in practice as well.

TG: What are thinking of, the Mandarins?

PR: I was thinking of Cosimo de Medici. Machiavelli's Prince is a highly cultured person with a great understanding of many things but would you like to have him as a role model for educational leaders?

TG: I'd rather have the Prince than the technocrats of today. Machiavelli helped him to understand what he was doing and why. I would prefer that to the people who are being swept over the precipice and don't realise it.

PR: He understands politics and people. Is that not an intensely control-orientated vision?

TG: Not in the technocratic sense. It is control in the political sense, the lawful sense.

PR: Is that an important distinction?

TG: I think so. Certainly organisations are control orientated, but my theme is that they should not work through a mechanistic kind of control, but rather through a lawful, personal, responsible form. That is the point emphasised in the title of this paper, the idea of wilfulness and non-natural order. The idea that the organisation is not natural, it is created out of somebody's intention, purpose and will, and the people who understand this and its implications for theory and practice are the ones who will control it. That is the nature of organisations. The people who run organizations ought to understand this. Therefore, I prefer the Prince even though he is selfish and egotistical. He does not pursue the best goals but he knows what goals he is pursuing and how to pursue them. Hodgkinson would say what we need is an amalgam of Machiavelli and Plato, a Prince with better ideals. We need a Prince who knows he is responsible, not one who thinks science removes his responsibility or who manipulates us behind the mask of a fraudulent science.

PR: Plato did not seem to have somebody like the Prince in mind as a model ruler in the *Republic*. He believes if you are egotistical and selfish you will become the most terrible prisoner of your own vices and desires. He propose a form of selection and training which would liberate his guardians from this danger but he was not too precise about how you might achieve this.

TG: I don't think there is a technology for that. All we can do is work with the character of leaders. This is a distinction which Hodgkinson makes. Whereas studies of leadership in the positivistic mode have looked at the characteristics of leaders, what is important is their character. I think we look at the Prince and deplore his character, but how do you get people of good character into leadership positions in organizations? That would be the answer.

PR: But isn't what Machiavelli proposed predicated on somebody who is like the Prince? Can you be other than the Prince if you operate in the kind of way that Machiavelli is proposing? Could Plato's Philosopher Guardian operate as Machiavelli's Prince is advised to do without becoming the Prince?

TG: We must hope it is possible. That is why I put emphasis on a withdrawal from the exercise of power so that leaders can examine what they are doing. The headlong pressure to act, to do, to be the leader militate against a reflective attitude – a stance that is needed for the growth of worthwhile values, of character. That is what I see as the ultimate in the nurture of leaders through training. It would be aimed at persons in power, fostering awareness of values and of the value choices that face them, and thereby perhaps assisting character growth.

PR: So the effort is not to make them effective leaders, but to make them good persons first?

TG: To make them good persons, yes. I'd remind you that in German, Machiavelli's genre is known as *Furtenspiegel*, writing from the 'mirror for princes'. Seeing himself in the mirror, the Prince is to be transformed.

PR: Even so what makes a good leader? What, for example, makes St Paul a good leader? Why was St Peter less effective as a leader than Paul? How do you help leaders to be better people *and* more effective leaders?

TG: Paul, is a perfect example. He receives a blinding vision on the road to Damascus with a new moral insight and thereafter he combines, what you might call political strategies with mystical experience. 'For now we see through a glass, darkly; but then face to face.' He shows us what it is to be a good leader. His combination of vision with untiring effort and endless recipes and advice for making things work, seeing where values require taking a stand on what matters, and working out their implications in practical reality. For example, his decision to make Christianity more than just another Jewish sect by his abandonment of the old Law and circumcision, opening the new way to *all*, to Gentile and Jew, to women, to men, to freeborn and slave, the insistence that redemption was open to all. That's leadership, and it has a political element woven with the visionary. He is filled with concern for the world as it is and how to change it and organise it but at the same time he is touched by, in this case, a transcendental vision. The role that I see for the arts is the one that gives us some insight into the larger values, and that I think leaders very much need.

PR: That is one thing the arts could do. They could also give leaders an insight into motive and intention and the operation of will and the relationship between each and all of these things and actions.

TG: One of the implications of accepting a world of multiple realities is that leaders need to appreciate the realities that they are overriding in the pursuit of those they seek to inculcate. Again this requires a kind of withdrawal from the immediate reality to understand the complexities and the alternatives. But the leader cannot contemplate forever, contemplation must stop sooner or later and action must begin. But there is no calculus for resolving a conflict of values, a conflict of separate realities, except through force, varying from psychic to physical.

PR: Can we examine 'Critical Perspective' of 1985. It offers an economical yet comprehensive account of your thinking on educational organisation.

TG: What it represents in terms of something new, is a study of the foundations of our field in the work of Herbert Simon and Chester

Bernard, especially Simon. Here is where I began to consider how Simon built up a foundation and pushed the field in a mistaken direction.

PR: What do you see as the mistaken direction?

TG: He established logical positivism as *the* methodology of the field. In doing so he understood it could not deal with values: there is no science of valuing. Simon recognised that. His solution removed valuing and purposing from the science of administration. His science came at the price of a neutered administrative practice, deploring on the one hand that administrators make choices out of their own values, creating on the other the administrative 'moral cipher' as the model for scientific action. In that sense, Simon is worse than Machiavelli, much worse.

PR: He had a very technicist view.

TG: He scientised the field by eliminating the value choice questions. His whole aim was to reduce decision making, to eliminate values in choice question. His whole aim it to reduce decision making to a calculable system. The only way you can calculate this is if there are values established within it. So Simon's perfect administrator is a neutered cipher. Interestingly, he began by trying to understand what he called the 'psychology of human choice'. But ultimately the thrust of his logic brought him to the study of artificial intelligence, as is seen in his model for choosing a diet that was maximally nutritious and of minimal cost, as though religious rules of diet were meaning-less, and as if food fads and fetishes had no force. The endpoint of Simon's thought is HAL of Kubrick's *2001*, the computer that is superrational, but non-human and non-humane, making up for the deficiencies of human thinking by obliterating the human power to have values to choose.

PR: What of Chester Barnard?

TG: Barnard saw the task of the executive officer as building a moral order. That is the nature of organisations – a moral order in action. The building of that order is, as I see it and as Barnard saw it, a wilful thing. So if you put Simon and Barnard together, you create the perfect combination. Barnard was much concerned about purpose and the building of commitment through communication. These were the foundations of his concept of administration, defining an administrator who was value-concerned and active on behalf of them. All that Barnard's administrator strove to create Simon assumed as givens in the administrator's world. Simon focused only on what the administrator has to be to achieve the values handed to him and to achieve them efficiently. But Barnard and Simon are not seen in a complementary sense within much of the subsequent literature. Rather Simon becomes a replacement for Barnard, as superior because he is scientific. If you look at early editions of Simon, there is an introduction by Barnard in which he says virtually the same thing. He too was dazzled by the promise of Science.

PR: Even Barnard?

TG: Even Barnard. He speaks of Simon's book as being the next wave, as something standing on the base of what he offered. I don't think he saw that as entailing a destruction of the base.

PR: To what extent is 'Decline and Fall' of 1986 concerned with similar issues?

TG: Very much. It takes up where the previous paper leaves off. It looks at what Simon offered, at the difference between Simon and Barnard.

PR: Is there anything else in this paper that we should note at this point?

TG: I mention the classic work, *The Consolation of Philosophy* by Boethius, and this is to make the argument on the need for reflection. The story of Boethius is touching. He was a Christian who stood at the hinge between the Roman World and the Middle Ages. He is an administrator, one caught between the Emperor and the Pope, or as it turned out, the wrong Pope. He is condemned, and as he awaits his death he thinks back on his career and writes, thus bringing new insight to the administrative task. Few of us will face the horror that Boethius did, but I am convinced that potentially there is that same dimension in all administrative rule, a kind of horror. The wielding of power is terrible, and the more power, the more terrible it becomes. If there is to be a kind of humanising of that power a contemplative, philosophical dimension must and should be brought to it. Perhaps to do the thing at all requires the kind of withdrawal which I have advocated, and a need for a meditation on values.

PR: Some of your work has an epistemological focus some deals with aspects of value and its place in the study and practice of educational administration. Both themes are present in the last two papers. Both were written in 1991. The first is 'Phoenix' and the second is 'Science and service'. They read, to an extent, as an *Apologia pro Vitae Sua*. Do you see it like this?

TG: I feel rather like Prospero, I guess, looking back on a career.

PR: Prospero voluntarily gives up the power of magic at the end of *The Tempest*?

TG: Shortly before I wrote this paper I retired. So this is a retrospective view of the controversy in which I have been involved for close on twenty years. I had these things that I wanted to say stored up.

PR: You try to look back over developments in the field as well as the debates in which you have been involved over the last two decades. You try to make sense of the field as a whole, but as you do that, new things come forward like the book from Evers and Lakomski.

TG: That's right!

PR: Which is a new challenge, a rather subtler one philosophically than the some that had come before?

TG: I finished the paper knowing that it was not a final testament after all. The debate wasn't finished. There's a whole new phase, a new era of issues and controversy, but that makes me feel good. I like to think I had some part to play in what's happening now.

PR: Certainly in this case, they much value your work.

TG: A surprise after all this time.

PR: I think *Knowing Educational Administration* is in many ways an exceptional book, But I can't help thinking that Evers and Lakomski have been brave or foolhardy or both. The scope of their thesis is immensely broad. They have been pretty reckless in the potential enemies they might make given the range of critiques they present. But of all the critiques, yours is the most understated. It is one of the longest in the book, but also one of the most tentative. Whilst they acknowledge its strengths, they seem rather more critical of Hodgkinson's work. They are also critical of the critical theorists.

TG: Perhaps they see Hodgkinson as the more dangerous opponent philosophically. His comment on the book was that the value–fact divide recognized over 2,500 years of philosophy is not so easily unhorsed, that naturalistic coherentism hasn't done it. I take great satisfaction from what they have said, not just because it is appreciative, although it is that, but because they pay attention to the text of what I have written. They pay attention to what I said, even though their view of it is rather selective. They don't look at all of my writing over the last twenty years and I wish they had looked at some of the other things. But what they look at, they look at squarely and carefully.

PR: And they're critical of others who don't.

TG: Exactly, And that is something which has aggrieved me most over the years. Too often I have been personally attacked rather than attacked on the basis of what I have written. That has been a cross to bear over the years. So it is satisfying at this juncture to find critics with whom I may disagree, and I'm sure I will, but who understand what I've said and deal with it.

PR: Your work has often been associated with that of Hodgkinson. How have you influenced each other's thinking and what kind of intellectual debt do you owe each other?

TG: The debt he may owe me is that mine was the initial breach in the wall. I began discussion of contentious issues. This opened up the field and he has marched through that breach. It was likely he would have done so anyway but this breach was there to use and I think he used it. He has gone much further with the questions of value than I did initially, and so what I owe to him is a better understanding of the world of values, and perhaps he has saved me – I'm not sure that I've been guilty of the relativism that some people have accused me of. I don't think I ever took that position, people misunderstood the fact that I wanted to look with open eyes at the different value positions that people live by, and to recognise where conflicts of values exist. I don't think this is to claim that there is no way of arbitrating between them, but my task has always been to put description first. That's the message I have tried to leave – description first and prescription second. And to emphasise that prescription does not logically follow from description, it cannot. I guess I largely set aside the question of how one is prescriptive, although I recognised that one must be ultimately. Hodgkinson has addressed such issues much more centrally and much more fully. There is a difference: Hodgkinson has said to me I am the better writer – perhaps or perhaps not. But I have been able to get attention that he does not. A kind of interaction occurs between us; together we are a kind of reciprocating intellectual machine.

PR: How are you alike in what you are trying to do?

TG: We're alike in our opposition to positivism, we're alike in our awareness of values generally. His appreciation of values tends to be more classical and philosophical, maybe Platonist. Whereas mine tends to be, perhaps 'artistic', because I draw upon roots to seek an understanding of value. I think it's also the case that I acknowledge a spiritual tradition more strongly than he does, although it's there with him as well.

Perhaps he draws on an eastern spiritual element whereas I am more likely to find it in Judaeo-Christianity. There is a religious or spiritual tradition in my work whereas this is less prominent in his other than in his references to the eastern religions. But even this he interprets in an almost secular way. But no one can read *The Philosophy of Leadership* with its orchestrated and plangent credos without knowing that this is a work of great moral architecture, profound and moving. There is a kind of flirtation in my work – an obsession even – with the religious, a sensitivity at least to the spiritual. Some readers have pointed out that Biblical imagery suffuses many of my texts, and these appeal strongly to those of a religious cast of mind. Even so I hope my work carries no stigma of a doctrinal emphasis, although in some sense it moves within the Western spiritual tradition.

What I have taken from Hodgkinson is his argument that a social science of organization can never replace an understanding of administration itself. He deals with the existential reality of the administrative act as virtually no other writer does. He is a fine philosopher, insightful, expressing the power of ancient and modern thought, revealing its essence in pungent human terms. His knowledge of the management literature is profound and he leads the way to deeper and deeper insights into it. He is relentless that technique, ancient or modern, can never supplant the wilfulness of human action or release human agents from responsibility for it. If there are ideas from Hodgkinson that have influenced me most, they are the irreducibility of value choice and the unavoidability of human responsibility for that choice. Free will in some measure at least, and that is where the struggle with Evers and Lakomski begins. They deny mind and free will, reducing everything to matter, arguing as Evers has said that it is easier to physicalise the mental than to mentalise the physical. In opposition to that dehumanizing proposition Hodgkinson and I are united.

PR: One sense in which I see you as somewhat similar is that you are both scholars in the traditional sense of the word. Neither of you is known now as a researcher.

TG: Yes, I accept that, but I would also argue that we ought not to draw a sharp line between non-empirical scholarship and empirical scholarship. I mean they are both enquiries, and one needs the other.

PR: I don't deny that for a moment but you did much of your research when your thinking was influenced by the traditions you have now spend many years challenging.

TG: Yes, though I have done more beyond that than people recognise. But I certainly accept the judgement that I am not an active empirical researcher.

PR: I have tried to frame a series of questions reflecting the criticism that your theories are invalid, since you have done little or no empirical research in the light of them. Can we consider them?

TG: I travel this ground reluctantly, for I have been over it many times before, most recently in 'Phoenix'. Before taking on the individual questions, let me suggest that they boil down to a single point: Why can't Greenfield abide by the rules of the game set down in the systems–empiricist paradigm, which is after all the only rational and desirable one? That question constitutes a strategic denial of my arguments, a strategy that rules them out of order before they are even considered. Do I again have to cite opinions to the contrary by Culbertson, Griffiths, Evers and Lakomski, and others? Do I have to make a defence in a court ignorant of those judgements or at least dismissive of them? Past pleadings in front of that court have been fruitless and give ample evidence that those who pose the charge often fail to hear the answers, let alone weigh them in balanced judgement.

The reason for this recalcitrance on the part of my critics is clear, as Hodgkinson shows in his Foreword: 'He touches the point with a needle'. The implications of my work are seen as so threatening and revolutionary in some quarters that the only defence against them is to deny that my positions carry sense or weight, to seek to invalidate them as having no empirical support. I *am* reluctant to push this analysis, but the recrudescence of such criticism in ever new forms and from varied sources makes it all the more important to address the issues again. And this, I know, is your argument. So let's look at it again in the separate aspects you enumerate.

PR: Let me put the questions as five propositions. That theory is valuable only insofar as it is useful in research?

TG: This proposition is cast within the assumptions of the systems–empiricist paradigm. It refuses to see any other kind of enquiry as a contribution to knowledge. As Schumacher says, even the slenderest knowledge of matters of profound importance is of great value. If 'adequate' standards of inquiry, as Schumacher describes them, are acknowledged, my work is a kind of research. While not profound itself, my work 'adequately' addresses issues that are. I hope it has yielded at least some slender knowledge of these issues, knowledge that other methods cannot generate.

PR: That your work is not and has not been useful by this crucial criterion of research as it is usually understood.

TG: Perhaps my work has not been useful by that criterion. But that is the heart of the issue. The whole thrust of my argument is that there are other more 'adequate' criteria for building knowledge.

PR: That there is a failure by the missing research criterion is demonstrated by the fact that to date not a single researcher has used your ideas.

TG: That no researcher has used the ideas I have espoused is true only if the criteria and assumptions of the systems–empiricist paradigm are imposed as a Procrustean bed for the whole field. That those who live encapsulated within the systems paradigm do not use these ideas is hardly surprising. But it is false to claim that my work has influenced no researchers to take up new modes of inquiry. There has been a 'sea change' in the field and 'turmoil' as Griffiths and others acknowledge: part of that transformation, as these commentators recognize, is due to my blazing the path.

PR: That in any case, it would be difficult to undertake research on the basis of your ideas, since these change significantly from paper to paper and lecture to lecture.

TG: Surely it is not to be seen as a negative quality of my work that it has changed and evolved over two decades, that the critique has not sprung Minerva-like and fully formed from the head of Zeus. Instead it has come slowly and with some pain from a human being struggling for understanding over two decades of work. Surely recognition of this struggle is not to be taken as serious criticism of the effort over those decades. It is possible to see a thrust in the development of ideas in my critiques. If there are changes in that critique, they are not

266

simply erratic and do not constitute abrupt or ill-founded changes to suit the ideological winds of the time. There are developing themes in the work and these have been identified most recently in 'Science and Service'. You have noted the other side of this coin, the face of it that says, 'You have tended to reproduce rather than advance significantly your ideas since the IIP '74 paper'. That I must face the inherent contradictions of these twinned criticisms suggests to me that they come from those who are acutely uncomfortable with what I have written. Their response is less reasoned argument than a reflex that rejects or ignores what lies behind them. They have another agenda to pursue.

PR: That these criticisms go a long way towards explaining why your work is not much quoted in the United States, is not popular, and has not 'caught on' there.

TG: The observation about the 'point of the needle' is explanation of why my critique has not 'caught on' in the United States. It is unpopular wherever what Frye describes as 'Mercantilist Whiggery' prevails. Writings such as 'Phoenix' where I critique the ill-effects on education of such a world view are unlikely to be received with joy and gratitude in cultures that accept the excesses of technocratic–pragmatic, systems–empiricist, individualist values as received and unopposable truth. But it should be noted that 'Phoenix' was commissioned by an American group and presented first from an American platform to a small but appreciative audience.

   On all of these points, a more balanced judgement will surely be possible after the results of the programme we are engaged in here appear in the Routledge collection. After its publication, I would hope to hear the opinions of those who may bring an open-mindedness to the issues and ultimately a balanced appreciation of them. *De quistibus non est disputandum.* I am willing to let the matter rest with a 'trial by what is contrary', as Milton described the process of truth making. In such a trial, I ask only an opportunity to present my defence, hoping not to be ruled out of order for wanting to argue it.

PR: What of the final paper in the collection? Why did you write it and what were you trying to achieve with it? How does 'Science and Service' relate to 'Phoenix?'

TG: 'Science and Service' was written six months after 'Phoenix', the two of them being a keystone in the arch of my writings. I did not set out to make them serve such a crucial role nor even conceived them as linked. As usual the papers arose from invitations. After word of my retirement spread I began to get invitations to write – anything at all, just write. The invitations to do these papers came early and as invitations to speak about issues that arose during the last two decades of controversy in administrative studies.

267

'Phoenix' is a synoptic statement revisiting the issues of the past two decades. It attempts to secure the ground that has been won and to extend the implications of the argument into new territory. I delivered 'Phoenix' not only at AERA in Chicago but in seminars at the Universities of British Columbia and Victoria. These presentations began the questioning anew.

'Science and Service' puts values central to its persuasive structure. It speaks from the heart, and in return has engendered strong reactions – for and against. It speaks to others' hearts too. The fundamental issue in both papers is the same: what place can values have in a science of the social world, in purposive, administrative action within it? If 'Phoenix' did not answer that question, it had at least pointed the direction in which the answer lies. In beginning to write 'Science and Service', I knew I had to speak to the challenge from Evers and Lakomski, but I did not want to make it only a response to their work. That may come later. Rather 'Science and Service' does a march around Evers and Lakomski, it outflanks their fact-driven position by making values central to the whole argument – or rather by making the chosing of values central to that argument. In Evers and Lakomski's argument, the choosing of values is reduced to a process that lies essentially outside human will: they solve the value problem by obviating it. As Evers says, their answer is to 'physicalise the mental'. Values are genetically encoded, I suppose, and scientifically discovered.

When I presented 'Phoenix' at a seminar at the University of British Columbia, I was surprised by a question that asked me to clarify *my* values. I was taken aback. I thought I had done so, and listed the various value positions I had taken in the latter part of that paper. Later I realized I had not spoken to the heart of that question, how one *values* values.

In 'Science and Service' I bring the fact–value dichotomy into the existential reality of making a value choice out of facts. I take seriously the Weberian argument that rationality itself stands upon a non-rational choice. The paper offers a leap, a leap upwards, a leap of faith perhaps. The argument shows what we must do if we are to avoid the Evers–Lakomskian trap. To be humane, to escape the fact-driven, calculable world, we must *be human*, reaching beyond our grasp, towards heaven, as Browning would say. And this of course takes us out of the limited world of fact and matter, out of synapses and programmed responses, into the world of culture, into true culture, a world that Evers and Lakomski deny, or accept only as an obverse of the physical. As I see it Evers and Lakomski's great contribution is to remind us of the world of fact, of the error of valuing too much. My Contribution and Hodgkinson's is perhaps to remind us of the mystery beyond fact, of the error of valuing too little. In 'Science and Service' I acknowledge contemporary problems in education where values inappropriately overwhelm the factual. One need not look far in education today to see many such problems: the view for example that all is to be discovered by the child pursuing its own needs, the conviction-driven exalting of the child-centred approaches that deny what we all know to be good and great teaching. There are facts in all of this that need more attention than they get, though I admit they are value saturated. All of this may leave us dismayed, overwhelmed even, before the fact–value gulf.

When I presented 'Science and Service' at a recent seminar at the University of Western Ontario, I was asked whether it represents a departure from previous relativist positions. My first response was to say that I hope there is *not* a single and even line of development through all my papers. They represent a groping towards understanding, not a uniform and logical line of extrapolation. But I also said I hoped that the position seen in 'Science and Service' is consistent with what has gone before, with positions that set out the realities of different perceptions of the world and that describes the realities of those views in conflict. Those differences are the basic stuff of the world, and much of my earlier work asserts them in the face of a mode of thought that would deny them or work them out in a flawed system that asserts technical progress is equivalent to moral progress. Such progress brings us to the world of authority and hierarchy, which my work has never denied, though I now see more clearly than I did where the redemption of authority and hierarchy must come from. I hope I have never taken the position that one value position is as good as another – the opposite indeed – though I have tried to show that looking at the world through the eyes of value holders reveals profound conflicts that reason itself fails utterly to resolve. I may have come close, but I never embraced the relativist horror. That's clear in the bonsai image from *Decline and Fall* where the educator shapes pupils' values even as the gardener shapes the bonsai tree. While I'm at it, I should say that I am dismayed at those who read my work as though it made nothing but a liberationist, egalitarian, and rights-of-the-individual argument, a position seen most vividly – and wrongly – in the stance of today's deconstructors, post-modernists and radical feminists. I yield no more to values calculated out of science than to values taken for granted or ignored. While it might be easier to throw up one's hands in the face of these difficulties, the way I have reached finds that each culture offers its own road upwards. Salvation, peace and reconciliation, if they are to be found, are to be found on that road, and we cannot deny our own road. I began 'Science and Service' with deliberately religious metaphors in mind, and these connect with others that suffuse much of my work. I finished the paper with a sense that the great conundrum we face is still unresolved. But perhaps we know better now what it is and which way to look to face it.

In pushing that position a little further I would refer to a work I have just come to know. In the Massey lecture series titled, *The Malaise of Modernity* (broadcast on CBC and published by Anansi), Charles Taylor has argued what he calls 'the view from Dover Beach'. In reference to Arnold's far-seeing poem and in contravention to Lasch and Bloom, he defends self-fulfilment as a goal of individual action. He argues that the ethic of the 'authentic' individual, as first stated by Nietzsche, the presumed villain of the piece, does not destroy the truth of ethical limits on human action. It simply moves the consideration of such limits to a new context. Nietzsche himself never gave up the moral perspective, calling for a yea-saying, a yes to the world. How can it be otherwise if we are not to perish with the individual in self-defeating doubt, agony, and destruction? Taylor's view is that the ebbing of the Dover tide is not absolute, it offers as much as it takes away. Hope lies at the bottom of Pandora's box. There remain the possible errors of liberalism in Taylor's argument. It must be made clear therefore that the authentic individual goes unredeemed – doomed within violence and self-destruction – without a sense of obligation, of altruism, of something beyond the individual. Taylor chronicles the trip the elite, modernist poets – Yeats and Eliot – took towards fascism, a charge that may be wrong at least in the case of Eliot, but who can deny the endpoint of individualism seen in Pound's broadcasts from Italy during World War II? These were not just madness, as they were treated as being after the War, but the end development of a line of thought, a line still alive today in the vicious and death-dealing actions of the skinheads of today. The strength of the individual perspective is the pause it gives for questioning, for dialogue and its stimulus for the creative, for the new vision. It seems clear to me now that dialogue cannot deny a conversation with the ultimate. That must temper the excesses and destructiveness of the otherwise unrestrained individual. There must be a yea-saying to the world. Ultimately – and this may be the point of greatest importance – art must be descriptive, mimetic, of the world not just creative of it, otherwise art and human action itself ends in self-defeat.

The hundredth anniversary of the birth of Henry Miller and a renewed critical appraisal of his work give reason to look again at these issues. Miller called the *Tropic of Cancer* 'a gob of spit in the face of art', as he revelled in his experience of Paris. But even in the *Tropic* he had something to say: he praised one culture and criticized his own. He moved to the Big Sur, but deplored the New Ageism that followed him there, even as he deplored the spirit of the larger

270

American culture. He was horrified that Linda Lovelace and *Deep Throat* could be seen as justified by his art, yes by his *Art*. Another gob of spit in the face of *Art*, and he ended by defending what he knew he had never attacked. We should remind ourselves that great art is moral. It is an ethical statement about the world, and that is what makes it great. Gobs of spit may besmirch it, but not deny its message. Art and ethics are ultimately united. So too the individual and his understanding of the world are ultimately united with ethics. That is the position I have come to, and it is the position I began with. *Macbeth* and *Faust* are not just fine words spread over five acts. Great art – and great social science too – must always have a moral content. And we judge their greatness by that content. Describing the world as it is can hardly deny or controvert this position. Indeed it makes the position. That's what I have been trying to do in my work: trying to describe the world as it is, and trying to contemplate the moral conundrums created thereby.

REFERENCES

Griffiths, D. (1957) 'Towards a theory of administrative behaviour'. In *Administrative Behaviour in Education*, eds R. Campbell and A. Gregg. New York: Harper.

Griffiths, D. (1988) 'Administrative theory'. In *Handbook of Research in Educational Administration*, ed. N. Boyan. New York: Longman.

Evers, C. and Lakomski, G. (1991) *Knowing Educational Administration*, London: Pergamon.

APPENDIX

Publications and papers

Greenfield, T. B. and Andrews, J. H. M. 1961. Teacher leader behaviour as related to pupil growth. *Alberta Journal of Educational Research* 7, 2: 93–103.

Greenfield, T. B. and Downey, L. W. 1961. *Leadership training for educational administrators.* Edmonton: Department of Educational Administration, University of Alberta.

Greenfield, T. B. 1961. A procedure for evaluation of the school program. *Skills of the effective principal.* Edmonton: Department of Educational Administration.

Greenfield, T. B. 1962. The principalship. *B.C. Principals' Journal* March, 17–23.

Greenfield, T. B. 1962. School athletics: Boon or blight? *CSA Bulletin* (Alberta) 2, 13–19.

Greenfield, T. B. and Baird, R. E. 1962. The politics of education: Practice and theory; The politics of education: Controversy and control. *The Canadian Administrator* 1, 7 and 8: 31–38.

Greenfield, T. B. 1964. Survey research: Design and analysis. *Planning for research.* Ottawa: Canadian Teachers' Federation.

Greenfield, T. B. 1964. Problems and prospects of the teacher research movement in Canada. *Third Canadian Conference on Educational Research,* Ottawa: Canadian Council for Research in Education.

Greenfield, T. B. 1964. *Collective bargaining by teachers' organizations in Canada: A description of practice and survey of opinion.* Ottawa: Canadian Teachers' Federation.

Greenfield, T. B. 1964. Administration and systems analysis. *The Canadian Administrator* 3, 7: 25–30.

Greenfield, T. B. 1964. *Teacher research on programmed instruction: A collection and critique of studies.* Ottawa: Canadian Teachers' Federation.

Greenfield, T. B. 1965. Some problems and methods in teacher conducted research. *Report of a workshop on classroom research.* Toronto: Ontario Educational Research Council.

Greenfield, T. B. 1965. *The consolidation of Ontario school districts.* Toronto: Ontario Teachers' Federation.

Greenfield, T. B. 1965. Classroom research and teacher decision-making. *Manitoba Journal of Educational Research* 1, November, 69–78.

Greenfield, T. B. 1966. *Teachers evaluate programmed instruction: A survey of attitudes and problems.* Ottawa: Canadian Teachers' Federation.

Andrews, J. H. M. and Greenfield, T. B. 1967. Organizational themes relevant to change in schools. *Ontario Journal of Educational Research* 9, 81–99.

Greenfield, T. B. 1968. Research on the behaviour of educational leaders: Critique of a tradition. *Alberta Journal of Educational Research* 14, 1: 55–86.

Greenfield, T. B., House, J. H., Hickcox, E. S. and Buchanan, B. H. 1969. *Developing school systems*. Toronto: OISE.

Greenfield, T. B. 1970. Creating effective school programs. *Orbit* 1, 1: 20–22.

Havighurst, R. J., Greenfield, T. B. and Janovitz, M. 1970. Institution building in urban education: A review symposium. *Interchange* 1, 1: 124–132.

Greenfield, T. B. 1972. Developing accountability in school systems. *Education Canada* 12, March, 21–29.

Greenfield, T. B. 1972. *Developing and assessing objectives for school system planning.* Toronto: Department of Educational Administration, OISE.

Greenfield, T. B., Hickcox, E. S., Ryan, D. W. and Scott, J. G. 1972. *The structure and process of decision making in a school system.* Toronto: Department of Educational Administration, OISE.

Greenfield, T. B. 1972. Relating educational objectives, programs and resources: Policy analysis for school systems. In *The planning process: A systems perspective for school boards*, eds J. G. Scott and D. J. Ducharme, 24–49. Toronto: OISE.

Greenfield, T. B. 1972. Policy analysis in education: Looking at the alternatives. *Orbit* 3, 4: 16–20.

Greenfield, T. B. 1973. Educational goals for a school system. *Canadian Administrator* 13, 13–17.

Greenfield, T. B. 1973. Organizations as social inventions: Rethinking assumptions about change. *Journal of Applied Behavioural Science* 9, 5, 551–574. Translated into German and reprinted in *Gruppendynamik* 6 (1975): 2–21.

Greenfield, T. B. *et al.* 1974. *Structure, decision-making, and communication in the Waterloo County school system: An evaluation report.* Toronto: Department of Educational Administration, OISE.

Greenfield, T. B. 1975. Theory about organization: A new perspective and its implications for schools. In *Administering education: International challenges*, ed. M. Hughes, 71–99. London: Athlone Press of the University of London. Reprinted in *The management of organizations and individuals*, eds V. Morton, R. McHugh, and C. Morgan, 59–84. London: Ward Lock.

Ryan, D. W. and Greenfield, T. B. 1975. *The class size question: Development of research studies related to the effects of class size, pupil/adult, and pupil/teacher ratios.* Toronto: Ministry of Education.

Ryan, Doris W. and Greenfield, T. B. 1976. *Clarifying the class size question: Evaluation and synthesis of studies related to the effect of class size, pupil–adult and pupil–teacher ratios.* Toronto: Ministry of Education.

Greenfield, T. B. 1976. Bilingualism, multiculturalism, and the crisis of purpose in Canadian culture. In *Bilingualism in Canadian education: Issues and research/Le bilinguisme dans l'éducation: la recherche et les problèmes*, ed. Merrill Swain, 107–136. Third Yearbook of the Canadian Society for the Study of Education. Edmonton: The Society.

Greenfield, T. B. *et al.* 1976. *Creating and changing curriculum in a school system: A design for development, implementation and evaluation.* Toronto: Department of Educational Administration, OISE.

Greenfield, T. B. 1976. Theory about what? Some more thoughts about theory in educational administration. *UCEA Review* 17, 2: 4–9.

Greenfield, T. B. 1977/78. Where does self belong in the study of organizations? *Educational Administration* 6, 1: 81–101.

Greenfield, T. B. 1978. Reflection on organization theory and the truths of irreconcilable realities. *Educational Administration Quarterly* 14, 2: 1–23.

Greenfield, T. B. 1979. Organization theory as ideology. *Curriculum Inquiry* 9, 2: 97–112. Published also in Hebrew in *Educational Organization and Administration* (Israel), 7–8 1978, 119–134 + xv–xvii.

Greenfield, T. B. 1979. Organisationen als Rede, Zufal, Handlung and Erfahrung. In *Die Psychologie des 20. Jahrhunderts: Lewin und die Folgen, Band VII*, eds A. Heigl-Evers and U. Streeck, 547–558. Zurich: Kindler Verlag. (Title in English: Organizations as talk, chance, action and experience.)

Greenfield, T. B. 1979. Ideas versus data: How can the data speak for themselves? In *Problem-finding in educational administration: Trends in research and theory*, ed. G. Immegart and W. Boyd, 167–190. Lexington, Massachusetts: D. C. Heath and Company.

Greenfield, T. B. 1979/80. Research in educational administration in the United States and Canada: An overview and critique. *Educational Administration* 8, 1: 207–245.

Greenfield, T. B. 1980. Is it true what he said about educational psychology? Comments on Travis. *Canadian Journal of Education* 5, 2: 87–90.

Greenfield, T. B. 1980. The man who comes back through the door in the wall: Discovering truth, discovering self, discovering organizations. *Educational Administration Quarterly* 16, 3: 26–59.

Greenfield, T. B. 1981. Gems in a dreary landscape. Review of R. H. Farquhar and I. Housego, eds, *Canadian and comparative educational administration. CSSE News/nouvelles SCEE*, 12–13.

Greenfield, T. B. 1981. Can science guide the administrator's hand? A critique of 'new movement' ideology in educational administration. In *Re-thinking education: Modes of enquiry in human sciences*, ed. T T. Aoki, 5–15. Monograph no. 3, Curriculum Praxis Monograph Series. Edmonton: Faculty of Education, University of Alberta.

Greenfield, T. B. 1982. Against group mind: An anarchistic theory of education. *McGill Journal of Education* 17, 1: 13–17.

Greenfield, T. B. 1983. Against group mind: An anarchistic theory of organization. *Reflective readings in educational administration*, 293–301. Victoria, Australia: Deakin University Press. (A revised and expanded version of Greenfield [1982]).

Greenfield, T. B. 1983. Environment as subjective reality. Paper presented to the Annual Meeting of the American Educational Research Association, Montreal.

Greenfield, T. B. 1984. Leaders and schools: Wilfulness and non-natural order in organizations. In *Leadership and organizational culture: New perspectives on administrative theory and practice*, eds T. J. Sergiovanni and J. E. Corbally, 142–169. Urbana: University of Illinois Press.

Greenfield, T. B. 1985. Theories of educational organization: A critical perspective. *International encyclopedia of education: Research and studies*, Vol. 9, 5240–4251. Oxford: Pergamon Press.

Greenfield, T. B. 1985. Trial by what is contrary. *Curriculum Inquiry* 14, 1: 1–6.

Greenfield, T. B. 1986. The decline and fall of science in educational administration. *Interchange* 17, 2: 57–80.

Greenfield, T. B. 1986. Waiting for an answer. *Curriculum Inquiry* 16, 3: 239–243.

Greenfield, T. B. 1986. The headache and the crown. *Curriculum Inquiry* 16, 4: 357–364.

Greenfield, T. B. 1987. The doing of research. *CASEA Newsletter* 16, 1: 24–30.

Greenfield, T. B. 1988. Writers and the written: Writers and the self. *Curriculum Inquiry* 18, 3: 245–253.

Greenfield, T. B. 1989. Still waiting for an answer. *Curriculum Inquiry* 19, 1: 1–9.

Greenfield, T. B. 1990. 'The ae thing needful': What is the meaning of this? *Curriculum Inquiry* 20, 4: 359–367.

Greenfield, T. B. 1991. Preface to *Educational leadership: The moral art* by C. Hodgkinson. Albany: SUNY University Press. [In press.]

Greenfield, T. B. 1991. Re-forming and re-valuing educational administration: Whence and when cometh the phoenix? Paper presented to the Organization Theory SIG, AERA Annual Conference, Chicago, 1991. Published in *Educational Management and Administration* 19, 4: 200–218.

Greenfield, T. B. 1991. Science and service: The making of one profession of educational administration. Papers presented at one Thirty-Fifth Anniversary Conference of the Department of Educational Administration, University of Alberta, Edmonton, September 1991.

INDEX

actions, 265; judgement and rationality of, 127; make organizations, 103–4
administration: active and passive, 128–9; ethics of, 154; as a moral art (Hodgkinson), 194–5; need for understanding of, 34, 264; as a normative discipline, 208; practical, 231; principles evolved by practitioners, 135–6; profession of, 2
Administration Science Quarterly, 108
administration theory, Litchfield, 108
Administrative Behavior in Education (Campbell and Gregg), 199, 200, 209
Administrative Behavior (Simon), 135, 136, 163
administrative behaviour, theory of, 106
administrative research, theoretical foundations of, 27–9
administrative science: alternative, 152–4, 155–8; devaluation of, 146–7; early studies in, 214; failure of, 26–7, 138–40, 151; flawed, 139, 147–9, 165; growing belief in, 145–6; new research agenda in, 157–8; power of, 206–7; as pure science, 211; and reality of organizations, 152; science of managing behaviour, 174; in texts, 42–3; and values, 147–9, 207
Administrative Science Quarterly, 43, 139
'Administrative Theory: The Fumbled Torch' (Halpin), 30
administrative theory: distinct from organizational theory, 43; Erickson's practical studies in, 47; flawed, 30–2; language of, 44–5; philosophical problems of, 166; Simon's vocabulary of, 136
administrators, 2, 157–8; dehumanized,

140–1, 261; *is* and *ought*, 202–3; and moral order, 222; need for judgement, 218; practical experience of, 135–6, 216, 249; research into behaviour of, 208; and science, 205; training of, 18–19, 111–13, 149–51, 258; and values and facts, 221; values and power for, 165; violent forces in, 86
Allison, D. J., 186, 187, 196
American Educational Research Association, 27, 59, 239
'Anarchy' (Greenfield), 254
Andrews, J. H. M., 36, 49
Aquinas, Thomas, 112
Aral, S. O., 191, 196
Arrow's General Impossibility Theorem, 48, 131n
art: as moral, 270–1; and social science, 256–7
artificial paradises (Huxley), 100
artists, ideas and reality, 75, 76, 77
asymmetries, in meaning and morality, 110
Atwood, Margaret, 167
Auden, W. H., 242

Bacon, Francis, 96, 97, 115, 237
Barnard, C., 15–16, 23, 261–2; commitment in administration, 153–4; practitioner-scholar, 136, 158
Barnes, J., *Flaubert's Parrot*, 183–4, 189
Baron, G., 18, 23, 240, 244
Bates, R. J., 138, 146, 158, 169, 196, 220, 227
Bauman, Z., 95, 114, 115, 138, 159; on understanding, 180, 196
Becker, H. S., 117

sociology: paradigms in, 178, *see also* social science
Sontag, Susan, 190, 198
Sovereign (Hobbesian General Will), 147, 149–50
Spady, W. G., 13, 19, 21, 25
specific: in administrative theory, 48; in social theory, 69
Spencer, H., 54
statistics: and chance, 249; use and misuse of, 59–62, 218–19, 236–7
Steiner, George, xi
Stout, R. T., 192, 197
Strauss, A. L., 11, 24
Strauss, G., 212
Street, C. M., 204, 211, 226; *see also* 'Developing a Value Framework. . . '
Structure of Scientific Revolutions (Kuhn), 177
Stufflebeam, D. L., 46, 52
subjectivism, 241; attack on, 158n
subjectivity: of experience, 70–1; and objective truth, 95; and understanding others, 113
Sullivan, W. M., 138, 161
Summers, A. A., 62
superintendents, training programmes for, 150–1
Suzuki, D. T., Zen and logic, 128, 133
Systems Analysis in Education (Greenfield), 233
systems theory, 6, 8, 202; administration in, 138; and organizations, 144–5; power in, 240; research as confirming theory, 11, 12; of society, 211, 217
systems–empiricist paradigm, 178–81
Szasz, T., 130, 131n, 133, 142; science and morality, 188, 198

Taylor, Charles, *The Malaise of Modernity*, 270
Taylor, W., 18, 23
texts, used in training programmes, 42–4
theory: academic isolation of, 44; administrative/organizational distinction, 43; and consistency principle, 65–6, 67; Greenfield on, 266; and human action, 28, 106; hypothetico–deductive, 117, 144, 210, 238; in New Movement, 31–2, 33–5, 143–4; observation and proofs, 64; and research, 1977 seminar on, 40–1; and social reality, 10–11, 217; stages of development of, 177; as super–reality (Marx), 82; in training texts, 42; and

wonderful ideas (Duckworth), 88; *see also* Theory Movement
Theory Movement, 164, 186; in Chicago, 231; and experience, 249; Greenfield's attack on, 171–2; Halpin and, 251; positivism of, 219, 229; *see also* New Movement; theory
Theory in Practice (Schon and Argyris), 49
Thomas, R., 186
Tipton, B. F. A., 4, 25, 146, 161
Tope, D. E., 3, 25, 149, 161
Toulmin, S., 138, 156–7, 161
Towards a Philosophy of Administration (Hodgkinson), 247, 248
'Towards a Theory of Administrative Behavior' (Griffiths), 206–7
training: of administrators, 18–19, 144; new models for, 155–6
training programmes: science–validated, 149–51; texts, 42–4
truth: facts and the definition of, 94; interpretation of, 118–19; knowledge of, 185; and positivist science, 94; problem of perceiving, 114

United States of America: distinct from Canada, 26, 27; Greenfield rejected by, xv, 172, 267; New Movement in, 4, 29; organizations in, 189; social programmes, 191
University of Alberta, Department of Educational Administration, 199, 200, 213–15, 216
University Council for Central Administration, 245
University Council on Educational Administration, 1977 seminar, 40–1

value systems (Graff and Street), 204; *see also* systems theory
value-free method, in decision-making, 135
value-free science of administration, 146, 210
value-judgements, in Weber, 182
value(s): in administration, 134, 142–3, 157, 168; cannot be measured, 182–3; conflicting, 221–2; denied by positivism, 137, 139, 140, 147, 261; excluded from administrative science, 136, 164; Greenfield on, 268–9; ignored in research paradigm, 47; institutional, 174; and methodology, 81–3, 175–6; and organizations, 104–5, 110; and problem of moral